Arminius on the Assurance of Salvation

Brill's Series in
Church History

(Formerly Known as Kerkhistorische Bijdragen)

Edited by

Wim Janse, Leiden/Amsterdam

In Cooperation With

Theo Clemens, Utrecht/Antwerpen

Oliver Fatio, Genève

Alastair Hamilton, London

Scott Mandelbrote, Cambridge

Andrew Pettegree, St. Andrews

VOLUME XXVII

ARMINIUS ON THE ASSURANCE OF SALVATION

KEITH D. STANGLIN

Arminius on the Assurance of Salvation

The Context, Roots, and Shape of the Leiden Debate, 1603-1609

By

Keith D. Stanglin

BRILL

LEIDEN • BOSTON
2007

Cover illustration: Portrait of Jacobus Arminius by Sebastian Furck (2nd half 17th century). Photo: Library of the Universiteit van Amsterdam (Remonstrantse Prentencollectie, Q00013362).

This book is printed on acid-free paper.

Library of Congress Cataloging-in Publication data

A C.I.P. record for this book is available from the Library of Congress.

ISSN: 1572-4107
ISBN-13: 978 90 04 15608 1
ISBN-10: 90 04 15608 9

To Amanda
and our children, Paul, Isaac, and Rachel

"In this present life there is no greater joy or contentment, nothing more certain or necessary for rising above all the difficulties we face, than to know and feel that we are the children of God."

(Jean Taffin, 1586, *The Marks of God's Children*, 35)

"The use of this doctrine [of predestination] handed down from the Scriptures is great. For it serves to establish the glory of God's grace, to comfort afflicted consciences, to upset the impious and drive away their security."

(Jacobus Arminius, 1604, *Disp. pub.* XV.xiv)

CONTENTS

PREFACE

The purpose of this essay is to examine Arminius's doctrine of the assurance of salvation in light of his own theology and in the context of the university debate that took place in Leiden. To be sure, to readers somewhat familiar with the Arminian controversy, the topic of this book, Arminius's doctrine of assurance, may sound like an oxymoron. As a number of my Reformed friends have quipped in reply, "Did Arminius even have a doctrine of assurance?" Many theologians and historians have been equally skeptical. However, not only did he have a doctrine of assurance, but this perennial issue in Reformation and Post-Reformation theology was also one of the great motivating factors behind Arminius's doctrine of salvation that became so contentious in the low countries and beyond. Arminius's struggle with the epistemological question of how one can be certain of one's own salvation binds him with the great theologians of the Reformation and Protestant scholasticism.

As a few scholars have pointed out, it is surprising that a figure who was so influential and controversial in his own day and continues to be invoked in a variety of theological and ecclesiastical communities in our day has nevertheless received such slight attention from historians. It may be the dearth of technical examinations of Arminius and his theology that contributes to the abundance of uninformed polemic as well as the tendency of modern theologians to stamp the name of Arminius on any system that modifies so-called classical theology. If the present essay contributes to greater interest in and knowledge of the historical Arminius and the contours of his thought, to the end of a more refined understanding of the historical debate and its application for present-day theology, then it will have accomplished its goal.

A note about primary texts and translations is appropriate. For primary sources that have a modern English translation, I have always checked the original language and generally altered the translation accordingly. Inasmuch as this monograph aims to examine the Leiden theology of a specific period, it relies heavily on academic disputations during the period under investigation. The disputations appearing in Arminius's *Opera* (*Disputationes publicae et privatae*) are numbered by uppercase Roman numerals. For all disputations, I refer to the thesis number within the respective disputation with lowercase Roman numerals.

The disputations other than those appearing in Arminius's *Disp. pub.* and *Disp. priv.* will be noted first by their long title, then in subsequent references by a short title. If two or more disputations are written on the same topic by the same author, they will be distinguished by the year of publication. All these disputations, again with the exception of those in Arminius's *Opera*, will appear in the first section of the final bibliography for easy reference.

This project would not have been possible without generous funding from several institutions. I express gratitude to Calvin Theological Seminary and the Christian Scholarship Foundation, who subsidized my research trip to Universiteit Leiden. I also would like to recognize Southside Church of Christ in Grand Rapids, which granted me a paid leave of absence during those months of research abroad. Throughout my family's stay in Leiden, many people, not least of which are the members of the Haarlem Gemeente van Christus, made our time more enjoyable by their hospitality.

It is no exaggeration to say that I had the privilege of carrying out my research at the best library in Europe and the best library in North America for this specific project. First, at the Universiteitsbibliotheek Leiden, thanks to Dr. Anton van der Lem and the staff of the Dousa Kamer, who were helpful in providing access to the rare disputations of the Leiden theologians. Second, at the Hekman Library of Calvin College and Seminary, Paul Fields and Lugene Schemper have been especially accommodating in granting me access to the rare book collection. In addition to all this assistance, Gerald Cox and the Interlibrary Loan Department of the Brackett Library of Harding University have helped me obtain a variety of necessary secondary sources. Thanks also to Universiteitsbibliotheek Amsterdam, Universiteit van Amsterdam, for permission to use the print from the Remonstrantse Prenten Collectie for the book cover.

I am grateful to Ronald Feenstra and Lyle Bierma, who read through and offered instructive comments on the manuscript. I also thank Professor Wim Janse of Leiden University and Vrije Universiteit Amsterdam for all his support. While I was in Leiden, he showed interest in my work and directed me to relevant sources; he also invited me to present portions of my research to the university's Kerkhistorisch Gezelschap (SSS). His meticulous reading and insightful suggestions have improved the quality of my manuscript, and I am honored that he requested my book for this esteemed series. I especially recognize my mentor, Richard Muller, for all his guidance and counsel over the past five years. He gets the credit for introducing me to the vast landscape of Reformation and Post-Reformation theology, for helping me find my specific areas of interest within it, for stimulating me to ask the right questions, and for encouraging me to seek the answers. The combination of his own unparalleled scholarship, his expectation of academic rigor from me, and his willingness to be a friend along the way has been a wonderful model for me.

My family and friends, especially my parents and in-laws, deserve my thanks for their constant encouragement and affirmation. Above all, I owe a debt of gratitude to my wife, Amanda, and our three children, Paul, Isaac, and Rachel. They have joyfully accompanied me from place to place in my academic pursuits throughout the States and Europe and graciously persevered with me through the highs and lows of graduate education and teaching. More importantly, they have loved me unconditionally, kept me grounded, and reminded me not to take myself or my work too seriously.

Soli Deo Gloria

Keith D. Stanglin

ABBREVIATIONS AND FREQUENTLY CITED MATERIAL

Ahsmann, *Collegia*	*Collegia en Colleges: Juridisch onderwijs aan de Leidse Universiteit 1575–1630 in het bijzonder het disputeren*
Amica col.	Arminius, *Amica cum Iunio de Praedestinatione, collatio*
Apologia	Arminius, *Apologia adversus Articulos quosdam [XXXI] Theologicos*
Art. non.	Arminius, *Articuli nonnulli diligenti examine perpendendi*
Bangs, *Arminius*	*Arminius: A Study in the Dutch Reformation* (1971; repr. 1998)
Beeke, *Assurance*	*Assurance of Faith: Calvin, English Puritanism, and the Dutch Second Reformation*
BLGNP	*Biografisch lexicon voor de geschiedenis van het Nederlandse Protestantisme*, 6 vols. (Kampen, 1978–2006)
Cap. VII Rom.	Arminius, *De vero et genuino sensu cap. VII Epistolae ad Romanos dissertatio*
Dec. sent.	Arminius, *Verklaring (Declaratio sententiae)*, ed. Hoenderdaal (1960)
Dekker, *Rijker*	*Rijker dan Midas: Vrijheid, genade en predestinatie in de theologie van Jacobus Arminius (1559–1609)*
Disp. priv.	Arminius, *Disputationes privatae*
Disp. pub.	Arminius, *Disputationes publicae*
Ep. ecc.	*Praestantium ac eruditorum virorum epistolae ecclesiasticae et theologicae*, 2nd ed. (1684)
Exam. Perk.	Arminius, *Examen modestum libelli, quem D. Gulielmus Perkinsius…edidit…de praedestinationis modo et ordine*
Exam. Gom.	Arminius, *Examen thesium D. Francisci Gomari de Praedestinatione* (1645)
Inst.	Calvin, *Institutio Christianae religionis* (1559 ed.), in *Ioannis Calvini opera*
Itterzon, *Gomarus*	*Franciscus Gomarus* (1929; repr. 1979)
Kendall, *Calvin*	*Calvin and English Calvinism to 1649*, 2nd ed. (1997)
LA	C. Brandt, *The Life of James Arminius, D. D.*, American ed. (1857)
Letham, 'Faith'	'Saving Faith and Assurance in Reformed Theology: Zwingli to the Synod of Dort' (Ph.D. diss., University of Aberdeen, 1979)

LSJ	Liddell, Scott, and Jones, *A Greek-English Lexicon* (1940)
LW	*Luther's Works*, American Edition (1955–86)
Muller, *DLGT*	*Dictionary of Latin and Greek Theological Terms*
Muller, *GCP*	*God, Creation, and Providence in the Thought of Jacob Arminius: Sources and Directions of Scholastic Protestantism in the Era of Early Orthodoxy*
Muller, *PRRD*	*Post-Reformation Reformed Dogmatics*, 4 vols. (2003)
NAKG	Nederlands Archief voor Kerkgeschiedenis (Leiden, 1829ff.)
Opera	Arminius, *Opera Theologica*, 1st ed. (1629)
Otterspeer, *Bolwerk*	*Groepsportet met Dame I. Het bolwerk van de vrijheid: De Leidse universiteit, 1575–1672*
PL	Migne, ed., *Patrologia Latina cursus completus*, 221 vols.
Platt, *Scholasticism*	*Reformed Thought and Scholasticism: The Arguments for the Existence of God in Dutch Theology, 1575–1650*
SCJ	Sixteenth Century Journal (St. Louis, 1972ff.)
SHCT	Studies in the History of Christian Thought (Leiden, 1966ff.)
ST	Thomas Aquinas, *Summa theologiae*, 61 vols. (1964–81)
Theo. disp.	Kuchlinus, *Theologicae disputationes de religionis Christianae capitibus praecipuis* (1613 ed.)
WA	*D. Martin Luthers Werke*, Kritische Gesamtausgabe (Weimar)
Workes of Perkins	Perkins, *The Workes of that Famous and Worthy Minister of Christ... Mr. William Perkins*, 3 vols. (1631–35)
Works	*The Works of James Arminius*, London edition (1825–75; repr. 1986)
Zachman, *Assurance*	*The Assurance of Faith: Conscience in the Theology of Martin Luther and John Calvin*

CHAPTER ONE

INTRODUCTION

"Without doubt or debate, Arminius is one of the most unfairly neglected and grossly misunderstood theologians in the story of Christian theology."[1] Indeed, the legacy of Jacobus Arminius (ca. 1559–1609), who is famous (or infamous) exclusively for his "anti-Calvinist" doctrine of conditional predestination, has suffered a double blow. First, the neglect by the scholarly community is evident. Despite the accessibility of Arminius's works and his undeniable status as a learned and thoughtful theologian—not to mention all the controversy that Arminius's theology and its opponents have generated—Arminius has not been given due scholarly attention. For example, although he has been a figure of intense controversy in Protestant circles for 400 years, no one has yet written a technical monograph completely devoted to his doctrine of salvation. Second, when his doctrine is discussed, it is too frequently done from an overtly biased theological perspective, resulting in confusion over what Arminius actually taught. Such misunderstanding, passed on by the internet and popular publications *ad nauseam*, perpetuates the Arminius of mythical lore—on the one hand, the free thinking, enlightened hero who put his Calvinist oppressors in their place with his irrefutable biblical theology, or, on the other hand, the deceptive heretic who resurrected Pelagianism and made anthropocentric religion, Enlightenment rationalism, and anti-Trinitarianism acceptable. The scholarly ignorance and popular misunderstanding can only be remedied by peeling away the layers and examining the "historical Arminius." To make progress toward this end, it is time for his doctrines of salvation and assurance to be analyzed in their historical context, not for the purpose of jumping to conclusions about his orthodoxy, but in order to show where and how Arminius's theology fits (or does not fit)

---

[1] Roger E. Olson, *The Story of Christian Theology: Twenty Centuries of Tradition and Reform* (Downers Grove, 1999), p. 455. See similar statements in Richard A. Muller, *God, Creation and Providence in the Thought of Jacob Arminius: Sources and Directions of Scholastic Protestantism in the Era of Early Orthodoxy* (Grand Rapids, 1991), p. 3.

with the theology of his contemporaries, on what sources his theology rests, precisely what generated the controversies with his own colleagues in the university, and, if possible, what was the foundation or starting point of his protest.

I. *The State of Arminius Scholarship and the Current Proposal*

In light of the tremendous impact of Arminius's theology on the subsequent history of doctrine along with the availability of his works in English, the scarce quantity and often deficient quality of scholarship dealing with Arminius are surprising.[2] Although there are many factors that contribute to this deficiency, I shall classify the scholarship under two particular weaknesses. The first limitation plaguing much of the scholarship on Arminius is a myopic use of sources. Included here are secondary works that fail to engage contemporary scholarship on developments in late sixteenth-century Protestant thought.[3] More prevalent and seriously flawed are the studies that neglect important primary documents of Arminius himself, and the texts they do cite are usually from translations.[4] Many of these surveys devote their sole attention to Arminius's *Declaratio sententiae* and ignore his other works of the academic genre. Unfortunately for them, it is impossible to fully comprehend some nuances of the *Declaratio* without a working knowledge of his broader theology revealed in his disputations and treatises. These studies

---

[2] For a more chronological survey of the scholarship on Arminius, see Muller, *GCP*, pp. 3–14. See also the survey in William Gene Witt, 'Creation, Redemption and Grace in the Theology of Jacob Arminius' (Ph.D. diss., University of Notre Dame, 1993), pp. 187–210.

[3] E.g., see F. Stuart Clarke, 'Arminius's Understanding of Calvin,' *Evangelical Quarterly* 54 (January–March 1982), 25–35.

[4] Most studies fail to ever consult Arminius in the original Latin, as Donald M. Lake confesses about his own work, 'He Died for All: the Universal Dimensions of the Atonement; Jacob Arminius' Contribution to a Theology of Grace,' in *Grace Unlimited*, ed. C. H. Pinnock (Minneapolis, 1975), pp. 223–42, there p. 236; see also, e.g., R. T. Kendall, *Calvin and English Calvinism to 1649*, 2nd ed. (Carlisle, UK, 1997); Howard A. Slaatte, *The Arminian Arm of Theology: The Theologies of John Fletcher, First Methodist Theologian, and His Precursor, James Arminius* (Washington, D.C., 1977). A host of other studies could be cited here, for those that refer to Arminius's Latin are far outnumbered by those that only use the translations. A few "scholarly" articles on Arminius fail to use Arminius's works at all, e.g., Charles M. Cameron, 'Arminius—Hero or Heretic?' *Evangelical Quarterly* 64 (1992), 213–27, who cites Arminius exclusively via C. Bangs's biography.

suffer the same flaws as some older Calvin scholarship that assumed the *Institutio* to be the sole and final statement of Calvin's theology.

The second weakness of much of the extant scholarship may be summed up as a failure to contextualize. We may identify three causes for such lack of historical and intellectual contextualization in Arminius studies. The first reason is directly connected to the weakness mentioned above, that is, a myopic use of sources. In other words, the accidental result of neglecting the language and vocabulary of Arminius's academic works is the creation of an ahistorical, English or American Arminius, whose rhetorical appeals to the laity in works such as *Declaratio sententiae*—over against the typical genre of Reformed scholasticism—tend to resonate with moderns. To bolster this view, Arminius's disputations and other writings belonging to the academic genre are largely neglected due to their incomprehensibility to most modern readers. One result of this situation is the still very prevalent assumption of a causal connection between scholasticism and supralapsarianism; that is, since Arminius was definitely not a supralapsarian, so the implicit argument goes, he must have been anti-scholastic.[5] However, far from being antischolastic, more recent scholarship has correctly shown that, in addition

---

[5] E.g., see Gerrit J. Hoenderdaal, 'The Life and Struggle of Arminius in the Dutch Republic,' in *Man's Faith and Freedom*, ed. Gerald O. McCulloh (New York, 1962), pp. 11–26, there p. 23, who opposes the "anti-Scholastic" theology of Arminius to "Scholastic" supralapsarianism. This assumption about the key difference between Arminius and his opponents underlies so much of older scholarship. It pervades the address given on the 300th anniversary of Arminius's death by H. Y. Groenewegen, *Jacobus Arminius op den driehonderd-jarigen gedenkdag van zijnen dood* (Leiden, 1909). Groenewegen pits biblical Christianity against speculative dogmatics. Many of these otherwise good studies fail to account for Arminius's scholastic context. Cf. G. J. Sirks, *Arminius' pleidooi voor de vrede der kerk* [Referatenreeks uit Remonstrantse Kring 11] (Lochem, 1960); J. N. Bakhuizen van den Brink, 'Arminius te Leiden,' *Nederlands Theologisch Tijdschrift* 15 (1960), 81–89; Richard F. Studebaker, 'The Theology of James Arminius,' *Reflections* 4 (1996), 4–17. Willem Otterspeer, *Groepsportet met Dame I. Het bolwerk van de vrijheid: De Leidse universiteit, 1575–1672* (Amsterdam, 2000), p. 212, may reflect similar assumptions: "In Arminius en Gomarus stond de academicus en rationalist tegenover de dogmaticus en mysticus." Slaatte, *Arminian Arm*, pp. 34 and 63, opposes the dialectical-realistic-existential Arminius to the "cold" Greek logic and rationalism of Calvin. D. M. Lake, 'He Died for All,' p. 230, distinguishes Arminius from his contemporaries as being a "biblical theologian."

For further examples of historical anachronism, inaccuracies, and unsupported generalizations, see Cameron, 'Arminius,' 213–27, who structures his essay around the TULIP acrostic (five points of which Arminius never conceived). Alan P. F. Sell, *The Great Debate: Calvinism, Arminianism and Salvation* (Grand Rapids, 1983), p. 7, concludes, "Arminius's debt was to some of the more liberal of the Renaissance humanists."

to being a biblical, humanist theologian, Arminius, like his contemporary friends and foes, was theologically trained in the scholastic method,
and was not opposed to using that training skillfully to his advantage.[6]
Even a cursory reading of the majority of his works demonstrates his
continuity with the development of Protestant scholasticism.

A second reason that several scholars have been slow to grasp the
intellectual context of Arminius may be due to their dubious comparative methodology. Rather than comparing him with his contemporaries,
some of these studies have been based on facile comparisons between
Arminius and other—often post-Enlightenment—theologians that have
little to do with Arminius's historical context. Such inquiries frequently
result not only in a superficial analysis of Arminius's thought, but also
in a failure to properly treat the theological categories of Arminius's
day, instead imposing categories from later thinkers into his system. This
problem is easily identifiable in the work of Slaatte, who sees no methodological problem in making the leap from Arminius to the Methodist
John Fletcher.[7] The point is not that one thinker cannot be compared

----

[6] Cf. Richard A. Muller, 'Arminius and the Scholastic Tradition,' *Calvin Theological Journal* 24/2 (November 1989), 263–77; *GCP*, pp. 3–4; with John Platt, *Reformed Thought and Scholasticism: The Arguments for the Existence of God in Dutch Theology, 1575–1650* [SHCT 29] (Leiden, 1982), pp. 119–76, who demonstrates the Leiden theologians' affinity for the scholastic method on the question of God's existence; and Ellis, 'Episcopius's Doctrine of Original Sin,' pp. 23–25, who, despite affirming Arminius as a true scholastic, still implicitly identifies scholasticism with rationalism and opposes it to humanism.

[7] Slaatte, *Arminian Arm*. See Muller's critique of Slaatte's method in *GCP*, p. 11. Other studies whose comparisons of Arminius necessarily de-contextualize him include Ronald Vincent Huggins, 'Romans 7 and the Ordo Salutis from Arminius to Ironside (1591–1928): With Special Emphasis on the American Revivalist Tradition in Its Trans-Atlantic Connection' (Th.D. diss., Wycliffe College [Canada], 1996), pp. 9–27, who uses Arminius as a point of departure to discuss American revivalism; Robert Thomas Dell, 'Man's Freedom and Bondage in the Thought of Martin Luther and James Arminius' (Ph.D. diss., Boston University Graduate School, 1962), in his comparison of Luther and Arminius, does not make use of Arminius's own context and contemporaries; William Kenneth Brown, 'An Analysis of Romans 7 with an Evaluation of Arminius' Dissertation on Romans 7' (Ph.D. diss., Bob Jones University, 1984), pp. 178–234, offers little in-depth analysis in his summary of Arminius on Romans 7, instead paying more attention to Paul himself and then comparing Arminius with modern Reformed and Arminian theologians. Cf. also Luke L. Keefer, 'Arminian Motifs in Anabaptist Heritage,' *Brethren in Christ History and Life* 13 (1990), 293–323. Rodney L. Reed, 'Calvin, Calvinism, and Wesley: The Doctrine of Assurance in Historical Perspective,' *Methodist History* 32 (Oct. 1993), 31–43, is another example of a study that, in its attempt to cover so much, says very little helpful for our discussion. Such studies could be multiplied here, most of which suffer from the weaknesses identified in the "Special, Diachronic" model and "Great Thinker" model discussed in James E. Bradley and Richard A. Muller, *Church History: An Introduction to Research, Reference Works, and Methods* (Grand Rapids, 1995), pp. 29–31.

with another figure from another era; the problem is the method's tendency to ignore the significance and implications of a figure's specific *Sitz im Leben*. Mitigating this problem are the existing comparative analyses of Arminius and later Dutch Remonstrants, which by definition are quite relevant to Arminius's context and not as likely to fall victim to this weakness.[8] Therefore, in contrast to comparative studies that oversimplify, misconstrue, or neglect historical and intellectual contexts, the comparison of Arminius with his faculty colleagues and Reformed contemporaries—that is, those who shared his context most proximately— is clearly of much greater relevance and interest for the understanding of Arminius.

A third cause that contributes to the neglect of Arminius's original context is that many studies, both popular and academic, are characterized by an overt partiality for or against Arminian theology. The point is not that a historian can or even should cast off all theological presuppositions, but instead that the question regarding the actual sources, motivations, and content of a particular figure's thought must be prior to the question regarding the orthodoxy of that figure. Otherwise, when the question of true understanding is explicitly subordinate to the question of orthodoxy or heresy, the door is open for the interpreter to read his own biases into the historical figure and ignore what the figure really said and why he said it. In the case of Arminius, many interpretations are not hesitant about their evaluations, with the result that the reader tends to discover more about the interpreter than about Arminius, who

---

[8] These studies include Mark Alan Ellis, 'Simon Episcopius's Doctrine of Original Sin' (Ph.D. diss., Dallas Theological Seminary, 2002); John Mark Hicks, 'The Theology of Grace in the Thought of Jacobus Arminius and Philip van Limborch: A Study in the Development of Seventeenth-Century Dutch Arminianism' (Ph.D. diss., Westminster Theological Seminary, 1985). With regard to the point of continuity and discontinuity between Arminius and his successors, Ellis, 'Episcopius's Doctrine of Original Sin,' pp. 72–123, who deals with Arminius's doctrine of original sin, argues for more continuity between Arminius and Dutch Remonstrantism than Hicks allows. On this point, see also G. J. Hoenderdaal, 'Arminius en Episcopius,' *NAKG* 60 (1980), 203–35; idem, 'The Debate about Arminius outside the Netherlands,' in *Leiden University in the Seventeenth Century: An Exchange of Learning*, ed. Th. H. Lunsingh Scheurleer and G. H. M. Posthumus Meyjes (Leiden, 1975), pp. 142–44; Lambertus Jacobus van Holk, 'From Arminius to Arminianism in Dutch Theology,' in Gerald McCulloh, ed., *Man's Faith and Freedom*, pp. 27–45; Geoffrey F. Nuttall, 'The Influence of Arminianism in England,' in Gerald McCulloh, ed., *Man's Faith and Freedom*, pp. 46–63. Cf. E. H. Cossee, *Arminius en de eerste Remonstranten in hun betrekkingen tot Rome* (Leiden, 1973). The focus of the present monograph is not on the later Remonstrants, but on Arminius and his contemporaries.

merely functions as the hero or foil.[9] In connection with the negative biases often goes the charge that Arminius's doctrine, if not wholly heretical itself, inevitably led to heresies of all kinds. Not only do these accusations taint the objectivity of the historical account, but they are generally overstated or completely false.[10] In sum, for the purpose of correct understanding and application, the prescriptive, theological question, important in its own right, must be subsequent to the descriptive, historical question.[11]

---

[9] E.g., cf. Robert A. Peterson and Michael D. Williams, *Why I Am Not an Arminian* (Downers Grove, 2004), pp. 98–133, passim, which contains numerous inaccuracies in its historical survey and theological analysis; with Jerry L. Walls and Joseph R. Dongell, *Why I Am Not a Calvinist* (Downers Grove, 2004). Robert Letham, 'Saving Faith and Assurance in Reformed Theology: Zwingli to the Synod of Dort' (Ph.D. diss., University of Aberdeen, 1979), pp. 319–20, shows his hand when he judges that Arminius's reaction against Bezan supralapsarianism "goes too far"; Louis Praamsma, 'The Background of the Arminian Controversy (1586–1618),' in *Crisis in the Reformed Churches*, ed. Peter Y. De Jong (Grand Rapids, 1968), pp. 22–38, there p. 30, refers to the "Arminian heresy."

[10] E.g., Praamsma, affirming that Arminius's objections were "centered in the doctrine of predestination" (ibid., p. 29), agrees with the assessment of H. Bavinck that "Arminianism prepared the way for rationalism" (ibid., p. 30). The rhetoric, if not the logic, of this common claim is appealing. However, if there is such a simple causal connection between the doctrine of conditional predestination and rationalism, then the Enlightenment should have followed on the heels of Irenaeus, Origen, Ambrose, and Chrysostom. For references to the doctrine of conditional predestination in patristic literature, see Keith D. Stanglin and Tom McCall, 'S. M. Baugh and the Meaning of Foreknowledge,' *Trinity Journal*, n. s. 26 (2005), 19–31, there 24 n. 26; and James Jorgenson, 'Predestination according to Divine Foreknowledge in Patristic Tradition,' in *Salvation in Christ: A Lutheran-Orthodox Dialogue*, ed. John Meyendorf and Robert Tobias (Minneapolis, 1992), pp. 159–69. That Arminius was a kind of proto-rationalist is a common claim of older scholarship. See Otto Ritschl, *Dogmengeschichte des Protestantismus: Grundlagen und Grundzüge der theologischen Gedenken- und Lehrbildung in den protestantischen Kirchen*, 4 vols. (Leipzig/Göttingen, 1908–27), 4: 320–21, who says that Arminius was a supernaturalist, despite his logical thinking and rationalism.

In addition to Enlightenment rationalism, Arminius's theology has often been linked with the Socinian heresy. For an early example of this charge, see Robert Baillie, *A Scotch Antidote against the English Infection of Arminianism* (London, 1652), pp. 18–22, who claims that Dutch Arminians "decline" to Socinianism, but English Arminians to "popery." Philip van Limborch, *Historical Relation concerning the Origin and Progress of the Controversies in the Belgic League, upon Predestination and its Connected Heads*, in L.W. P., 'Arminian Controversy in the Low Countries,' *Methodist Review* 26 (1844), 425–60 and 556–87, there 572–77, defends the later Remonstrants against the charge of Socinianism. C. Bangs, 'Arminius and Socinianism,' in *Socinianism and Its Role in the Culture of the XVIth to XVIIIth Centuries*, ed. Lech Szzucki (Warsaw, 1983), pp. 81–84, demonstrates the lack of direct connection between Arminius himself and Socinianism.

[11] See Bradley and Muller, *Church History*, pp. 48–52. Admittedly, the degree of interpretive objectivity decreases when moving from simple description to explanation to questions of larger significance. At the same time, even if this more subjective question of historical and theological significance is the most interesting aspect of historical theology (see ibid., p. 52), the questions must be posed and treated in this progressive order.

Despite the shortcomings of much of the extant scholarship, some features of Arminius's life and theology have received recent, objective, erudite treatment. The definitive biography of Arminius, based largely and necessarily on the 1609 funeral oration given by Petrus Bertius and the later biography by Caspar Brandt, but also scattered with illuminating archival research, was written by Carl Bangs.[12] As an example of early Protestant scholasticism, Muller has provided a detailed account of Arminius's doctrines of God, creation, and providence.[13] Consistent with his thesis that Arminius proposed a thoroughly alternative theological system to the emerging Reformed codification, Muller has also given briefer treatments of Arminius's Christology, possible intellectualism, and covenant theology, the latter of which is complemented by Raymond Blacketer's article.[14]

Considering that the whole of Arminius's theology has sometimes been reduced to a doctrine of predestination[15] (an unfortunate characterization to which Arminius would have undoubtedly objected), one might expect the secondary analysis of his doctrine of predestination

---

[12] Carl Bangs, *Arminius: A Study in the Dutch Reformation* (1971; repr. Eugene, OR, 1998). An example of the illuminating results of archival research is the discovery that Arminius was probably born in 1559, not 1560. Overall, the strength of C. Bangs lies in the biographical information and story telling. For a well-informed review and summary of Bangs, see John C. Godbey, 'Arminius and Predestination,' *Journal of Religion* 53 (1973), 491–98. All biographies of Arminius are heavily dependent on Petrus Bertius, *De vita et obitu reverendi & clarissimi viri D. Iacobi Arminii oratio*, in *Opera*, fols. 001–0004; *Works* 1:13–47; these subsequent biographies are Caspar Brandt, *The Life of James Arminius, D.D.*, trans. John Guthrie, with an intro. by T. O. Summers (Nashville, 1857); Nathan Bangs, *The Life of James Arminius, D.D., Compiled from His Life and Writings, as Published by Mr. James Nichols* (New York, 1843); and Jan Hendrik Maronier, *Jacobus Arminius, een biografie* (Amsterdam, 1905). See also *BLGNP* 2:33–37.

[13] Muller, *GCP*.

[14] Muller, 'The Christological Problem in the Thought of Jacobus Arminius,' *NAKG* 68 (1988), 145–63; idem, 'The Priority of the Intellect in the Soteriology of Jacob Arminius,' *Westminster Theological Journal* 55 (1993), 55–72; idem, 'The Federal Motif in Seventeenth Century Arminian Theology,' *NAKG* 62/1 (1982), 102–22; Raymond A. Blacketer, 'Arminius' Concept of Covenant in Its Historical Context,' *NAKG* 80/2 (2000), 193–220, focuses more deliberately on Arminius himself than does Muller's study on Arminian covenant theology.

[15] Peter White, *Predestination, Policy, and Polemic: Conflict and Consensus in the English Church from the Reformation to the Civil War* (Cambridge, Eng., 1992), p. 13, says, "Arminianism was nothing if not a doctrine of predestination." The contrary mistake is often made as well, namely, asserting that Arminius simply rejected predestination. E.g., G. C. Berkouwer, *Faith and Justification*, trans. Lewis B. Smedes [Studies in Dogmatics] (Grand Rapids, 1954), p. 161, classifies "Arminianism" among those systems that "have denied election."

to be more complete than it is. Yet in-depth attempts to understand Arminius on this controversial point are limited. The most comprehensive treatment of Arminius's doctrine of predestination is by Evert Dekker.[16] Connected with predestination, Dekker and Muller have also clearly shown Arminius's appropriation of the Jesuit doctrine of *scientia media* and its implications for his theology.[17] Most extant studies of Arminius on predestination still fail to take this important modification of the divine knowledge into account.

Apart from the doctrines of God and his acts of creation, providence, and predestination, there have been no monographs devoted to other important aspects of Arminius's theology. Two noteworthy dissertations have investigated grace in the thought of Arminius.[18] Occasionally, modern discussions of "Arminian" soteriology will attempt to recover the views of the "historical Arminius," but, as noted above, such efforts often de-contextualize Arminius from his *Sitz im Leben*, use him to promote a modern theological agenda, and generate as many questions as answers about Arminius.[19]

---

[16] Evert Dekker, *Rijker dan Midas: Vrijheid, genade en predestinatie in de theologie van Jacobus Arminius, 1559–1609* (Zoetermeer, The Netherlands, 1993). Dekker's greatest strength is his exposition of the philosophical background of and modalities within Arminius's doctrine. See also idem, 'Jacobus Arminius and his Logic: Analysis of a Letter,' *Journal of Theological Studies*, n.s. 44 (1993), 118–42. See briefer summaries of Arminius's doctrine of predestination with some analysis in Richard A. Muller, 'Grace, Election, and Contingent Choice: Arminius' Gambit and the Reformed Response,' in *The Grace of God and the Bondage of the Will*, ed. Thomas Schreiner and Bruce Ware, 2 vols. (Grand Rapids, 1995), 2: 251–78, there 254–59; Arthur Skevington Wood, 'The Declaration of Sentiments: The Theological Testament of Arminius,' *Evangelical Quarterly* 65 (April 1993), 111–29, there 115–22; Bangs, *Arminius*, pp. 308–13 and 350–55; White, *Predestination*, pp. 22–32; D. M. Lake, 'He Died for All,' pp. 236–39; Clarke, 'Arminius's Understanding,' pp. 30–35; Cameron, 'Arminius,' 217–21; Emmanuel D. Mbennah and J. M. Vorster, 'The Influence of Arminian Conception of Predestination on the 18th-century Wesleyan Revival,' *Studia Historiae Ecclesiasticae* 24 (1998), 169–72; these latter two are heavily reliant on Bangs, *Arminius*.

[17] Dekker, 'Was Arminius a Molinist?' *SCJ* 27/2 (1996), 337–52; Muller, *GCP*, pp. 154–66. Witt, 'Creation,' pp. 336–70, argues against interpreting Arminius as a Molinist. Cf. Luis de Molina, *On Divine Foreknowledge (Part IV of the Concordia)*, trans. Alfred J. Freddoso (Ithaca, 1988).

[18] See Witt, 'Creation,' and Hicks, 'Theology of Grace,' in which Hicks demonstrates the discontinuity between the doctrine of grace taught by Arminius and the subsequent development of the doctrine in Dutch Remonstrantism, represented by Limborch; idem, 'The Righteousness of Saving Faith: Arminian versus Remonstrant Grace,' *Evangelical Journal* 9 (Spring 1991), 27–39, provides a summary of his argument.

[19] E.g., see Stephen M. Ashby, 'A Reformed Arminian View,' in *Four Views on Eternal Security*, ed. J. Matthew Pinson (Grand Rapids, 2002), pp. 135–87; Peterson and Williams, *Why I Am Not an Arminian*.

In contrast to the shortage of material on Arminius's doctrines of salvation and assurance, there is a substantial literature investigating these doctrines as they appear in Reformation and Post-Reformation Reformed theology. These studies are often concerned with either defending or challenging the once prevalent "Calvin versus the Calvinists" assumption of older scholarship.[20] In many of the studies defending this older hypothesis, if Arminius is discussed at all, it is to attempt to show how far Reformed theology had strayed from Calvin and how close it had come to Arminius.[21]

Given this present state of scholarship, the present essay will supplement the current literature available both on Arminius's theology (which has not yet dealt adequately with his doctrines of salvation and especially assurance) and on the early Reformed orthodox understanding of the doctrines of salvation and assurance in the period of early Protestant orthodoxy (which has not yet dealt adequately with Arminius).[22] These two fields of research intersect in this topic of Arminius's doctrine of the assurance of salvation. In addition, this essay will seek to avoid the pitfalls mentioned above by placing Arminius in his proper *Sitz im Leben*, comparing him with his most proximate colleagues, and taking into account Richard A. Muller's reappraisal of Arminius as a scholastic theologian in continuity with the methodology of the early period of Protestant orthodoxy.[23]

---

[20] On the one hand, R. T. Kendall, *Calvin*, and M. Charles Bell, *Calvin and Scottish Theology: The Doctrine of Assurance* (Edinburgh, 1985), both argue for the vast discontinuity between Calvin and subsequent Reformed theology. John S. Bray, *Theodore Beza's Doctrine of Predestination* (Nieuwkoop, 1975), also underscores the supposed discontinuity from Calvin to Beza in the doctrine of assurance, among other doctrines. Letham, 'Faith,' somewhat backing off of the discontinuity bandwagon, argues for two distinct strands of covenant theology, faith, and assurance in Reformed theology. On the other hand, Joel R. Beeke, *Assurance of Faith: Calvin, English Puritanism, and the Dutch Second Reformation* (New York, 1991), sees substantial continuity between Calvin and Reformed orthodoxy on these soteriological issues. For a comparison of Luther and Calvin on assurance, see Randall C. Zachman, *The Assurance of Faith: Conscience in the Theology of Martin Luther and John Calvin* (Minneapolis, 1993).

[21] E.g., see Kendall, *Calvin*, pp. 143–44.

[22] Letham, 'Faith,' pp. 311–20, who in some ways comes closer to my topic than any other study, deals in only a few pages with Arminius's doctrine of faith and assurance, and, significantly, attempts to compare Arminius with his Reformed contemporaries, including his Leiden colleague, Gomarus.

[23] I follow the proposed periodization of Protestant orthodoxy in Muller, *PRRD* 1:30–32.

This book specifically will seek to demonstrate at which points Jacobus Arminius's soteriology and doctrine of the assurance of salvation exhibit continuity as well as discontinuity with those of his Reformed predecessors and contemporaries, notably his colleagues on the theological faculty in Leiden, and then argue that his teaching on assurance coheres well with the rest of his theology. The essay, then, rather than tracing the impact of Arminius's teaching in later Dutch Remonstrantism or English anti-Calvinism, will focus on the debate during Arminius's years as a professor in Leiden (1603–09). This study will reveal the central importance of assurance as a decisive factor in the thought and polemic of Arminius and explore the connection between assurance, predestination, and the doctrine of God. It will also demonstrate, contrary to certain scholarly readings of Arminius's thought and its impact, that Arminius's soteriological system did not attenuate the possibility of the assurance of salvation, but instead was intended to grant full assurance of salvation to Christian believers. Indeed, this book will show that Arminius's interest in the doctrine of assurance and his engagement in the significant debate over this issue may very well be an important foundation and driving force of his polemic against certain aspects of the Reformed theology of his time. His reaction against supralapsarianism, traditionally regarded as the starting point of Arminius's polemic, is itself the consequence of his thought concerning true assurance of salvation.

II. *The Importance of Arminius and Assurance*

For several reasons it is important to fill the scholarly gap and offer an analysis of Arminius's doctrine of the assurance of salvation. First, on a purely historical level, it further illuminates the shape of this most significant theological debate in Leiden, whose repercussions quickly spread geographically and have continued down through the centuries. Examining the roots of this controversy will reveal exactly what the key issues of contention were and what they were not. It will be seen that the position and function of the topic of assurance were crucial in the Arminian debate, with the implication that modern appraisals of historical Arminianism that ignore the problem of assurance require modification. Second, to bring the historical question into its present day relevance, this essay will help today's "Arminians" and "Calvinists" to see what is at stake in their respective theological viewpoints and to understand their respective theological heritage on the topic of assurance, and it ought to challenge crude notions of the lack of the assurance of salvation in the thought of Arminius. The essay should help historians and theologians understand and appreciate the rich heritage of the Dutch Reformation and what the Arminian controversy was and is all about. As noted above, neither practical, contemporary application nor an assessment of doctrinal orthodoxy is within the scope of this essay; however, since historical inquiry need not be completely theoretical, it is appropriate for modern theologians to take into account and wrestle with the categories of historical theology in general and of the Arminian dispute in particular.

III. *Methodology and Outline*

This project is in the field of intellectual history, the history of contextual theology.[24] Therefore, the primary mode of research will involve a detailed analysis of Arminius's theological treatises and disputations. Arminius's *Declaratio sententiae*, his mature apologetic and polemical statement on the topics of controversy, delivered before the States of Holland in Dutch on 30 October 1608, is perhaps the most important document for understanding Arminius.[25] However, as merely a starting point and

---

[24] See Heiko A. Oberman, *The Reformation: Roots and Ramifications*, trans. Andrew Colin Gow (Grand Rapids, 1994), pp. 1–2, who distinguishes between the broad history of ideas and the more specifically contextual history of thought. See also the helpful distinctions in Bradley and Muller, *Church History*, pp. 4–11. Furthermore, the social and political history impacting Arminius, which are integrated well and can be consulted in the work of C. Bangs, will not play a significant role in this book.

[25] Jacobus Arminius, *Verclaringhe Iacobi Arminii Saliger ghedachten, in zijn leven Professor Theologiae binnen Leyden: Aengaende zyn ghevoelen* (Leiden, 1610); *Verklaring van Jacobus Arminius, afgelegd in de vergadering van de staten van Holland op 30 Oktober, 1608*, ed. G. J. Hoenderdaal (Lochem, 1960) (*Dec. sent.*); *Declaratio sententiae I. Arminii de praedestinatione, providentia Dei, libero arbitrio, gratia Dei, divinitate Filii Dei, et de iustificatione hominis coram Deo*, in *Opera Theologica*, pp. 91–133; *The Just Mans Defence, or, The Declaration of the Judgement of James Arminius . . . concerning the Principal Points of Religion, to which is added, Nine Questions Exhibited by the Deputies of the Synod . . .*, trans. Tobias Conyers (London, 1657); and in *The Works of James Arminius*, London Edition, trans. James Nichols and William Nichols, 3 vols. (London, 1825, 1828, 1875; repr. with an intro. by Carl Bangs, Grand Rapids, 1986) 1:580–732. For a useful introduction to the historical background of *Declaratio*, see, in addition to the standard biographies of Arminius, Hoenderdaal, 'Inleiding,' in *Verklaring van Jacobus Arminius, afgelegd in de vergadering van de staten van Holland op 30 Oktober, 1608*, ed. G. J. Hoenderdaal (Lochem, 1960), pp. 8–41. Translations from the original Dutch *Declaratio* are mine. Latin references to this Dutch document will only be

succinct guide to the controversies, the *Declaratio* was in no way intended
to be a statement of Arminius's whole theology. This document should
be supplemented first with the disputations of Arminius contained in
the collection of *Disputationes publicae et privatae*, found in Arminius's
Opera. Here the reader has access to many more topics that never came
under controversy, but, as will be seen in this essay, nevertheless contribute significantly to understanding Arminius on the controversial topics.
These works must then be supplemented by the numerous treatises and
letters that Arminius wrote during his pastorate and professorship.[26] In
addition to the works translated into English and the letters transcribed
and published by the Remonstrants in the seventeenth century,[27] there
exist at least 35 public disputations by Arminius that were not included
in his *Opera* and that remain untranslated. Analysis of these disputations
will further aid our understanding of Arminius's theology.[28]

given when the terminology is deemed important; although not translated into Latin
by Arminius, Latin terminology can serve as a clue to the thought of the author, given
the theological precedence and sophistication of Latin over early seventeenth-century
Dutch. Page references to Arminius's other documents will be given to the Latin *Opera*
and English *Works* (with volume number). Nichols's translation is extremely helpful, but
I have in each quotation checked the original and usually altered the translation based
on the original Dutch or Latin.

[26] The *Opera* of 1629 (2nd edition, 1631; 3rd edition, 1635) contains all of the major
treatises translated in the London edition of the *Works*, with the exception of *Examen
Thesium D. Francisci Gomari de Praedestinatione* ([Amsterdam,] 1645), in *Works* 3:522–658.
Useful introductions and historical background to these pieces can be found in *Works*,
passim, and in Bangs, *Arminius*, passim. Arminius's letters are found in *Praestantium ac
eruditorum virorum epistolae ecclesiasticae et theologicae*, 2nd ed., preface by Philip van Limborch (Amsterdam, 1684). Several of the letters have been translated by Nichols in the text
and notes of the London edition of the *Works*.

[27] These letters are found in *Ep. ecc.*

[28] These hitherto unused disputations of Arminius, along with those of his Leiden
colleagues, are cited by the thesis number (in lowercase Roman numerals) within the particular disputation. If it is necessary to distinguish, the short references in the footnotes
will include the year of the disputation, and, in rare cases, the name of the respondent.
In the final bibliography, the disputations not appearing in Arminius's *Opera theologica*
are organized alphabetically by title under the author's name (rather than chronologically or according to *locus* treated). Two of the most important of these disputations by
Arminius pertaining to this study have been transcribed in Appendices 2 and 3. The
disputations by the Leiden faculty were mostly separate documents. However, a massive
collection of the regent Johannes Kuchlinus's disputations is found in the posthumous
collection, *Ecclesiarum hollandicarum et Westfrisicarum catechismus... disputationibus theologicis,
a quaestionum et responsionum catecheticarum initio ad finem, in unum volumen redactis* ([Geneva,]
1612), which is actually the second edition. The third edition is *Theologicae disputationes
de religionis Christianae capitibus praecipuis: in collegio theologico Illustr. DD. Ordinum Hollandiae et
Westfrisiae* ([Geneva,] 1613).

Throughout this study, the thought of Arminius will be compared and contrasted with the thought of important contemporaries of Arminius on certain topics relating to salvation and assurance. The most important of these contemporaries include William Perkins—who wrote extensively on assurance and whose treatise on predestination generated a response from Arminius—and Arminius's colleagues on the theological faculty at Leiden—specifically, Franciscus Gomarus, the younger Lucas Trelcatius, and the regent Johannes Kuchlinus. This comparison should reveal not only the similarities and differences between Arminius and a major representative of the Cambridge Reformed theology, but it will also illuminate for the first time the shape and character of the "Leiden theology" during Arminius's tenure. The public disputations of Arminius's colleagues at Leiden are an essential source for knowledge of the debates at Leiden University, and examination of the debates is a useful way to discover the theology behind them. Alongside of these contemporaries, it will be appropriate on occasion to note the thought of predecessors influential to both Arminius and his opponents.[29] These figures will only be used to indicate early Protestant orthodoxy's dialogue with the Christian theological tradition, and to keep the debates pertinent to this essay in their historical and theological context.

In addition to the primary method of analyzing the relevant works of Arminius and the secondary method of comparison with contemporaries and predecessors, this essay will interact with recent scholarship that deals with Arminius and the doctrines of salvation and assurance. As indicated above, secondary scholarship has provided little opportunity for dialogue on this point; therefore, the majority of critical interaction will be with those works examining issues of soteriology and assurance in the thought of Calvin and subsequent Reformed theologians. Of these works, primary attention will be given to the studies of J. Beeke and R. T. Kendall, the latter of which has been a flashpoint of controversy for over two decades.

Before proceeding to a summary of this book's contents, a matter of terminology should be addressed. Throughout this study, the thought of Arminius is juxtaposed with the thought of the "Reformed." This usage

---

[29] Of particular interest are the theologians known to have been an influence on Arminius. A good, albeit not infallible, indication of this influence is the list of books from Arminius's personal collection, documented in *The Auction Catalogue of the Library of J. Arminius*, a facsimile edition with an introduction by Carl O. Bangs (Utrecht, 1985).

of "Reformed" is not intended as a denial of the fact that Arminius and the Remonstrants before the Synod of Dort (1618–19) considered themselves to be Reformed. It is clear that Arminius taught and died in good standing with the Reformed Church. However, given that the Dutch Reformed Church expelled the Arminians, and that the Arminians in turn quickly distanced themselves from the Reformed, it still seems appropriate (or at least less complicated) to use "Reformed" to represent the theological opponents most closely associated with Arminius. At any rate, since the Lutherans and Roman Catholics paid no attention to Arminius during his life, his opponents were nothing other than Reformed. The question of the legitimacy of calling Arminius "Reformed" will be raised in the conclusion of the essay.

Having now introduced the aim and method of this study, a general outline will show the progression of the project. Part one of the essay, "Background of the Debate," serves as an introduction to the context of Arminius. It consists of chapter two, "Arminius and His Academic Context," which offers a brief biography of Arminius with emphasis on his university setting and interaction with colleagues in Leiden. This chapter will conclude with a discussion of two issues relevant for a proper understanding of Arminius's soteriology—namely, the nature and authorship of the disputations that played such a vital role in the Leiden debate, and the nature and use of Aristotelian causality in discussions of salvation.

The essay is then divided into two more parts. Part two, "The Ontology of Salvation," which includes chapters three and four, describes and analyzes certain features of Arminius's doctrine of salvation. Chapter three, "Grace, Predestination, and the *Ordo Salutis*," provides an overall survey of the soteriological issues in Arminius's theology. Arminius continually stressed that predestination is the foundation both of salvation and of the certainty of salvation, and that the pastoral purpose of predestination is to effect assurance of salvation. This brief examination of the shape of Arminius's soteriology is necessary for the following, more detailed discussion of the soteriological problems raised by Christian living.

Chapter four, "Sanctification, Perfection, and Apostasy," begins the more precise discussion of Arminius's soteriology as it relates to Christian living. First, Arminius and his colleagues are compared on basic issues of sanctification and good works. In light of modern misunderstandings concerning Arminius's views, his discussion of the possibility of moral perfection is then examined. Finally, I reach a conclusion regarding his opinion on the possibility of apostasy, paying careful attention to his examination of Perkins and his statements regarding David's sin.

Part three of the monograph, "The Epistemology of Salvation," consisting of chapters five and six, addresses the central problem of this essay, namely, how a person knows he is saved, and the degree of certainty to which it can be known. Chapter five, "The Undermining of Assurance," explores what Arminius calls the "two fiery darts of Satan," the pests of religion and of souls: namely, despair and security. It is first necessary to define assurance, a basic point of departure often overlooked by modern discussions. Then the chapter proceeds to look at the theological tradition of this dialectic between despair and security that was so important to Arminius. Arminius was convinced that certain aspects of Reformed soteriology, ultimately expressed in unconditional predestination—especially the supralapsarian variety—led to either one of these two harmful dispositions. Along with other "anti-Calvinists," he was disturbed by the overall neglect of the danger of *securitas*.

Chapter six, "The Grounding of Assurance," reveals how Arminius sought to make assurance possible for the Christian believer. After an initial survey of certainty in general, Arminius's thought is compared with the typical Reformed *a posteriori* testimonies of salvation and the "practical syllogism." Then the *a priori* grounds of assurance are illustrated and contrasted. For Arminius, the ultimate ground of assurance is the twofold love of God.

Chapter seven concludes the essay by drawing some of the principal themes together. The distinction and connection between the ontology and epistemology of salvation are restated, and final comparisons and contrasts between the thought of Arminius and his Reformed contemporaries are summarized. Finally, the results of the research call for a modification of how interpreters ought to view the position and function of assurance in Arminius's theology.

PART ONE: BACKGROUND OF THE DEBATE

CHAPTER TWO

ARMINIUS AND HIS ACADEMIC CONTEXT

Because the biography of Arminius is readily accessible to modern readers, it is not desirable to summarize Bertius, C. Brandt, or Bangs. It is appropriate, however, to position Arminius in the context of his colleagues on the theological faculty of Leiden University and in the context of their standard pedagogical and theological methods. Thus, rather than a traditional biographical sketch of Arminius with passing reference to Leiden University, we shall offer a narrative of some aspects of university life as they relate to the context of Arminius. This chapter—consisting of a brief "biographical" sketch of the theological college at Leiden, an analysis of the disputation method within the curriculum, and a survey of Arminius's theological method—will help fill in some gaps, especially for English readers, in our knowledge of the details of Arminius's academic life and professorial career. Attention to his university context will illuminate the nature of the debate during the first decade of the seventeenth century.[1]

The history of Leiden University is well documented.[2] Its history goes back to 1574, when Spanish troops lifted their siege of Leiden

---

[1] This biographical sketch supplements those found in Bertius, *Vita*; Gerard Brandt, *The History of the Reformation and Other Ecclesiastical Transactions in and about the Low-Countries*, 4 vols. (London, 1720–23); *LA*; A. W. Harrison, *The Beginnings of Arminianism to the Synod of Dort* (London, 1926), pp. 16–130; Bangs, *Arminius*; *BLGNP* 2:33–7; Edwin Rabbie, 'Introduction,' in Hugo Grotius, *Ordinum Hollandiae ac Westfrisiae Pietas (1613)*, trans. Edwin Rabbie (Leiden, 1995), pp. 1–92, there pp. 2–10. A decent summary of the vital records of Arminius is in A. A. Bantjes, ed., *De Leidse hoogleraren en lectoren 1575–1815. 1. De theologische faculteit* (Leiden, 1983), pp. 4–6. Equally important, but beyond the scope of this essay, is the political context of the Arminian debate. In addition to the information in Bangs, *Arminius*, a good survey of the political landscape is available in Jonathan Israel, *The Dutch Republic: Its Rise, Greatness, and Fall, 1477–1806* (Oxford, 1995); Christine Kooi, *Liberty and Religion: Church and State in Leiden's Reformation, 1572–1620* [Studies in Medieval and Reformation Thought 82] (Leiden, 2000). See also Michael Abram Hakkenberg, 'The Predestinarian Controversy in the Netherlands, 1600–1620' (Ph.D. diss., University of California at Berkeley, 1989).

[2] Otterspeer, *Bolwerk*, is the first volume of a multi-volume history of Leiden University; idem, 'Leiden, University of,' in *The Dictionary of Seventeenth- and Eighteenth-Century Dutch Philosophers*, vol. 2 (Bristol, Eng., 2003), 603–14; Henrike L. Clotz, *Hochschule für Holland: Die Universität Leiden im Spannungsfeld zwischen Provinz, Stadt und Kirche, 1575–1619*

and retreated. In reward for their bravery and perseverance, William of Orange offered the citizens of Leiden either tax relief or a university; they chose the latter. Thus, the first northern Dutch university opened there in 1575. According to university records, "Jacobus Hermannus ex Veteribus Aquis" was the twelfth student to enroll, matriculating on 23 October 1576 as a student of liberal arts.[3]

I. *Arminius in the Staten College*

Between the time of Arminius's brief sojourn as a student in Leiden and his return as professor in 1603, the university went through many changes. The most important addition was the establishment of the Staten College, or theological college, in 1592, for the purpose of training ministers. The wish of university curator Jan (van der Does) Dousa was that the college would be a temple of rest and harmony, "a true wet nurse for the church."[4] The history and character of the college would be determined by the personalities of its regents, sub-regents, and faculty.[5]

A. *Regent, Sub-regent, and Faculty*

In light of the high expectations for the college, great care was taken in choosing a regent to lead it. Before and during the years of Arminius's tenure as a professor, the Staten College was headed by the former Amsterdam pastor, Johannes Kuchlinus.[6] On 6 October 1592, the

---

(Stuttgart, 1998); Heinz Schneppen, *Niederländische Universitäten und Deutsches Geistesleben von der Gründung der Universität Leiden bis ins späte 18. Jahrhundert* (Münster, 1960); G. D. J. Schotel, *De Academie te Leiden* (Haarlem, 1875); Albert Eekhof, *De theologische faculteit te Leiden in de 17de eeuw* (Utrecht, 1921); Margreet J. A. M. Ahsmann, *Collegia en Colleges: Juridisch onderwijs aan de Leidse Universiteit 1575–1630 in het bijzonder het disputeren* (Groningen, 1990) is an examination of pedagogical method in the early law faculty of Leiden. For first hand reports and archival transcripts, see P. C. Molhuysen, *Bronnen tot de geschiedenis der Leidsche Universiteit*, 7 vols. (The Hague, 1913–24).

   [3] W. du Rieu, ed., *Album Studiosorum Academiae Lugduno Batavae MDLXXV–MDCCCLXXV, Accedunt Nomina Curatorum et Professorum* (The Hague, 1875), col. 1.

   [4] Schotel, *Academie*, p. 26.

   [5] On the Staten College, cf. Otterspeer, *Bolwerk*, pp. 151–63; Clotz, *Hochschule*, pp. 67–76.

   [6] For biographical information on Kuchlinus, see Lucas Trelcatius, Jr., *Oratio funebris in obitum reverendi et clarissimi viri D. Iohannis Kuchlini*, ad diem 5 July 1606 (Leiden, 1606); *BLGNP* 5:317–19; B. Glasius, *Godgeleerd Nederland: Biographisch Woordenboek van Nederland-*

college was initiated with Kuchlinus's inaugural address in Latin.[7] However, because of his responsibilities as a pastor in Amsterdam, Kuchlinus took a hiatus from the college, during which time Jeremias Bastingius was appointed regent and Petrus Bertius as sub-regent. By 1595, Kuchlinus was freed from his pastoral duties in Amsterdam and he resumed his position as regent, which he would hold until his death in 1606. Under Kuchlinus, the Staten College was in stable hands. Kuchlinus, who studied under Zacharias Ursinus at Heidelberg and was himself an expert on the Heidelberg Catechism, was a thoroughly Reformed theologian, and by all accounts, serious and reliable. He was a well-recognized scholar of philosophy, languages, and the sacred letters.[8] Like Dousa, Kuchlinus wanted the college to be a cultivating ground of the foundations of learning and of all virtues. He hoped it would be a beehive from which the bees would swarm out to the churches, schools, and republics to make honey.[9]

Of special interest are the changes that Kuchlinus's family experienced after his permanent move to Leiden. On 10 December 1596, Kuchlinus married his fifth wife, Geertgen Jacobsdochter of Oudewater. She was the sister of Arminius's father. By the time of this wedding, Kuchlinus and Arminius were already well acquainted. A decade earlier, Kuchlinus had written a letter in the name of the Amsterdam presbytery to Arminius while the latter was studying in Geneva.[10] In addition, from the time Arminius was ordained as pastor in Amsterdam in 1588 until Kuchlinus left Amsterdam for Leiden in 1595, they were colleagues in ministry. This wedding in 1596 made Kuchlinus Arminius's new uncle by marriage, a relationship that would be further

---

sche Godgeleerden, 3 vols. ('s-Hertogenbosch, 1851–56), 1: 319; *Biographisch Woordenboek van Protestantsche Godgeleerden in Nederland*, ed. J. P. de Bie and J. Loosjes, 6 vols. (The Hague, 1919–49), 5: 289–96; L. van Poelgeest, ed., *Addenda Hoogleraren en Lectoren Theologie, Regenten Statencollege, Regenten Waals College, Bibliothecarissen, Secretarissen van de Curatoren* (Leiden, 1985), pp. 32–33.

[7] Johannes Kuchlinus, *Oratio reverendi doctissimíque viri D. Iohannis Kuchlini, ecclesiae Amstelrodamensis pastoris, electi et vocati primi praesidis Collegii Theologici* (Leiden, 1593). Some significant points of this discourse are summarized in Paul Auguste Georges Dibon, *L'Enseignement philosophique dans les universités néerlandaises à l'époque pré-cartésienne (1575–1650)* (Amsterdam, 1954), pp. 22–23; Platt, *Scholasticism*, pp. 82–85.

[8] Trelcatius, *Oratio funebris*, fol. B4v: "Magna in illo fuit Artium liberalium et Philosophiae cognitio, major linguarum, sacrarum litterarum maxima."

[9] Otterspeer, *Bolwerk*, p. 162.

[10] The letter, dated Kal. June 1586, is transcribed in Herman de Vries, ed., *Genève pépinière du Calvinisme hollandais*, vol. 2 (The Hague, 1924), pp. 31–33.

solidified when Arminius joined the Leiden faculty less than seven years later. Furthermore, the wedding was the occasion of the young pastor Arminius meeting and commencing a discussion with the experienced Leiden professor, Franciscus Junius.[11] Thus began Arminius's famous work, *Amica cum Iunio collatio* (published, 1613).

The daughters of Kuchlinus also contributed to the interesting new shape of the Kuchlinus household in the 1590s. On 17 February 1596 his daughter Marijtge married Petrus Bertius, and on 26 November 1599 his daughter Jannetje married Festus Hommius. Bertius was professor of ethics and philosophy at Leiden, and he was sub-regent of the Staten College under Bastingius (1593–95) and then under his father-in-law Kuchlinus (1595–1606).[12] After Kuchlinus's death, Bertius then became regent in 1606, a post which he held until 1615. Notably, he also was a friend of Arminius and Hugo Grotius. Bertius delivered the oration at Arminius's funeral, which was published, and to which Gomarus responded in writing. He was a signer of the Remonstrance of 1610. When the Remonstrants were dismissed in 1619, Bertius went to Paris and became a Roman Catholic, working and teaching under the king. During his tenure in the college, at the least, Bertius was "one of the most controversial Arminians;" at the most, he was charged with heterodoxy.[13] Hommius, the other son-in-law of Kuchlinus, was a preacher in Leiden, and was one of the most outspoken opponents of Arminius and later Remonstrants.[14] He occasionally confronted Arminius in the presence of others.[15] After Arminius's death, Hommius began conducting *collegia* of disputations with university students.[16] Hommius went on to become secretary at the Synod of Dort, and he later became regent of the Staten College in 1619. Thus, in the space of less than four

---

[11] See a biographical sketch of Junius in *BLGNP* 2:275–78.

[12] Cf. the biographical sketch of Bertius in *BLGNP* 2:63–64.

[13] Otterspeer, *Bolwerk*, pp. 158–59, reports that Bertius was also rumored to be a homosexual. This charge, although it is likely untrue, demonstrates how controversial Bertius was as sub-regent and later regent. Schotel, *Academie*, p. 30, says that during Bertius's tenure as regent (1606–1615), the Staten College was known as the "hotbed of the Jesuits."

[14] The standard biography of Hommius is P. J. Wijminga, *Festus Hommius* (Leiden, 1899). Cf. also *BLGNP* 2:251–54.

[15] *Ep. ecc.* 77, p. 145; *Works* 1:469–70.

[16] Wijminga, *Hommius*, pp. 73–76. His "collegium antibellarminum" was published in 1614 as *LXX Disputationes*. See the laws and roster of this particular *collegium* in Wijminga, *Hommius*, Bijlage H, pp. xv–xvii.

years, three weddings brought together opposite ends of the theological spectrum in Leiden. Kuchlinus was Arminius's new step-uncle; Bertius and Hommius were brothers-in-law, and the husbands of Arminius's new step-cousins. Otterspeer remarks, "Seldom have family relations been less representative of ideological sympathies."[17]

In 1602, when the plague came to the low countries, Leiden University lost two-thirds of its theological faculty, namely, Franciscus Junius and Lucas Trelcatius, Sr. François Gomaer, better known as Franciscus Gomarus, who had been on the faculty since 1594, was the sole survivor.[18] Arminius and Lucas Trelcatius, Jr., would replace the two vacant positions. After Trelcatius died in 1607 and Arminius in 1609, Gomarus found himself the sole survivor at Leiden again. Gomarus then left for Middelburg in 1611, after the appointment of the controversial Conrad Vorstius. These three—Gomarus, Arminius, and Trelcatius, Jr. (in order of seniority)—were the core of the faculty during the often unsettled first decade of the seventeenth century.

B. *Working Relationships*

Now that the Staten College has been briefly introduced, it is important to consider it from the perspective of a working environment, for behind the academic, theological curriculum stand four men— Kuchlinus, Gomarus, Arminius, and Trelcatius, Jr. Each man had his own background, biases, experiences, personality, and idiosyncrasies. Because of the lack of primary source material regarding the question of working relationships, our conclusions in this section must be cautious. The existing evidence is really a combination of clues that come from primary and secondary sources, from anecdotal testimony and official documentation.

It might be tempting to point to the scant evidence of the personal interaction within the Staten College as an indicator that this question is insignificant. On the contrary, the matter of the working relationship at Leiden is important for seeking answers to two important questions that

---

[17] Otterspeer, *Bolwerk*, p. 158: "Zelden waren familierelaties minder representatief voor ideologische sympathieën."

[18] The standard biography of Gomarus is Gerrit Pieter van Itterzon, *Franciscus Gomarus* (The Hague, 1929). Cf. Bangs, *Arminius*, pp. 245–48; *BLGNP* 2:220–25.

arise when one considers Arminius's tenure there. The first question is how did Arminius survive in an environment in which all of his colleagues viewed his theology as heterodox? Second, how did the personal and theological polemic affect further development of theology and the theological curriculum? The evidence and the conclusions yielded by this biographical sketch of the theological college will be important for discovering the roots of the debate in Leiden.

The tense working association at Leiden began before Arminius was appointed professor.[19] Professors at Leiden were normally called by the curators of the university after the university Senate (which included ordinary, but not extraordinary, professors) and faculties had been consulted.[20] The curators wanted Arminius to be the replacement for Junius. Many influential people supported this decision, including Johannes Uytenbogaert, Arminius's good friend and pastor in The Hague and future Remonstrant leader. However, Arminius's imminent arrival drew opposition from several ministers. More importantly, his proposed appointment was opposed by his step-uncle Kuchlinus, the regent of the Staten College. Speaking before the curators, Kuchlinus exclaimed, "Pray, what shall I, an old man, do? Shall I suffer my pupils to attend the Academy, and hear and carry away with them new doctrines every day? I will not bear it: I will not suffer it: I will rather shut up my college."[21] The appointment was also opposed by Gomarus, the senior faculty member. Gomarus told the curators that Junius's dying request was that Arminius not replace him at Leiden. The curators did not believe the story; rather, they felt that Gomarus, who had only greeted Arminius once from a distance and never read Arminius's correspondence with Junius, had no authority to speak on the matter (unlike Kuchlinus, who at least knew Arminius fairly well).[22]

Arminius, who was not initially seeking this professorship, was cleared by the church and city of Amsterdam to accept the call to Leiden. On 6 May 1603 a conference took place at The Hague to provide Arminius an opportunity to answer charges from Gomarus and defend his ortho-

---

[19] See G. Brandt, *History* 2:26–28; and Caspar Brandt, *The Life of James Arminius, D.D.*, trans. John Guthrie, with an intro. by T. O. Summers (Nashville, 1857), pp. 132–59, on Arminius's call and the support and opposition to it.

[20] See Schotel, *Academie*, p. 228.

[21] *LA*, p. 137.

[22] *LA*, pp. 137–39.

doxy before witnesses of church and state.[23] This would be the first of many conferences between Arminius and Gomarus at The Hague. It is evident that the intention of this conference was to determine whether Arminius was orthodox. Until he was cleared, his appointment was not guaranteed. Arminius answered all the charges of Gomarus to the satisfaction of the audience, and thus overcame the final obstacle standing in his way. Therefore, in response to the favorable outcome of the conference, the curators named Arminius as Professor of Theology on 8 May 1603.[24]

It was subsequently urged by the university authorities that Arminius be invested with the title of doctor. Universities conferred doctorates on anyone who excelled in the arts or sciences, and especially in theology, since it was thought to transcend all other disciplines.[25] Arminius consented, and his doctoral examination was conducted by Gomarus on 19 June 1603. Arminius reported that the private examination, which took place with two others present, went smoothly. In a letter to Uytenbogaert, Arminius commended Gomarus for acting honorably and fairly.[26] Three weeks later, on 10 July, Arminius successfully defended a public disputation for his degree entitled *De natura Dei*.[27] Among the four designated opponents were Bertius and Hommius. The next day, following his public lecture on the priestly office of Christ, Arminius was awarded the doctorate from Leiden University. After the act of promotion, as was customary, Arminius prayed to God and then addressed Gomarus before the audience. Arminius humbly thanked Gomarus for his role in promoting him, and said he hoped Gomarus "could never justly repent of the conferring of this honor" on Arminius.[28] According to the Acts of the Senate, Arminius was officially promoted to Professor Ordinarius on 11 October 1603.[29] He began presiding over public disputations on 28 October.

---

[23] See *LA*, pp. 172–80.

[24] Molhuysen, *Bronnen* 1:150.

[25] *LA*, p. 182.

[26] *LA*, pp. 180–81. The original text of the letter, 21 June 1603, is not extant. See Dekker, *Rijker*, p. 257.

[27] *Disp. pub.* IV.

[28] Arminius, *Oratio de sacerdotio Christi habita a D. Iacobo Arminio cum publice doctor s. theologiae crearetur*, in *Opera*, p. 25; *Works* 1:432.

[29] Molhuysen, *Bronnen* 1:148.

With reference to Gomarus's approval of Arminius for the doctorate and his public disputation on God's nature (which included theses
on *scientia media*), it should be pointed out that, even if Gomarus was
not thrilled with Arminius, his best opportunity to stop the appointment had passed with the conference in May. By this time, the job was
Arminius's to lose. This is not to imply that Arminius was now tenured
above the possibility of dismissal, for it seems that Gomarus would keep
his eyes open for later opportunities.

It was not long before tension began to appear. The new professors
Arminius and Trelcatius, Jr., both plugged into the third repetition cycle
of public disputations in the Staten College. Disputation number 30 in
the cycle, which happened to be on predestination, fell to Arminius on
7 February 1604.[30] Gomarus did not approve of what was said in the
disputation, for he responded on 31 October 1604 with his own public
disputation on predestination.[31] Gomarus's move to publish theses on a
topic that had just been covered eight months earlier in the curriculum
was viewed as insulting, for he did it "out of his turn, and contrary to
the method that had been before agreed upon."[32] The very next day,
Arminius wrote a letter to Uytenbogaert, calling Gomarus *offensissimus*.[33]
That Arminius took Gomarus's disputation as a polemical refutation of
his own is demonstrated by the fact that Arminius responded directly to
Gomarus's disputation point by point in writing.[34] Other interested parties also saw these disputations as counter to each other, for they were
translated into Dutch and published together.[35] Thus, the theological
differences and personality conflicts had an immediate effect on the curriculum and public disputations.

The conflict continued a few months later when one of Arminius's
students was set to offer objections at a disputation under Gomarus on
30 April 1605. Gomarus incorrectly viewed the student's objections as

---

[30] *Disp. pub.* XV.

[31] Franciscus Gomarus, *Theses theologicae de praedestinatione Dei*, Samuel Gruterus
respondens, ad diem 31 October 1604 (Leiden, 1604).

[32] G. Brandt, *History* 2:31. Stephen Curcellaeus, 'Praefatio Christiano lectori,' in
Exam. Gom., fols. 02r–04v, there fol. 03r; *Works* 3:523, reports that Gomarus composed
the theses "extra ordinem." By contrast, to propose theses within the *repetitio* order is to
propose them *ex ordine*. See *Ep. ecc.* 76, p. 143.

[33] *Ep. ecc.* 74, p. 141.

[34] *Exam. Gom.* See also his description of Gomarus's disputation in *Ep. ecc.* 74,
p. 141.

[35] Arminius and Gomarus, *Twee disputatien vande goddelücke predestinatie* (Leiden, 1610).

being prompted by Arminius, and Gomarus then defended his own theses against the objections. At the same time, according to Arminius, who was present at the disputation, Gomarus said things against Arminius, who he thought was behind the objections.[36]

About this same time, Kuchlinus was taking action of his own against Arminius's teachings. He "resisted hand and tooth against the influence of Arminius."[37] Consistent with his statement before the curators that he did not want his students to hear Arminius, Kuchlinus moved to change the hour of his own lectures on the Belgic Confession to eight in the morning, the same hour as Arminius's lectures. He then urged all his "bursalen," or students receiving scholarships, to be present at his own lectures instead of Arminius's. Arminius filed a complaint to the burgomasters of Leiden, who ordered that the lectures remain unchanged until the curators arrive.[38] Kuchlinus seems to have had some control over the academic schedule, but he still had to answer to his superiors.

The problem is that these conflicts were hard to keep secret. To the degree that the debates spilled over into the public disputations, students were involved in these professorial disagreements. The churches began to speak of the "novelty fanatics" (*nieuwigheyt-drijvers*) at the university.[39] Even Kuchlinus's attempt to lecture during Arminius's hour was mentioned in a letter from Werner Helmichius to Arnoldus Cornelius, dated 30 April 1605.[40] This correspondence between churchmen is evidence of what would soon become known to the Staten College—the churches were beginning to talk about the problems at Leiden University. The church's involvement became official when the *classis* (that is, the governing body of clergy and elders) of Dordrecht issued a "gravamen," or grievance, saying that, because of the reports of "differences" in the church and university at Leiden, their next synod would discuss ways to stop the schisms and scandals.[41]

---

[36] *Ep. ecc.* 76, p. 143; *Works* 1:658–59; *LA*, p. 219.

[37] Otterspeer, *Bolwerk*, p. 159.

[38] G. Brandt, *History* 2:33; *LA*, pp. 220–21.

[39] Itterzon, *Gomarus*, p. 107; Otterspeer, *Bolwerk*, p. 244.

[40] The letter is transcribed in H. Q. Janssen and J. J. van Toorenenbergen, eds., *Werken der Marnix-Vereeniging III/4: Brieven uit Onderscheidene Kerkelijke Archieven* (Utrecht, 1880), pp. 281–83, there p. 282: "D. Cuchl. hadde sijn ure in't collegie verandert op de ure als Armin. leest, om sijn studenten te houden wt de lesse Arminij: het is Arm. gebootschapt door twee wt den Colleg., hy heefft aen de Burgem. gelopen, die D. Cuchl. hebben de wete gedaen geen innovatie in de uere te maken voor de comste der Curatoren."

[41] *LA*, pp. 231–32.

The curators of the university and magistrates of Leiden approached the theological faculty about the Dordrecht allegation, and the faculty responded with a statement of solidarity that refuted the Dordrecht accusation. After describing the complaint, the faculty said that "they knew not of any difference among the professors of the Faculty of Theology, so far as related to fundamental points of doctrine."[42] They went on to promise that they would work to silence any controversies that the students might be causing. This document was signed on 10 August 1605 by Arminius (who was rector of the university at the time), Gomarus, and Trelcatius, Jr. Then, in the very next paragraph, Kuchlinus signed in agreement with what was stated.

Thus, even after the initial controversies, there is evidence of some degree of a collegial working relationship. C. Brandt notes that it astonished many people that Gomarus would sign such an amicable statement.[43] It should be no less surprising that Kuchlinus and Arminius signed it as well. This document is evidence of something that is seldom noted in the Arminius-Gomarus relationship: namely, there were moments of collegiality. Just a few weeks after the Gomarus and Kuchlinus incidents of April, 1605, and two months before this faculty statement, Arminius wrote privately to Uytenbogaert on 7 June, "I have peace with Gomarus."[44] It was reported also that Gomarus desired to be at peace with Arminius, but was pressured by influential churchmen to oppose Arminius for the sake of Reformed orthodoxy.[45]

---

[42] Molhuysen, *Bronnen* 1:417*: "…maer dat sy nyet weten dat voor soe veel de fondamenten der leere aengaet onder den professoren der Faculteit der Theologien enich geschil is…"; *Works* 1:39.

[43] *LA*, p. 234. Bertius, in his writing against Gomarus, expresses his surprise over Gomarus's action. The signed statement is discussed in Gomarus, *Bedencken over de Lyck-Oratie van Meester P. Bertius*, in *Verclaringhe, over de vier hooftstucken, der leere, waer van hy met sijn weerde mede—Professore D. Iacobo Arminio, gheconfereert heeft, voor de E. E. moghende Heeren Staten van Hollandt ende Westvrieslandt: overghelevert den achtsten Septembris* [Leiden, 1609], p. 43; and Petrus Bertius, *Aen-spraeck aen D. Fr. Gomarum op zijne Bedenckinghe over de Lijck-oratie ghedaen na de Begraefenisse van D. Jacobus Arminius zaligher* (Leiden, 1601 [1610]), fols. B3v–B4v. Bertius asks Gomarus, "Was de Predestinatie op die tijt dat is in t'jaer 1605 gheen fundament: waerom is het nu in t'jaer 1609 een fundament gheworden…?" (ibid., fol. B4v).

[44] *Ep. ecc.* 77, p. 147: "Cum D. D. Gommaro mihi pax est.…" It was during Arminius's tenure as rector of the university that he delivered his famous speech on religious divisions and his plea for unity in *Oratio de componendo dissidio religionis inter Christianos, habita ab auctore VIII. Feb. 1605 cum Rectoratum deponeret*, in *Opera*, pp. 71–91. For a brief commentary on the ideas behind this address from the perspective of older scholarship, see Sirks, *Arminius' pleidooi*.

[45] Grotius, *Ordinum pietas*, pp. 150–51; *LA*, p. 235.

On the one hand, there can be no doubt that the actions of pastors such as Hommius and Petrus Plancius had a negative influence on the behavior of Gomarus. Gomarus himself admitted that his first objections before Arminius's faculty appointment originated with Plancius.[46] Furthermore, ministers were present as witnesses, and perhaps as influences, when Gomarus and Arminius faced one another before the states in 1609. On the other hand, blame for the unfriendly nature of the conflict cannot completely rest on these pastors. Gomarus was often described as an irascible individual not only by his opponents, but also by more objective first-hand observers. His biographer, Itterzon, after noting how difficult it is to form a fair opinion of Gomarus, admits that he indeed possessed a "fiery temperament" (*vurig temperament*).[47] This volatile disposition was manifest on several occasions.[48] One example of Gomarus's occasional petulance was his behavior at Arminius's final public disputation on 25 July 1609.[49] Gomarus was visibly agitated during the disputation and, immediately after its conclusion, went into the hall, engaged in a heated exchange with Arminius, and charged him with teaching papist doctrine. It is for this incident and others like it that Otterspeer has called Gomarus the hammer and Arminius the anvil.[50]

It is perhaps not overly speculative to wonder whether envy contributed to Gomarus's occasionally harsh attitude toward Arminius. It is known that, as Professor Primarius, Gomarus felt somewhat threatened by Arminius. C. Brandt, whose history is consciously pro-Arminian, reports that as early as 1604, Gomarus was offended that Arminius was also lecturing on the New Testament, so he exclaimed to Arminius, "You have invaded my professorship!" Arminius assured Gomarus that he was not trying to invade his territory, but that he was given permission by the curators to lecture on any biblical book as long as the specific topic did not overlap with Gomarus's lectures.[51] As he did when he encountered a scheduling conflict with Kuchlinus the next year, Arminius was appealing to the authority of the curators. It could not have helped the situation that people like Josephus Scaliger, famous scholar-in-residence at

---

[46] *LA*, p. 139.
[47] Itterzon, *Gomarus*, pp. 376–79.
[48] See Bangs, *Arminius*, pp. 248 and 261.
[49] See Borrius's eye-witness account in *Ep. ecc.* 130, pp. 226–28; cf. G. Brandt, *History* 2:55.
[50] Otterspeer, *Bolwerk*, pp. 211 and 213.
[51] *LA*, pp. 193–94.

Leiden, made their opinions known. Although he remained aloof from the theological controversies, Scaliger was not fond of Gomarus's scholarship; however, he called Arminius a very great man (*vir maximus*).[52]

Gomarus was not the only theological opponent of Arminius on the faculty. About the other faculty member, Lucas Trelcatius, Jr., there is comparatively little known.[53] Born in London, he studied at Leiden in the 1590s under his father, Lucas Trelcatius, Sr. He could preach equally well in Dutch and in French.[54] Like his father, he preached at the Walloon church in Leiden. This often overlooked and much less controversial faculty member still made his share of charges against Arminius.[55] Trelcatius, Jr., apparently did not impress Arminius on an intellectual level. Concerning Trelcatius, Otterspeer notes that "according to Arminius he was an incoherent thinker, according to Scaliger an outstanding speaker. Those things can go together well."[56]

Nichols records that Arminius considered it audacious that Trelcatius, Jr., published a whole body of divinity at such a young age in 1604. Furthermore, Arminius found some things in Trelcatius's *Loci communes* to be well written, but many other things to be novelties that detract from the truth.[57] Arminius disagreed with Trelcatius on the description of Christ's divine nature as αὐτόθεος.[58] After Trelcatius's death,

---

[52] Itterzon, *Gomarus*, p. 148; G. Brandt, *History* 2:28.

[53] See Glasius, *Godgeleerd Nederland*, 3:441; Platt, *Scholasticism*, pp. 127–31; *Nieuw Neder-landsch Biografisch Woordenboek*, ed. P. C. Molhuysen and Fr. K. H. Kossman, 10 vols. (Leiden, 1911–1937), 10:1039–40.

[54] G. Brandt, *History* 2:46.

[55] G. Brandt, *History* 2:46; Bangs, *Arminius*, p. 292.

[56] Otterspeer, *Bolwerk*, p. 212. Among Trelcatius's works is a homiletical handbook, *Ecclesiastes, sive methodus et ratio formandi sacras conciones*.

[57] Cf. *Dec. sent.*, p. 120; *Works* 1:693; with *Ep. ecc.* 88, pp. 160–61; and J. Nichols, in *Works* 1:311.

[58] See *Ep. ecc.* 88, pp. 160–61; *Dec. sent.*, pp. 118–23; *Works* 1:691–95; and *LA*, pp. 257–61; Bangs, *Arminius*, pp. 281–82. Arminius defends himself against Christological heterodoxy in *Apologia*, art. XXI; *Dec. sent.*; and *Epistola ad Hippolytum a Collibus*, in *Opera*, pp. 935–47. For a theological analysis of this controversy, see Muller, 'Christological Problem,' 145–63. There is a chronological problem in identifying which disputation was the source of this controversy. In *Dec. sent.*, Arminius mentions a thesis "vande Godtheyt des Soons" which was part of a disputation. C. Brandt has erroneously taken this to be the title of the whole disputation, but there is no extant disputation that corresponds to this title, and nothing even close to this topic is handled by Arminius in 1606, when Brandt places this event. Brandt no doubt places it here because it is first mentioned in *Ep. ecc.* 88, which was written 1 September 1606. However, Arminius's mention of the disputation does not imply that it had recently occurred. Rather, the disputation in question may be *Disp. pub.* V, *De persona Patris et Filii*, which was held 23

when Arminius addressed this Christological controversy in the *Declaratio sententiae*, he intimated that his relationship with Trelcatius was at times as icy as his relationship with Gomarus. Rather than speaking directly with Trelcatius himself, Arminius explained the incident to a mutual friend who preached in Amsterdam, in effect asking him to relay the information to Trelcatius, which he apparently did.[59] In addition, Arminius was particularly uninspired by Trelcatius's *locus* on predestination and his attempt to consider it partly before the fall and partly after the fall. According to Arminius, Trelcatius's theses are asserted wrongly (*perperam*), badly (*male*), and absurdly (*insulse*).[60] Trelcatius's disputation on predestination ends with a somewhat conciliatory statement on tolerating different conceptions of the doctrine of predestination.[61] It is unclear whether Trelcatius intended to include Arminius's doctrine under those to be tolerated; this is unlikely, though, given that he rules out predestination based on foreseen faith.[62] However, based on the language cited above, it is quite clear that Arminius did not tolerate the view of Trelcatius.

Having surveyed these men and their contact with Arminius, we can make some summary observations about the working environment in Leiden. First, it often goes unmentioned that the theological faculty agreed on the majority of theological topics; the differences they may have had on many topics would not have been unusual in any contemporary university, and either were slight enough to go unnoticed in disputations or were routinely considered to be indifferent matters. This is

---

February 1605. The particular thesis where the Son's divinity would come up is difficult to isolate. The word αὐτόθεος is not mentioned, but it could come up in objections to thesis iv on the *fons divinitatis*, or a number of other places. In *LA*, p. 262, C. Brandt then mentions this disputation on the person of the Son separately. The best solution is to see this controversy beginning with *Disp. pub.* V in 1605, with Arminius then reporting it in the 1606 letter, a comment probably due to the increasing chatter among the students, confirmed by Arminius's repeated defenses in his final years.

[59] *Dec. sent.*, p. 120; *Works* 1:692. For whatever reason, Gomarus did not confront Trelcatius either. In *Ep. ecc.* 88, p. 161, Arminius writes, "Intelligo D. Gommarum in privato suo collegio Trelcatii sententiam confutasse."

[60] Arminius, *Articuli nonnulli diligenti examine perpendendi, eo quod inter ipsos Reformatae religionis professores de iis aliqua incidit controversia*, in *Opera*, p. 956; *Works* 2:717–18. Perhaps because of his youth, Junius did not support the proposed appointment of Trelcatius, Jr., to the faculty. See *BLGNP* 2:277; Bangs, *Arminius*, p. 232.

[61] Trelcatius, *Disputationum theologicarum quarto repetitarum trigesima de aeterna Dei praedestinatione*, Daniel Guerinellus respondens, ad diem 19 April 1606 (Leiden, 1606), xxiv.

[62] Trelcatius, *De praedestinatione* (1606), xii.

not to say that Arminius's theological system was not distinctive in many ways, for it was; rather, it is an acknowledgment that outside of issues touching the doctrine of salvation and one fine point of Christology, the differences rarely became controversial. Viewing Arminius's life in light of the subsequent Remonstrant controversy, it is understandable why the moments of conflict, rather than the times of peace, dominated the histories on both sides of the controversy. Yet because of vast areas of agreement, the faculty could sign declarations of unity such as the 1605 statement, and they could work together for the common cause of training students and building up the church. Arminius and his colleagues survived in such an environment by establishing and working together within a curriculum that, with few exceptions, ran smoothly.

Second, despite the broad agreement among the faculty on many theological issues, clearly there were troublesome times as well, especially when it came to issues touching the doctrine of salvation. Even if the conflicts did not dominate the university landscape, the occasionally contentious environment had an effect on the Leiden curriculum. For example, rather than one public disputation on predestination in 1604, Gomarus's response ensured that there were two that year. It is impossible to know how often personal theological debates among the faculty shaped the disputation topics and the disputation content during the first decade of the seventeenth century, but the 1604 controversy proves that these debates occasionally did make a difference.

Third, examination of Arminius's environment in Leiden further illuminates the context of his own theology and writing. Past scholarship has attempted to demonstrate that Arminius's theology was a reaction or response to teachings he encountered earlier in his life. Bertius and C. Brandt, whose biographies of Arminius focus almost entirely on the predestinarian controversy, claimed that Arminius, who studied under Beza in Geneva, began his ministry as a Bezan supralapsarian. Then around 1589, as the story goes, in light of the Dirck Coornhert controversy, Arminius suddenly became disenchanted with supra- and infralapsarian types of unconditional predestination. However, Bangs has shown that this story of a supralapsarian Arminius suddenly converting to conditional predestination is implausible.[63] Therefore, the subsequent shape of Arminius's theology cannot be rationalized by appealing to this story.

---

[63] Bangs, *Arminius*, pp. 138–41.

Bangs himself posits Arminius's theology to be a reaction to the supra-lapsarianism of Theodore Beza, Arminius's teacher in Geneva. After summarizing Beza's doctrine during Arminius's time as his student, Bangs writes, "It was the insistence on the details of [Beza's supralapsarian] system as essential to Reformed orthodoxy which had a great deal to do with the precipitation of the so-called Arminian controversy."[64] Although Bangs does note that Beza tolerated other predestinarian views at Geneva, Muller stresses even more Beza's acknowledgment that supralapsarianism need not be the confessional norm.[65] It is indeed clear that Arminius was not fond of the doctrine later known as supra-lapsarianism. Most of his polemic in the *Declaratio sententiae* is aimed at this type of predestination, as the other two types are briefly dismissed for their inability to avoid the main problem of supralapsarianism.

What is often overlooked is how the context of Arminius's university setting contributed to his polemic. Every one of his academic colleagues who conducted regular disputations in the Staten College was a supralapsarian. Gomarus's doctrine is well known from the examination that Arminius applied to his theses. Trelcatius, Jr., in his disputation on predestination, proposes a view of predestination that can consider the object as either *homo simpliciter* or *homo peccator*.[66] At the least, he viewed supralapsarianism as a coherent, biblical option. With regard to Kuchlinus, Bangs describes him as a moderate Calvinist who "was not one to speculate on the order of the decrees."[67] On the contrary, although Kuchlinus does not explicitly mention the order of decrees, he implies the order when he describes the *massa* of Romans 9. This mass, Kuchlinus says, is not to be understood as the corrupt human race, but denotes a "rude and indistinct material" (*rudem atque indistinctam materiam*). God is compared to a potter—not one who considers vessels distinctly made and formed, but who has power "according as he wills them to be created" (*prout vult condendi*). Otherwise, asks Kuchlinus, how can the vessels of wrath be said to be formed for dishonor if they are already corrupt?[68]

---

[64] Bangs, *Arminius*, p. 68.
[65] Cf. Bangs, *Arminius*, p. 75, with Muller, *GCP*, p. 19.
[66] Trelcatius, *De praedestinatione* (1606), xiv, xxi.
[67] Bangs, *Arminius*, p. 116.
[68] Kuchlinus, *Theses theologicae de divina praedestinatione*, M. Gerardus Vossius respondens (Leiden, 1600), xii. A. J. Lamping agrees with this assessment: "In zijn lessen becommentarieerde hij de Heidelbergse Catechismus vanuit een standpunt dat als supralapsaristisch getypeerd zou kunnen worden." *BLGNP* 5:319.

In the Staten College, then, only Bertius agreed with Arminius against their colleagues' supralapsarianism, but Bertius presided over disputations in philosophy and ethics, not usually in theology. The supralapsarianism extended also to Arminius's other Leiden agitator, the pastor Hommius.

It cannot be doubted that Arminius reacted strongly against unconditional predestination in general and supralapsarianism in particular. The point here is that, if one wants to identify a certain theologian to whom Arminius is responding, we can find examples more proximate than the usual culprit, Beza. Calvin and Beza considered together are indeed mentioned frequently by Arminius. It was Arminius's present working environment in Leiden, however, that provides a better context for understanding his polemic. It is not that his Leiden colleagues were forcing supralapsarianism on Arminius; but, since it was the norm in that environment, he found it to be especially worthy of refutation. If Arminius seems to devote an inordinate amount of time and energy against supralapsarianism, then one should remember the people whom he faced on a daily basis.

Finally, there is the question of how the faculty held it all together during this unsettled time. The simplest explanation is that, although Arminius was hired against the wishes of Kuchlinus and Gomarus, as with any work situation, most of the time the faculty attempted to make the best of it. Another factor has to do with the pressure on the faculty to get along with each other. This pressure came from all corners—the church *classes*, the curators of the university, the burgomasters of Leiden, and the states of Holland. As soon as rumbling began among the churches, the curators and civic leaders approached the faculty and urged them to resolve it and mollify the churches. Despite their differences, no one on the faculty departed to another work during this decade. Indeed, the polemic only became unbearable in 1609 with the commencement of the pamphlet war, which took place primarily after Arminius's death.[69] Now rival theologians, including Bertius and Gomarus, who were colleagues in the Staten College, began addressing and denouncing one another through mass printing in the vernacular. It was two years later when Gomarus finally left for Middelburg.

---

[69] For accounts of the pamphlet war, see Itterzon, *Gomarus*, pp. 151–89; and Hakkenberg, 'Predestinarian Controversy,' pp. 320–79, who stresses the importance of the Dutch pamphlets for understanding the theological and social ramifications of the Remonstrant/Contra-Remonstrant controversy in the decade preceding Dort.

Kuchlinus should also be recognized as someone who contributed to the stability of the Staten College. From the beginning of his tenure, he was known for his clear-headedness and sound judgment. The fact that he got along well with his sub-regent and son-in-law, Bertius, despite their theological differences, is evidence that he was instrumental in keeping the theological college together. Furthermore, after Kuchlinus died on 3 July 1606 and was succeeded by the more controversial figure Bertius—who did not command the high degree of respect and authority that his father-in-law Kuchlinus did—there is a noticeable increase in the degree of polemical rhetoric from Gomarus and Arminius. Perhaps the two men had simply had enough of one another; but it is also plausible that the authoritative presence of Kuchlinus either implicitly or explicitly kept the faculty cautious. Particularly after Arminius's death, Gomarus and Bertius, who were not nearly as cautious as Kuchlinus and Arminius, lowered the level of discourse to personal attacks. Gomarus brought Kuchlinus into the controversy by suggesting to Bertius that if Kuchlinus, the "faithful teacher" (*trouwe leeraer*), were still alive, he would reprimand his son-in-law Bertius who took his place as regent and who was causing the once blooming Staten College now to lead its students astray.[70] Bertius then responded to Gomarus with his own speculation of what his father-in-law would say against Gomarus.[71] My guess is that Kuchlinus would have had something to say to both Gomarus and Bertius. The fact that both rivals appeal to Kuchlinus for posthumous support indicates not only the commanding influence of his memory still four years after his death, but also his impressive influence as a mediating figure during his tenure over the Staten College. When disagreement broke out in 1605, Kuchlinus did his best to quell the rumors and maintain the integrity of the Staten College by uniting the faculty with a statement of agreement. When disagreement broke out after Arminius's death in 1609, a pamphlet war ignited outside the walls of the university and the controversy was literally taken to the pulpits and the streets. One wonders if the decade before Dort would have gone differently if Kuchlinus had still overseen the Leiden Staten College.

---

[70] Gomarus, *Bedencken*, pp. 47–48.
[71] Bertius, *Aen-spraeck*, fols. D2r–D3r; cf. Itterzon, *Gomarus*, p. 182.

II. *Arminius and the Leiden Pedagogy*

Since the Arminian debate took place within a university context, it is
surprising that scholarship has paid such scarce attention to the pedagogical context at Leiden University as a means for illuminating that
controversy. Understanding the broad contours of the course of study
in the Staten College, with particular attention to the disputation, is
necessary for placing Arminius in his context as a professor.

A. *Education in General*

After noting the Arminian and later Cartesian controversies as evidence
of the Staten College's failure to provide the intended stability for the
church, Otterspeer claims that the college's meaning for the university
was in its reputation for education and advancement of the curriculum.
Perhaps the most important contribution of the college to the university
was its discipline in general.[72] According to records, students still enjoyed
their time off, which consisted of about 13 weeks total per year. After
1631, days off included 1 February for the nomination of the new rector, 8–21 February for review ("recensie"), two weeks for Easter, a week
and a half for Pentecost, 16 July–1 September for summer recess, two
days in September for the Valkenburg annual market, 3–10 October for
the celebration of Leiden's deliverance, and two weeks for Christmas.[73]
It would be unwarranted to retroject this schedule onto the theological
college under Kuchlinus, for all three professors frequently conducted
disputations as late as 1 August, as well as on 1 February and 21 February. Perhaps this is an indication of the famous academic rigor of the
seminary.

According to the statutes of 1592, when the Staten College was
established, the *bursalen* in the theological college applied the first two
and a half years to the study of philosophy, Latin, and Greek. A sample
schedule of lectures has Bredius teaching Latin at 9:00 in the morning, Trutius teaching physics at 10:00, Merula teaching history at 11:00,
Ramsaeus teaching logic at 1:00, Vulcanius teaching Greek at 2:00, and
Snellius teaching fundamental mathematics at 4:00. Concerning the
theological part of the curriculum, each day at 5:00 Kuchlinus gave
instruction in the catechism. In addition, at 8:00 in the mornings the

---

[72] Otterspeer, *Bolwerk*, pp. 162–63.
[73] Otterspeer, *Bolwerk*, p. 226.

advanced students heard Trelcatius, Sr., reading *loci communes* and Junius lecturing on Isaiah at 9:00.[74] The busy, structured schedule for students is consistent with the fact that a *collegium* such as the theological college bears similarities to the clerical pattern of a cloister.[75] According to Otterspeer, this schedule probably comes from the hand of Kuchlinus. If so, this provides further evidence that one of Kuchlinus's duties was to establish and organize the curriculum and schedule for the college. Moreover, judging from Arminius's differences with Kuchlinus and Gomarus over curriculum and schedule boundaries, Kuchlinus's authority on these issues was subject to the university curators. It is also worth noting the vast opportunities Kuchlinus had to influence the theological students. It seems that all the students took catechism theology under him every day for their first two and a half years.

B. *The Disputation*

B.1. *Background*

There were two major components of late medieval university education. The first of these was reading, or the lecture.[76] In this *lectio/praelectio*, the professor led students through a careful exposition of some canonical text (for example, Aristotle, Lombard's *Sententiae*, or Scripture). These lecture notes and comments often became the source for published commentaries on any of these texts.

The lecture, inasmuch as it required little active participation on the part of the student, was incomplete without the second component

---

[74] Otterspeer, *Bolwerk*, p. 162. Cf. other *series lectionum* from 1587, 1599, and 1601, reprinted in Molhuysen, *Bronnen* 1:157*–58*, 384*–85*, 400*–01*. Cf. also the information on Staten College pedagogy in Dibon, *L'Enseignement philosophique*, pp. 23–26. For a general idea of Arminius's daily schedule, see Bangs, *Arminius*, p. 243.

[75] Friedrich Paulsen, *The German Universities and University Study*, trans. Frank Thilly and William W. Elwang (New York, 1906), p. 27. Leiden's Staten College in particular was modeled after Heidelberg's *Collegium Sapientiae*, in which Kuchlinus participated as a student under Zacharias Ursinus. Kuchlinus's personal knowledge of the theological college in Heidelberg was one factor in the curators' choice of Kuchlinus as regent. Cf. Otterspeer, *Bolwerk*, p. 152; Platt, *Scholasticism*, p. 82; *BLGNP* 5:317–18; Eike Wolgast, 'Das Collegium Sapientiae in Heidelberg im 16. Jahrhundert,' *Zeitschrift für die Geschichte des Oberrheins* 147 (1999), 303–18.

[76] John Marenbon, *Later Medieval Philosophy (1150–1350): An Introduction* (New York, 1987), pp. 16–19; Paulsen, *German Universities*, p. 24. General aspects of German universities, like those noted in Paulsen's study, can generally be applied to Dutch universities. Paulsen, *German Universities*, p. 2, notes that universities in the Netherlands inherited the German model, as opposed to the English or French models.

of the educational process, the *disputatio*.[77] The Middle Ages laid great stress on the disputation as a supplement to what was gained through the lecture. The purpose of the disputation was to address and resolve some debated *quaestio*. The demanding nature of the disputation was advantageous for training students. Its performance required a sharp wit, good memory, and rhetorical skill. Such intense training made for more thorough assimilation of the knowledge in students' minds. In addition, the excitement of a contest and anticipation of objections and responses added pressure to the participants.[78] The potential thrill of victory and agony of defeat drew a crowd and tended to ensure good preparation on the part of the students.

The disputation had great import in the curriculum of Leiden University. In 1587, Professor Everardus Bronchorst praised this pedagogical method in the law school: "The use of disputations is great and incomparable."[79] In a disputation, a student respondent (or defendant) would defend a number of theses, answering the objections of variously appointed opponents, all under the oversight of the presider (usually a professor, but sometimes a student). This form of disputation was called *disputatio sub praeside*.[80] The text of the disputation theses was printed for each person present. The opponents were sought out beforehand, and apparently given some freedom in posing objections. C. Brandt records how one student, Vliet, the appointed opponent in a disputation under the presiding of Gomarus, objected to the theses and thus angered Gomarus. Arminius defended the student's right to object, that he was performing his appointed duty.[81] Moreover, the other professors in attendance also had the right to raise objections.[82]

---

[77] For general information on disputations, see Anthony Kenny and Jan Pinborg, 'Medieval Philosophical Literature,' in *The Cambridge History of Later Medieval Philosophy*, ed. Norman Kretzmann, et al. (Cambridge, Eng., 1982), pp. 19–29; Marenbon, *Later Medieval Philosophy*, pp. 19–20; Paulsen, *German Universities*, pp. 24–26; Ahsmann, *Collegia*, pp. 274–323. On the relationship between the *lectio* and *disputatio*, see Beryl Smalley, *The Study of the Bible in the Middle Ages* (New York, 1952), pp. 196–213.

[78] See Paulsen, *German Universities*, pp. 24–25.

[79] Molhuysen, *Bronnen* 1:151*: "Disputationum magnus et incomparabilis est usus."

[80] Ahsmann, *Collegia*, p. 275.

[81] *LA*, pp. 219–21. Cf. Arminius's testimony in *Ep. ecc.* 76, p. 143; *Works* 1:658–59. Itterzon, *Gomarus*, p. 108, and Bangs, *Arminius*, pp. 266–67, who, in this particular case, identified the defendant as the opponent, apparently misunderstood the role of the opponent. The opponent (in this case, Vliet), whose task is to object to the theses, is distinct from the respondent (in this case, Vassianius), whose task is to defend the theses.

[82] Otterspeer, *Bolwerk*, p. 237.

Disputations can be categorized in different ways. *Disputationes pro gradu* were for obtaining the degree or doctorate; *disputationes exercitii gratia* were meant purely for practice.[83] The practice disputation was introduced in Leiden by the philosopher Trutius.[84] A distinction also exists between public and private disputations. Private disputations, which were authored by the professors, took place in *collegia privata* "surrounded by private walls" (*inter privatos parietes*). Because they were closed to the public, it is difficult to know the exact division of tasks between professor and student while they were being conducted.[85] In the case of Arminius, we at least know that the collection of his private disputations served as the groundwork of the theological system he never finished writing.[86] In contrast, we know a little more about public disputations. Public disputations took place mostly on Wednesday and Saturday mornings at 9:00 in the auditorium of the theologians, open to anyone who wanted to hear. The gathering lasted for two hours. The *pedel* (registrar) made sure that either the Bible, Hippocrates, or the *corpus iuris civilis* was present for a theological, medical, or law disputation, respectively.[87] The attendance of a public disputation could vary according to the importance of the theses and the size of the respondent's circle of friends and family. Each person present would have a copy of the theses; there were usually between 100 and 150 copies printed by the university printer.[88] On 20 May 1587, the university curators and Leiden burgomasters decreed that theology students would defend public disputations at least every 14 days.[89] Professors who presided over public disputations received one guilder as compensation.[90]

---

[83] Ahsmann, *Collegia*, p. 288. Cf. Dibon, *L'Enseignement philosophique*, pp. 33–43. Most of the disputations examined in the present study are practice disputations.

[84] Otterspeer, *Bolwerk*, p. 163.

[85] Ahsmann, *Collegia*, pp. 289–90 and 323. As with all of Ahsmann's findings concerning the law faculty, application to the theological faculty should be done with great caution.

[86] This fact is evident in the full title, *Disputationes privatae, de plerisque Christianae religionis capitibus, incoatae potissimum ab auctore ad corporis theologici informationem*. Cf. Nichols's preface in *Works* 2:318.

[87] Otterspeer, *Bolwerk*, p. 237.

[88] Ahsmann, *Collegia*, p. 280; Otterspeer, *Bolwerk*, p. 237. Bangs, 'Introduction,' in *Works* 1:xviii, posits smaller numbers of attendees and disputations printed. The sheer scarcity of these documents today may indeed suggest a smaller number for most theological disputations.

[89] Molhuysen, *Bronnen* 1:148*.

[90] Ahsmann, *Collegia*, pp. 308–10.

B.2. *Structure*

The titles of the theological disputations varied somewhat. In addition to *theses*, they were often entitled *aphorismi, assertio, decades, disputatio, disquisitio, dissertatio, enuntiata*, or *positiones*. In the early days of the university, the disputation texts were printed down the length of one folio page. Each thesis was between one and four lines in length; because of their brevity, they were known as *theses nudae*. After September, 1593, the external form of the disputation text was transformed. They began to be printed on quarto pages, and they could now be several pages long and put together as a sort of booklet. Because of the extra space for printing, disputations soon contained more theses, as well as longer, expanded theses, known as *theses vestitae*.[91] Biblical, patristic, and other references could now be printed in the margins. Furthermore, each disputation came with its own title page, along with a dedication on its verso side. On the verso page, students would often dedicate the disputation to pastors or teachers who were influential in the students' lives, past or present. Sometimes they were dedicated to the members of the Leiden theological faculty. These dedications reveal much about a student's connections and influences. In addition, congratulatory poems (*carmina gratulatoria*) composed by fellow students for the respondent were sometimes printed at the end of the disputation.

Before the first thesis, the disputation would customarily begin with a preface describing the rationale for discussing the topic at hand at this particular point in the disputation cycle. This brief preface served to set the topic in its context with the *locus* that preceded it. The opening theses serve to locate the topic and work toward an initial definition, which would appear near the beginning of the disputation (usually the first or second thesis). The initial definition, which answers the question *quid sit*, was normally a summary of the causes and effects, or, from the opposite perspective, the lining out of causes and effects was the expansion of the definition. The *quid sit* often took up the bulk of a theological disputation, for this is where the more detailed questions were proposed, questions which reveal the context in which disagreements would take place in this scholastic form of teaching, namely, the context of definitions, causes, and effects. In the course of the argumentation, scholastic

---

[91] Ahsmann, *Collegia*, pp. 294–95.

distinctions, appeals to biblical and patristic authority, answers to objections, and polemic against contemporary Roman Catholicism were all common elements of the post-Reformation disputation.

B.3. Repetitiones

With regard to the public practice disputations, a distinction was made between a disputation over a randomly chosen subject that held no connection with the material being handled at that time—thus, *quaelibet materia*—and a disputation in a series, in which a number of connected problems were handled. The random disputations—which have medieval antecedents in the quodlibetal questions handled by Aquinas, Scotus, and Ockham, among others—were held at Leiden University about twice a month at an *ad hoc* assembly.[92] In the Staten College, these disputations were most commonly called *theses theologicae*. These random disputations gave professors an opportunity to deal with any topics that arose in their own reading or interaction with one another. In contrast to the randomly chosen subjects, the disputations handled in a series were part of a *collegium*.[93] The *collegia disputationum* were the most intensive types of *collegia* available (as opposed to the *collegia explicatoria* and the *collegia examinatoria*).[94] In the theological college, this series of disputations was known as a *repetitio*, and is indicated in the disputation title by the number it occupies in the cycle.

While the regent, Kuchlinus, was conducting his own *collegium disputationum* on the Heidelberg Catechism, the three theological faculty members impartially shared in the task of presiding over the *repetitio* disputations. The third *repetitio* of the theological faculty was disrupted by the untimely deaths of Junius and Trelcatius, Sr., in 1602, and Gomarus was left to preside over every disputation until Trelcatius, Jr., and Arminius joined in. The fifth *repetitio* was disrupted by the death of Trelcatius, Jr., in 1607, after which Gomarus and Arminius evenly split the disputations. Then, after Arminius's death in 1609, Gomarus was left alone again to oversee the disputations of the fifth *repetitio*. Thus, the fourth *repetitio* of disputations, conducted in the middle of that decade, was the only one completed by Gomarus, Arminius, and Trelcatius, Jr.

---

[92] Ahsmann, *Collegia*, pp. 288–89; Otterspeer, *Bolwerk*, p. 238.
[93] Ahsmann, *Collegia*, pp. 289 and 296.
[94] Otterspeer, *Bolwerk*, p. 238.

The fourth *repetitio* of disputations lasted just over two years, from 4 December 1604 to 13 January 1607.[95] As with each cycle, the duties of presiding in the fourth *repetitio* went in order of faculty seniority. Thus, Gomarus presided over the first disputation, Arminius the second, and Trelcatius, Jr., the third. Then the fourth disputation came back to Gomarus, and so on down to the 47th and final disputation under Arminius. It is probable that the disputation topics were not ordered in such a way to correspond to any particular professor. Thus, the disputation on predestination in the third *repetitio* ended up falling to Arminius (who had only recently been plugged into a cycle that began before his appointment), and predestination in the fourth *repetitio* went to Trelcatius. Gomarus had to wait until the fifth *repetitio* to discuss predestination in the order of *loci*. Perhaps it was the unpredictability of which professor would preside over which topic that prompted Gomarus to conduct his *quaelibet* predestination disputation in 1604. Nevertheless, it is also possible that predestination in the fourth *repetitio* went to Trelcatius precisely because Arminius and Gomarus had each done one in 1604. Otterspeer notes that in a *collegium* such as this, the order of respondents and opponents was determined by lot.[96] Beyond this statement, there is not much information regarding how this significant process of determining the curriculum actually worked; furthermore, it is a matter of debate how firmly Otterspeer's general observations should apply to the Staten College of this time.

It is not known precisely how the topics for any given *repetitio* series were chosen. Since G. Brandt noted that Gomarus's 1604 disputation on predestination was "out of his turn, and contrary to the method that had been before agreed upon,"[97] it is implied that the faculty sat down to select and order the topics for disputation before the *repetitio* began. Concerning the third *repetitio*, in which Arminius's 1604 disputation on predestination appeared, the younger Brandt explicit says that the "professors of theology had entered into a mutual arrangement as to the order and succession in which the disputations were to be held, and the lot had fallen to Arminius to dispute on the subject of predestination."[98] Thus, even if we cannot know for sure how the dis-

---

[95] See Appendix 1 for a table of the disputations in the fourth *repetitio*.
[96] Otterspeer, *Bolwerk*, p. 238.
[97] G. Brandt, *History* 2:31. See *Ep. ecc.* 74, p. 141; *Works* 1:261.
[98] *LA*, p. 194.

putations were assigned to which students, we can be fairly certain that the faculty agreed on the cycle of disputation topics to be covered in a given *repetitio*. The decision would be based not only on the standard theological *loci* and the interest of the professors, but also on what they viewed as being essential for the theological education of their students. It would be illuminating to compare the 47 topics of the fourth *repetitio* with those of the fifth, which were both determined by the same three faculty members. Then, after further comparison with the third *repetitio* and even the later *Synopsis purioris theologiae*, as well as contrasting it with other university collections, a general sense of the shape of the "Leiden theology" might come into view.

The Leiden theology represented in the fourth *repetitio* was judged to be a significant statement of academic theological curriculum, for it was published as the *Syntagma disputationum theologicorum* in 1615.[99] Other universities had published similar collections of disputations. This collection served as a sort of Leiden system of theology, inasmuch as these topics were selected and written by a collaboration of the Leiden professors. It is initially perplexing that, as late as 1615, this fourth *repetitio* would still be considered and publicized as representative of the Leiden theology. After all, none of the three professors was still teaching at Leiden, and the faculty that produced these disputations was, at best, full of tension, and at worst, plagued by heresy. In response, it should be noted that the faculty of the fourth *repetitio* was not radically discontinuous with the faculty a decade later. The names were different, but Johannes Polyander and Simon Episcopius, who had been just recently appointed, still represented two different sides of the Remonstrant controversy. The faculty of 1615 was no less turbulent than the earlier faculty. Bertius was now regent, Conrad Vorstius had nearly been hired before he was rejected as a professor, and the Remonstrant controversy was raging, but not yet decided. Therefore, it is in some sense appropriate that the *Syntagma* should serve as an accurate portrayal of the Leiden faculty up to Dort. Moreover, what made the Leiden theology distinctive and cohesive was greater than the controversy over predestination. In fact, with Trelcatius's unique (in Leiden) view of predestination being represented in the fourth *repetitio*, controversy and polemical theology

---

[99] *Syntagma disputationum theologicorum, in Academia Lugduno-Batava quarto repetitarum… Francisco Gomaro, Iacobo Arminio, et Luca Trelcatio Iuniore* (Rotterdam, 1615).

are hardly noticeable in the *Syntagma* itself. The written form of disputations tended to be less controversial than the public performances, where opponents were expected to raise objections and press respondents for more doctrinal precision.

B.4. *Importance for the Leiden Debate*

A careful study of the theological disputations at Leiden is a necessary component for knowing the full story of the Arminian controversy, even if current scholarship has largely ignored these documents.[100] The disputations are important, first, because they are a principal means for discovering the contours of any given professor's theology. Trelcatius, Jr., wrote a system of *loci communes* that can be consulted to determine his thoughts concerning many theological topics. However, Arminius and Gomarus never wrote such a work. We know that Arminius had intended to compose a system of the whole Christian religion, but he never completed it due to his untimely death.[101] In fact, as noted above, the collection of *Disputationes privatae* was written as the groundwork for the system he intended to write. In 1612, Uytenbogaert said that the disputations of Arminius contain a sort of "brief system of divinity."[102] Thus, along with his occasional and apologetic treatises, the disputations of Arminius provide a fundamental window into his thought.[103]

Because the disputations are key for understanding a professor's theology, modern interpreters' negligence of these theological disputations creates a wide gap in the research of the Leiden theology and debates, for there are many topics covered in these Leiden disputations not covered in the collected *Opera omnia* of Gomarus or the *Opera theologica* of Arminius. For example, there are at least 35 known public disputations of Arminius that were not collected and do not appear in any edition of

---

[100] Over half a century ago, Dibon underscored the importance of these disputations for understanding the Leiden debate (*L'Enseignement philosophique*, p. 33): "Il est évident que la série des disputes théologiques soutenues à Leyde sous la présidence de Gomarus ou d'Arminius dans les premières années du 17e siécle, au moment même où se durcissaient les positions théologiques des futurs protagonistes de la rencontre de Dordrecht, offre à l'historien une documentation des plus précieuses."

[101] See the preface to *De vero et genuino sensu cap. VII. Epistolae ad Romanos dissertatio*, in *Opera*, p. 822; *Works* 2:486; cf. also Bangs, 'Introduction,' in *Works* 1:xviii.

[102] *Works* 1:lxii.

[103] Cf. Muller, *GCP*, pp. 49–50. Cf. also Dibon, *L'Enseignement philosophique*, p. 33: "Nous croyons au contraire qu'elles constituent une source, sans doute modeste, mais qui présente, en l'absence quasi totale d'autres documents, le plus haut intérêt."

the *Opera*. Given the importance of disputations for understanding his theology, and in light of the fact that there are only 24 public disputations in the *Opera*,[104] it is a significant scholarly lapse that most interpreters have never even read half of his public disputations. After noting the problem of the missing public disputations, Bangs concludes that the *Opera* "provide a sufficient body of material for understanding Arminius's theology."[105] What Bangs explicitly declares has been tacitly affirmed by centuries of scholars who have neglected these disputations.[106] On the contrary, although we may have a large representation of Arminius's theology, it is incomplete and perhaps even insufficient. Without the disputations, we can, at best, only maintain a cautious confidence in our interpretation of Arminius. For these missing and untranslated disputations contain Arminius's thoughts on topics not discussed elsewhere, including disputations dealing with the doctrines of creation, sin, restoration, Christ, good works, Roman Catholicism, and the last things.[107]

Second, the disputations are important because they reveal not only a professor's own theology, but also his thought at the particular time that he authored the disputation. It is not uncommon for a theological shift to take place when a thinker is shaped by years of polemical engagement, collegial interaction, and continued reading and learning. Even if the shift seems minor, it is not for that reason always insignificant to the debate. In the instance of Gomarus, the disputations contained in his *Opera theologica omnia* do not correspond to his own Leiden disputations.[108]

---

[104] The collection of *Disputationes publicae* included in the *Opera* contains 25 disputations, but *Disp. pub.* IV is actually the disputation Arminius wrote and defended for his doctorate. Thus, the *Opera* includes only 24 of the at least 59 disputations he presided over as professor. Bangs, 'Introduction,' in *Works* 1:xviii, says there were 60 public disputations, but I have located only 59 extant (24 in the *Opera*, 35 outside). Perhaps Bangs is counting Brandt's report of a 1606 disputation on the divinity of the Son as a separate disputation not in the *Opera*. However, since there is no evidence of any such disputation in 1606, I take this Christological thesis to be a reference to the extant 1605 *Disp. pub.* V.

[105] Bangs, 'Introduction,' in *Works* 1:xx.

[106] The existence of these disputations has been documented in modern scholarship. See Louis D. Petit, *Bibliographische lijst der werken van de Leidsche hoogleeraren van de oprichting der Hoogeschool tot op onze dagen: Faculteit der godgeleerdheid*, Eerste Aflevering (Leiden, 1894).

[107] In addition to these public disputations, other important material by Arminius was not included in the *Opera*. The most accessible materials are the many letters of Arminius included in *Epp. ecc.* Beyond this printed collection of Latin letters, there are several other letters and Tronchinus's notes on Arminius's Galatians lectures that have never been transcribed, much less translated.

[108] See Gomarus, *Opera theologica omnia, maximam partem posthuma; suprema autoris voluntate*

It would be a mistake, therefore, when analyzing the Leiden debates before 1609, to interpret the Gomarus of Arminius's day through the disputations of the older, and presumably wiser, Gomarus.[109] Stephen Curcellaeus underscores this point when he observes that Gomarus's disputation on predestination which Arminius examined is not the one he later wrote and was published in his *Opera theologica omnia*.[110] It could also be instructive to track any developments through the decade, say from Gomarus's 1604 disputation to his 1609 disputation on predestination, considering the polemical exchanges that went on in the intervening five years. Again, the public disputations missing from Arminius's *Opera* that duplicate topics covered elsewhere are still important, for they will allow interpreters to do a comparative analysis and then determine shifts in Arminius's thought or assess the impact from his contemporary circumstances, if any such shifts are present.

Finally, it is necessary to remember that the disputations increasingly became a platform for airing theological opinions in an acceptable academic context. The primary use of theological disputations was clearly to educate the ministers of the next generation; we might call this the "official function" of disputations. Increasingly, however, the secondary, "unofficial function" of the disputations, especially on potentially controversial *loci*, was to provide an opportunity for the professor to defend his view of orthodoxy. This functional context should always be considered when analyzing the disputations.[111]

---

a discipulis edita (Amsterdam, 1644). Cf. the comments of the editors of Gomarus's *Opera omnia*, who deliberately omitted the Leiden disputations and included the latest editions, in ibid., fol. o4v: "Disputationes etiam eas, quae cum aliis, Professorum Leidensium, impressae sunt, omisimus: quod eas se non ἀκριβῶς, sed ut studiosis disputandi materiam praeberet, levi opera conscripsisse autor dictitaverit. Earum verò Disputationum, quas hic damus, ultimas secuti editiones sumus." Adolphus Sibelius, one of the editors of Gomarus's *Opera omnia*, produced an abridgement of Gomarus's theology in *Locorum communium theologicorum, epitome* [ed. Adolphus Sibelius], (Amsterdam, 1653). Likewise, the disputations of Junius examined in this essay do not correspond to those collected in his *Opera theologica* (Geneva, 1607).

[109] With the exception of Itterzon's use of the Dutch translation of Gomarus's 1604 disputation on predestination, Itterzon, *Gomarus*, and Letham, 'Faith,' rely on the *Opera omnia* without using the Leiden disputations.

[110] Curcellaeus, 'Praefatio,' fol. o3r; *Works* 3:523.

[111] In other university contexts, the disputation was not intended to necessarily represent the professor's thought, but instead to provide a means for theological discussion and resolution of debatable topics. As will be seen below, the context of the Leiden disputations did not lend itself to this use of disputations.

B.5. *Authorship*

Of utmost importance in the use of disputations for interpretation is the problem of disputation authorship. Secondary scholarship on Arminius has generally assumed that he was the author of the *Disputationes publicae*, but this fundamental assumption has never been directly supported in the case of Arminius.[112] The fact that no one has addressed this issue does not mean it is insignificant or that Arminius's authorship is indisputable, for there may be reason to doubt professorial authorship. The significance of this question is obvious, for if the student defendants wrote the theses for disputation at Leiden, we then would have little ground for thinking that the disputations represent the thought of Arminius and his faculty colleagues. Consequently, the disputations would provide little assistance in analyzing Arminius's theology, and we would have only modest interest in what they say. In the analysis up to this point, I have assumed professorial authorship, and I will argue the legitimacy of this assumption. However, since this assumption is not without its problems, we must first survey the evidence against professorial authorship.

The most recent and comprehensive study of the Leiden University curriculum is the book by Margreet Ahsmann, which is specifically a study of the law school up to 1630. In her section discussing the authorship of disputations, she cautions that it is difficult to give a uniform answer as to whether the presider, student, third party, or any combination of these should be considered the author.[113] In contrast to what was once the scholarly assumption, Ahsmann argues that "in this period in Leiden the rule was that the student in principle formulated his theses himself."[114] Although Ahsmann's study directly relates to the law faculty,

---

[112] E.g., Platt, *Scholasticism*, pp. 79–85 and 130–31, passim, assumes professorial authorship of all the theological disputations at Leiden during the period under question.

[113] Ahsmann, *Collegia*, pp. 311–12, also gives a brief survey of scholarship on this question.

[114] Ahsmann, *Collegia*, p. 313. Appealing to the custom of other universities is not especially helpful for resolving this issue at Leiden. However, we do know that Johannes Piscator acknowledges his authorship of the theses on justification over which he presided at Herborn. See Piscator, *A learned and profitable treatise of mans iustification* (London, 1599), fol. A3v. Professorial authorship must have been the custom at Heidelberg and Neustadt; see theses in Girolamo Zanchi, *De religione Christiana, fides* (London, 1605), pp. 393–456. Professorial authorship was also customary at Wittenberg; see Johannes Haussleiter, *Aus der Schule Melanchthons: Theologische Disputationen und Promotionen zu Wittenberg in den Jahren 1546–1560* [Festschrift der Königlichen Universität Greifswald zu Melanchthons 400 jährigem Geburtstag] (Greifswald, 1897), pp. 4–6.

her thesis statement seems to apply to the whole university during the period in question, 1575–1630. Otterspeer accepts her judgment that the defendant, and not the presider, was the author.[115]

Ahsmann offers several pieces of evidence to support her conclusion of student authorship. I shall organize her evidence into four arguments and then assess them. First, many unprinted disputations have been found that are in the handwriting of the defendants. Ahsmann acknowledges that the student defendant could have simply copied them from someone else, say, the professor. Yet, Ahsmann judges that, given her other arguments, it is more likely that the student wrote them himself.[116] Second is the testimony of law student Willem de Groot, who, in correspondence with his brother Hugo (Grotius), apparently claims to be writing the theses of his disputations (1615–16). Ahsmann herself admits that this evidence may seem incidental, but again finds it to concur with the additional evidence.[117] These data are especially dependent on a third argument, which is the testimony of the law faculty at Leiden. Petrus Cunaeus, professor of law, repeatedly cites the disputations of students, without ever mentioning the name of the presider. Bronchorst's diary entry in October, 1596, says that the student who had disputed under him "wrote (*conscripserat*) 156 theses." Presumably, the reason this fact made it into the diary was not that the student wrote them, but the great number of theses he wrote.[118]

Before moving to Ahsmann's fourth piece of evidence, an assessment of these first three arguments is in order. Her admittedly cautious deductions with respect to the first two facts show the weakness of her cumulative case. Unfortunately, the first argument about handwritten copies cannot support any conclusion concerning authorship. In fact, if we were to assume professorial authorship, we would expect the student to make a handwritten copy for his own review while the master copy, perhaps from the professor's hand, was being sent to the university printer.[119] What really connects these three arguments—and what distinguishes Ahsmann's study as a whole—is that they pertain only to the

---

[115] Otterspeer, *Bolwerk*, p. 236.
[116] Ahsmann, *Collegia*, p. 315.
[117] Ahsmann, *Collegia*, pp. 312–13.
[118] Ahsmann, *Collegia*, pp. 317–18.
[119] I have seen a manuscript of Arminius's 1604 disputation on predestination (published as *Disp. pub.* XV) that does not appear to be in his handwriting. This evidence alone does not constitute proof against his authorship.

law faculty at Leiden. Ahsmann is appropriately wary about applying the studies of Horn and Schubart-Fikenstscher to disputations by the law faculty at Leiden, for they are about German universities at a different time period.[120] This recognition shows that her book itself, which draws evidence from the Leiden law faculty, may not totally apply to the Leiden theological faculty. To regard these arguments as conclusive for the theological Staten College at Leiden would require testimony from its own faculty or students.

Ahsmann's fourth argument is more relevant for our purposes, for it applies to all disputations conducted at the university. She points to the dedication page of the disputations as evidence of student authorship.[121] As mentioned above, on the verso side of the title page, the student respondent gives, says, and dedicates *hasce theses* to people who had been influential in his life.[122] It must be acknowledged that, if there were no other evidence about disputation authorship, the fact that the student is the one dedicating the theses seems conclusive for student authorship. After all, to dedicate something is to take some kind of credit for it. Furthermore, the *carmina gratulatoria* often appended at the end of the disputation were written in Latin or Greek by fellow students to praise the erudition of the student respondent.[123] How could a student dedicate or be praised for something he did not compose?

Again, as far as this argument is meant to apply to the theological faculty, the evidence falls short. Rather than indication of his authorship, the student is merely dedicating and being praised for his performance in the face of opposition. Recall that the opponents were scheduled ahead of time, and were no doubt expected to arm themselves with a range of objections to which the defendant must extemporaneously respond. The texts of the theses themselves, even after their expansion in 1593, were still often general, at times brief, and sometimes did not take objections into account; a respondent could say much to expand on the theses. Otterspeer notes that much attention was given to the manner in which the respondent defended the theses. The arrangement of the defense depended on the personality and talent of the student.

---

[120] Ahsmann, *Collegia*, p. 312.
[121] Ahsmann, *Collegia*, pp. 316–17.
[122] At the bottom of the verso page, a formulaic "D. D. D." often appears. It means the student "dat, dicat, dedicat" the theses.
[123] Cf. Ahsmann, *Collegia*, p. 298.

According to Bronchorst's diary, he described student respondents variously as being clever, accurate, prompt, scholarly, or subtle, but also
sober, cold, or shy during their defenses.[124] Thus, even if the text of
the disputation theses did not originate with the student, the success
of the disputation depended on the student's ability to defend against
objections with appeals to proper scriptural or traditional authority and
with clever, logical argumentation. His performance, the culmination
of years of education, was rightly dedicated to those who influenced
the training that made the defense possible. Therefore, the dedications
and congratulatory poems, rather than providing evidence for student
authorship, can be seen as consistent with the following evidence for
professorial authorship.

We can affirm that, even if they have given no reasons for their sup-
position, modern Arminius interpreters have been correct in accepting the disputations as accurate representations of his theology. The
convincing evidence will be summarized in four arguments. The first
proof is the testimony of Arminius himself. When he sought to defend
himself against heterodoxy in a letter to the noble Hippolytus à Collibus, he appealed three times to his *theses publice in Academia disputatae*.[125] In
his *Declaratio sententiae* before the States of Holland, Arminius defended
his orthodox doctrine of God's providence by appealing to his Leiden
disputation.[126] Without doubt, Arminius would not point the magistrates
inquiring about his theology to the composition of students.

In addition to his testimony to public officials, Arminius's correspondence with his friends contains his own claims to authorship. In his personal letters, he sometimes sent the texts of his public disputations to his
friends for review. In a letter to Uytenbogaert, 30 July 1604, Arminius
said he was sending along the theses on the first sin that had been disputed on 24 July. He told his friend, "I composed the theses myself, as
you will easily see from the style and order; I have used liberty in them,
but more so in this disputation."[127] In another letter to Uytenbogaert, he

---

[124] Otterspeer, *Bolwerk*, p. 237.

[125] *Epistola*, in *Opera*, pp. 938, 942, and 944; *Works* 2:690, 698, and 701.

[126] *Dec. sent.*, p. 112; *Works* 1:658.

[127] *Ep. ecc.* 70, pp. 134–35; *Works* 2:150–51: "Theses ipse conscripsi, ut facile videbis
ex stilo et ordine; libertate in iis usus sum, sed in ipsa disputatione majori." J. Nichols
incorrectly dates this letter as 3 August. Knowing that "3 Kalend. Augusti" is 30 July is
important, for this letter falls between two public disputations of Arminius, the texts of
which he sends along with the letter to Uytenbogaert.

notes that he is sending him theses on providence (*Disp. pub.* IX), and he asks Uytenbogaert to read and critique them vigorously, and to indicate to Arminius where they are wanting.[128]

Arminius's letter to Adrianus Borrius on 25 July 1605 is even more revealing. He wrote,

> I send to you theses *de libero arbitrio*, which I so composed, because I was of the opinion that they conduce to peace. I placed nothing that I am of the opinion is near to a falsity. But some truths, which I could say, I passed over in silence, knowing that there is the one condition of passing over something true, the other of saying something false; of which the latter is never permitted, the former sometimes, and is indeed very often expedient.[129]

Arminius is referring to *Disp. pub.* XI, conducted two days before writing this letter to Borrius. He says he told the truth, but not the whole truth;[130] that is, he deliberately withheld some points that would be controversial—to be sure, a common tactic in an era of rising confessionalism—yet again showing his own precise authorship. Elsewhere, referring to his public disputation on predestination in the third *repetitio* of the *collegium*, Arminius said that he deliberately ordered (*jusserim*) the thesis to be composed according to the words of the confession.[131] This case seems to imply a very close supervision in the composition of the disputation, perhaps supervision over another writer. If the student, Wilhelmus Bastingius, did collaborate on the writing of this disputation, his was a minimal contribution, subject to the oversight of Arminius. In all of these instances, Arminius never mentioned the student respondent

---

[128] *Ep. ecc.* 77, p. 145.

[129] *Ep. ecc.* 78, p. 147: "...At nonnulla vera, quae dicere poteram, tacui: sciens aliam esse rationem verum tacendi, aliam falsum dicendi; quorum hoc nunquam licet, illud aliquando, imo et saepissime expedit."

[130] A revealing statement such as this tends to bring the polemicists and apologists out of the woodwork. On the one hand, Abraham Kuyper, *De Leidsche Professoren en de Executeurs der Dordtsche Nalatenschap* (Amsterdam, 1879), p. 36, represents many opponents of Arminius when he refers to him as a "looze vos" (crafty fox). Cf. Praamsma, 'Background,' p. 28: "We must also agree with the charge often leveled against him that he was not free from a certain kind of duplicity." Cf. also Gomarus, *Bedencken*, pp. 43–44. On the other hand, Clarke, 'Arminius's Understanding,' 25, represents many defenders of Arminius when he claims that interpreters must assume "Arminius was a normally honest man and a Christian theologian who had a proper sense of his responsibility to tell the truth as he saw it." Neither of these interpretations does justice to what Arminius wrote to Borrius. Maronier, *Arminius*, p. 222, offers a more nuanced historical picture of a very cautious individual caught in a volatile situation. Thus, we should view Arminius as being both honest and crafty, as much as these two traits can cohere together.

[131] *Dec. sent.*, pp. 107–08; *Opera*, pp. 119–20; *Works* 1:654.

or acknowledged that the student had any input (in contrast to law professor Cunaeus, who never mentioned the presider). Whatever argument could be conceived against professorial authorship would have to contend with these claims of Arminius himself.

The second piece of evidence supporting professorial authorship is that the presiding professor often stepped in to defend the theses in response to an opponent. In a letter to Uytenbogaert, 1 September 1606, Arminius said that he himself answered the opponent, hardly something a professor would do in defense of a student's theses.[132] In a letter to Simon Episcopius, 30 July 1609, Borrius gives an eye-witness account of the final public disputation of Arminius that had taken place five days earlier, a disputation on the calling of people to salvation (*Disp. pub.* XVI). The silence of Borrius concerning the respondent that day, Jacobus Bontebal, would be remarkable if that respondent had been responsible for the content of the disputation. On that particular occasion, it is Arminius who responds to the student opponents and other *ad hoc* opponents.[133] The defense that Arminius gives is not in order to rescue the student's reputation, but to deliver his own theses from charges of heterodoxy.[134]

The third factor in support of professorial authorship is that the disputations of Arminius and his colleagues were ubiquitously viewed by their contemporaries as their own compositions. First of all, Arminius and his colleagues often used the disputations as opportunities to make their opinions known in the presence of one another.[135] We have already noted that Uytenbogaert considered the collection of Arminius's disputations as a kind of systematic theology. As cited above, since Arminius assumed that Uytenbogaert could distinguish his writing style, it is unlikely that Uytenbogaert would have endorsed the publication of the

---

[132] *Ep. ecc.* 88, p. 160, italics mine: "Ego in disputatione publico-privata, quum opponens diceret Christum non habere essentiam sibi a Patre communicatam, *monstravi id falsum esse....*"

[133] *Ep. ecc.* 130, pp. 226–28, excerpted and summarized in *Works* 1:300–02. According to Otterspeer, *Bolwerk*, p. 237, by 1647, there was a complaint that presiding professors were defending the theses and not allowing the respondents an opportunity, which defeated the purpose of the disputation.

[134] Gomarus did the same thing, defending his own theses against the student opponent, Vliet. See *LA*, pp. 219–20; Itterzon, *Gomarus*, p. 108.

[135] According to *Ep. ecc.* 70, p. 134; *Works* 2:150, Arminius relished the opportunity to assert his views in the presence of Gomarus and Trelcatius. Cf. *LA*, p. 221; J. Nichols, in *Works* 1:258 and 266.

disputations if he thought Arminius did not compose them. Therefore, this authorial assumption is further proved by the publication of disputations under the names of their respective authors. Although the title pages of the original disputations contained the names of both the presiding professor and the respondent,[136] the professors themselves were praised or blamed for the content in the disputations. A professor's responsibility for thetical content was not limited to a kind of general oversight of the shape of the disputation, but his responsibility extended to the minutest details. For example, in the Christological controversy, Arminius appealed for support to Gomarus's 1605 disputation on the Trinity of persons, noting that Gomarus in three separate places also disagrees with their colleague Trelcatius.[137] Again, when Arminius examined Gomarus's 1604 disputation on predestination, he held it to detailed scrutiny, assuming it to be the exact opinion of the professor.[138] Furthermore, Arminius's and Gomarus's 1604 disputations on predestination were published in Dutch as representative of their thought.[139] When Gomarus and Arminius met before the States at The Hague in 1608, Gomarus cited Arminius's disputation on justification to argue his heterodoxy.[140] In the controversies over the content in disputations, whether in response to opponents present at the disputations or in polemical writing, the professors never blamed the content of the disputations on student input. This silence would seem to preclude any notions of students contributing anything meaningful to the actual text of the printed theses.

Finally, when comparing a professor's disputations with his other writings, the striking similarities point to an identical author. Two separate public disputations under the same presiding professor on the same topic frequently demonstrate much verbal similarity, and are at times verbatim.[141] It is possible that this verbal correspondence is the result

---

[136] This may explain the tradition of some university catalogues (such as Universiteitsbibliotheek Leiden) that list the respondent as the primary author and the presider as secondary author.

[137] *Dec. sent.*, pp. 120–21; *Works* 1:693.

[138] *Exam. Gom.*, pp. 1, 10, and 157; *Works* 3:526, 533, and 657, passim, Arminius refers to Gomarus as the *author*.

[139] Arminius and Gomarus, *Twee disputatien*.

[140] *LA*, p. 319.

[141] E.g., cf. Kuchlinus, *Theses theologicae de peccato originali*, ad quaest. 7 catechesios, Henricus Henrici Geesteranus respondens (Leiden, 1602); with idem, *Theses theologicae de peccato originali*, Lambertus de Riick respondens, in *Theo. disp.* 19, pp. 107–12.

of student plagiarism from previous disputations, but this is unlikely, for Arminius's public disputations also correspond very closely to his private disputations, and scholars agree that private disputations were authored by the professors.[142] Not only do the disputations concur among themselves, but disputations also show similarities with other treatises by the same professor. These similarities often go beyond mere consistency, pointing instead to verbal dependence.[143]

Having considered the evidence supporting professorial authorship of the disputations, I must now address two genuine caveats regarding this position. The first caution is a report by Bertius that the first two disputations over which Arminius presided in the fall of 1603 contained some things not exactly in accord with his own opinions.[144] The story goes that two students, Carronus and Jacchaeus, wanted the new professor Arminius to preside over their disputations on justification and original sin, respectively.[145] Having agreed to fulfill this duty, Arminius never had to step in to defend the theses with which he did not precisely agree, for the students were up to the task. If Bertius's testimony is taken seriously, then there are public disputations over which Arminius presided that he neither composed nor completely endorsed. If, indeed, either of these early disputations was not written by Arminius, how can we be confident about the authorship of any of his public disputations?

As an initial response to this caveat, it is important to note why Bertius mentions this story in the first place. In polemic against Bertius's funeral oration for Arminius, Gomarus had first recalled that he had high hopes for Arminius, especially after his first public disputation, which was on justification. Gomarus says that in this disputation Arminius had taught correctly (*suyverlick*) on election, faith, justification, certainty of salvation, and perseverance.[146] In response, Bertius then claims that this particular disputation had been an extraordinary situation where Arminius left the

---

[142] Ahsmann, *Collegia*, p. 313 n. 194 and p. 323; Otterspeer, *Bolwerk*, p. 236.

[143] E.g., cf. the *materia* question in Trelcatius, *De praedestinatione* (1606), with his *Scholastica, et methodica, locorum communium s. theologiae institutio* (London, 1604), pp. 32–37.

[144] Bertius, *Aen-spraeck*, fols. B3v and B4v–C1r. C. Brandt propagates this report in *LA*, pp. 191–92.

[145] Arminius, *Disputationum theologicarum vigesima-quarta, de iustificatione hominis coram Deo per solam fidem*, Theodorus Carronus respondens, 4 Calend. November 1603 (Leiden, 1603); idem, *Disputatio theologica de peccato originali*, Gilbertus Iacchaeus respondens, 5 November 1603 (Leiden, 1603).

[146] Gomarus, *Bedencken*, pp. 43–44.

theses unchanged (*onverandert*). Bertius proceeds to ask whether Gomarus would like to be held responsible for everything students placed in their theses, and then he chides Gomarus for suggesting that Arminius contradicted himself (*Arminius teghens Arminium strijdich is*).[147]

Some conclusions can be drawn from this exchange between Gomarus and Bertius. First, Gomarus presupposed that Arminius wrote the 1603 disputation, which implies that professorial authorship was the assumed norm. In C. Brandt's report of Bertius's story, he writes that Gomarus had on some occasions presided over disputations with which he would not agree in every respect. He then reports that this practice was not unusual in the universities.[148] Far from saying that this was the norm at Leiden, Brandt's description and his very mention of this incident imply that the norm was professorial, not student, authorship. Second, Bertius notes that this situation is *extraordinarie* in that Arminius let this disputation go unaltered. Since the two disputations in question both appear at the very beginning of Arminius's career, and given that the disputations themselves increasingly became a means of polemic among the faculty, it is a safe assumption that Arminius only tolerated student authorship as a concession for students who were not yet used to his oversight. Third, since Bertius employed this account in a heated exchange in order to defend an alleged contradiction in Arminius, and since I have found no first-hand evidence from Arminius's letters verifying this account, the veracity of the story is not above question.

Finally, with regard to the 1603 public disputations, it is appropriate to actually compare these early disputations with Arminius's undisputed opinions and writings. There does seem to be patent discontinuity between the disputation *De peccato originali* of 1603 and Arminius's later thought on the topic.[149] Although intellectual development is always a possibility, it is highly unlikely that Arminius's thought altered so drastically in the eight months between these contradictory public disputations, the latter of which represents Arminius's normative concept of original sin (*Disp. pub.* VII). With regard to the disputation on justification mentioned by Bertius, in my own estimation, and despite Gomarus's

---

[147] Bertius, *Aen-spraeck*, fols. B4v–C1r.

[148] *LA*, p. 191.

[149] Arminius, *De peccato originali* (1603), v–vii, directly contradicts *Disp. priv.* XXXI. ix–x and *Disp. pub.* VII.xvi (1604) on the issue of original sin as a lack of original righteousness and as *poena* only. On Arminius's thoughts regarding original sin, cf. Hicks, 'Theology of Grace,' pp. 30–31, 31 n. 20, pp. 37 and 41; Bangs, *Arminius*, pp. 339–40.

claims to the contrary, there does not appear to be any significant discontinuity between the 1603 disputation on justification (Carronus
respondens) and Arminius's own *Disputatio privata* on the same topic.[150]
The only other public disputation of 1603 under Arminius, *De bonis
operibus*, bears much similarity with his 1609 disputation on the same
topic; although there does seem to be more emphasis on the necessity
of good works in the latter document, it is not improbable to see such a
minor shift in the nearly six year interval.[151] Because the 1603 disputation on original sin demonstrates discontinuity with the later thought of
Arminius, we can accept Bertius's story regarding this one disputation
without succumbing to agnosticism about the authorship of all disputations. Bertius's account alone does not refute our position.

More potentially damaging to the defense of professorial authorship
is the first-hand evidence from Arminius's letter to Uytenbogaert, 30
July 1604. In this letter, Arminius tells his friend that he is sending him
the theses *de peccato primorum parentum* which were disputed a few days
earlier on 24 July. He goes out of his way to mention that he himself
wrote the theses, and that Uytenbogaert should be able to easily see his
authorship by the "style and order" in which they were composed.[152]
Although his claim of authorship of this disputation supports professorial authorship, one is left wondering why he felt the necessity to point
out the ordinary. Then, in the postscript, Arminius said, "I also add

---

[150] Instead, the *continuity* between the 1603 disputation in question and Arminius's
Disp. pub. XIX, and especially *Disp. priv.* XLVIII, is convincing. The attribution of causes
correspond, the notes contra Bellarmine are present, and the 1603 disputation describes
the elect as "credentes," a favorite point of Arminius. Even thesis xxxviii, which connects *fiducia* to *fides*, does not transgress Arminius's manner of describing the relationship
between the two. Cf. Arminius, *Disputationum theologicarum quarto repetitarum vigesima-tertia
de fide*, Ricardus Ianus Neraeus respondens, 21 December 1605 (Leiden, 1605), xiv–xv.
See Appendix 3 for the text of *De fide* (1605).

[151] Cf. Arminius, *Disputationum theologicarum vigesima-septima, de bonis operibus, et meritis
eorum*, Christopherus Hellerus respondens, ad diem 17 December 1603 (Leiden, 1603);
with idem, *Disputationum theologicarum quinto repetitarum vigesima-nona, de bonis operibus et meritis eorum*, Christianus Sopingius respondens, ad diem 28 February 1609 (Leiden, 1609).
Arminius, *De bonis operibus* (1609), x, says that good works are a *caussa* in salvation, "inasmuch as without which the possession of salvation is impossible to be obtained." See
Appendix 2 for the text of *De bonis operibus* (1603).

[152] *Ep. ecc.* 70, p. 134; *Works* 2:150. It is interesting that Arminius assumes Uytenbogaert could distinguish his writing by the "style and order." I posit that he means
the style and order peculiar to the subject of this disputation, namely, the first sin.
That is, Arminius is not saying that his friend can discern his authorship of just any
disputation.

other theses to be disputed tomorrow, which not I, but the respondent himself put together, only with very few things changed and added by me."[153] The disputation of which he spoke is on the human nature of Christ. In any event, here is solid firsthand testimony that some disputations were written by the professor and at least one disputation written by the student respondent.[154] Does this admission confirm a position of agnosticism with regard to the authorship of any given disputation?

Inasmuch as this statement does present a caveat, caution should certainly be exercised; however, Arminius's statement still falls short of overturning my hypothesis. First, it is likely that Arminius went out of his way to tell Uytenbogaert that he authored the disputation *De peccato primorum parentum* because he was also sending him another disputation that he did not primarily author. In other words, professorial authorship may still be the norm and student authorship the exception, but he had to specify the respective origins of the two documents that accompanied his letter. Second, the fact that he made some changes and additions confirms that Arminius reviewed and approved each disputation, and that what was written in the disputations did not contradict his own opinion. Third, this letter provides evidence that Arminius granted latitude of authorship on less controversial topics, such as the human nature of Christ. It is hard to imagine him allowing a student to compose theses on predestination or any other explicitly soteriological topic that would likely come under the sharp scrutiny of his faculty colleagues.[155]

In light of the overwhelming evidence that professorial authorship of the public practice disputations in the Leiden faculty of theology was the rule during the time of Arminius, we may confidently affirm that the disputations are accurate portrayals of the presiding professor's

---

[153] *Ep. ecc.* 70, p. 135: "Addo etiam alias theses cras disputandas, quas non ego, sed ipse Respondens confecit, pauculis a me tantum mutatis et additis." He was referring to Arminius, *Theses theologicae de vera humana Christi natura*, Sebastianus Damman respondens, 31 July 1604 (Leiden, 1604).

[154] Another example may be in Franciscus Junius, *Theses theologicae de differentia inter iustificationem et sanctificationem*, Lambertus de Riick respondens, 12 July 1600 (Leiden, 1600), fol. A1v, where the respondent says, "inscribo, do, dico, consecro..." this disputation. The student respondents commonly gave, said, and consecrated disputations, but rarely acknowledged inscribing them.

[155] Whether a public disputation appeared in the regular *repetitio* does not seem to be a factor regarding authorship. The disputation Arminius sent to Uytenbogaert was not part of the *repetitio*, but neither was Gomarus's 1604 disputation on predestination that Arminius picked apart. Subject matter, along with student ability, seems to be the determining factor.

thought.[156] This confidence is tentative inasmuch as there was disagreement even between Gomarus and Bertius on this issue, two figures who ought to know more about it than anyone; nevertheless, the two bits of evidence supporting student authorship are far outweighed by the testimonies of professorial authorship. Only when a disputation is in open contention with another undisputed writing of the same professor may we have cause for doubt. Using this criterion of continuity, there is ample reason to affirm the norm of professorial authorship, even if we may doubt Arminius's authorship of the disputation *De peccato originali* (1603). Consequently, there is warrant for employing the 1603 disputation on justification as a reliable guide to the thought of Arminius on justification. This general conclusion presumably neither affects the law faculty at Leiden (the subject of Ahsmann's inquiry) nor the later theological faculty at Leiden. Furthermore, a distinction between primary and secondary authorship may be helpful in some instances. However, we can only say the disputations under discussion here were written by the student respondents if we qualify it by affirming that absolutely nothing contained in the theses would contradict the professor's opinion.

III. *Arminius and Theological Method*

When the modern reader first encounters the theological works of Arminius and his contemporaries, there is an immediate sense of unfamiliarity with their approach to doing theology. Indeed, the theology may even appear vastly different from a sixteenth-century writer like Calvin. This predicament is due to the gradual shift in methodology which took place in early Protestant orthodoxy (ca. 1565–ca. 1640). The relationship between Reformation and Post-Reformation theology has been described, in its simplest form, as one of "broad doctrinal continuity together with methodological discontinuity."[157] In other words, the successors of the Reformation expounded and developed the inherited doctrinal content of the Reformation increasingly by means of the scholastic method. This method, which was borrowed directly from the

---

[156] This conclusion concurs with that of Albert Eekhof, *Theologische faculteit*, p. 32*; and P. Dibon, *L'Enseignement philosophique*, pp. 43–44.

[157] Muller, *PRRD* 1:46.

academic context of the universities and traditional Catholic theology, provided both a much-needed order for theological investigation and a certain academic quality to Protestant polemical and constructive theology. Since Arminius employed this method carefully, grasping its main contours is imperative for clearly understanding Arminius's thought.

A. *Asking the Right Questions*

The questions that a scholastic method asks are usually quite similar, but the answers to the questions are as diverse as the perspectives of the theologians using the method.[158] In other words, the method more or less determines the questions without determining the theological conclusions. Two of the most frequently addressed questions about a given topic were *an sit* and *quid sit*. This common mode of beginning theological or philosophical inquiries in the period of medieval scholasticism was used by both Arminius and his colleagues.[159] After all, the existence of a thing must be determined before discussing its essence and quality. Following the treatment of these questions, various other questions might be addressed, including *qualis* (what kind of), *quantum* (how much), and *quomodo* (how), depending on the nature of the topic under consideration and the needs that arise from it.

Under the issue of *quid sit*, the question of causality in particular, as proposed originally by Aristotle and filtered through an influential philosopher like Francisco Suárez, became a quickly recognizable characteristic of scholastic theology and philosophy, and it deserves brief attention here. By the end of the sixteenth century, sufficient handling of many theological topics required that the manifold causes of that particular point of Christian doctrine be resolved and defended. Arminius's assumption that one learns about an issue by defining and discussing its causes was shared by his contemporaries.[160] For the purposes of this

---

[158] For brief discussions of Reformed use of scholastic methodology, see Richard A. Muller, *The Unaccommodated Calvin: Studies in the Foundation of a Theological Tradition* [Oxford Studies in Historical Theology] (New York, 2000), pp. 42–44; idem, *After Calvin: Studies in the Development of a Theological Tradition* [Oxford Studies in Historical Theology] (New York, 2003), pp. 27–33 and 81–83; *PRRD* 1:60–66.

[159] For explicit examples of this method being used, cf. *Exam. Gom.*, 21; *Works* 3:543; with Kuchlinus, *De praedestinatione* (1600), viii; and idem, *De peccato originali* (Geesteranus, 1602).

[160] Arminius, *De bonis operibus* (1603), i.

larger study of soteriology, it is necessary to recognize that causality
was especially important in topics concerning salvation, for much of the
debate centered on what part of salvation, if any, should be attributed
to humanity. The importance of understanding causality for orthodox
theology and especially soteriology is demonstrated by the fact that even
Calvin, who generally avoided explicit use of scholastic terminology,
enumerated the four causes of salvation.[161]

Widespread understanding of metaphysical terminology in general
and the categories of causality in particular declined rapidly with the
spread of the Enlightenment. As early as 1726, J. L. Mosheim noted,
as if from a great distance, the "scholastic jargon of that age" which he
found in Arminius's disputations.[162] Not even a century after Mosheim,
Nichols, standing closer to Arminius's context than to ours, already
found it necessary to translate an excerpt from J. Wallis's text on logic, in
order to give his readers an introduction to the strange world of Aristotelian causality.[163] Because the attribution of causes was hotly contested
then and is seldom understood now, it is appropriate to offer a brief
description and analysis.

When investigation is made into a certain subject, one naturally
inquires concerning its "causes," that is, the broad causal questions
about the "how" and "why" of a given thing. Why do things change?
What is responsible for something being this way instead of that way?[164]
Aristotle wrote, "For then do we assume to know, [only] when we recognize the causes."[165] Further, to avoid a skepticism that never arrives

---

[161] *Inst.* 3.14.17.

[162] Quoted in *Works* 1:lv.

[163] Johannes Wallis, *Institutio logicae, ad communes usus acommodata* [*sic*] (Oxford, 1687),
58–60. See *Works* 2:77–79. Although it is initially helpful, Nichols's notes on causality
will not suffice for our purposes. Not only does this excerpt fail to include the original
Aristotelian background, but since Wallis was not considering Arminius, his categories
do not correspond exactly to those of the Leiden professors.

[164] Because some things were called "causes" that we normally do not think of as
being causes, it is important to convey the broad semantic ranges of the noun αἰτία
(responsibility, cause) and the adjective αἴτιος (responsible, culpable). Aristotle used the
two interchangeably, the neuter adjective (αἴτιον) functioning as a substantive (literally, a
responsible thing, cause). There is no exact English equivalent, although the translation
"reason [for]" may help in some cases. See also LSJ, q.v.

[165] Aristotle *Metaphysics* [Loeb Classical Library] (Cambridge, Mass., 1961) 994 b
30–31: "τότε γὰρ εἰδέναι οἰόμεθα, ὅταν τὰ αἴτια γνωρίσωμεν." Cf. *Metaphysics* 982 a
12–14: "ἔτι τὸν ἀκριβέστερον καὶ τὸν διδασκαλικώτερον τῶν αἰτίων σοφώτερον εἶναι
περὶ πᾶσαν ἐπιστήμην." "Further, the one who is more accurate and more able to teach
about the causes is wiser concerning all knowledge." Cf. also Virgil *Georgicon* [Loeb
Classical Library] (Cambridge, Mass., 1953) 2.490: "Felix qui potuit rerum cognoscere
causas."

at knowledge, Aristotle assumed the number of causes to be finite.[166] The classic fourfold causality based on the teaching of Aristotle became the standard heuristic model from the Aristotelian renaissance of the thirteenth century until the seventeenth century. In one sense, wrote Aristotle, a cause is "that from which something comes about inherently (τὸ ἐξ οὗ γίνεταί τι ἐνυπάρχοντος), as the bronze of the statue and the silver of the bowl."[167] It is the *materia* of which something consists, or the *causa materialis*. Second is "the form and the pattern (τὸ εἶδος καὶ τὸ παράδειγμα),"[168] the essence of a thing that makes it what it is, for example, a statue or bowl. It is the *forma*, or the *causa formalis*, that gives the shape to the *materia*. These two causes are known as the internal causes (*causae intrinsecae*), for the form and matter are inherent to the substance of a thing.[169] The third meaning of cause is that "from which is the first beginning of change or of rest (ὅθεν ἡ ἀρχὴ τῆς μεταβολῆς ἡ πρώτη ἢ τῆς ἠρεμήσεως),"[170] such as the sculptor or the smith who works with the *materia*. This agent of change is known as the *causa efficiens*. Finally, there is "the end; that is, the because of which (τὸ τέλος: τοῦτο δ' ἐστὶ τὸ οὗ ἕνεκα)."[171] This *finis*, or *causa finalis*, is the overall purpose for the changes that are produced. The statue is for enjoyment or commemoration, and the bowl is for holding food or drink. These latter two causes are known as external causes (*causae extrinsecae*), for they affect the substance from without. The order in which these causes are named varies depending on the perspective. For example, although *causa finalis* is the ultimate goal which is fulfilled logically and chronologically *a posteriori*, and thus may be named last, it is also the beginning in the sense that the purpose of a thing comes prior to its production, and can thus be placed in the first position.[172] The main point is that all four of these causes serve to answer the "how" and "why" questions from different angles.

---

[166] Aristotle *Metaphysics* 994 b 28–30. For a brief but reliable discussion of Aristotle's metaphysics, see Frederick Copleston, *A History of Philosophy*, 9 vols. (Garden City, 1962–75), vol. 1, part 2:30–61.

[167] Aristotle *Physics* [Loeb Classical Library] (Cambridge, Mass., 1963) 194 b 24–26.

[168] Aristotle *Physics* 194 b 27.

[169] Francisco Suárez, *Disputationes metaphysicae*, in *Disputaciones metafísicas*, 7 vols., Ediciòn de Sergio Rábade Romeo, et al. (Madrid, 1960–66), 17.1.6; cf. Aristotle *Metaphysics* 1070 b 22–24.

[170] Aristotle *Physics* 194 b 30–31.

[171] Aristotle *Physics* 194 b 33–34.

[172] Cf. Suárez, *Disputationes metaphysicae* 12.3.4: "licet finis sit postremum in exsecutione, tamen est primum in intentione...."

As Aristotelianism developed in the high and late medieval period, the intricacy of the fourfold causality model increased. The most influential metaphysician of the early modern period was the Jesuit Francisco Suárez (1548–1617). His *Disputationes metaphysicae* were employed not only by the Roman Catholic Church, but also by Protestant theologians and philosophers throughout Europe. Suárez, often labeled as a staunch defender of neo-scholastic Aristotelianism, propounded a more critical and eclectic Aristotelianism than his high medieval scholastic predecessors. He does not simply repeat the philosophy of medieval scholasticism, but methodologically approaches Aristotle as a post-Renaissance humanist, modifying and explaining Aristotle with frequent appeals to Aquinas and Averroes over against the interpretation of Italian secular Aristotelianism. For Suárez, Aristotle "has ceased to be an authority and has become a source."[173] One example of the shift away from Aristotelian thinking during this period is the increasing doubt that was cast on the legitimacy of the final cause. Suárez claims there are six reasons to doubt the legitimacy of the final cause, before he comes around to accept it; only a few decades later Gideon Harvey outright denies it.[174] Another important thinker during this period of eclectic Aristotelianism, Franco Burgersdijk, who studied and taught philosophy at Leiden in the decades after Arminius's death, is a good representative of a Reformed philosopher who revised Aristotelian causality in light of Suárez's work.[175] Burgersdijk observes that a number of subordinate

---

[173] Charles H. Lohr, 'Jesuit Aristotelianism and Sixteenth-Century Metaphysics,' in *Paradosis: Studies in Memory of Edwin A. Quain*, ed. G. Fletcher and M. B. Schuete (New York, 1976), pp. 203–20, there p. 219.

[174] Suárez, *Disputationes metaphysicae* 23.1; Gideon Harvey, *Archelogia philosophica nova, or New Principles of Philosophy* (London, 1663), Bk. 2:73. The shift in methodological and philosophical presuppositions visible from Aquinas to Suárez should not be exaggerated. See Alfred J. Freddoso, 'Introduction,' in Francisco Suárez, *On Creation, Conservation, and Concurrence: Metaphysical Disputations 20, 21, and 22*, trans. Alfred J. Freddoso (South Bend, 2002), pp. xi–cxxiii, there pp. xviii–xxv, who underscores the continuity of Suárez with high medieval scholasticism.

[175] For an introduction to the thought of Burgersdijk, see E. P. Bos and H. A. Krop, eds., *Franco Burgersdijk (1590–1635): Neo-Aristotelianism in Leiden* [Studies in the History of Ideas in the Low Countries 1] (Amsterdam, 1993); and Dibon, *L'Enseignement philosophique*, pp. 90–119. On Burgersdijk's chastened use of Suárez, see J. A. van Ruler, 'Franco Petri Burgersdijk and the Case of Calvinism within the Neo-Scholastic Tradition,' in *Franco Burgersdijk (1590–1635)*, pp. 37–65; and H. A. Krop, 'Natural Knowledge of God in Neo-Aristotelianism. The Reception of Suarez's Version of the Ontological Argument in Early Seventeenth Century Leiden,' in *Franco Burgersdijk (1590–1635)*, pp. 67–82.

causes exist under each general cause,[176] a point taken for granted by the Leiden theologians. Burgersdijk's discussion of causality, simpler and more accessible than that of Suárez, serves as a helpful introduction to the thought of the Leiden professors.

What concerns us in this essay is the use that Arminius and his contemporaries made of fourfold causality. In his disputations, Arminius, like his contemporaries, demonstrated his concern for causes by employing a version of the fourfold model. His frequent adherence to this method is made explicit at the beginning of his disputation *De magistratu*: "For a broader explanation of this definition, we will consider now the object, then the external causes of this function, [namely] the efficient and final; and the internal, [namely] the material and formal, from which [causes] we will derive the rest."[177] Included in "the rest" are other causes Arminius repeatedly examines in his disputations, such as προηγουμένη, προκαταρκτική, *causa obsignans et conservans, causa dispositiva, causa instrumentalis, finis summum et subordinatus*, and *finis proximus et remotus*. The expansion and complexity of the fourfold model show the influence that the new sixteenth-century Aristotelianism had on early Reformed orthodoxy.[178]

The widespread assumption among the later sympathizers and opponents of Arminius alike was that Arminius used scholastic categories and particularly the language of causality remarkably less than did his contemporaries. Speaking in the context of causality, Nichols claimed that, although Arminius was well versed in logic and metaphysics, nevertheless in his *Works* "appears far less of this metaphysical refinement, than in those of any other contemporary divine."[179] According to some later Arminian opponents, the reason for this scarcity is that, as William Twisse claimed, Arminius "was totally incompetent," and "he used Logic and Scholastic Theology in a manner the most puerile."[180] On

---

[176] Franco Burgersdijk, *Institutionum logicarum libri duo ad juventutem Cantabrigiensem* (Cambridge, Eng., 1637), pp. 61–63; *Monitio logica, or, An abstract and translation of Burgersdicius his logick by a gentleman* (London, 1697), pp. 50–52.

[177] Arminius, *Disp. pub.* XXV.ii: "Ad cujus definitionis latiorem explicationem, tum objectum, tum causas hujus functionis externas, efficientem et finem; et internas, materiam et formam considerabimus, ex quibus reliqua derivabimus."

[178] Current scholarship needs to address in more detail the origins and sources of this intricate causality schema and its comparatively rapid entrance into Reformed orthodoxy.

[179] *Works* 2:77.

[180] According to J. Nichols, in *Works* 1:251–52.

the contrary, Arminius's own contemporaries widely acknowledged his skill in logic. One church deputy who opposed Arminius's appointment to Leiden had only one good thing to say about him—Arminius was "an expert logician."[181] After Nichols proved Arminius's competence in metaphysical knowledge, he claimed that Arminius "conscientiously avoided all displays of it, except when the sinuosities of his opponents' arguments demanded an exposure, and then he was compelled to oppose his own syllogisms and definitions to theirs."[182] If Nichols was correct, then the reader of Arminius should notice a competent but comparatively chastened use of causality, as well as its use being confined primarily to those theological topics that were most contentious.

However, the common judgment that Arminius seldom employed causality is unwarranted. It parallels the more general claims of older scholarship that Arminius was more of a biblical humanist than a scholastic. Rather than simply making assumptions about the differences between Arminius's methodology and that of his colleagues, it is better to actually compare the ways they used causality.[183] Judging from the disputations and documents examined for this essay, there is no remarkable difference in the frequency or the mode of the causality employed in Arminius's writings in comparison with those of his contemporaries. Arminius neither restricted his use of causality, nor did he confine it to controversial topics. For example, Arminius's disputation on the comparatively non-controversial topic of Christian liberty exhibits some of his most detailed scholastic terminology.[184] Elsewhere, in a non-controversial letter to a friend, which he says contains his

---

[181] *LA*, p. 136.

[182] *Works* 1:253–54. Conversely, C. Graafland, *De zekerheid van het geloof: Een onderzook naar de geloofsbeschouwing van enige vertegenwoordigers van reformatie en nadere reformatie* (Wageningen, 1961), p. 85, explains that Gomarus's use of scholastic method was a response to Arminius's scholasticism: "Maar omdat zijn tegenstander [Arminius] eveneens wapenen hanteerde die aan de wijsbegeerte waren ontleend, werd ook Gomarus steeds verder op deze weg gedreven." In light of these contradictory assumptions, therefore, such explanations for the apparent "excess" of scholasticism are dubious. Neither Arminius nor Gomarus reluctantly gave in to the methodological presuppositions of the other.

[183] For a summary of and annotations on the following analysis, see Appendix 4, which compares the uses of causality in Arminius, Kuchlinus, and Gomarus. The results of this specific research on causality supplement what Muller and Dekker have established about Arminius and his use of scholastic methodology in general. Cf. Muller, 'Arminius and the Scholastic Tradition'; *GCP*; Dekker, 'Was Arminius a Molinist?'; idem, *Rijker*.

[184] *Disp. pub.* XX.

"slight musings and meditations" and "rough notes," Arminius retains the scholastic terminology, and it is one of the few places he discusses the *causa impulsiva*.[185] Thus, the thesis that Arminius only used causal terminology sparingly, or primarily to defeat his opponents, must be overturned in face of the evidence. Uytenbogaert wrote in his diary that, although Arminius was not seeking the faculty position at Leiden, Arminius himself said he preferred "the scholastic mode of speaking." In his major polemical and apologetic works, Arminius never criticized his opponents for using the scholastic method or for excessive speculation. The appeal to rely on Scripture alone, the plea to avoid *pointless* speculation, and the critique of certain scholastic distinctions are not only characteristic of Arminius's writings, but are also marks of Reformed orthodoxy in general. Even if it were proved that Arminius used causality terminology less, he used it enough for us to conclude that he shared the same metaphysical presuppositions as his colleagues.

Although specific terminology occasionally varied among the professors, there was broad consensus on the categories employed. At times, there are terms appearing in the Leiden theological disputations that do not appear in Burgersdijk; on the other hand, Burgersdijk occasionally mentions causes that do not appear in the disputations.[186] Overall, the Leiden theology professors' use of fourfold causality roughly corresponds to the analysis of Burgersdijk. First, efficient causality was the most refined of the four causes; after stating that "the efficient cause extends very broadly," Burgersdijk mentions eight different ways the efficient cause can be distinguished.[187] The most common distinctions under *efficiens* in the Leiden theological disputations are the *primaria* and *secundaria* efficient causes, with the latter generally consisting of προηγουμένη, προκαταρκτική, and *instrumentalis*.[188] Second, Arminius, Kuchlinus, and Gomarus generally followed a threefold division of *materia* into *ex qua, in*

---

[185] *Ep. ecc.* 45, pp. 89–90; *Works* 2:732 and 735.

[186] See the discussion of causes in Burgersdijk, *Institutionum libri duo*, pp. 59–83; *Monitio*, pp. 48–71. Cf. Thomas Spencer, *The art of logick delivered in the precepts of Aristotle and Ramus* (London, 1628), pp. 28–57, who discusses the causes and gives numerous biblical examples as illustrations.

[187] Burgersdijk, *Institutionum libri duo*, pp. 69–78; *Monitio*, pp. 58–68: "causa efficiens latissime patet." Cf. Suárez, *Disputationes metaphysicae* 17–22, on efficient cause. See Alfred J. Freddoso, 'Introduction,' in Suárez, *On Creation*, pp. xi–cxxiii, for a helpful introduction to efficient causality in Suárez.

[188] Curiously, Suárez does not mention προηγουμένη or προκαταρκτική in his discussion of the types of efficient cause. See Suárez, *Disputationes metaphysicae* 17.2.

qua (subjectum), and *circa quam (objectum)*, a division in which Burgersdijk concurred.[189] Third, concerning the formal cause, Burgersdijk noted that it may be divided in four different ways: between *forma materialis* and *immaterialis, forma substantialis* and *accidentalis, forma naturalis* and *artificialis*, or *forma principalis* and *disponens*.[190] However, Arminius, like his contemporaries, had an undeveloped formal causality. The only occurrence that may reflect an expansion of the formal cause is Arminius's *causa dispositiva*, which may correspond to Burgersdijk's *forma disponens*.[191] The final cause, according to Burgersdijk, can be divided in three different ways: between *finis cujus* and *cui, finis principalis* and *secundarius*, or *finis subordinatus* and *ultimus*.[192]

Far from determining the outcome of a doctrine, this heuristic device was simply designed to help define a doctrine more precisely.[193] The theological disputations exhibit some variations in their uses of causality. A careful reading of the disputations demonstrates overlap in some terminology and flexibility concerning which causes to discuss.[194] The eclectic use of subordinate causes shows that, beyond the basic four causes, the causes to be chosen for examination were influenced by the topic at hand. For example, it would be unnecessary and usually impossible to divide the efficient cause eight ways for any topic, but eight different ways were available to choose from to best suit the needs of the topic.

The reason that causality dominates several of the disputations, but is scarcely found in a famous document such as the *Declaratio sententiae*, is simply a question of genre. The former were conducted in Latin, and in an academic context where the scholastic method was normative; the latter was delivered in Dutch to laymen. We see that Arminius

---

[189] Burgersdijk, *Institutionum libri duo*, p. 64; *Monitio*, p. 53. Cf. Suárez, *Disputationes metaphysicae* 13–14, on material cause.

[190] Burgersdijk, *Institutionum libri duo*, pp. 66–8; *Monitio*, pp. 56–7. Cf. Suárez, *Disputationes metaphysicae* 15–16 on formal cause.

[191] Cf. also Trelcatius, Jr., *Disputationum theologicarum quarto repetitarum vigesima-quarta de iustificatione hominis coram Deo*, Bernherus Vezekius respondens, 21 January 1605 [1606] (Leiden, 1605 [1606]), xix, who speaks of *negativa* and *affirmativa* under formal cause.

[192] Burgersdijk, *Institutionum libri duo*, pp. 80–1; *Monitio*, pp. 68–9. Cf. Suárez, *Disputationes metaphysicae* 23.2, who divides the final cause in six different ways.

[193] Cf. Muller, *PRRD* 2:224–28, for a brief discussion of causality in the doctrine of the divinity of Scripture. Muller agrees that the use of causality questions does not determine a doctrine, but merely is "the application of a heuristic principle."

[194] Suárez, *Disputationes metaphysicae* 27, discusses the relationship of the four causes among one another.

asked the causality question not only because he properly fits into this early orthodox context of increasingly scholastic methodology, but also because it is often quite useful for explaining and defending doctrine, as Nichols also admitted: When this science "is not carried to extremes and does not degenerate into *excessive refinement*, it affords mighty aid to the interests of Truth, and cannot justly become an object of reprehension to the most fastidious among the lovers of simplicity."[195] If we allow Arminius to escape modern charges of "excessive refinement" in his use of this heuristic device, then it would be inaccurate to apply the same charges to his contemporaries, who used the same refined system. The difference between Arminius and his contemporaries lies not in *whether* they used the metaphysics of causality, but *how* they applied this commonly received causality. Arminius considered not the use or non-use of causal categories, but the attribution of causes, to be at times a fundamental difference between his theology and that of his opponents.[196]

B. *Handling the Right Topics*

Another feature typical of the late medieval and early modern periods is the *locus* method.[197] A collection of theological *loci*, similar to the medieval gatherings of *sententiae*, was simply an orderly arranged discussion of common doctrinal topics arising out of Scripture. With few exceptions, by the time of Arminius there was a standard set of *loci* that a theologian was expected to handle. Despite his intention to do so, Arminius never ordered and gathered his *loci* into a separate book for publication, an exercise, if it had been accomplished, which would doubtless have shed light on his thought. Thus, one must be cautious when referring to Arminius's theological "system," since some standard *loci* were never handled by Arminius in writing. However, because there is such a close relationship between *loci* and the *disputationes* in which Arminius did engage, these terms may be used interchangeably when referring to the theological topics Arminius treated in the university setting.

---

[195] *Works* 2:79, italics mine.
[196] *Exam. Gom.*, p. 74; *Works* 3:589.
[197] On the *locus* method in general and its use in theological and biblical studies in particular, see Muller, *After Calvin*, pp. 57–60 and 83–4; idem, *Unaccommodated Calvin*, pp. 108–11; *PRRD* 1:177–81; Robert Kolb, 'Teaching the Text: The Commonplace Method in Sixteenth Century Lutheran Biblical Commentary,' *Bibliothèque d'Humanisme et Renaissance* 49 (1987), 571–85; Otterspeer, *Bolwerk*, pp. 43–45.

One will quickly notice that the designation "soteriology" was never employed by Arminius and his contemporaries; neither was there a separate *locus* on salvation. Therefore, soteriology, or the doctrine of salvation, can be an ambiguous term, touching anything from the doctrine of God to eschatology, and hence demanding qualification. Soteriology can more properly have reference to doctrines such as that of atonement or of the Holy Spirit. However, when this essay speaks of "soteriology," it will comprise primarily the doctrines of sin, free choice, grace, predestination, calling, faith, justification, repentance, and good works, each of which affects the others. These topics arise when one asks the most basic questions about the ontology of individual salvation, including: How is a person saved? Who can be saved? How is salvation applied? What can one do to obtain or lose salvation?

C. *Establishing the Right Order*

Once the correct *loci* had been determined, it was equally important to place these in the correct order. Theologians who employed the scholastic method of investigation and education were concerned about proper order (*ordo recte docendi*). Disputations often began with a statement justifying why this certain topic should be examined now, placing it in the proper order of theology.[198] Reformed orthodox theologians were particularly intent on establishing an orderly doctrine of salvation. The term *ordo salutis* was used already in the ninth century to suggest God's arranged plan of salvation through the person and work of Christ.[199] Although it did not take on its more technical meaning until the late seventeenth century, one can speak of the *ordo salutis* in a general way to refer to the structure and sequence of the doctrine of salvation.

The concern for establishing a correct *ordo salutis* in this sense is characteristic of the early orthodox period. An excellent example is William Perkins, who proposed the order of effectual calling (exhibited in preaching and effectual hearing of the word, a mollification of the heart, and faith), justification (exhibited in remission of sins and imputation of righteousness), sanctification (exhibited in mortification,

---

[198] E.g., see Kuchlinus, *De praedestinatione* (1600), i.
[199] Jaroslav Pelikan, *The Christian Tradition: A History of the Development of Doctrine*, 5 vols. (Chicago, 1971–89), 3:108.

vivification, repentance, and new obedience), and glorification.[200] Perkins opposed his order of the causes of salvation to that taught by the Roman Catholic Church.[201] That the Leiden theologians were concerned about the proper *ordo salutis* is clear from their writings as well. Kuchlinus, for example, spoke of the chain (*catena*) of the causes of our salvation, taking it straight from Rom. 8,30,[202] which was the *locus classicus* on this topic.

The principal distinction between the soteriology of Arminius and that of his Reformed contemporaries was not in questions asked or topics handled, but in the specifics of the *ordo salutis* itself. That Arminius was just as concerned as his contemporaries with the right *ordo salutis* is clear from his debates about soteriology. In his *Amica collatio*, Arminius demonstrated his concern for the correct order as it is represented in Scripture.[203] In a private disputation on justification, he asked a series of questions concerning the *ordo*.[204] It is also readily apparent that Arminius's proposed *ordo* was significantly different from that of his Reformed contemporaries. His opinion on predestination and salvation, claimed Arminius, establishes "the order by which the gospel must be preached,"[205] whereas the order described by opponents such as Perkins and Gomarus is "a straight reversal of the doctrine of the holy gospel."[206]

IV. *Conclusion*

Modern theologians who seek answers to their various questions about "Arminianism"—usually as distinct from "Calvinism," and generally with a view to determine which system is "right"—too often approach

---

[200] William Perkins, *Armilla aurea, id est, theologiae descriptio*, 2nd ed. (Cambridge, Eng., 1591). Richard A. Muller, 'Perkins' *A Golden Chaine*: Predestinarian System or Schematized *Ordo Salutis?*' *SCJ* 9/1 (1978), 68–81, discusses the theology of this piece.

[201] Perkins, *Armilla aurea* cap. 51: "De ordine causarum salutis."

[202] Kuchlinus, *Theses theologicae de sanctorum perseverantia in fide*, ad quaestionem catech. 58, Iacobus Paulides respondens (Leiden, 1603), vi.

[203] Arminius, *Amica cum D. Francisco Iunio de praedestinatione, per litteras habita collatio*, in *Opera*, p. 462; *Works* 3:23: "Hunc ordinem nobis infinitis locis demonstrat Scriptura."

[204] Arminius, *Disp. priv.* XXIII.vii–xvi.

[205] Arminius, *Dec. sent.*, p. 110; *Works* 1:655: "de ordre deur welcke het Evangelium moet gepredict worden."

[206] Arminius, *Dec. sent.*, p. 88; *Works* 1:633: "Een rechte omkeeringhe vande leere des H. Evangelij."

Arminius without setting him within his historical context. It is not that theologians should refrain from asking their questions, but all interpreters should be careful about reading Arminius apart from his context and through the lens of a particular agenda. Interpretations that uncritically lionize or demonize Arminius generally fail to consider the social context of his life in the university and fail to grasp the intellectual context of his theological literature. Arminius's interaction with his supralapsarian colleagues, the function of disputations in the Staten College, and the methodological presuppositions of early modern Leiden theology all contribute to our understanding of the roots of the debate on salvation and the assurance of salvation. Although much more could be written about the context of Arminius, this chapter is an attempt to supplement the classic biography by Bangs by offering this biographical sketch of Arminius's academic context. Keeping this context firmly in one's grip is the first step that will enable the interpreter to proceed with an appropriate examination of Arminius's own work and theology.

PART TWO: THE ONTOLOGY OF SALVATION

CHAPTER THREE

GRACE, PREDESTINATION, AND THE *ORDO SALUTIS*

As an examination of Arminius's doctrine of the assurance of salvation, this essay is primarily concerned with what we may call the epistemological question concerning soteriology, that is, how one *knows* whether one is saved. Such a discussion presupposes at least a cursory familiarity with Arminius's doctrine of salvation in general, especially the ontological question, that is, what is salvation, or how one is saved. For the purpose of laying a foundation for the assurance discussion, in this chapter I shall briefly set soteriological debate in its theological and historical context, after which the broad contours of Arminius's soteriology in its Leiden context will be surveyed. Although not an attempt to describe and analyze Arminius's doctrine of salvation exhaustively, this chapter will reveal certain significant features of Arminius's theology and give the reader a sense of the shape of his soteriology, especially as it relates to the topic of assurance.

I. *The Importance of Soteriology in the Sixteenth Century*

Controversy drives the development and codification of Christian doctrine. Not only did controversy spark the writings of the New Testament canon, but the course of church history from the subapostolic period to the present day can hardly be considered apart from the debates and debaters that mark the chapters of Christian thought. History has shown that some disputes have had a longer life than others. Whereas the doctrines of God and Christ were codified in the ecumenical church councils, the Western Church, more overtly than the Eastern Church, continually struggled with its soteriology. From the letters of Paul through the treatises of Augustine to the Canons of Dort, soteriology has played a constitutive and ongoing role in the character of the Western Church.

The Western Church of the sixteenth century was, of course, marked by the Protestant Reformation, the causes of which were as many and varied as the debates and debaters of that era. However, when we inquire into the theological impetus of the Reformation, our attention must turn eventually to the broad subject of soteriology, which became the primary flashpoint and driving force of conflict.[1] To claim that soteriology was the theological starting point for the Reformation is not to say that all other theological topics were uncontested. Rather, soteriology was the principal point of contention, whereas the classical doctrines of God and Christ enjoyed wide, though by no means unanimous, consensus among Roman Catholics and Protestants.[2] Neither do I claim that soteriology stands alone and disconnected from the other theological *loci*, for it undoubtedly affects every conceivable topic of theology. To the degree that soteriological systems differed, systems of anthropology, ecclesiology, eschatology, Christology, and theology proper were all diversely influenced.

Soteriology has always been a key point of departure for theological discussion. In the East, the doctrine of salvation has frequently functioned in defense of other theological topics, but in a subordinate way. For example, the fourth-century fathers who defended Nicaea, although they emphasized and may have begun with the soteriological implications of various Christologies, were primarily deliberating about Christology, a topic which was still being codified in the creeds.[3] In the West, soteriology has more often functioned as the τέλος of debate.[4] For

---

[1] Cf. Reinhold Seeberg, *Text-book of the History of Doctrines*, 2 vols., trans. Charles E. Hay (Grand Rapids, 1977), 2:224–25 (emphasis mine): "Luther's decisive religious experiences were gained in connection with the sacrament of repentance, under the stress of a false conception of repentance for which he struggled to find a substitute. This was the *starting-point from which his fundamental religious ideas were developed....* All his ideas in regard to penitence and faith, faith and works, sin and grace, law and gospel, together with his new ideal of life, constitute a complex of religious conceptions which were developed under the pressure of and in opposition to the sacrament of repentance. This brings his work, however, into the very centre of the current of religious development in the West. *The controlling thought in the latter is always the salvation of souls (salus animarum).*" See also Carter Lindberg, *The European Reformations* (Oxford, 1996), pp. 56–70.

[2] Cf. Seeberg, *History*, 2:303 and 323–25; Lindberg, *European Reformations*, pp. 191–97 and 267–69; Muller, *PRRD* 1:97.

[3] E.g., Athanasius, *Contra Gentes and De Incarnatione*, ed. Robert W. Thomson (Oxford, 1971); Gregory of Nazianzus, Λογοι Θεολογικοι, ed. Joseph Barbel (Düsseldorf: Patmos-Verlag, 1963), 29.18; 30. Indeed, as noted in Seeberg, *History*, 1:207, the Arian theology opposed by Athanasius and Nazianzus had troubling consequences for the assurance of salvation. On the connection between Christology and soteriology in the patristic debates, see also Wolfhart Pannenberg, *Jesus—God and Man*, 2nd ed., trans. L. Wilkins and Duane A. Priebe (Philadelphia, 1977), pp. 124, 164, and 172–73.

[4] Cf. Seeberg, *History*, 1:199. For example, one may simply consider the significance of the Pelagian controversy in the West and its comparative irrelevance in the East.

example, Martin Luther's understanding of the *iustitia Dei* was prompted by and applied to his well-known concern for salvation by grace through faith alone. Even ecclesiology, the context of much of Luther's polemical energy, took a subordinate place to the more pressing concern of salvation.[5] Theological reflection done by the church and for the church generally deals first with the practical, pastoral problem of salvation. Once questions of salvation have been addressed, then the topics of God and humanity are further informed.

Although the controversy over soteriological issues in the sixteenth century is famous for the interchanges between notable Protestants such as Luther or Calvin and notable Catholics such as Erasmus or Pighius, the two sides did not divide along neat Catholic versus Protestant lines. Debates over soteriology and its connection with the divine attributes dominated the Roman Church, with Dominicans emphasizing God's sovereignty and Jesuits and Franciscans highlighting human freedom.[6] A parallel dispute began to appear within the Reformed churches during the period of early Protestant orthodoxy. The shift from the Reformation to the period of early orthodoxy was characterized by the need for confessionalization, resulting in the institutionalization of the Reformed church and the gradual codification of its doctrine, especially the doctrine of salvation.[7] As the problem of soteriology took on a more definite shape during this period, the debates among the Reformed were no less contentious than the polemic between the Protestants and the Roman Catholics. Indeed, Protestants often leveled the charge of "popery" against fellow Protestants who manifested any signs of perceived Roman Catholic influence in matters pertaining to salvation. It is in this highly charged polemical context that the Arminian debate at Leiden University took place.

---

[5] See Luther, *Disputatio pro declaratione virtutis indulgentiarum* (1517), in *WA* 1:233–38, which chiefly questions soteriology, not the pope. The implication, at least in 1517, is that Luther could more easily tolerate the papal office if the pope would change the church's policy on indulgences. Heiko A. Oberman, *The Dawn of the Reformation: Essays in Late Medieval and Early Reformation Thought* (1986; repr. Grand Rapids, 1992), pp. 97–103, traces the development of Luther's rejection of the *facere quod in se est*, his major soteriological issue.

[6] See Alfred J. Freddoso, 'Introduction,' in Luis de Molina, *On Divine Foreknowledge (Part IV of the* Concordia*)*, trans. Alfred J. Freddoso (Ithaca, 1988), pp. 1–81, there pp. 1–46; see also J. A. van Ruler, 'Calvinism within the Neo-Scholastic Tradition,' pp. 44–45; and Muller, *GCP*, p. 7.

[7] See Muller, *PRRD* 1:46–73.

II. *The Shape of Arminius's Soteriology*

Because most popular and even scholarly treatments of Arminius and
Arminianism are concerned primarily with issues that relate to soteriology, one may wonder whether another survey of Arminius's doctrine of
salvation is necessary. This survey, however, is an attempt to avoid two
weaknesses that plague most existing surveys of his soteriology, weaknesses that reflect the deficiencies of Arminius studies in general. Many
studies demonstrate a myopic, severely limited use of primary and secondary sources, and they exhibit a failure to contextualize Arminius
and compare him with his contemporaries; specifically, they ignore the
many disputations of Arminius not collected in the *Opera theologica* and
neglect the disputations of his colleagues during their Leiden years. A
third rationale is based on the few existing quality discussions of Arminius's doctrine of salvation, which are not weak in themselves, but are
limited in scope and focus their surveys toward a specific goal other than
assurance.[8] This survey is not intended to be an exhaustive account of
soteriology in Arminius, but it will treat the central topics relating to
salvation, focus on the issues that will better inform Arminius's doctrine
of the assurance of salvation, and demonstrate the concord and conflict
between Arminius and his colleagues.

Given the potentially enormous range of topics that could fall under
soteriology and the variety of possibilities for ordering such a discussion, it is appropriate to follow as closely as possible the topics and order
proposed by Arminius in his *Disputationes privatae*, which served as the
groundwork for his system. *Disputationes privatae* XL–XLIX, which all
relate to salvation, move in order through the topics of predestination
(XL–XLI), vocation (XLII), repentance (XLIII), faith (XLIV), union
with Christ and justification (XLV–XLVIII), and finally sanctification
(XLIX). This order does not necessarily represent Arminius's *ordo salutis*,
for he says that a certain kind of faith precedes repentance. These disputations simply form the basis for the structure of our survey, but are
naturally not the only sources for the discussion. The major treatises and
public disputations (including the ones never before used) of Arminius
will provide necessary context and supplemental material for this survey.

---

[8] E.g., Hicks, 'Theology of Grace,' aims his survey at Arminius's doctrine of saving
grace.

In addition, the topic of free choice, which does not appear in the *Disputationes privatae*, does appear in the *Disputationes publicae* before the other soteriological topics. Therefore, this survey will begin with the topic of free choice and issues related to this topic that were not proposed for separate disputations. The topic of sanctification, which deals with the Christian life and the topic of assurance more directly, will be handled in the next chapter.

A. *Human Freedom and Divine Grace*

Theologians during the period of early orthodoxy tended to agree that humans have freedom. Gomarus, for example, categorically denied a forced, metaphysical determinism. Whatever one wills, one wills it freely, not forcibly. For neither the eternal decree of God nor the temperament of a person introduce any force (*vis*) upon the will.[9] The question is whether a person is free to choose the good, and the answer depends on how "freedom" and "good" are defined and to what extent grace impinges on the human situation.

A.1. *Free Choice*

The Leiden theologians all agreed that human free choice can find itself in one of three diverse positions in this world, corresponding to the three conditions of humanity in this life. The first condition is the pre-lapsarian state of innocence; second, the post-lapsarian state of corruption; and third, the state of regeneration.[10] Also, there are three different kinds of good things: natural goods, which pertain to animal life; moral goods, which pertain to external obedience and conservation of the human race; and spiritual goods, which pertain to spiritual life and beatitude.[11] All agreed that Adam, in the state of innocence, truly

---

[9] Gomarus, *Disputationum theologicarum decima-quarta, de libero arbitrio*, Samuel Gruterus respondens, 19 March 1603 (Leiden, 1603), vi.

[10] *Disp. pub.* XI.iii; Gomarus, *De libero arbitrio* (Gruterus, 1603), vii. Gomarus, *De libero arbitrio* (Gruterus, 1603), xxi, in continuity with Reformed orthodoxy, adds a fourth condition corresponding to the next age, when the state of free choice will enjoy a better position than it did in Eden, for it will not be able to will evil (*non posse peccare*). Furthermore, these states correspond to the states of the *imago Dei*. See a description of *imago Dei* in Gomarus, *Disputationum theologicarum repetitarum decima quinta, de creatione hominis ad imaginem Dei*, Symeon Ruytingius respondens, 29 July 1598 (Leiden, 1598), iii: "*Integra*, ut fuit antelapsum: *Corrupta*, ut est per lapsum: *Restituta*, ut est post lapsum, inchoate in hac vita, perfecte in altera."

[11] Gomarus, *De libero arbitrio* (Gruterus, 1603), xi; Kuchlinus, *Theses theologicae de statu*

had free choice and ability for either spiritual good or evil, and that he sinned by his own free choice, persuaded by Satan.[12] Gomarus here insisted that God was not the author of evil, a charge that Arminius would apply to Gomarus's doctrine of predestination.

The point becomes more complex with the descriptions of the two conditions possible in this present, post-lapsarian age, namely, the positions of freedom with regard to the corrupted and the regenerate individual. In the position of corruption, according to Gomarus and Kuchlinus, humanity can will and do natural goods by the general helping (common) grace of God (*gratia generalis*). Humanity can further perform externally moral goods, irrespective of the internal motives, only by the special grace of God (*gratia specialis*).[13] However, with regard to spiritual goods, there is no free choice left to the corrupt individual for penitence and justification.[14] Arminius agreed that, after the fall, without the help of God's grace, the will to spiritual good is useless, the darkened and perverted mind pursues only evil, and one's whole life is dead in sin.[15] By contrast, the person in the state of regeneration can, by the singular grace of the Holy Spirit, will and do spiritual good, although he will still be susceptible to temptation and sin.[16]

The most important issue that concerns us here is the process by which the corrupt, unregenerate person becomes regenerate, and what role free choice plays in this process of conversion. On the surface there appears to be general concurrence among these disputations. It should be noted that, although Arminius wrote nothing that he considered incorrect, he did admit to withholding some points in this particular disputation *De libero arbitrio* that were more likely to stir controversy.[17]

---

hominis non regeniti post lapsum, ad quaest. 8 catecheseos, Franciscus Petrus respondens (Leiden, 1603), i. In *Disp. pub.* XI.iii, Arminius calls the second category "animal."

[12] *Disp. pub.* VII.iii; XI.v; Gomarus, *De libero arbitrio* (Gruterus, 1603), x (*posse peccare*).

[13] Gomarus, *De libero arbitrio* (Gruterus, 1603), xii; Kuchlinus, *De statu hominis* (1603), i.

[14] Gomarus, *Disputatio theologica de libero arbitrio*, Gilbertus Iacchaeus respondens, 28 June 1603 (Leiden, 1603), xx; idem, *Disputationum theologicarum quinto repetitarum decimasexta de libero arbitrio*, Hieronymus Vogellius respondens, ad diem 24 November 1607 (Leiden, 1607), ii: "Ad quod respondemus, hominem corruptum non renatum nihil boni spiritualis posse velle aut eligere suis viribus...."

[15] *Disp. pub.* XI.vii–xi; cf. *Dec. sent.*, pp. 112–13; *Works* 1:659–60.

[16] *Disp. pub.* XI.xii; Gomarus, *De libero arbitrio* (Gruterus, 1603), xviii; Kuchlinus, *De statu hominis* (1603), i. The third condition of a regenerate free choice, which relates more directly to the doctrine of sanctification, will be discussed at more length in chapter four.

[17] *Ep. ecc.* 78, p. 147; *Disp. pub.* XI.

Thus, it should not be surprising that Arminius's silence hints at the difference between his colleagues and him on this point. In the disputations, the matter is not an outright contradiction or a disagreement over words, but it is a degree of emphasis. Gomarus went out of his way to stress that God makes unwilling people into willing people.[18] Kuchlinus stressed that God distributes the Holy Spirit to whomever he wills, not as people will, and, by his immutable decree, establishes the rest in sin and abandons them to destruction.[19] For Gomarus and Kuchlinus, there is no free choice in matters of salvation prior to regeneration. Although Arminius would equally stress the necessity of divine grace in initiating conversion, he was careful to avoid language implying that humanity is an unwilling participant in conversion.[20] The difference of emphasis between Arminius and his colleagues becomes clearer when Arminius discusses the grace involved in conversion.

A.2. Grace

Gratia is a word that comes theologically loaded and often ambiguous. Arminius and his Reformed contemporaries acknowledged various distinctive uses of the word *gratia*.[21] The differences between Arminius's conception of grace and the conception of grace found in the thought of his Reformed colleagues should not conceal the similarities between them. In his discussion of God's will, Arminius describes grace in general: "God is affected to communicating his own good and to loving (*amandumque*) creatures, not from merit or debt, nor that it may add anything to God himself; but that it may be well with him on whom the good is bestowed (*tribuitur*), and who is loved."[22] Saving grace in particular is first the affection of God to adopt sinners, then infusion of gifts for the purpose of regeneration and sanctification.[23] Arminius's goal is not

---

[18] Gomarus, *De libero arbitrio* (Gruterus, 1603), xix.

[19] Kuchlinus, *De statu hominis* (1603), ix.

[20] *Disp. pub.* XI.xii, xiv. Cf. idem, *Theses theologicae de imaginis Dei in nobis restitutione*, Theodorus Tronchinus respondens, ad diem 2 July 1605 (Leiden, 1605), viii: "Haec facit Deus nobis, sed non perficit sine nobis, agit nobis ut nos agamus." This sentiment echoes the thought of Augustine, *Sermones ad populum omnes* 169.11.13; *PL* 38:923: "Qui ergo fecit te sine te, non te justificat sine te. Ergo fecit nescientem, justificat volentem."

[21] E.g., see *Apologia*, art. XVI, in *Opera*, p. 158; *Works* 2:18. Cf. Muller, *DLGT*, pp. 129–33. For a more detailed discussion of Arminius's doctrine of grace, see Hicks, 'Theology of Grace;' Dekker, *Rijker*, pp. 157–77.

[22] *Disp. pub.* IV.lxix.

[23] *Dec. sent.*, p. 113; *Works* 1:661–64.

to undermine divine grace in the least. He frequently describes grace in terms consistent with his Reformed colleagues.

> I ascribe to God's grace the origin, the continuance, and the fulfillment (*het beghinsel, den voorgangh, ende de volbrenginghe*) of all good, also so far that the regenerate person himself, without this prevenient and stimulating, following, and co-operating (*medewerckende*) grace, can neither think, will or do good, nor also resist any evil temptation. From this it appears that I do not diminish God's grace by attributing too much to humanity's free will (*vryen wille*).[24]

Arminius was willing to elevate grace as much as possible, provided that it does not undermine the free choice that God has justly granted to humanity; in other words, like many of his contemporaries, he was attempting to strike a balance between divine grace and human freedom in salvation.

> We do not wish to do injury to divine grace, by taking from it anything that is of it; but let my brothers watch (*videant*), lest they themselves do injury to divine justice by attributing to it what it refuses, or rather to divine grace by transforming (*transmutando*) it into something else which cannot be called grace. That I may in a word signify what must be proved by them, namely, that the grace that is necessary, sufficient, [and] efficient for salvation is [also] "irresistible," or acts with such power (*potentia*) that it cannot be resisted by a free creature.[25]

---

[24] *Dec. sent.*, pp. 113–14; *Works* 1:664. This passage is quoted exactly in *Articuli Arminiani sive Remonstrantia*, art. 4, in Philip Schaff, *The Creeds of Christendom, with a History and Critical Notes*, 3 vols., 6th edition (1931; repr., Grand Rapids, 1998), 3:545–49. Cf. the similarity of Desiderius Erasmus, *De libero arbitrio* διατριβη *sive collatio*, in *Desiderii Erasmi Roterodami Opera Omnia*, 10 vols. (Leiden, 1703–06), 9: col. 1244 b; *On the Freedom of the Will: A Diatribe or Discourse*, trans. E. Gordon Rupp, in *Luther and Erasmus: Free Will and Salvation* [Library of Christian Classics 17] (Philadelphia, 1969), p. 90: "That is to my mind the advantage of the view of those who attribute entirely to grace the first impulse which stimulates (*exstimulatur*) the soul, yet in the performance allow something to human will which has not withdrawn itself from the grace of God. For since there are three parts in all things—beginning, progress, and end (*initium, progressus, et summa*)—they attribute the first and last to grace, and only in the progress say that free choice does (*agere*) anything, yet in such a way that in each individual action (*opus*) two causes concur, the grace of God and the will of man: in such a way, however, that grace is the principal cause and the will secondary, which can do nothing without the principal cause, since the principal is sufficient in itself."

[25] *Apologia*, art. 27 (7), in *Opera*, p. 177; *Works* 2:52. Cf. *Dec. sent.*, p. 114; *Works* 1:664; with idem, *Epistola*, in *Opera*, p. 944; *Works* 2:700–01. Some popular interpretations fail to do justice to Arminius's nuanced doctrine of grace. E.g., see the description of Arminius's doctrine in Peterson and Williams, *Why I Am Not an Arminian*, p. 116: "Grace is not causal but rather persuasive in nature. And such a notion of grace is demanded by Arminius's doctrine of the free human will." On the contrary, as is evident from the

Therefore, Arminius was adamant that saving grace, though a complete gift from God, is nevertheless a resistible gift. The resistibility of grace is the key difference between Arminius and his associates on the doctrine of grace.

> But the only difference is located here, whether God's grace be an irresistible force (*onwederstandelijcke cracht*). That is the difference and it is not concerning deeds or operations which may be attributed to grace (which, after all, I acknowledge and teach so much as anyone ever did), but only concerning the mode of operation (*maniere der werckinghe*), whether it is irresistible or not.[26]

Thus, according to Arminius, the controversy is not about what grace does in its operation, but whether a person can resist its operation. For Arminius, "Grace is not an irresistible force."[27] God is certainly able to determine human wills, but this would in effect remove the freedom of choice.[28]

Arminius felt that too many passages of Scripture made it plain that humanity can and often does freely resist God's grace. Rather than destroying free will, God's grace governs and steers the human will in the right direction.[29] It is, to be sure, a direction that fallen humanity would never consider without God's grace. Nevertheless, it is synergistic in the sense that the human will either cooperates by not resisting, or by resisting it refuses to cooperate. Borrius reports Arminius saying that "humanity determines itself, but not without grace: for free choice concurs with grace."[30] "No one," claims Arminius, "comes to

---

passage of Arminius cited above, causality does not entail *irresistible* causality; in other words, there is a definite distinction between *causa* and *coactio*. It is not illogical that a cause may be resisted and thus may fail to be a cause leading to the desired end. For those who do not resist God, grace may be said to be causal.

[26] *Dec. sent.*, p. 114; *Works* 1:664.

[27] *Art. non.*, in *Opera*, p. 959; *Works* 2:722: "Gratia est non vis irresistibilis." As noted above, Arminius's colleagues agreed that God does not impose *vis* on the will. Arminius, however, did not feel that such denials actually resolved the problem. On the Jesuit doctrine of resistible grace in Molina, Suárez, and Bellarmine, see Dekker, *Rijker*, pp. 157–61.

[28] *Apologia*, art. 5, in *Opera*, p. 142; *Works* 1:755. In this context, Arminius does not deal with the eschatological state (*non posse peccare*) and its relation to free choice.

[29] *Dec. sent.*, p. 83; *Works* 1:628–29. The fact that *liberum arbitrium* was sometimes used interchangeably with *libera voluntas* is seen in the Latin translation of this paragraph of *Dec. sent.* In two places, Arminius said "vrije wille," which was translated in the first place as "libertate voluntatis" and second as "liberum arbitrium."

[30] *Ep. ecc.* 130, p. 226: "hominem se determinare, sed non sine gratia: concurrere enim liberum arbitrium cum gratia."

the knowledge of the truth—that is, faith—involuntarily or unwillingly (*invitus sive nolens*)."[31] Nothing can hinder the possibility of mercy being extended to the sinner except the sinner's own refusal to believe and repent.[32] Arminius recognizes that there are differences among those who hear the gospel. Unlike the majority of his Reformed contemporaries, however, he is not willing to place the cause of those differences at the feet of God's decree.[33] Arminius can therefore declare that election is *ex gratia*.[34] Sufficient grace is offered to all, but the grace becomes efficacious for those who do not refuse it, the elect.[35] In sum, humanity is totally unable to be saved without God's grace.[36]

A.3. Facere quod in se est

Because of his stress on the resistibility of grace and freedom of choice contra most of his Reformed contemporaries, Arminius was accused of teaching, "God will deny his grace to no one who does what is in himself (*facienti quod in se est*)."[37] This saying made famous by the late medieval nominalist disciples of William of Ockham, particularly by Gabriel Biel, represented well the object of the Protestant polemic against Roman Catholic, "semi-Pelagian" soteriology. By linking Arminius with this catch-phrase, his opponents were implying Catholic (or, more precisely, non-Augustinian) influence on him—at least, the influence of the Jesuits; at most, the influence of Pelagius himself.[38] Arminius claims that his opponents have misunderstood his own doctrine of grace. He disagrees

---

[31] Arminius, *Examen modestum libelli, quem D. Gulielmus Perkinsius...edidit ante aliquot annos de praedestinationis modo et ordine*, in *Opera*, p. 751; *Works* 3:444.

[32] *Dec. sent.*, p. 92; *Works* 1:637.

[33] *Apologia*, art. 8, in *Opera*, p. 145; *Works* 1:763.

[34] E.g., see *Amica col.*, in *Opera*, p. 532; *Works* 3:124.

[35] *Apologia*, art. 28 (8), in *Opera*, p. 177; *Works* 2:53. Cf. idem, *Exam. Perk.*, in *Opera*, p. 665; *Works* 3:315.

[36] See *Dec. sent.*, pp. 112–13; *Works* 1:659–60; Hicks, 'Theology of Grace,' pp. 53–69.

[37] *Apologia*, art. 17, in *Opera*, p. 158; *Works* 2:19: "Deus gratiam suam nemini negabit facienti quod in se est."

[38] Accusations that Arminius was influenced by Roman Catholic—especially Jesuit—writers were not uncommon. Bertius, *Aen-spraeck*, fols. D3v–D4v, notes that Junius and Gomarus both utilized the same sources, including Biel. Cf. the summary of Bertius's statement in Itterzon, *Gomarus*, p. 182: "De Roomsche scholastieken werden reeds vóór Arminius door Junius gelezen en worden nog veel vaker door Gomarus zelf geciteerd."

with the exact statement because it nowhere includes prevenient grace (*gratia prima*). If the *facere quod in se est* were preceded, accompanied, and followed by grace, then Arminius would assent. "For if the expression be understood in this sense, *to the one who does what he can* (potest) *by the first grace already conferred on him*, then there is no absurdity in saying *God will bestow further grace on him who profitably uses what is first*."[39] The necessity of prevenient grace is what distinguishes Arminius's apologetic use of the *facere quod in se est* from the accusation of his opponents.[40] It is important to point out distinctions such as this, for Arminius was accused of papism in general and of following an apparent distortion of Biel's phrase in particular.[41]

B. *Predestination*

From the time of Arminius to the present, a great deal of ink has been spilled on Arminius's doctrine of predestination, primarily because it was the most debated topic of the controversies at Leiden. The older assumption that an analysis of this doctrine alone provides a sufficient picture of Arminius's theology has been overturned by recent studies.[42] Nevertheless, since the more recent studies of Arminius's doctrine of predestination do not have in mind his doctrine of assurance, a survey of the main contours of Arminius's thoughts on predestination and

---

[39] *Apologia*, art. 17, in *Opera*, p. 159; *Works* 2:20. Cf. idem, *De imaginis Dei restitutione* (1605), viii.

[40] For a discussion of Biel's own doctrine, cf. Oberman, *The Harvest of Medieval Theology: Gabriel Biel and Late Medieval Nominalism* (1963; repr. Grand Rapids, 2000), pp. 133 and 194, with Harry J. McSorley, 'Was Gabriel Biel a Semipelagian?' in *Wahrheit und Verkündigung*, ed. Leo Scheffczyk, et al. (Munich, 1967), pp. 1109–20; and Steinmetz, *Luther*, pp. 52–56. If Arminius reintroduced the *facere quod in se est* into Protestant thought as Muller claims (*DLGT*, p. 113), it was definitely distinct from what his opponents accused him of and apparently took to be Roman Catholic doctrine, as represented by the lack of any *gratia* language in the stated article. A firm resolution to this problem would require a thorough examination of the use and meaning of this phrase in the period between Biel and Arminius, particularly in polemics, which is beyond the scope of this monograph. Furthermore, Arminius should not be portrayed as attempting to rescue an orthodox meaning for the phrase. He seems to have no positive affinity for it, but only uses it here apologetically contra his opponents. Cf. Muller, 'Federal Motif,' 107.

[41] Gomarus, *Waerschouwinghe over de Vermaninghe aen R. Donteclock* (Leiden, 1609), pp. 35–38 and 49, cites the origins of Arminius's teaching in Pighius, Bellarmine, Biel, Molina, and the Council of Trent.

[42] E.g., see Muller's survey and critique of scholarship in Muller, *GCP*, pp. 3–14.

their connection with assurance is necessary, given the *foundational* connection Arminius perceived between these two doctrines.[43]

B.1. *Conditional Predestination*

The crucial difference between Arminius's doctrine of predestination
and that of most of his Reformed contemporaries was his belief that
predestination is conditional on a person's free acceptance or rejection of
God's saving grace, that is, one's faith or unbelief. Arminius accepts the
judgment of the Danish Melanchthonian, Nicolaus Hemmingius, who
said that the controversy boils down to one of two questions, "whether
the elect believe, or believers are elect."[44] Arminius affirmed the latter
expression, for he defines election as God's decree to save *fideles*.[45] One is
reprobate for rejecting the offered grace of God.[46] In defending the conditional nature of predestination, Arminius stands in continuity with
many Protestant predecessors, both Lutheran and Reformed.[47]

---

[43] For a detailed study of Arminius on predestination, see Dekker, *Rijker*. The present
section is intended as a supplement to Dekker's essay. Cf. C. Graafland, *Van Calvijn tot
Barth: Oorsprong en ontwikkeling van de leer der verkiezing in het Gereformeerd Protestantisme* (The
Hague, 1987), pp. 85–119, who focuses on Arminius's *Exam. Perk.* and *Dec. sent.*

[44] *Dec. sent.*, p. 95; *Works* 1:642–43. Cf. Kuchlinus, *De perseverantia* (1603), vi: "soli credentes sunt electi."

[45] *Disp. pub.* XV.ii; *Disp. priv.* XL.ii; *Apologia*, art. 4, in *Opera*, p. 139; *Works* 1:748. Idem,
Exam. Gom., p. 151; *Works* 3:652, says Gomarus is guilty of *confusio intolerabilis* for speaking of faith as both an effect and a condition of election.

[46] *Exam. Perk.*, in *Opera*, p. 747; *Works* 3:438–39. Cf. *Exam. Gom.*, p. 77; *Works* 3:591.

[47] Arminius notes his predecessors who acknowledged conditional predestination,
among other places, in *Dec. sent.*, pp. 94–96; *Works* 1:639–44. Cf. Keith D. Stanglin,
"Arminius *avant la lettre*": Peter Baro, Jacob Arminius, and the Bond of Predestinarian
Polemic,' *Westminster Theological Journal* 67 (2005), 51–74, there 63–66. In addition to
Hemmingius (whose influence will be noted more fully below), if Arminius's library is
any indication, Hemmingius's teacher Philip Melanchthon was one of Arminius's most
revered authors. Among other works, Arminius owned Melanchthon's *Corpus doctrinae
Christianae* (see *Auction Catalogue*, pp. 13 and 21), which contained the 1543 edition of
his *Loci Communes*. In it, Melanchthon's thoughts on conditional predestination broadly
harmonize with those of Arminius. Cf. Melanchthon, *Loci praecipui theologici* (1543), in
Corpus doctrinae Christianae. Quae est summa orthodoxi et catholici dogmatis (Lipsiae, 1565), pp.
299–672, there on predestination pp. 557–64; *Loci Communes 1543*, trans. J. A. O. Preus
(St. Louis, 1992), pp. 172–75: "Ideo Petrus est electus, quia est membrum Christi, sicut
ideo iustus est, id est, Deo placens, quia fide factus est membrum Christi" (p. 559).

See also, from the Dutch context, Ioannes Anastasius Veluanus, *Kort Bericht in allen
principalen punten des Christen geloves . . . und is des halven genant der Leken Wechwyser* (1554), in
Bibliotheca Reformatoria Neerlandica: Geschriften uit den tijd der hervorming in de Nederlanden, ed.
S. Cramer and F. Pijper, vol. 4 (The Hague, 1906), pp. 123–376, there 155–56: "Die
geordeniert waren ten ewigen leven, zynt gelovich worden." Veluanus's doctrine of conditional predestination was typical of mid-sixteenth-century Dutch piety and influential
on successive generations of Dutch clergy and laity. Veluanus's works do not appear in

B.2. *Predestination, Assurance, and the Consistency of Theological System*
It is impossible to isolate the topic of predestination from other topics
of soteriology in particular and broader theological topics in general.
To acknowledge a fundamental shift in any one of these topics will have
repercussions throughout a given theological system. This observation did not go unnoticed by Arminius and his opponents. Arminius
declared that there are many articles of Christianity that have a "great
commonality (*gemeenschap*) with the doctrine of predestination and that
are in a great measure dependent on it."[48] The relation of predestination to other *loci* is indeed crucial to his apologetic, and is seen in the
very structure of his speech before the States of Holland. The overall
shape of Arminius's mature argument about predestination in the *Declaratio sententiae* is not directly constructed around the interpretation of
individual biblical texts, although they are interspersed throughout his
speech. By not structuring his argument around Scripture, he is tacitly acknowledging that both parties in the debate have their favorite
scriptural proof texts and are equally adept at explaining away their
respective problem passages. He aims his speech at laymen and assumes
a common knowledge of the major points of the gospel. Furthermore,
the occasion of this speech was not the appropriate place for detailed
exegesis, a task that he had accomplished in earlier treatises.

Rather, the section on predestination in the *Declaratio sententiae* is structured around four distinct types of predestination taught in Reformed
churches.[49] Arminius gives attention primarily to the first option, later

---

Arminius's personal library, but his indirect influence on Arminius is almost certain. On
Veluanus, see Gerrit Morsink, *Joannes Anastasius Veluanus (Jan Gerritsz. Versteghe, levensloop
en ontwikkeling)* (Kampen, 1986). Morsink documents the influence of Veluanus's *Wechwyser* on seventeenth-century Remonstrants in ibid., pp. 107–11.

  Cf. Hoenderdaal, 'Arminius en Episcopius,' 212: "Later zullen de verdedigers van
Arminius dan ook telkens wijzen op zijn verwantschap met de theologen die hem zijn
voorgegaan, waarbij Melanchton genoemd wordt naast Bullinger en Anastasius Veluanus. Uytenbogaert geeft in zijn Noodighe Antwoordt van 1617 in twee kolommen het
standpunt van Melanchton weer in de eerste en in de latere edities van diens Loci Communes, die sterk afwijken op het punt van de vrije wil. Hiermede wil hij de legitimiteit
van het Remonstrantse standpunt adstrueren. De Remonstranten willen uitdrukkelijk
blijven binnen de reformatie."

[48] *Dec. sent.*, p. 111; *Works* 1:657.

[49] Arminius distinguishes three different predestinarian options in *Amica col.*, in *Opera*,
pp. 459–60; *Works* 3:18. In contrast, he distinguishes five different lapsarian options in
Epistola, in *Opera*, p. 943; *Works* 2:699. This letter was written only six months before the
Declaratio sententiae, which demonstrates the flexibility of predestinarian typologies and
multiple modes of distinguishing the available options. The four types delineated in the
Dec. sent. are thus not intended to represent a comprehensive list of every conceivable
nuance. See Stanglin, 'Arminius *avant la lettre*,' 58–66.

known as supralapsarianism, and the fourth option, his own view, passing comparatively quickly over the second and third types. Within his
discussion of these two views, he deals with the question of their respective cohesion with other theological topics and traditions. Thus, the
bulk of his predestination argument is that supralapsarianism *pugnat
cum* twenty different points gleaned from Scripture and tradition, twenty
points that Arminius felt were vital to healthy doctrine. Then, when he
assesses his own doctrine of predestination, he finds that it measures up
to the twenty standards. For Arminius, one's opinion on predestination
stands or falls by its consistency with the normative theological system,
represented in his case by the twenty points.[50]

It is true that the terminology and definitions of Arminius's theology
cohered with Reformed theology on the majority of issues. As recent
scholarship has shown, however, the theological system of Arminius was
at some points quite distinct from that of his Reformed contemporaries.[51]
For example, for the majority of Reformed theologians, making the
eternal decree of God subordinate in any way to the free decisions of
human creatures—actual or counterfactual—undermines the free sovereignty of God. Yet according to Arminius, the decree of predestination is still determined and eternal. It is based on the divine *scientia media*,
that is, that God knows what a person would do in any given set of circumstances, even if that set is never actualized.[52] Arminius's proposed
order of four divine decrees is as follows:

> I. The first precise and absolute (*precijs ende absoluyt*) decree of God, con-
> cerning the salvation of sinful men, is that he has decreed to appoint (*stel-
> len*) his son Jesus Christ as a Mediator, Redeemer, Savior, Priest, and King,
> who might destroy sin through his death, obtain (*verwerve*) the lost salvation
> through his obedience, and communicate it through his power.

---

[50] For the twenty points, see *Dec. sent.*, pp. 71–96 and 106–10; *Works* 1:618–45 and
654–56.

[51] See especially Muller, *GCP*. Cf. the work of Muller and Dekker with studies that
ignore the differences. E.g., Clarke, 'Arminius's Understanding,' 25–35, suggests that
Arminius followed Calvin on mostly everything except the doctrine of predestination.
The tacit assumption of studies like Clarke's is that predestination does not relate significantly to the rest of a given theological system.

[52] See Arminius's use of *scientia media*, which is essential to his doctrine of conditional
predestination, in *Disp. pub.* IV.xxxvi–xlv; *Disp. priv.* XVII.xi; idem, *Amica col.*, in *Opera*,
p. 491; *Works* 3:65; idem, *Exam. Perk.*, in *Opera*, pp. 752–53; *Works* 3:446–47. See analyses
of Arminius's use of *scientia media* in Muller, *GCP*, pp. 143–66; Dekker, 'Was Arminius
a Molinist?'; and idem, *Rijker*, pp. 77–84. Dekker, ibid., p. 236, says Arminius can cau-
tiously be called a "Protestant Molinist."

II. The second precise and absolute decree of God is that he has decreed to receive in grace those who repent and believe, and in Christ, for Christ's sake, and through Christ, to save those who persevere (*volherdende*); and to leave in sin and under wrath, and to damn, the impenitent and unbelieving as foreign from Christ.

III. The third decree of God is by which he resolved to administer (*beleyden*) the means necessary for repentance and belief, sufficient and efficient; which administration (*beleydinghe*) happens according to God's wisdom, by which he knows what is proper to his mercy and severity, and according to his righteousness, by which he is prepared (*bereyt*) to follow what his wisdom prescribes and to perform it.

IV. Here follows the fourth decree, in order to save and to damn certain particular (*sekere bysondere*) persons; which decree depends on (*steunt op*) the foreknowledge of God, by which he has known from eternity which persons—according to such administration of the means proper for repentance and faith—through his prevenient grace would (*souden*) believe, and through subsequent grace would persevere, and also which would not believe and not persevere.[53]

From the first decree, it is clear that this schema concerns the salvation of sinful people. The decree of creation and permission of the fall is already presupposed, and his system is therefore infralapsarian. The second decree demonstrates the conditional nature of predestination, that God will save believers and condemn unbelievers.[54] The fourth decree finally has particular individuals as its object, based on God's *scientia media*. The intention of this sequence is to give due attention to reconciling divine omniscience, grace, and human freedom.

Not only does this position agree with Arminius's doctrine of God, but it is also, from Arminius's perspective, more consistent with resolving the problem of evil. Arminius, in the tradition of Augustine, is concerned about any philosophical or theological dogma that would seem to assign direct culpability for sin to God himself. Without such contingent human freedom, Arminius (and virtually every other "anti-Calvinist") cannot see how God can justly reprobate or damn sinners. With unconditional predestination, especially of the supralapsarian variety, God seems to work so that humanity necessarily sins. If this necessity is

---

[53] *Dec. sent.*, pp. 104–06; *Works* 1:653–54. The same four decrees are in idem, *Art. non.*, in *Opera*, p. 957; *Works* 2:718–19. Arminius only mentions three decrees, in effect omitting the first one, in *Ep. ecc.* 81, p. 151; *Works* 2:69.

[54] Dekker, *Rijker*, pp. 183–84, passim, refers to Arminius's doctrine that God will save believers as "eigenschappen-predestinatie."

so and one cannot speak of a robust divine permission of sin, then God, not humanity, is the real sinner. The frequency with which Arminius pressed this point indicates how central it was to his polemic and that the resolution of the problem of evil was a formative factor in his own doctrine of predestination.[55] Not surprisingly, his colleagues consistently denied that their doctrine implied that God is the author of sin.

The kind of contingent necessity at the heart of Arminius's opinion on predestination introduced a modality into the eternal divine decree with which his Reformed colleagues were not comfortable. It was, however, completely consistent with Arminius's emphasis on the doctrine of creation. For Arminius, there can be no divine decree that affects creation before the decree of creation itself. Creation, as a "perfect act of God," is not subordinate to any other decree.[56] Many "supralapsarian" accounts of predestination position reprobation not only logically before the fall, but also before creation. In contrast, Arminius contends that any actions of God that tend to the damnation of people are "alien works of God."[57] God's first act toward his creature cannot be its reprobation, for God loves primarily.[58] The assumption is that the first decree should concern God's *actio propria*, which Arminius describes as creation. Arminius defines creation as "a real communication of good after the intention of God."[59] The final cause (*finis cui*) of creation is the good of humanity.[60] Creation is an act of God's love, not of hatred, and it is intended that humanity may know, love, worship, and live with God

---

[55] *Dec. sent.*, pp. 84–85 and 101–02; *Works* 1:630 and 647–48. *Apologia*, art. 23 (3), in *Opera*, pp. 169–70; *Works* 2:39–40; *Amica col.*, in *Opera*, pp. 478, 571, 583, and 591–92; *Works* 3:44–45, 179, 196–97, and 208–09; *Exam. Perk.*, in *Opera*, pp. 644–50; *Works* 3:283–92; *Exam. Gom.*, pp. 154–58; *Works* 3:654–58; *Epistola*, in *Opera*, p. 942; *Works* 2:697–98. Hoenderdaal, 'Arminius en Episcopius,' 230, associates this "uitgangspunt" of Arminius with the nominalistic tradition of Gabriel Biel. Ironically, according to *Dec. sent.*, p. 112; *Works* 1:658, Arminius himself was once accused of implying that God is the author of sin. Interpreters have easily recognized that Arminius's doctrine sought a resolution to this problem. E.g., cf. Dekker, *Rijker*, p. 104: "Zo kan he took geen verbazing wekken al seen theorie waarin een ongedifferentieerde goddelijke al-wil naar voren komt, die geen ruimte overlaat voor de menselijke vrijheid, leidt tot een predestinatieleer die impliceert dat God de 'auteur van het kwaad' is."

[56] *Dec. sent.*, p. 81; *Works* 1:627.

[57] *Dec. sent.*, p. 81; *Opera*, p. 108; *Works* 1:627: "vreemde wercken Gods (*alienae Dei actiones*)"; idem, *Exam. Gom.*, p. 90; *Works* 3:602. See *Disp. pub.* IV.lix, on the distinction between *opus proprium et opus alienum Dei*.

[58] *Exam. Gom.*, p. 76; *Works* 3:590.

[59] *Dec. sent.*, p. 109; *Works* 1:654–55.

[60] *Disp. priv.* XXIV.ix.

forever.[61] Thus, Arminius agrees that predestination (that is, election) is caused by the divine *beneplacitum*, which he describes as the "benevolent affection of his will."[62] To the degree that Arminius's creation theology and anthropology influence predestination and soteriology, his system can be called a theology of creation.[63]

The foregoing discussion is by no means a comprehensive account of how predestination relates to other doctrines. Many more examples could be added from the twenty criteria, and the implications perhaps reach far beyond the twenty standards that Arminius enumerates. However, of special significance to our topic is the connection that Arminius draws between predestination and assurance. In the *Declaratio sententiae*, only two times Arminius speaks of *fundamentum* in the twenty points. If we bar the twentieth point, which functions in some ways as a summary point about the agreement of the broader Christian historical tradition with Arminius, the *fundamentum* language appears only at the beginning (point one) and at the end (point nineteen) of his argument. Both of these points on predestination, positioned and worded for maximum rhetorical effect, have to do with the assurance of salvation. At point *one*, Arminius asserts that supralapsarianism is not the "foundation of Christianity, of salvation, nor of the certainty of salvation," but that his doctrine of predestination is.[64] Then at point *nineteen*, Arminius claims that supralapsarianism is opposed to the foundation of (Christian) religion, which is the *tweederley liefde Godes* (*duplex Dei amor*), but on the contrary, that his own doctrine harmonizes this twofold love.[65] According to Arminius, it is God's love that serves as the basis for pious assurance of salvation; therefore, if supralapsarianism undermines God's twofold love, then it undermines assurance as well.

---

[61] *Exam. Gom.*, pp. 87–90; *Works* 3:599–602.

[62] *Disp. pub.* XV.iv: "benevolum affectum voluntatis suae." This explanation of God's *beneplacitum* parallels the explanation which allowed the anti-Calvinist Peter Baro to subscribe to article 2 of the Lambeth Articles. Related to this point, Baro and Arminius both appealed to the distinction in God's will between antecedent and consequent will. See Stanglin, 'Arminius *avant la lettre*,' 56 n. 26.

[63] See Richard A. Muller, 'God, Predestination, and the Integrity of the Created Order: a Note on Patterns in Arminius' Theology,' in *Later Calvinism*, ed. Fred W. Graham (Kirksville, MO, 1994), pp. 431–46.

[64] *Dec. sent.*, pp. 71 and 106; *Works* 1:618 and 654: "fondament des Christendoms, der salicheyt, noch der seeckerheyt vande salicheyt."

[65] *Dec. sent.*, pp. 90–4 and 110; *Works* 1:634–38 and 656.

Further investigation reveals that, far from being an isolated reference in the *Declaratio sententiae*, Arminius underscores both of these "foundational" points throughout his works, demonstrating the important connection he envisioned between predestination and assurance. Point one in the speech about the foundational nature of predestination was a recurring theme in Arminius. It is a direct quote from the last thesis in his private disputation on predestination: "This predestination is the foundation of Christianity, of salvation, and of the certainty of salvation."[66] He says exactly the same thing about predestination in a letter to Uytenbogaert, 1 September 1606, in the letter to Hippolytus à Collibus, 5 April 1608, in *Articuli nonnulli*, in *Apologia*, and in *Examen thesium Gomari*.[67] "The foundation on which the certainty of particular election to salvation, and of reprobation to death, rests, is the true definition of predestination, election, and reprobation."[68] In addition, point nineteen about the twofold love of God is a doctrine that was apparently dear to Arminius.[69] In his last conference at The Hague with Gomarus, 12–22 August 1609, Arminius again stressed in the first point concerning predestination, "The foundation of all religion is the twofold love of

---

[66] *Disp. priv.* XL.ix: "Haec praedestinatio est fundamentum Christianismi, salutis, et certitudinis de salute."

[67] *Ep. ecc.* 88, p. 160: "...dogma quod fundamentum est Christianismi, salutis, et certitudinis nostrae de salute nostra...." Arminius, *Epistola*, in *Opera*, p. 943; *Works* 2:698. In idem, *Art. non.*, in *Opera*, p. 957; *Works* 2:719, he specifies that it is the second decree concerning God's election to save penitent believers because of Christ that qualifies as the "Fundamentum Christianismi, salutis et certitudinis de salute." In *Apologia*, art. 4, in *Opera*, p. 139; *Works* 1:748. In idem, *Exam. Gom.*, pp. 34–35; *Works* 3:554, Arminius says that predestination "dicitur esse Christianismi, salutis nostrae et certitudinis de salute fundamentum." It is unclear to me who, if anyone, else exactly referred to predestination in this way, as Arminius implies in this last passage that it is not original to him. Nicolaus Hemmingius, whose work was influential on Arminius, said in *Enchiridion theologicum, praecipua verae religionis capita breviter et simpliciter explicata continens* (London, 1580), p. 233: "Nam aeterna Dei *praedestinatio est fundamentum* et prima causa bonorum omnium, quae a Deo percipimus" (italics mine). Arminius owned this and other titles by Hemmingius (see *Auction Catalogue*, pp. 14 and 16–17), and acknowledged his influence in soteriological matters (see *Dec. sent.*, p. 95; *Works* 1:642–43). Hemmingius also influenced the anti-Calvinist Peter Baro (see Baro, *Summa trium de praedestinatione sententiarum*, in *Ep. ecc.* 15, pp. 29–32; *Works* 1:89–100).

[68] *Exam. Gom.*, p. 149; *Works* 3:650: "Fundamentum quo nititur certitudo singularis electionis ad salutem, et reprobationis ad mortem, est vera praedestinationis, electionis et reprobationis definitio." Cf. idem, *Exam. Gom.*, p. 150; *Works* 3:651.

[69] The connection between God's love and assurance of salvation will be explored further in chapter six.

God." He went on to declare under the topic of free choice, "Irresistible grace disagrees with that twofold love of God."[70] Arminius also uses this twofold love of God as the basis for the doctrine of atonement.[71]

The connection between predestination and assurance is again made clear in Arminius's public disputation on predestination. Inasmuch as doctrine is practical and not merely an end in itself, Arminius identifies the uses of predestination, and two of the three uses are directly related to assurance. "For it serves to establish the glory of God's grace, to comfort afflicted consciences, to upset the impious and to drive away their security."[72] Arminius wanted to return to the historic use of the doctrine of predestination, namely, as a support for the assurance of salvation.[73] Moreover, even if he emphasizes more than his contemporaries the doctrine's purpose of driving away security, Arminius's colleagues would have agreed in principle with these stated uses of predestination.[74] The watershed for Arminius would be whether a given doctrine of predestination adequately fulfills its obligation to assurance and the Christian life of sanctification. In this way, for Arminius, assurance functions as a point of departure and is a fundamental criterion for the orthodoxy of a predestinarian system.

I conclude two things from this brief survey of predestination in Arminius. First, predestination is an important doctrine for Arminius, even foundational to the Christian religion. It would not be accurate to dismiss the idea that predestination was a significant issue for Arminius

---

[70] "Fundamentum omnis Religionis est duplex Amor Dei.... Gratia irresistibilis pugnat cum duplici illo Dei amore." The account of Arminius's statements at The Hague conference of 1609 is taken from the eye-witness report of Hommius, who was one of the four ministers that accompanied Gomarus. The account is in a letter addressed to Sibrandus Lubbertus, 4 September 1609, reprinted in Wijminga, *Hommius*, Bijlage G, pp. xi–xv.

[71] *Disp. pub.* XIV.xvi.

[72] *Disp. pub.* XV.xiv: "Hujus doctrinae ita ex Scripturis traditae magnus est usus. Servit enim gloriae gratiae Dei adstruendae, afflictis conscientiis solandis, impiis percellendis et securitati illorum excutiendae."

[73] Cf. Seeberg, *History*, 2:424.

[74] E.g., Kuchlinus, *De praedestinatione* (1600), xxiii, observes that the doctrine of predestination gives humility, *fiducia*, and patience, and it excites to good works. See also Zacharias Ursinus, *Doctrinae christianae compendium: seu, commentarii catechetici* (Cambridge, Eng., 1585), pp. 492–93; *The summe of Christian religion: Delivered by Zacharias Ursinus in his Lectures upon the Catechism* (Oxford, 1587), p. 649, who says that predestination gives consolation, but, at best, only implies a use for discouraging human sin. Ursinus was an important influence on the Leiden theology, having a direct impact on Kuchlinus and an indirect impact on Arminius. Cf. Platt, *Scholasticism*, pp. 79–85 and 150–54.

based on the suggestion that he was merely responding to polemical attacks. His earlier interaction with Junius and Perkins seems to indicate that he was the one seeking greater clarification on this foundational topic before the intense polemic began. Moreover, the fact that predestination does touch so many other topics makes it an important *locus* in its own right within early Reformed orthodoxy. This is not to suggest that predestination functioned as a central dogma for Arminius, for it is one foundation among many; instead, it draws its great import from its connection with other topics.

For too long, historians and theologians have located the starting point of Arminius's conditional predestination in a reaction against Bezan supralapsarianism. I have already argued that the culprit may very well be supralapsarianism, but it would more likely be the supralapsarianism located in Leiden, not Geneva. In other words, it is the presence of supralapsarianism all around Arminius in Leiden, not just Geneva or Cambridge, that continues to drive the intensity of his polemic against all forms of unconditional predestination.[75] Arminius's conditional predestination arises from the need to reconcile divine grace with human willing and resolve the problem of evil that he detected in supralapsarianism.

Second, the link Arminius attaches between this most controversial topic of predestination and the doctrine of assurance of salvation is indicative of the prominence of *assurance* in Arminius's theology. Furthermore, we propose the view that the doctrine of assurance was just as much the point of departure for Arminius's distinctive soteriology as any other issue. The question of whether a doctrine leads to true assurance is an important criterion that has been overlooked by previous scholarship. Proof that Arminius's doctrine of assurance has been almost completely ignored as an underlying reason for his doctrine of predestination can be seen in C. Bangs's following comment:

> In the earlier part of his *Declaration* Arminius had criticized his opponents at length. From that criticism there emerge implicitly some parameters within which the four decrees must be defined. Predestination must be understood Christologically; it must be evangelical; it must not make God

---

[75] Cf. the assessment of Letham, 'Faith,' 1:312: "Essentially, his [Arminius's] criticism centres around the speculative elements in the supralapsarianism that he had learned from Beza at Geneva and with which he had been confronted by William Perkins."

the author of sin; it must not make man the author of salvation; it must be scriptural, not speculative; and it must not depart from the historic teaching of the church, by which Arminius means the faith of the first six centuries, the confessions of the Reformation, and particularly the Belgic Confession and the Heidelberg Catechism. That is a big order....[76]

Although these aspects indeed form the boundaries for Arminius, it should be clear that Bangs has neglected an essential criterion for Arminius's doctrine of predestination. Since predestination is the foundation of assurance and the use of the doctrine is to comfort the afflicted and terrify the secure, a quintessential condition for Arminius's assessment of a doctrine of predestination is whether it truly accomplishes its intended use of healthy, biblical assurance. Any conception of predestination that undercuts such assurance is found wanting by Arminius. The priority of place for assurance in Arminius's theology is conspicuous to the observant reader of his works. Not only is assurance emphatically positioned in the *Declaratio sententiae*, but, as we will see in chapter five, it also served as one of Arminius's key criticisms against Reformed soteriology, and it was a recurring theme in many of his works, as will be demonstrated in chapter six.

C. *Vocation*

According to Arminius, vocation is God's calling sinful people out of their animal life into the fellowship of Jesus Christ for the purpose of giving them life and eternal salvation. In continuity with his colleagues, Arminius affirmed that the primary efficient cause of this calling is God the Father in his Son Jesus Christ; the Holy Spirit is the one who makes the calling effective.[77] The instrumental cause of this calling to salvation is the word of God, and it can happen in two ways. First, vocation happens ordinarily through the means of humans who communicate the word by preaching or writing. Vocation occurs extraordinarily when the word is immediately communicated to someone from God without human means. Arminius was careful to say that even this extraordinary method of calling is done by the word of God, thereby emphasizing the

---

[76] Bangs, *Arminius*, p. 350.

[77] *Disp. pub.* XVI.ii–iii. Cf. Trelcatius, *Disputationum theologicarum trigesima-prima, de vocatione hominum ad salutem*, Hermannus H. Montanus, ad diem 18 February 1604 (Leiden, 1604), iv.

unity of word and Spirit.[78] As Arminius acknowledges, this distinction between ordinary and extraordinary means of vocation was in common use among his Reformed contemporaries.[79]

Vocation is for all people, and the main purpose of vocation is for the salvation of those called; whomever God calls, he calls them *serio*.[80] However, it is one's future contingent belief that determines more proximately whether the calling is effectual. Because the unregenerate are able to resist the Holy Spirit and divine grace, they may not open the door to the Savior who knocks. Conversion is passive on the part of the one being converted, but it is nevertheless resistible.[81] Therefore, although the proximate goal of vocation is that the called will become God's covenant people, the *eventus per accidens* is that, for some, vocation results in the hardening of one's heart and the rejection of grace and the Holy Spirit.[82] This accidental end is the point of conflict with Arminius's Reformed colleagues, who are silent about any such consequence. For example, Trelcatius distinguishes between efficacious and inefficacious vocation. The final cause of efficacious calling is the salvation of those called, but the final cause of inefficacious calling is the condemnation of those called.[83]

D. *Repentance*

The order of the *Disputationes privatae* reveals the shape of Arminius's *ordo salutis*. Here it reflects a traditional formula of a threefold obedient response to God's calling, namely repentance, faith, and observance of

---

[78] *Disp. pub.* XVI.v, vii, xiii; *Disp. priv.* XLII.iv; idem, *De Fide* (1605), vii. Arminius insists on the presence of the word even in such extraordinary cases of vocation apart from the human means of proclamation, contra Zwingli. See *Apologia*, art. 18, in *Opera*, pp. 159–60; *Works* 2:21–22.

[79] *Apologia*, art. 18, in *Opera*, p. 160; *Works* 2:21. Gomarus, *Theses theologicae de fide salvifica*, Elias de Monier respondens, Kal. March 1603 (Leiden, 1603), viii: "Interim non inficiamur, etiam absque his mediis extraordinarie, Spiritum Sanctum fidem in cordibus Electorum gignere posse: Sed ideo dicimus, quia divinae sapientiae ac bonitati visum est...." Gomarus goes on to declare that it is a work of God done "supra naturam." Cf. idem, *Disputationum theologicarum quarto repetitarum trigesima-prima de vocatione hominis ad salutem*, Laurentius Pauli respondens, ad diem 29 April 1606 (Leiden, 1606), iv.

[80] Cf. *Canons of the Synod of Dort* 3 and 4.8–9, in Schaff, *The Creeds of Christendom* 3:550–97.

[81] *Art. non.*, in *Opera*, pp. 958–59; *Works* 2:721–22; cf. idem, *Amica col.*, in *Opera*, p. 463; *Works* 3:23.

[82] *Disp. pub.* XVI.ix, xiv; *Disp. priv.* XLII.viii–ix, xii.

[83] Trelcatius, *De vocatione* (1604), x. See also Gomarus, *De vocatione* (1606), x. Cf. Hicks, 'Theology of Grace,' p. 51.

God's commands.[84] Arminius proceeds to define repentance as sorrow
for sin, desire to be delivered from sin, and actual avoidance of sin, a
threefold process that involves the intellect, affections, and the whole
of life.[85] The primary efficient cause of repentance is God, and the
proximate, less principal efficient cause is the person himself.[86] Gomarus
agrees when he asserts that God is the efficient cause and that the faculties of our soul are the internal, ordinary, instrumental cause.[87] The
fruit of repentance is twofold, encompassing God's part and humanity's
part: God forgives and the person does good works.[88] Again, Gomarus
is in perfect agreement on this point as well.[89]

E. *Faith*

Arminius acknowledges that the word *fides* can bear a variety of mean-
ings. In a disputation *De fide*, after listing fourteen different connotations
of *fides*, he locates his topic in the fifteenth definition: Faith is the "assent
of the soul" (*assensus animi*) produced from the Holy Spirit by the gospel
in sinners, by which they recognize Jesus Christ as Savior destined and
given to them by God; *fiducia* then arises as the result of this assent.[90]
This faith, along with repentance, is the obedient response to the call to
salvation. Faith consists in *adsensus* to divinely revealed truth, an *adsensus
animi* which is given by the Holy Spirit, its author, infused "above the
order of nature" (*supra naturae ordinem*). It also consists of *notitia*, which

---

[84] *Disp. priv.* XLIII.iii. Hemmingius proposed the same order in Hemmingius, *Enchirid-ion*, pp. 118–19: "Ex his patet, tres esse partes poenitentiae: Contritionem, Fidem, et novam obedientiam. Quarum prima et secunda substantiales partes poenitentiae recte dicuntur, quibus necessario tertia pars tanquam inseparabilis proprietas, adjicitur." In *Art. non.*, in *Opera*, p. 960; *Works* 2:723, Arminius says that repentance comes in order between faith that God is willing to give grace to the sinner and actual saving faith in Christ. This nuance precludes facile comparison with orders found in Kendall, *Calvin*, pp. 146 and 150, and Bell, *Calvin*, p. 11. For further indications of Arminius's *ordo salutis*, see *Dec. sent.* p. 110; *Works* 1:655; *Amica col.*, in *Opera*, pp. 462–63; *Works* 3:22–3. Cf. also Perkins, *Armilla aurea*, chart, with Beeke, *Assurance*, pp. 109–16.

[85] *Disp. pub.* XVII.ii; *Disp. priv.* XLIII.iv; idem, *Art. non.*, in *Opera*, p. 960; *Works* 2:722.

[86] *Disp. pub.* XVII.v–vi.

[87] Gomarus, *Disputationum theologicarum quarto repetitarum vigesima-quinta de resipiscentia*, Matthaeus Cotterius respondens, 1 February 1606 (Leiden, 1606), ix–x.

[88] *Disp. pub.* XVII.x.

[89] Gomarus, *De resipiscentia* (1606), xiii.

[90] Arminius, *De fide* (1605), i. Cf. idem, *Disputationum theologicarum quinto repetitarum vigesima-quinta, de fide*, Iacobus Massisius respondens, ad diem 26 July 1608 (Leiden, 1608), i.

is antecedent to faith as its internal foundation.[91] Much could be said
about Arminius's definition of faith, but I shall limit the discussion to
three aspects—the first two for their role in the Leiden debate, and the
third for its importance in modern interpretations.[92]

E.1. *Faith as a Gift*

Arminius underscored that saving faith is the gift of God to humanity.
Its principal efficient cause is "God the Father in the Son by the Holy
Spirit; for the works of the Trinity *ad extra* are indivisible." He went
on to say, "It is a supernatural, not natural, work and gift" (*Est opus et
donum supernaturale non naturale*). Faith is a theological virtue infused by
the Holy Spirit, not by a human exercise of reasoning, for it surpasses
all intellect.[93] God produces, preserves, and confirms faith in us by illuminating our intellect, mollifying our heart, and impressing the desire
for salvation.[94] Arminius insisted that although predestination is based
on and in a sense posterior to foreseen faith, nevertheless it is God's
grace that causes this faith, for "salvation and faith are God's gifts."[95]
The claim that faith is a pure gift of God was paralleled by Arminius's
colleagues. Gomarus agreed that the principal efficient cause of faith is
God the Father, Son, and Holy Spirit, begetting it in the elect "above
the order of nature" (*supra naturae ordinem*). It is the gift and work of God,
an infused theological virtue.[96]

---

[91] *Disp. priv.* XLIV.i–iii, v–vi.

[92] Cf. discussions of Arminius's doctrine of faith in Hicks, 'Theology of Grace,' pp.
92–105; Muller, 'Priority of the Intellect,' 55–72; and Ritschl, *Dogmengeschichte* 3:332–
39.

[93] Arminius, *De fide* (1605), ii.

[94] Arminius, *De fide* (1608), v: "Caussa itaque efficiens principalis est Deus Pater in
Filio per Spiritum sanctum qui fidem in nobis producit, eam conservat ac confirmat,
illuminando intellectum nostrum per cognitionem et scientiam gloriae suae in facie Iesu
Christi, cor nostrum lapideum emolliendo et desiderium salutis illi imprimendo, ver-
tatemque in verbo revelatam mentibus, ac cordibus persuadendo, ut Christum oblatum
videamus et in illum certa fide ut salvatorem nostrum credamus."

[95] *Apologia*, art. 4, in *Opera*, pp. 139–40; *Works* 1:749–50: "salutem et fidem esse dona
Dei." Cf. idem, *Exam. Gom.*, p. 137; *Works* 3:640: "Ergo Christus praedestinatione prior:
quia fides in illum prior eadem praedestinatione: et Christus fide prior." Cf. Veluanus,
Wechwyser, p. 168: "Hier is to mercken, dat nymant sich selves mit eighene macht kan
ghelovich maken. Mer dat Gott de ghelove in ons maket, mit sijnen woirt unde hillighen
geest."

[96] Gomarus, *De fide salvifica* (1603), vi. Cf. idem, *Disputationum theologicarum vigesima-tertia, de fide iustificante*, Henricus H. Geisteranus, Jr., respondens, ad diem 15 October 1603
(Leiden, 1603), iv; with Kuchlinus, *Disputatio theologica de fidei iustificantis causa efficiente, et
instrumentali. Et de sacramentis in genere*, complectens explicationem quaestionum catecheticarum 65. 66, Tobias a Gellinchuisen respondens, in *Theo. disp.* 85, pp. 532–42, i–ii.

To defend himself against the charge that he did not suppose faith to be a pure gift of God, and to show the harmony between human freedom and divine grace, Arminius employed a comparison (*similis*).

> A rich man gives a poor and famishing beggar (*egeno*) alms by which he may be able to sustain himself and his family. Does it cease to be a pure, undiluted gift (*donum purum putum*) because this beggar extends his hand for receiving (*accipiendum*)? Can it be said with propriety (*commode*) that the alms depended partly on the liberality of the one giving and partly on the liberty of the one receiving, though the latter would not have had the alms unless he had received it by extending the hand? Can it be rightly said, because the beggar is always prepared for receiving, that he can by [any] mode will (*velit*) to have the alms or not have it? If these cannot be truly said, how much less about the gift of faith, for whose receiving many more acts of divine grace are required.[97]

In a similar vein, Arminius asks:

> Who has merited that the blessing be offered to himself; who has merited that any grace whatsoever be conferred on himself for embracing (*amplectendam*) that [blessing]? Are not all those things of gratuitous divine favor? And if they are, is not God to be celebrated on account of those things with perpetual praises by those who, being made participants of this grace, have received (*acceperunt*) the blessing of God?[98]

Elsewhere, Arminius asserts that "faith is the effect of God illuminating the mind and sealing the heart."[99]

---

[97] *Apologia*, art. 27 (7), in *Opera*, p. 176; *Works* 2:52. Luther also describes the recipient of grace as a beggar. In Luther, *De captivitate Babylonica Ecclesiae praeludium*, in *WA* 6:519, he offers a similar analogy, supposing that a rich man gives gold to "mendico aut etiam indigno et malo servo." After receiving the alms, the beggar says, "I receive what I receive not by my merit nor by the right of something of my own. I know that I am unworthy and that I receive (*accipio*) more than I merit, in fact contrary to what I merit, but by the right of the testament and of the goodness of another I claim (*peto*) what I claim." This reference indicates precedence for Arminius's analogy; it is not to claim that Arminius agreed with Luther on the beggar's "role" in salvation. More proximate to Arminius's intention is Erasmus's analogy of a father helping his son. See Erasmus, *De libero arbitrio*, cols. 1244 e–1245 a; *On the Freedom of the Will*, p. 91. Erasmus offers other analogies in *De libero arbitrio*, col. 1238 a–b; *On the Freedom of the Will*, p. 79. Coornhert also employed a beggar analogy. See Dekker, *Rijker*, p. 173 n. 51.

[98] *Exam. Perk.*, in *Opera*, pp. 751–52; *Works* 3:445.

[99] Arminius, *Quaestiones numero novem cum responsionibus et anterotematis, nobiliss. DD. Curatoribus Academiae Leidensis exhibite a deputatis synodi... mense Novembri anni 1605*, resp. 6, in *Opera*, p. 185; *Works* 2:67: "fidem esse effectum Dei illuminantis mentem et cor obsignantis."

Thus, the main point is that even if faith is received and resistible, it does not cease to be a pure gift. The *actus/actio* of believing, as faith is described by Arminius[100]—to whatever degree passive acceptance of a gift can be considered an action—is not a work of merit, nor is it given according to merits. "God destines these means [to salvation] to no one because of or according to his own merits, but from pure, undiluted (*pura puta*) grace."[101] Faith, in effect, comes as the result of a person not resisting God's grace. To say that a person is saved through the gift of faith is not to acknowledge salvation by any merits, for "faith and merit are opposed in the Scriptures."[102]

E.2. Fides *and* Fiducia

The element of faith that deals with assurance is *fiducia*, or confidence. Reformed orthodoxy generally described faith as consisting of *assensus, notitia*, and *fiducia*.[103] Calvin has been described as considering fiducial assurance to be "of the essence of faith."[104] His definition of faith and subsequent descriptions of faith in the *Institutio* demonstrate the inseparability of faith and assurance.[105] Assurance does not follow faith as a logical consequence, but is integral to it.[106]

All of Arminius's colleagues said that true *fides* consists not only of *notitia* and *assensus*, but also of *fiducia*. Gomarus said that salvific faith is not only certain *notitia*, by which the elect firmly assent to all things revealed in God's word, but also certain *fiducia* from the Holy Spirit by the ministry of the Word.[107] Kuchlinus defined faith as follows: "Justifying

---

[100] *Apologia*, art. 26 (6), in *Opera*, pp. 175–76; *Works* 2:50–51.

[101] *Disp. priv.* XLI.x.

[102] *Disp. priv.* XLVIII.cor.iii. Cf. idem, *Exam. Gom.*, pp. 68–69; *Works* 3:583. Contra Berkouwer, *Faith and Justification*, p. 87, who describes Arminianism as an "over-estimation of faith as a spiritual achievement." To the degree that this description is intended to apply to Arminius, it is simplistic and inaccurate.

[103] E.g., Zacharias Ursinus and Caspar Olevianus, *The Heidelberg Catechism*, in Schaff, *Creeds of Christendom* 3:307–55, Q&A 21.

[104] Beeke, *Assurance*, p. 49. Cf. Bell, *Calvin*, p. 22; Kendall, *Calvin*, p. 19. See *Inst.* 3.2.7 and 3.2.14–15.

[105] See *Inst.* 3.2.7 and 3.2.15–16.

[106] See the discussions in Anthony N. S. Lane, 'Calvin's Doctrine of Assurance,' *Vox Evangelica* 11 (1979), 32–54; Beeke, *Assurance*, pp. 47–78.

[107] Gomarus, *De fide salvifica* (1603), ii; cf. idem, *De fide iustificante* (1603), vii. Cf. the contrary statements and quotations in Itterzon, *Gomarus*, p. 293; Letham, 'Faith,' 1:299–302; and Graafland, *Zekerheid*, pp. 85–98, which all indicate that Gomarus believed that *fiducia* follows *fides*. Since Itterzon, Letham, and Graafland only rely on Gomarus's later disputations included in the *Opera omnia*, their analysis of Gomarus is therefore of little

faith is not only *notitia*, by which I firmly assent to all things, which God discloses to us in his word, but also certain *fiducia* kindled in my heart from the Holy Spirit by the Gospel, by which I find rest in God."[108] Kuchlinus notes that defining faith as *fiducia* is one of the distinguishing characteristics of the Heidelberg Catechism.[109] Thus, the faithful are those who have not merely been gifted with a bare knowledge and assent (*nuda notitia et assensu*), but by a true *fiducia* they descend into God's grace by and because of Christ.[110] Trelcatius, Jr., divided these parts of faith in the standard way, placing *notitia* and *assensus* in the intellect and *fiducia* in the will.[111] In the preceding decade at Leiden, Trelcatius, Sr., presiding over a disputation to which his son responded, wrote that saving faith consists of two parts—*notitia* and *fiducia*.[112]

In contrast, Arminius dissented from this view, holding that *fiducia* is the consequent of *fides*, for it is through faith that confidence is placed in Christ, and through him in God. That is, *fiducia* cannot be identified as a component of faith, for faith, as a separate and preceding phenomenon, gives rise to *fiducia*, or assurance.[113] In a letter to Uytenbogaert, Arminius writes that *fiducia* is a necessary consequence of *fides*, but that it scarcely pertains to the substance of *fides*.[114]

The question naturally arises whether Arminius's doctrine of faith as *assensus* and *notitia* sans *fiducia* really amounts to a mere *fides historica*,

---

relevance to the Leiden debate. Although the issue will not be pursued here, Gomarus's later disputation on faith may indicate a shift of perspective in Gomarus. Cf. Gomarus, *Opera omnia*, 3:99.

[108] Kuchlinus, *Theses theologicae de salvandis et fide*, Henricus Adamus Billichius respondens, in *Theo. disp.* 76, pp. 476–80, viii: "Iustificans fides est non tantùm notitia, qua firmiter assentior omnibus, quae Deus nobis in suo verbo patefecit, sed etiam certa fiducia a Spiritu S. per Evangelium in corde meo accensa, qua in Deo acquiesco...."

[109] Kuchlinus, *De salvandis*, ix, xii. It is worth noting that Gomarus's and Kuchlinus's definitions of faith seem to rely on the Heidelberg Catechism, Q&A 21.

[110] Kuchlinus, *Theses theologicae de certitudine salutis fidelium*, Isaacus Ioannis F. respondens (Leiden, 1603), iii.

[111] Trelcatius, Jr., *Scholastica*, pp. 212–13; *A briefe institution of the common places of sacred divinitie* (London, 1610), pp. 557–58.

[112] Lucas Trelcatius, Sr., *Theses theologicae de fide electorum*, Lucas Trelcatius, Jr., respondens, 14 March 1592 (Leiden, 1592), x. Letham, 'Faith,' 1:295–96; 2:157, asserts that Junius considered assurance of salvation to be an *effect* of faith. However, this does not comport with the passages quoted by Letham that demonstrate Junius considered *fiducia* as a component of saving faith.

[113] *Disp. priv.* XLIV.v. Cf. idem, *De fide* (1605), i; idem, *De fide* (1608), iii. Arminius does not follow Hemmingius here, who says in *Enchiridion*, p. 119: "Fides autem est noticia et assensus promissae et expetitae misericordiae, et in eandem firma fiducia."

[114] *Ep. ecc.* 70, p. 134; *Works* 1:176–77, note. Cf. Muller, 'Priority of the Intellect,' 60–3.

which would be non-justifying. Indeed, Uytenbogaert himself asked
Arminius how his doctrine avoids this charge. Arminius responded by
writing, "A demon believes because he knows it is true; but a person
believes because he knows it is true and good for himself, for this reason, that he may obey the God who is commanding, and may obtain
the added promise. The former therefore is historical faith; the latter
justifying, which is also called the obedience of faith."[115] It is similar to
the difference between *credere Deo* and *credere in Deum*, the latter of which
is "for our good" (*nostro bono*).[116] Thus, far from being a historical faith,
the faith that justifies is more than the mere assent or knowledge that
demons share, but actually looks to Christ for salvation.

It is clear that although Arminius distinguishes *fiducia* from the essential components of *fides*, he still did not see *fiducia* as an unessential part
of the Christian life. Arminius's notion of *fiducia* being the normative
consequence of *fides* is analogous to the Reformed view of good works
following justification. Good works have no causal relation whatsoever
to justification; thus, the good fruit should not be confused with the
tree or its good nature.[117] In the same way, whereas Arminius avoids
confounding *fiducia* and *fides*, he does not consider *fiducia* to be in any
way insignificant to the life of faith, but to be the normative consequence of it.[118]

E.3. *Intellectualism and Voluntarism*

For Arminius, as with his contemporaries, the soul consists of two faculties, *intellectus* and *voluntas*. Arminius describes these as the essential

---

[115] *Ep. ecc.* 81, p. 152; *Works* 1:179, note: "...daemon credit quia verum novit: at
homo credit quia verum novit et sibi bonum, hac causa, ut Deo obsequatur jubenti, et
obtineat additam promissionem. Illa itaque fides est historica; haec justificans, et quae
obedientia fidei dicitur."

[116] *Ep. ecc.* 70, p. 134; *Works* 1:177, note. Cf. Oberman, *Harvest*, pp. 464–65.

[117] Trelcatius, Sr., *De fide* (1592), xii: "...bona opera Fidei testes sunt, non causae....
Nec filios Dei faciunt bona opera: Sed Filii Dei faciunt bona opera." Cf. Gomarus,
Disputationum theologicarum repetitarum trigesima sexta, de bonis operibus et meritis eorum, Iacobus
Vervestius respondens, 14 July 1599 (Leiden, 1599), preface; idem, *Theses theologicae de
hominis perfectione in hac vita*, Cornelius Burchvliet respondens, 18 March 1601 (Leiden,
1601), v and viii; Trelcatius, Jr., *De iustificatione* (1606), xviii and xxv.

[118] This specific assurance (*fiducia*) of election or remission of sins is similar in meaning to ἀσφάλεια, πληροφορία, παρρησία, πεποίθησις, ὑπόστασις, and ἔλεγχος, which
Arminius said are attributed to faith. See Arminius, *Orationes tres de theologia, quas ordine
habuit auctor cum lectiones suas auspicaretu, Oratio tertia*, in *Opera*, p. 61; *Works* 1:382–83; idem,
De fide (1605), xv. Moreover, *fiducia*, which can refer to trust in Christ, is not always used
interchangeably with *certitudo*, which can refer specifically to assurance of forgiveness.

content of the *imago Dei*; as essential, even if harmed, they were not lost after the fall.[119] The intellect inclines toward and assents to the true, as the will inclines toward and chooses the good.[120] Modern scholarship has posed the question of the priority of intellect or will in Arminius's doctrine of faith, a question that Arminius never explicitly addressed. R. T. Kendall, in an effort to show the similitude between the doctrine of faith as taught by Arminius and Reformed orthodoxy over against that doctrine taught by Calvin, has attempted to prove that Calvin taught an intellectualist view of faith and Arminius a voluntarist view.[121] Kendall defines voluntarism as "faith as an act of the will," and intellectualism as faith as "a passive persuasion in the mind."[122] M. C. Bell agrees that Calvin considered faith to be passive and centered in the intellect, but that voluntarism "stresses the action of man, especially in the work of faith." Thus, according to Bell, the voluntarists are one-sided in their doctrine of faith, inasmuch as faith becomes about what humanity, not God, does. Therefore, the claim is that voluntarism is preparationist, which means "sinners are prepared for faith by a law work."[123] Kendall and Bell both consider intellectualism to entail passivity in receiving salvation, and voluntarism to entail an autonomously human act of preparation for salvation.

This basic misunderstanding of what makes a doctrine of faith intellectualist or voluntarist has been roundly criticized.[124] Neither intellectualism nor voluntarism entails preparationism, (semi-)Pelagianism, Augustinianism, or rationalism.[125] In soteriology, the question concerns

---

[119] Arminius, *De imaginis Dei restitutione* (1605), iv, claims that even after the fall, sparks of the primeval wisdom remained in the intellect.

[120] *Disp. priv.* XXVI.v; *Art. non.*, in *Opera*, p. 952; *Works* 2:712; *Amica col.*, in *Opera*, p. 524; *Works* 3:112–13. Cf. Gomarus, *De libero arbitrio* (Gruterus, 1603), iii; with Muller, *DLGT*, pp. 157 and 330–31.

[121] See Kendall, *Calvin*, pp. 19, 34, and 211, passim.

[122] Kendall, *Calvin*, p. 3.

[123] Bell, *Calvin*, pp. 8 and 11.

[124] E.g., see George W. Harper, 'Calvin and English Calvinism to 1649: A Review Article,' *Calvin Theological Journal* 20/2 (1985), 258–60; Muller, 'Priority of the Intellect,' 55–72. See also a relevant critique that could apply to the work of Kendall and Bell in Norman Fiering, *Moral Philosophy at Seventeenth-Century Harvard: A Discipline in Transition* (Chapel Hill, 1981), pp. 104–27 and 137: "Sometimes it is mistakenly assumed that it is voluntarism that is conducive to a Pelagian potency of will, a confusion that is due to a failure to distinguish between the Molinist liberty of will and the Augustinian liberty that subordinates the will to either divine or satanic influence."

[125] Cf. Muller, *Unaccommodated Calvin*, p. 162: "Neither view leads naturally to the assumption of a human act prior to the work of grace."

the causal priority of either intellect or will in the soul's conversion to God by faith. Whether intellectualist or voluntarist, all "anti-Pelagians," including Calvin, Beza, Arminius, and the Reformed orthodox, would agree that God is the one enlightening the intellect and persuading the will and that humanity is the passive recipient of salvation.[126]

Although Arminius and his colleagues disagreed vehemently regarding the relationship between predestination and faith, their language regarding intellect and will was quite similar. Arminius said that faith is placed in the *assensus*, and he goes on to describe this assent as more than an *assensus intellectivus*, but an *assensus affectivus*. That is, the assent of faith involves both intellect and will.[127] This reflects the description of faith as *assensus animi* common to Arminius and Trelcatius.[128] This human soul that consists of *mens* and *voluntas* is, according to Arminius, the *materia in qua*, or common subject, of faith. "For we ought to recognize (*agnoscere*) the object of faith not only as true, but also as good." It pertains to both the theoretical intellect and the practical affections.[129] Thus, the role of the intellect and will in accepting faith was not a fundamental point of contention in the debate. The main difference in Arminius's doctrine of faith is his placement of *fiducia* subsequent to *fides*. Because *fiducia* is solely a movement of the will, on this basis one may conclude that Arminius's doctrine of *fides* sans *fiducia* leaned toward intellectualism.[130] Given that neither intellectualism nor voluntarism determines one's soteriology, perhaps the more relevant difference between Arminius and his colleagues in the discussion of intellect and will is not the question of causal priority, but the degree to which the intellect and will were affected by the fall and restored after regeneration.

---

[126] Contra Kendall, *Calvin*, p. 211 (italics mine): "In any case, faith as an act of the will *necessitates certain theological conclusions*, all of which are those of Arminius: (1) the demise of faith as a persuasion; (2) the separation of faith and assurance; (3) the need for two acts of faith: the direct and reflex acts; and (4) assurance by the employment of the practical syllogism." Kendall, *Calvin*, p. 142, also claims that it was Arminius's voluntarism that made him "suspect because of his modification of predestination."

[127] *Ep. ecc.* 70, p. 134; *Works* 1:177, note.

[128] Arminius, *De Fide* (1605), i; *Disp. priv.* XLIV.iii; Trelcatius, *Disputationum theologicarum quarto repetitarum vigesima-septima de bonis operibus et meritis eorum*, Ricardus Ianus Neraeus respondens, ad diem 4 March 1606 (Leiden, 1606), ix.

[129] Arminius, *De fide* (1605), xi. In *Disp. pub.* XI.i, Arminius says that *mens* and *voluntas* are connected by *arctissima unio*.

[130] Contra Kendall, Muller, 'Priority of the Intellect,' 55–72, also leans toward an intellectualist interpretation of Arminius's soteriology. In *GCP*, pp. 71–79, Muller argues more emphatically for Arminius's priority of the intellect regarding the beatific vision in the context of Arminius's consideration of theology as "practical."

F. *Union and Communion with Christ*

Because Christ is the "Savior of believers," and also because he will only communicate his blessings to those who are united with him, Arminius next treats the topic of union with Christ, which he calls "the first and immediate effect of faith."[131] The significance of this topic is evident in Arminius's definition of the concept.

> We may define or describe it [union] as a spiritual and very close, and therefore mystically essential conjoining, by which the faithful, being connected immediately to Christ himself by God the Father himself and Jesus Christ through the Spirit of Christ and of God, and to God through Christ, are made one with himself and with the Father, and participants of all his good things, to their salvation and the glory of Christ and God.[132]

Arminius describes a robust, mystical union of believers with the Trinity which results in benefits for those who are thus united. Emphasizing again the strength of this union, he writes, "For the union that is between Christ and faithful people is closer and stricter than that which is between the same and angels, because of the consubstantiality of human nature, from which angels are alien."[133] In his oration on the author and goal of theology, Arminius qualifies and clarifies the nature of this union. "The union is not essential, as if the two essences—to be sure of God and of humanity—are joined together (*compingantur*) into one, or that by which humanity is absorbed into God." He also denies that the union is formal, that is, that God might be made in the form of humanity. Rather, the union is objective and immediate in the sense that God shows himself clearly (*convincit*) to humanity by his faculties and actions, so that God is said to be all things in all (*omnia in omnibus*).[134] Arminius therefore emphasizes the union, but not to the detriment of the distinction between divine and human. The parties that are united

---

[131] *Disp. priv.* XLV.i.

[132] *Disp. priv.* XLV.iii: "Quam definire seu describere possumus spiritualem eamque arctissimam, et propterea mystice essentialem conjunctionem, qua fideles ab ipso Deo patre et Iesu Christo immediate, et per Christum Deo connexi unum cum ipso et cum patre fiunt, et omnium bonorum eius participes, ad suam salutem et Christi Deique gloriam." Cf. Arminius, *De Fide* (1605), xiii; idem, *Orationes tres, Oratio secunda*, in *Opera*, p. 47; *Works* 1:358.

[133] *Amica col.*, in *Opera*, p. 537; *Works* 3:132: "Unio enim quae inter Christum est et homines fideles arctior est et strictior, quam illa quae inter eundem est et Angelos, propter humanae naturae consubstantialitatem, a quo Angeli sunt alieni."

[134] Arminius, *Orationes tres, Oratio secunda*, in *Opera*, p. 49; *Works* 1:362.

are Christ and every sinner who believes in Christ, bonded to each
other by God's Spirit and humanity's faith in Christ. The formal cause
of this union is compacting and joining together (*compactio et coagmentatio*)
in covenant.[135]

Although it has not been one of the classic, popular topics for analysis among the interpreters of Arminius, union with Christ is in some
ways the central point of Arminius's soteriology, for this union is one of
the goals of predestination and salvation. Arminius says that faith "is
the necessary means of our union with Christ."[136] Vocation, which to
Arminius is the beginning of the execution of the *ordo salutis*, is so that
sinners may be united with Christ and enjoy (*frui*) the communion of his
benefits.[137] "The remote final cause [of vocation] is the salvation of the
called, and the glory of God and of Christ who calls; which [salvation
and glory] are located in the union of God and humanity."[138] Indeed,
union with God is the goal of religion itself and of theology, which is
the goal that makes theology a practical science.[139] Although Arminius's
colleagues do not appear to have given quite as much explicit attention
to the topic of union with Christ as he did, they nevertheless regarded
it as a necessary part of salvation. Kuchlinus calls union with Christ the
fundamentum of justification.[140] Kuchlinus also agrees with Arminius that
mystical union with Christ is the "proximate cause" (*caussa proxima*) of
the benefits that believers receive, and that the union is bound by God's
Spirit and true faith in Christ.[141] According to Trelcatius, the ultimate
final cause of election is communion with God.[142]

---

[135] *Disp. priv.* XLV.v–vii.
[136] *Exam. Perk.*, in *Opera*, p. 762; *Works* 3:460: "...necessarium est medium unionis
nostri cum Christo."
[137] *Disp. priv.* XLII.i.
[138] *Disp. priv.* XLII.ix: "Finis remotus est salus vocatorum, et gloria Dei et Christi
vocantis, quae posita sunt in unione Dei et hominis." Cf. *Disp. priv.* XL.vi; idem, *Amica
col.*, in *Opera*, p. 614; *Works* 3:241.
[139] *Disp. priv.* I.iii; II.i; III.iv; XXXII.i; idem, *Orationes tres, Oratio secunda*, in *Opera*, p. 50;
Works 1:364. The practical (as opposed to speculative) nature of Arminius's theology is
underscored by Hoenderdaal, 'De theologische betekenis van Arminius,' *Nederlands Theologisch Tijdschrift* 15 (1960), 90–98, there 98; idem, 'The Life and Thought of Jacobus
Arminius,' *Religion in Life* 29/4 (1960), 540–47, there 542–43; idem, 'Inleiding,' p. 34;
idem, *BLGNP* 2:34; idem, 'Arminius en Episcopius,' 230.
[140] Kuchlinus, *Theses theologic [sic] de iustificatione hominis coram Deo*, quaest. catech. 59.
60. 61, Raphael ab Allendorp Clivius respondens, in *Theo. disp.* 74, pp. 459–65, xviii.
[141] Kuchlinus, *De perseverantia* (1603), vii.
[142] Trelcatius, *De praedestinatione* (1606), xvi. Cf. Gomarus, *Theses theologicae de iustificatione hominis coram Deo*, Isaacus Diamantius respondens, ad diem 20 March 1604 (Leiden,
1604), vi. This attitude is quite typical of later Reformed orthodoxy as well.

It is clear that union with Christ is both a present reality for the regenerate as well as an anticipation for eschatological fulfillment. This union that has already been seized will one day be consummated and perfected.[143] Thus, Arminius speaks of the *ratio* of the "last and supreme (*postremae et supremae*) union." In this final union, God unites himself to the intellect and will of his creature, enabling the beatific vision, that is, to see God face to face.[144] The effect of union with the Trinity is *supernaturalis felicitas*.[145]

As far as this life is concerned, communion with Christ, which consists of the benefits (*beneficia/bona*) of union with Christ, begins now. This communion with Christ is the fruit of the union; the communion flows immediately from the union. Communion entails a common sharing of Christ's benefits, yet preserves the distinction between the one communicating the benefits and those participating in them.[146] The first part of this communion is participation in the benefits of Christ's death, which includes the abolition of the effects of death, sin, and the law on the faithful.[147] The other part of communion is participation in the power of the risen, glorified Christ, both now and in the eschaton.[148]

G. *Justification*

From union with Christ result two spiritual benefits in this present life, comprehended together as the whole promise of the new covenant that God will both forgive sins and write his laws on the hearts of the faithful; these two benefits are called justification and sanctification,[149] the latter of which will be dealt with in the next chapter. Justification is the just and gracious action of God to absolve a person from sins because of the obedience and righteousness of Christ, for the salvation of that sinner.[150] Not mentioned in the private disputation, but noted in the

---

[143] Arminius, *Orationes tres, Oratio secunda*, in *Opera*, p. 52; *Works* 1:366. Again, this eschatological dimension is prevalent in Reformed piety.

[144] Arminius, *Orationes tres, Oratio secunda*, in *Opera*, pp. 49–50; *Works* 1:362–63.

[145] Arminius, *Amica col.*, in *Opera*, p. 544; *Works* 3:143.

[146] *Disp. priv.* XLVI.i–ii. This distinction that Arminius maintains should help inform the strong definition of union cited above in *Disp. priv.* XLV.iii.

[147] *Disp. priv.* XLVI.vi–ix.

[148] *Disp. priv.* XLVII.

[149] *Disp. priv.* XLVIII.i.

[150] *Disp. priv.* XLVIII.ii.

1603 public disputation on justification, is the efficient cause of justification, which is God alone.[151] Arminius proceeds to elaborate on this efficient causality:

> The cause of our justification that internally moves and precedes God is the sole and mere grace of God.... The cause of our justification that externally moves or predisposes God is Jesus Christ, not according to the divine nature only, as Osiander wished, nor according to the human [nature] only, as Stancarus opined, but according to both.[152]

Christ, through his obedience and righteousness, is the meritorious and material cause of justification.[153] "The material cause (*materia*) *in qua*, or receiving subject, are all the elect, indeed by nature sinners and impious, nevertheless believers and incorporated into Christ by faith."[154] The instrumental cause of justification is twofold. "From the part of God who offers and confers" (*Ex parte Dei offerentis et conferentis*), it is the ministry of the word and sacraments; "from the part of man who apprehends and receives" (*ex parte hominis apprehendentis et recipientis*), it is faith. Faith is the instrument or action by which Christ's propitiation is apprehended for justification.[155] The formal cause of justification is the remission of sins and the gracious estimation of God whereby he imputes faith to us for righteousness. The *finis cujus gratia*, or *finis proximus*, is the salvation of those justified and peace of their consciences, and the *finis qui*, or *finis summus et ultimus*, is the glory of God from the demonstration of divine justice and grace.[156]

The single most notable feature of comparative analysis is the indisputable fact that, with regard to the assignment of causes, which was

---

[151] Arminius, *De iustificatione* (1603), viii.

[152] Arminius, *De iustificatione* (1603), xi, xv: "Causa interne Deum movens et προηγουμένη nostrae justificationis, est sola et mera Dei gratia.... Causa externe Deum movens sive προκαταρκτική nostrae justificationis est Iesus Christus, non secundum divinam naturam tantum, ut voluit Osiander, neque secundum humanum tantum, ut opinabatur Stancarus, sed secundum utramque." Even if one were to argue, based on Bertius's story, that Arminius did not compose these particular theses, these points on efficient and impulsive causality do not disagree with Arminius's soteriology. On authorship, see my discussion in chapter two, II.B.5.

[153] *Disp. priv.* XLVIII.v; idem, *De iustificatione* (1603), xviii.

[154] Arminius, *De iustificatione* (1603), xx: "Materia in qua sive subjectum recipiens sunt omnes Electi, natura quidem peccatores et impii, credentes tamen et fide Christo insiti."

[155] Arminius, *De iustificatione* (1603), xxix and xxxi; *Disp. priv.* XLVIII.vii.

[156] Arminius, *De iustificatione* (1603), xxi–xxviii and xxxix; *Disp. priv.* XLVIII.viii–ix.

the most obvious context of doctrinal debate in disputations, Arminius's disputations on justification exhibit no meaningful differences with those of his colleagues. They cohere and, even more, they demonstrate identical lines of thought. They all assign God as the principal efficient cause of justification. Kuchlinus declares, "Therefore the principal *efficient cause* of our justification before God is God."[157] They all attribute the προηγουμένη (preceding cause) to God's grace and mercy, and the προκαταρκτική (predisposing cause) to the righteousness and satisfaction of Jesus Christ.[158] The *materia ex qua* or *circa quam*, which is regarded here as identical to the προκαταρκτική, is again the righteousness of Christ. The only difference is that Gomarus explicitly mentions in the material cause the satisfaction of Christ as well, thus emphasizing the active and passive obedience of Christ.[159] Like Arminius, the others do not mention the satisfaction of Christ, although they clearly regarded it as necessary for justification. We do know, however, that Arminius was not keen on getting involved in the debate over the active and passive obedience of Christ.[160] The *materia in qua* are the elect believers, just as

---

[157] Kuchlinus, *De iustificatione*, viii. Cf. idem, *Theses theologicae de natura iustificationis in caussis*, Ioannes Arnoldus respondens, March 1603 (Leiden, 1603), v; Junius, *De differentia* (1600), vii; Gomarus, *De iustificatione* (1603), vi; idem, *De iustificatione* (1604), vii: "But the first of these [causes] is efficient. The principal is God alone." Idem, *De iustificatione* (1605), viii: "Caussa justificationis activa, est Deus." Trelcatius, *De iustificatione* (1604), vii; idem, *De iustificatione* (1606), vii: "Causa efficiens hujus iustificationis est Deus, is .n. quia solus est, in quem peccatur. Solus etiam peccata remittere potest."

[158] Gomarus, *Theses theologicae de iustificatione hominis coram Deo*, Laurentius Boenaert respondens, 12 March 1603 (Leiden, 1603), vii–viii; idem, *De iustificatione* (1604), viii–ix: "The impulsive is duplex: προηγουμένη and προκαταρκτική. The former is the grace of God."…"The latter is the righteousness and satisfaction of Christ." Idem, *Theses theologicae de iustificatione hominis coram Deo*, Henricus Slatius respondens, ad diem 19 February 1605 (Leiden, 1605), x and xii; idem, *Disputatio theologica de hominis coram Deo per Christum iustificatione*, Ioannes Perreus respondens, ad diem 26 April 1608 (Leiden, 1608), xiii and xv. Kuchlinus, *De iustificatione*, ix; idem, *De natura iustificationis* (1603), vi–viii. Trelcatius, *Disputatio theologica de iustificatione hominis coram Deo*, Ioannes Bocardus respondens, 21 January 1604 (Leiden, 1604), ix–x; idem, *De iustificatione* (1606), ix–x, thesis x of which on προκαταρκτική contra Osiander and Stancarus is nearly verbatim with Arminius's point cited above. The mention of these two opponents is formulaic, appearing in nearly every Leiden disputation dealing with Christ's mediation as the προκαταρκτική of justification. This fact further demonstrates the remarkable continuity between the thought of Arminius and the Reformed.

[159] Gomarus, *De iustificatione* (1604), xi; idem, *De iustificatione* (1605), xv–xvi. Cf. Kuchlinus, *De iustificatione*, xiii; Trelcatius, *De iustificatione* (1606), xii: "Materia Iustificationis Ex Qua, aut Circa Quam, est eadem justitia Christi, quatenus ea est qua per fidem apprehensa, in judicio Dei justi censemur."

[160] *Dec. sent.*, pp. 123–24; *Works* 1:695–96. Cf. idem, *Art. non.*, in *Opera*, pp. 962–63; *Works* 2:726–27.

Arminius asserted. Kuchlinus affirmed, "The material cause (*materia*) *in qua* are only those who truly believe: *He who believes has eternal life*."[161] Although Kuchlinus elsewhere emphasizes the "elect," Arminius especially would have appreciated his uncle's emphasis here on "believers" as those who have eternal life. The formal cause is the remission of sins and the imputation of righteousness. In agreement with Arminius, Trelcatius wrote, "The formal cause (*forma*) of justification consists in gracious imputation, which is twofold. One is negative, and is the remission of sins. The other is affirmative, and is the imputation of Christ's righteousness."[162] Arminius certainly does not fall under Trelcatius's critique of the "adversaries," who "wish the formal cause to be righteousness inherent and infused in us."[163] The final cause is also twofold: for God's glory and for humanity's salvation and peace. Gomarus said, "The final cause (*finis*) of justification is the praise of God's glorious grace by a holy life, peace of consciences, and eternal life."[164]

The correspondence in the disputations even extends to the placement of faith as the human part of apprehending justification. The instrumental cause is regarded by Arminius as twofold: from the part of God, his offering through the word and sacraments, and from the part of humanity, apprehending it by faith. Even here, all four Leiden theologians concur. Trelcatius's statement is representative, "So the instrumental cause is considered in a twofold way: either with respect to God who justifies us, or with respect to the person who receives justification." He goes on to mention that from God's part, he justifies through the

---

[161] Kuchlinus, *De iustificatione*, xiii: "*Materia* in qua, sunt soli vere Credentes: *Qui credit, habet vitam aeternam*." Cf. idem, *De natura iustificationis* (1603), xviii; Gomarus, *De iustificatione* (1605), xviii; Trelcatius, *De iustificatione* (1606), xiii.

[162] Trelcatius, *De iustificatione* (1606), xix: "Forma justificationis consistit in gratiosa imputatione. Quae duplex est. Una Negativa, et est Remissio Peccatorum. Altera Affirmativa, estque justitiae Christi imputatio." In thesis xxii, Trelcatius seems to say that human faith is part of the formal cause, but then denies that it properly belongs there. Cf. Kuchlinus, *De iustificatione*, xv: "*Forma* est imputatio iustitiae & satisfactionis Christi." Gomarus, *De iustificatione* (1603), ix; idem, *De iustificatione* (1604), xiii; idem, *De iustificatione* (1605), xviii.

[163] Trelcatius, *De iustificatione* (1604), xv: "Adversarii...volunt formam esse justitiam nobis inhaerentem et infusam."

[164] Gomarus, *De iustificatione* (1605), xxv: "Finis justificationis, est laus gloriosae gratiae Dei sancta vita; pax conscientiarum, et vita aeterna." Cf. idem, *De iustificatione* (1603), xvi; idem, *De iustificatione* (1604), xv; Kuchlinus, *De iustificatione*, xix; idem, *De natura iustificationis* (1603), xix; Trelcatius, *De iustificatione* (1606), xxvi.

word and sacraments, and from our part, by faith.[165] As Arminius in
his private disputation omits God's instrumentality and only mentions
the instrument of faith, so also Kuchlinus only mentions the instrument
of faith in his disputation on justification: "The instrumental cause is
true faith, which alone is not without works, but alone justifies without
works."[166]

Given that the role of faith was the main controversy surrounding
Arminius's doctrine of justification, it is remarkable to find that the
Leiden disputations are substantially identical on this point. Arminius
was criticized for teaching that faith, as the *actus apprehensionis* that apprehends Christ and his righteousness, is actually imputed for righteousness. For Arminius, faith, as the instrumental cause of justification, is
thus prior to justification. In this instrumental sense, faith can thus be
considered a condition of justification.[167] Arminius did not make it a
matter of great import how exactly faith acts as the instrument, whether
it is imputed for righteousness or apprehends righteousness.[168] When
he was accused of teaching that faith is not the instrument of justification, but an act, he said that faith is certainly both. As the instrument
of justification, faith "accepts and apprehends the promises given by
God.... But apprehension is an action: Therefore faith not as an instrument, but as an action is imputed for righteousness."[169] Therefore, it is

---

[165] Trelcatius, *De iustificatione* (1606), xiv–xv: "Instrumentalis Causa itidem dupliciter consideratur: vel respectu Dei nos justificantis: vel respectu hominis justificationem
recipientis." Cf. idem, *De iustificatione* (1604), xviii–xix: "nam id quod apprehendit non
justificat nos, sed quod apprehenditur." Junius, *Disputatio theologica de iustificatione peccatoris coram Deo*, Benjamin Basnageus respondens, 16 November 1600 (Leiden, 1600),
ix, xi; Gomarus, *De Iustificatione* (1603), xi; idem, *De iustificatione* (1604), x: "Instrumentalis remota in adultis, est duplex: offerens, Evangelium: recipiens, fides vera et salvifica,
eaque sola." Idem, *De iustificatione* (1605), xix–xx. Indeed, faith as the means of justification is standard fare in Reformed orthodoxy. See also Wolfgang Musculus, *Common places
of the Christian Religion* (London, 1563), fols. 226v–227v. Piscator, *Treatise*, p. 91.

[166] Kuchlinus, *De iustificatione*, x. Cf. idem, *Theses theologicae continentes exegesin et assertionem theorematis hodie controversi, sola fide absque operibus nos iustificari coram Deo*, Ioannes Arnoldus respondens, March 1603 (Leiden, 1603), iv and ix; *Disp. priv.* XLVIII.vii.

[167] *Art. non.*, in *Opera*, pp. 963–64; *Works* 2:727–28. Cf. idem, *Epistola*, in *Opera*, p. 945;
Works 2:701. See also Perkins, *Armilla aurea*, chart, who likewise puts *vocatio efficax* and
fides before *iustificatio*.

[168] *Dec. sent.*, pp. 123–25; *Works* 1:695–700. Cf. Hicks, 'Theology of Grace,' pp.
79–92.

[169] *Apologia*, art. 26 (6), in *Opera*, p. 175; *Works* 2:49–51: "...promissiones a Deo datas
accipiat et apprehendat....Apprehensio autem est actio: itaque fides non qua instrumentum, sed qua actio imputatur in iustitiam" (reading *iustitiam* for *iustititiam*). Cf. *Apo-*

not contradictory to consider faith as both an instrument and an action. Suffice it to say that the source of the debate was not that Arminius was unwilling to call faith the instrument of justification, for this is exactly what he called it; neither did the debate turn on Arminius's calling faith an act, for Gomarus himself refers to the "action of faith."[170]

After comparing the causes of justification among the disputations of the four Leiden theologians, the agreement is striking and the variations are rare. Therefore, when Arminius states that "some doctors of our profession" incorrectly assign faith as the formal cause of justification, he may be referring to a tendency of Trelcatius, but it is in no way a strike against his Leiden colleagues on the whole.[171] Attempts to implicate Arminius as un-Reformed by appealing to his statements on justification are finally unsuccessful, no less now as they were then.[172] If there was to be debate over the doctrine of justification, it must be located in divergent definitions of the key terms that each professor unanimously employed. For example, the professors may have had different views of grace and faith and the grounds of election, but Arminius still considered grace and faith and the elect to all function in the same causal way as his colleagues considered them to function.

---

logia, art. 24 (4). Contra Kendall, *Calvin*, p. 148: "Arminius sees that retaining the term 'instrument', which seems to be but a remnant of Calvin's theology, is without sound reason."

[170] Gomarus, *De fide iustificante* (1603), i and ix. Contra Kendall, *Calvin*, p. 148.

[171] *Disp. priv.* XLVIII.cor.ii. Cf. Trelcatius, *De iustificatione* (1606), xxii.

[172] E.g., see the unsuccessful attempt to demonstrate Arminius's doctrine of justification as outside Reformed orthodox bounds in Peterson and Williams, *Why I Am Not an Arminian*, p. 109 (italics mine): "[Arminius] consistently affirmed that the initiative in salvation is God's, that salvation is a response to God's preceding grace, and that salvation is by grace alone through faith alone. Yet the *faith* that saves (the "*instrumental cause*" of justification) *properly belongs to human beings*. Between the universal love of God for the world and the application of salvation to particular persons stands the active *faith* of the sinner as the *essential determining cause of salvation....*" As the documents show, the Leiden theologians agreed that faith is the instrumental cause that properly belongs to human beings, even if it is given by God. In addition, Arminius never isolated human faith as the essential determining cause of salvation over and above the other essential causes he enumerates. For his contemporaries, human faith was no less "essential" a cause of salvation than it was for Arminius. Cf. the comment in Hoenderdaal, 'Theologische betekenis,' 92: "In hoofdzaken hangt Arminius een rechtvaardigingsleer aan, die gelijk is aan die van Calvijn." Contra Ritschl, *Dogmengeschichte* 3:338, who sees Arminius's doctrine of faith and justification as a Catholic tendency.

III. *Conclusion*

A. *The Similarities*

In retrospect, not only is there correspondence between the broad shape of Arminius's soteriology and that of his Reformed contemporaries, but there is also conformity in many of the detailed soteriological issues of their respective systems. Popular interpretations, uninformed about one or both of these theological systems and frequently driven by theological agendas of their own, have too often exaggerated the differences and overlooked these undeniable affinities. These similarities, which have been enumerated throughout this chapter, are due to several factors. First and foremost, the similarities are due to the common cause of the Leiden theology within the Staten College of Leiden University. The diverse collection of Reformed theologians teaching at Leiden was united, especially in matters of soteriology, against the Roman Catholic Church. The primary controversy, for example, in justification was not between Arminius and his colleagues, but between the Reformed and the *Pontificii*, the latter of whom did not ascribe to justification by faith alone, but assigned faith as the formal cause of justification.[173] Leiden University, home of the cutting edge Reformed seminary, was in direct rivalry with the older, prestigious Catholic Louvain University to the south. Reformed theology in Leiden demonstrated solidarity in its opposition to Roman Catholicism.

Furthermore, there is a degree of ambiguity inherent within the disputation genre itself. As pointed out above, the theses are frequently stated so succinctly that they require a great deal of unpacking and context to uncover the latent divergences of thought, which undoubtedly would have been more conspicuous when the disputation was publicly defended. Inasmuch as Protestant theologians relied on biblical language and categories that are ambiguous and imprecise, the terminology in the disputations often underdetermined the contested issues. Thus, Arminius may be employing nomenclature and causes identical to those of the other Leiden theologians, but not necessarily intending an identical meaning at each point. A quick glance through Arminius's *Apologia*, for example, shows his typically scholastic defense to charges

---

[173] See Piscator, *Treatise*, pp. 91–92, passim.

of heterodoxy; namely, that he agrees with a certain way of putting a doctrine if only it is explained and understood in the correct, orthodox manner.

B. *The Differences and Motivations*

Just as popular interpretations have tended to exaggerate the differences or even create some that never existed between Arminius himself and his contemporaries, it would be unwise to react to this trend by over-looking the fundamental variations that did exist. The most commonly employed matrix for summarizing the diversity is the famous acrostic "TULIP" and the five Arminian articles to which Dort responded. It would be anachronistic, however, to impose the five Remonstrant arti-cles as a summary of Arminius's distinctives, even if he would have agreed with them in principle.

In my estimation, the distinctive points of Arminius's soteriology boil down to two interrelated points. The first difference is the prior-ity of faith, or, stated another way, conditional election, for faith is the condition. Faith is the primary dividing line between the saved and the unsaved. Arminius underscored the difference as the priority of faith in the order of salvation: "For the faithful are adopted, the adopted are not gifted with faith."[174] In other words, do you believe because you are elect (opponents), or are you elect because you believe (Arminius)? This harmonizes with the twofold love of God that Arminius emphasized, that is, that God would not reprobate a human creature, the object of his love, unconditionally.

The second point of difference concerns the resistibility of grace. If we take Arminius at his word, grace still operates in the same way as his Reformed opponents taught; the only difference is that grace is resistible. Faith is therefore a gift of God, but it is a resistible gift. Arminius insisted that accepting a resistible gift does not make salvation an earned work, as his Reformed contemporaries presumed. Reflecting back over our brief survey of soteriological topics in the thought of Arminius, it is the priority of faith, along with the themes of God's love and prevenient,

---

[174] *Amica col.*, in *Opera*, pp. 462–63; *Works* 3:22–23: "*Adoptantur enim fideles, non donantur fide adoptati.*"

but resistible, grace that prove to be the prominent and distinctive features of Arminius's soteriology.[175]

It is also fitting to summarize the possible motivating factors that propelled the distinctive features of Arminius's soteriology. In addition to his own exegesis of Scripture and the tradition,[176] I shall mention two primary impelling factors. The first is the problem of evil. Unconditional election implies unconditional reprobation, the latter of which Arminius believed to be in conflict with God's love. Even more, according to Arminius, determinism in salvation and damnation means that human freedom is destroyed and that God is the author of sin. Since he felt that supralapsarianism particularly falls victim to this flaw, the problem was reinforced not so much by the supralapsarian tendency in Beza's Geneva as by the supralapsarianism all around him at Leiden University. The motivation to resolve the problem of evil drove Arminius to reconcile God's grace and omniscience with human freedom (per Molina), which affected the doctrines of creation, predestination, salvation, and God.

The other motivating factor was the doctrine of assurance. The fundamental importance of this issue is apparent in Arminius's criteria for a right doctrine of predestination. If one's doctrine, and especially praxis, of assurance is skewed, it reflects a flaw in the broader soteriological and theological system, an issue that will be discussed below. In a sense, assurance is the impetus and *sine qua non* of the debate, the root of the controversy. Arminius's system has been called a theology of creation; perhaps it could also be called a theology of assurance. Ironically, Arminius is often remembered as one who undermined assurance.

---

[175] These two chief differences reflect the "U" and the "I" (and their contraries) in the famous "TULIP." The "T," "L," and "P" (and their contraries) flow from the other two points.

[176] Although it is beyond the scope of this essay, the present focus should not detract from the fact that Arminius found significant motivation and basis for his soteriology in his exegesis of Scripture, which was firmly rooted in the history of interpretation that preceded him. Arminius thus stands in continuity with the great reformers who preceded him in viewing Scripture as the primary source and the Christian tradition as a significant—albeit, subordinate—source of theology and hermeneutical lens. Graafland, *Van Calvijn tot Barth*, p. 90, implies that Arminius only cited the patristic and medieval sources because this was expected in the theological discourse of his day. To be sure, Arminius saw the advantage of citing the tradition, and was eager to employ it against his opponents. E.g., five of Arminius's twenty points against supralapsarianism appeal to the majority view of the Christian tradition. See *Dec. sent.*, pp. 71–96; *Works* 1:618–45.

Noting the problem of evil and the problem of assurance as chief motivations of Arminius's soteriology is not to say that these were his only concerns. As with any complex thinker living in complex times, Arminius and his theology are understood fully by appealing to multiple causes—social, emotional, and literary. However, the problems of evil and assurance not only go a long way in explaining the distinctive concerns of Arminius's theology, but also place him firmly in the tradition of Augustine, Luther, and others who were driven to refine their theology based on these cardinal issues.

CHAPTER FOUR

SANCTIFICATION, PERFECTION, AND APOSTASY

By its very nature, the problem of the assurance of salvation does not concern the unregenerate person, but rather the believer who lives as a Christian and considers himself to have experienced the causes of salvation briefly discussed in the last chapter. Inasmuch as assurance is a question strictly for the Christian life, our analysis must focus on that aspect of the *ordo salutis* that deals with the already regenerate person, namely, the topic of sanctification. Therefore, before delving into the epistemological question of salvation in particular, it is necessary first to complete our exploration of the ontological question and to describe Arminius's thought regarding the Christian life of sanctification. This chapter will begin by investigating Arminius's general doctrine of sanctification, and then proceed to a more detailed examination of his opinions concerning the possibility of Christian perfection and the possibility of apostasy. Consistent with the method employed throughout this essay, I shall engage in a comparative analysis between Arminius and his colleagues in the Staten College by means of the public disputations that were essential to the debate, albeit little known today. This comparison will provide additional context for understanding Arminius, the debate over assurance, and the Leiden theology.

I. *Sanctification in General*

A. *The Nature of Sanctification*

According to Arminius's definition, justification and sanctification comprise the spiritual benefits that believers enjoy in this life, corresponding to the twofold promise that God will pardon sins and write his laws on the hearts of believers.[1] Sanctification, as much as justification, is a blessing

---

[1] *Disp. priv.* XLVIII.i.

that naturally flows from union with Christ.[2] In fact, one recognized goal of justification is "holiness of life and the pursuit of righteousness."[3] Sanctification in general, according to Arminius, is the separation of anything from its common use for the purpose of divine use.[4] Arminius describes the sanctification of a person as when God purifies a sinful yet believing person and then grants him the Spirit of knowledge, righteousness, and holiness, in order that he might live the life of God (*vita Dei*), for the end of God's praise and his own salvation.[5]

Sanctification consists in the mortification of the old person and the vivification of the new person. The object of such sanctification is both the person as a sinner (inasmuch as sin contaminates one from service to God) as well as the person as a believer (inasmuch as the person united with Christ is therefore holy).[6] Arminius draws on the imagery of the Old Testament use of sacrificial blood to describe what the blood of Jesus Christ accomplishes. Not only does the sprinkling of the blood effect the expiation of sins, which is the cause of justification, but it also sanctifies those who have been justified, further enabling them to offer worship and sacrifices to God through Christ.[7]

B. *The Necessity of Good Works*

Because of the Protestant insistence on justification by faith alone apart from works, along with the sharp rhetoric of Luther and some of his followers against the efficacy of good works for salvation, Reformed theologians recognized their vulnerability to Roman Catholic charges of antinomianism.[8] Thus, in its teaching on sanctification, Reformed orthodoxy firmly declared the necessity of good works in the Christian

---

[2] *Disp. pub.* XXIV.i.

[3] Arminius, *De iustificatione* (1603), xxxix: "sanctimonia vitae et studium justitiae." As noted in the last chapter, all the Leiden theologians agreed on the final cause of justification.

[4] *Disp. priv.* XLIX.i.

[5] *Disp. priv.* XLIX.iv.

[6] *Disp. priv.* XLIX.v and vii.

[7] *Disp. priv.* XLIX.xi. On these general issues, Arminius is in step with the Reformed theology of his era. Cf. Amandus Polanus a Polansdorf, *Partitiones theologicae iuxta naturalis methodi leges conformatae duobus libris* (London, 1591), pp. 57–61; *The substance of Christian religion, Soundly Set Forth in two bookes, by definitions and partitions* (London, 1595), pp. 94–100; Junius, *De differentia* (1600).

[8] See Arminius, *De bonis operibus* (1603), xiii; idem, *De bonis operibus* (1609), x; Gomarus, *De bonis operibus* (1599), xii.

life. So also, according to Arminius, the formal cause of sanctification is conformity with God, and one of the goals of sanctification is to live the life of God and serve him in newness of life.[9]

The Leiden theologians devoted attention periodically in their disputation cycles to the topic of good works, that is, what it means to live, as Arminius calls it, "the life of God." The Leiden professors were all in agreement on the topic of good works and their causes. The efficient cause of good works is God, and the secondary efficient, or instrumental, cause is *homo regenitus* and his faith. Gomarus put it succinctly, "Therefore the efficient cause of good works is God working in us by faith."[10] The material cause of good works is whatever is prescribed in the moral law of God and summed up in the Decalogue. Again, Gomarus wrote, "The material cause (*materia*) of good works is whatever God commands to be done in his moral law (which is the true rule of discerning the good)."[11] The formal cause of good works is perfect conformity to that prescribed law. Kuchlinus asserted, "The formal cause (*forma*) of good works is perfect conformity with the law in all its parts and degrees."[12] The general conclusion that is drawn from this cause is that even the works of the regenerate are imperfect, for sin is not totally extinguished in this life. The final cause is consistently attributed in a threefold way, as Arminius declared, *ex parte Dei*, *ex parte nostra*, and *ex parte proximi*. Good works are for God's glory, they contribute to our own certainty of salvation, and they are for the good of one's neighbors, encouraging them to also glorify God.[13] This general assumption that good works contribute

---

[9] *Disp. priv.* XLIX.iv, ix–x.

[10] Gomarus, *De bonis operibus* (1599), iv: "Causa itaque efficiens bonorum operum, est Deus per fidem in nobis operans." Cf. Arminius, *De bonis operibus* (1603), iii–iv; idem, *De bonis operibus* (1609), ii–iv; Kuchlinus, *Theses theologicae de bonorum operum conditionibus*, expl. quaest. 91 catech., Ioannes Arnoldus respondens, in *Theo. disp.* 83, pp. 516–22, iii–iv; Trelcatius, *De bonis operibus* (1606), viii–ix.

[11] Gomarus, *De bonis operibus* (1599), vii: "Materia bonorum operum, est quicquid Deus lege sua morali, (quae vera dignoscendi boni regula est) fieri jubet." Cf. Arminius, *De bonis operibus* (1603), vi; idem, *De bonis operibus* (1609), v. Kuchlinus, *De conditionibus*, ix: "*Materia bonorum operum, lex Dei est*, seu quicquid divina lege praecipitur, sive in specie, sive in genere." Trelcatius, *De bonis operibus* (1606), x: "Materia bonorum operum est, quicquid in lege Dei morali, in tota Scriptura V. et N. Testamenti sparsa, et cujus summa in decalogo continetur, vera et sola dignoscendi bona regula immutabilique, precipitur."

[12] Kuchlinus, *De conditionibus*, xi–xii: "Forma bonorum operum est omnibus suis partibus et gradibus perfecta conformitas cum lege." Cf. Arminius, *De bonis operibus* (1603), vii–viii; idem, *De bonis operibus* (1609), vii–viii; Gomarus, *De bonis operibus* (1599), ix; Trelcatius, *De bonis operibus* (1606), xi.

[13] Arminius, *De bonis operibus* (1609), ix; idem, *De bonis operibus* (1603), x; idem, *De*

to one's certainty of salvation is of utmost concern for our overall investigation, and we will explore it later. For now, it is important to note the unanimous agreement on the causes of good works in the regenerate.

Arminius and his contemporaries all agreed that a person is not justified by works; thus, good works have no efficacy for justification, but instead are the fruit of faith. Junius reasoned, "Therefore when we profess that we are justified by faith alone, we exclude all our works and merits as most foreign to the cause of justification."[14] In a disputation of pure polemic against the Roman Catholic view of working to merit salvation, Kuchlinus refers—with both wit and irony—to the "works of supererogation" as "works of super-arrogance."[15] In other words, to think that a person can go above and beyond the divine call of duty and contribute to justification is indeed arrogant. Trelcatius claimed, "Good works do not precede justifying, but follow having been justified."[16] At the same time, as Trelcatius indicates, there appears to be a firm emphasis on the necessity of good works for salvation. Arminius said that good works are a *caussa* and assistance in the mode of salvation, a *sine qua non* of the saved. Good works are a condition to be performed by us if we wish to be saved, "inasmuch as without which the possession of salvation is impossible to be obtained."[17] This strong necessity language is not restricted to Arminius, for Gomarus used similarly strong language, calling good works the way to the heavenly kingdom.[18] According to Kuchlinus, justification and sanctification are inseparable gifts of God.[19] The Leiden theologians stressed that, since the Holy Spirit lives in believers as his temple, he cannot be idle, as it were, on vacation (*otiosus*).[20] In its effort to steer clear of justification by works on the

---

imaginis Dei restitutione (1605), viii; Gomarus, *De bonis operibus* (1599), x–xi; Kuchlinus, *De conditionibus*, xiii; Trelcatius, *De bonis operibus* (1606), xii. Cf. *Disp. pub.* XII.v. This threefold end corresponds with Ursinus and Olevianus, *Heidelberg Catechism*, Q&A 86. Cf. Zacharias Ursinus, *Compendium*, p. 648; *Summe*, p. 811.

[14] Junius, *De differentia* (1600), x: "Quum igitur sola fide nos justificari profitemur, omnia opera et merita nostra a caussa justificationis alienissima excludimus."

[15] Kuchlinus, *Disputatio* ἐλεγτικὴ[*sic*] *de meritis bonorum operum*, Isebrandus Guilielmius respondens, in *Theo. disp.* 84, pp. 522–32, xv: "opera Supererogationis...opera Superarrogationis." Cf. Arminius, *De bonis operibus* (1609), xi–xii.

[16] Trelcatius, *De iustificatione* (1604), xx: "Bona opera non praecedunt justificandum, sed sequuntur justificatum."

[17] Arminius, *De bonis operibus* (1609), x.

[18] Gomarus, *De bonis operibus* (1599), xi.

[19] Kuchlinus, *De certitudine* (1603), xv.

[20] Junius, *Disputatio theologica de salutis fidelium certitudine pro asserenda fiducia*, Ioannes vander Haghe respondens, 3 February 1601 (Leiden, 1601), x. Cf. Kuchlinus, *Theses*

one hand and antinomianism on the other hand, Reformed orthodoxy described good works as a necessary consequence of justification, but avoided confusing good works with justification. As the necessary fruit of justification, good works were thought to provide a sign of one's election, which is how they contributed to assurance. Here, too, Arminius's formulations are consistent with those of his colleagues and representative of the Leiden theology of his day.

C. *Sanctification as Cooperative and Progressive*

Sanctification is a cooperative effort between the Spirit of God and the regenerate person. According to Kuchlinus, the Spirit living in the believer is freshened and enlivened by good works so that the person can continue to resist the temptations of the devil.[21] For Arminius, it is by the Spirit who is present in our midst that we are able to walk in God's statutes.[22] Arminius declares, "God does this in us, but he does not perfect without us; he acts in us so that we might act."[23] Thus, God does not sanctify a person against that person's will, which corresponds with Arminius's view of justification.

Sanctification is also a progressive part of the Christian life—progressive in the sense of steady, ongoing, gradual improvement. Arminius explains that this sanctification for service is not completed in a single moment. For sin, which is still present, must go through a daily weakening process at the same time that the inner person is being daily renewed.[24] Junius declares that those who possess the Holy Spirit have mortified the works of the flesh and put on the new person. This penitence is not completed in one moment, day, or year, but it is gradual.[25] Kuchlinus writes, "He also sends his Holy Spirit, by whose virtue the lusts of the flesh are mortified; but we are regenerated, and day by day we are more and more sanctified."[26]

---

theologicae de bonorum operum necessitate, Ioannes Arnoldus respondens, in *Theo. disp.* 82, pp. 510–16, xii.

[21] Kuchlinus, *De necessitate*, ix.

[22] Arminius, *De imaginis Dei restitutione* (1605), vii.

[23] Arminius, *De imaginis Dei resititutione* (1605), viii: "Haec facit Deus in nobis, sed non perficit sine nobis, agit nobis ut nos agamus."

[24] *Disp. priv.* XLIX.xii; *Disp. pub.* XI.xiii.

[25] Junius, *De certitudine* (1601), xi.

[26] Kuchlinus, *De necessitate*, xi: "Mittit etiam Spiritum suum sanctum cuius virtute carnis concupiscentiae mortificantur: nos vero regeneramur, et indies magis ac magis sanctificamur."

II. *The Efficacy of Sanctification*

Two controversial issues frequently accompany discussions of the topic
of sanctification. These issues—namely, perfection and perseverance—
both concern the extent of sanctification, and they directly affect the
doctrine of the assurance of salvation. The first issue, the possibility
of perfection, concerns the extent of the transformational efficacy of
sanctification in the life of the regenerate. The epistle of First John, a
document devoted to the assurance of salvation, can be appealed to as
a summary of the tension involved in the issue of perfection. "If we
say that we do not have sin, we deceive ourselves and the truth is not
in us" (ἐὰν εἴπωμεν ὅτι ἁμαρτίαν οὐκ ἔχομεν, ἑαυτοὺς πλανῶμεν καὶ ἡ
ἀλήθεια οὐκ ἔστιν ἐν ἡμῖν) (1 Jn. 1,8). This simple, generally accepted
truth is juxtaposed in the same letter with straightforward statements
such as the following: "Everyone who has been begotten of God does not
do sin, because his seed remains in him, and he cannot sin, because he
has been begotten of God" (Πᾶς ὁ γεγεννημένος ἐκ τοῦ θεοῦ ἁμαρτίαν
οὐ ποιεῖ, ὅτι σπέρμα αὐτοῦ ἐν αὐτῷ μένει, καὶ οὐ δύναται ἁμαρτάνειν,
ὅτι ἐκ τοῦ θεοῦ γεγέννηται) (1 Jn. 3,9). Based on this verse, at the very
least, there is some kind of change in a person's relationship to sin after
regeneration; the most direct reading, of course, denies the very possibility of sin in the regenerate.

A. *The State of the Unregenerate*

In light of the above texts and the historical debates preceding the Reformation, how, then, did the Reformed orthodox deal with the problem of Christian perfection? It is important to understand, first of all,
that the perfection of the unregenerate was ubiquitously regarded as
impossible.[27] Legal justification, by which those who perfectly observe
the law are justified, is impossible. Legal justification would mean that
God justifies out of debt; rather, evangelical justification is out of mercy.
According to Arminius, even Roman Catholics denied the possibility
of legal justification by perfection.[28] However, many Catholics con-
tended that free choice in spiritual matters had not been completely
extinguished. They based this assertion on, among other things, the

---

[27] Gomarus, *De perfectione* (1601), iii–v.
[28] Arminius, *De iustificatione* (1603), vi; *Disp. pub.* XIX.vii–ix.

parable of the good Samaritan. According to Lk. 10,30, the man who fell among robbers was left ἡμιθανής (*semivivus*). This parable had long been used in church tradition as an allegory of a sinner (half-dead man) being justified or healed by Christ (Samaritan). This interpretation can be seen at least as early as Origen, who also described the beaten man as *seminex* and *semianimis*.[29] The application of this parable to Christ healing a sinner remained the standard interpretation even for the reformers.[30] On the one hand, according to Augustine's interpretation, the *semivivus* man represents humanity losing the power of free choice after the fall.[31] In other words, Augustine's interpretation of the parable has a definite anti-Pelagian flavor to it. On the other hand, according to a prominent late medieval Catholic interpretation, the fact that the man was only half-dead meant he was still spiritually half-alive and that he retained some spiritual ability, contra the interpretation of Augustine.

Once again, the Leiden theologians were in agreement against the use of this parable to describe the spiritual condition of a corrupt, unregenerate person as half-alive and somewhat able to choose the good. Gomarus insisted that the *pontificii* "shamefully err" when they contend that free choice in spiritual things has not been taken away, but has merely been troubled and is only half-dead or half-alive.[32] According to Kuchlinus, the *pontificii* "gravely hallucinate" when they teach from the parable on the man left half-alive (*de homine semivivo relicto*) that something sane remained in human nature.[33] When Arminius describes this corrupt state of free choice, he asserts that the will to good is useless if it is not assisted by divine grace, and that fallen humanity's mind, affections, will, capability, and life itself are all captive and destroyed.[34] In fact, he declares that in this state humanity is "entirely dead in sins."[35] This allusion employed against a common Catholic use of the parable of the semi-dead man shows Arminius's solidarity with his colleagues on the issue of the total inability of fallen humanity regarding salvation.

---

[29] Origen, *In Lucam homiliae*, 34, in *Origenis opera omnia*, vol. 4 (Berlin, 1834).

[30] E.g., see Luther, *In Epistolam Pauli ad Galatas M. Lutheri commentarius*, in *WA* 2:495; *LW* 27:227.

[31] Augustine, *Sermo* 131.6; *PL* 38:732.

[32] Gomarus, *De libero arbitrio* (Gruterus, 1603), xvii. Idem, *De libero arbitrio* (1607), iv, specifies that "totum hominis esse corruptum."

[33] Kuchlinus, *De statu hominis* (1603), xii.

[34] *Disp. pub.* XI.vii.

[35] *Disp. pub.* XI.xi.

B. *The State of the Regenerate*

Since the issue is about the life of sanctification, the relevant question of perfection concerns the sinner who has been justified by grace through faith. Exactly how much progress can a justified sinner make in this life on the road of sanctification? One place to find an answer to this question is in the question *de libero arbitrio*, specifically with regard to the regenerate, or third, state. As has been pointed out already, there is a difference between the corrupted and the regenerate *arbitrium*, that is, between the second and third states of humanity. Although it is in this context that the beginning of differences concerning sanctification may be perceived between Arminius and the other Leiden theologians, the Leiden disputations on this topic are very similar to one another. According to Gomarus, the transition from the second state to the third and last state in this age, namely, the state of regeneration, happens by conversion, the conversion of the Spirit to humanity and then humanity to God.[36] The change occurring at regeneration, however, is only partial. "We assert that, in this state, humanity has a mixed choice, partly to good, partly to evil."[37] The intellect and will still function, but have been irrevocably damaged in the fall, an injury that regeneration does not remedy by itself. Justification is perfect, but sanctification will only be perfected after this life. Gomarus goes on to say, "But also the free choice of the regenerate person is said to be carried to evil, because the intellect knows the good only in part, and the will still inclines to evil."[38] Kuchlinus affirmed that the free choice of saints still living in the flesh is never perfectly free, for it sometimes does good, but other times declines to evil; living saints cannot perfectly carry out good deeds.[39] Arminius agreed that even the regenerate person still carries around the remains of sin, and so is far from perfection and complete conformity to the law.[40]

Further evidence against the actuality of perfection in this life revolves around the common use of what I designate the "*lucta* theme."

---

[36] Gomarus, *De libero arbitrio* (Gruterus, 1603), xviii–xix.

[37] Gomarus, *De libero arbitrio* (Gruterus, 1603), xviii: "In hoc statu hominem mixtum arbitrium partim ad bonum partim ad malum habere asserimus."

[38] Gomarus, *De libero arbitrio* (Gruterus, 1603), xx: "Ad malum vero etiam dicitur hominis regenerati liberum arbitrium ferri, quia intellectus ex parte tantum bonum cognoscit, et voluntas ad mala etiamnum inclinat."

[39] Kuchlinus, *De statu hominis* (1603), viii.

[40] Arminius, *De bonis operibus* (1603), viii; idem, *De bonis operibus* (1609), viii.

Lucta, or wrestling, although not found in the Latin Vulgate, was a word that became a common description of the relationship between flesh and Spirit. The idea of the Christian life as a wrestling match is in the New Testament. According to Eph. 6,12, believers are in a wrestling match (πάλη) (*conluctatio*) with rulers, authorities, and cosmic powers. The struggle between the flesh and the Spirit particularly is felt in Gal. 5,17, where the flesh lusts (*concupiscit*) against the Spirit, and the Spirit against the flesh. Although *lucta* is not mentioned in this famous passage from Galatians, the description of this lust between flesh and Spirit as a wrestling (*lucta*) is an influential metaphor that goes back at least to Augustine, who says of this passage, "there is seen as if a kind of *lucta* of two enemies, between the flesh and the Spirit."[41]

The Leiden theologians continued the tradition of describing the Christian life as a *lucta* between the flesh and Spirit, and, for that reason, the Christian life is a participation in sanctification that remains incomplete and imperfect in this life. Arminius, like his predecessor Junius, said there is a *lucta* of the Spirit against the flesh, and he described consciences *luctantes* with temptation.[42] Gomarus remarks that the flesh always lusts against the Spirit, so that it is perpetually wrestling (*luctandum*) against it. He thus concludes that even the regenerate cannot perform any command from a whole heart, and their obedience is not perfect, for sin cannot be removed from this obedience.[43] Kuchlinus notes that sacred Scripture urges all Christians "to the wrestling (*Luctam*) against lusts."[44] This *lucta* Kuchlinus takes as proof of the imperfection of even the most holy people.[45] Kuchlinus elsewhere specifies that the *lucta* takes place between the Holy Spirit and the flesh.[46] In sum, both Arminius and his colleagues stressed the traditional notion that the Christian life is a wrestling between the flesh and Spirit (or spirit). We can conclude at this point that, whether or not perfection is theoretically possible in this

---

[41] Augustine, *De utilitate jejunii sermo* 4; *PL* 40:710; idem, *De continentia* 2.5; *PL* 40:352. Cf. idem, *Contra secundam Juliani responsionem imperfectum opus* 6.14; *PL* 45:1527: "Unde et in sanctis, in hujus vitae agone luctantibus, caro concupiscit adversus spiritum, et spiritus adversus carnem."

[42] Arminius, *De fide* (1605), xv; *Disp. pub.* XV.xiv. Cf. Junius, *De differentia* (1600), iii.

[43] Gomarus, *De perfectione* (1601), vii. Cf. idem, *De libero arbitrio* (1607), x.

[44] Kuchlinus, *De peccato originali* (de Riick), xxii: "...ad Luctam contra concupiscentias."

[45] Kuchlinus, *Disputatio* ἐλεκτικὴ[*sic*] *de perfectione hominis in hac vita*, ad quaest. catechet. 114 & 115, Ioannes Narsius respondens, in *Theo. disp.* 129, pp. 818–23, vi.

[46] Kuchlinus, *De statu hominis* (1603), viii.

life, it is at least deemed practically unrealistic. Furthermore, up to this point, there is no considerable divergence between Arminius and the other faculty members.

In addition to the overall concurrence among the Leiden faculty on the issue of progress in the life of sanctification, subtle differences can be detected between Arminius and his colleagues. Despite the fact that the Leiden theologians all describe the Christian life as *lucta* and the regenerate person as still carried to evil, Arminius seems to imply a greater contrast between the second and third states of *liberum arbitrium* than his colleagues recognize. After depicting in great detail the inability of the unregenerate to move toward salvation apart from God's grace, Arminius transitions to the regenerate state of sanctification with the phrase, "But far different..." (*At vero longe*).[47] This suggestive transition indicates how Arminius laid more emphasis on the difference between the unregenerate and the regenerate state of free choice, thus maintaining the total inability of the unregenerate but also placing more stress on the possibility of progress in the regenerate Christian life than did some of his Reformed contemporaries. In his short summary of the issue before the states of Holland, Arminius declared that the regenerate person is made free (*vry ghemaeckt*) from sin and, with the help of God's grace, able to think, will and do good.[48] As far as the language in the disputations goes, Arminius's Reformed colleagues would not disagree with his assertions, for Arminius represents here a difference of emphasis and not a difference of core content.

Arminius's difference of content, along with his greater emphasis on the possibility of moral progress, is more explicit in his interpretation of Romans 7.[49] Arminius provides a long and detailed exegesis, but his chief point can be easily summarized for this discussion. Many of his Reformed contemporaries, following the later Augustine, interpreted the *ego* of Romans 7 as a regenerate person who continues to struggle with sin.[50] Arminius rejected this interpretation, claiming that Paul was

---

[47] *Disp. pub.* XI.xii.

[48] *Dec. sent.*, p. 113; *Works* 1:660.

[49] See *Cap. VII Rom.*, in *Opera*, pp. 809–934; *Works* 2:471–683, passim.

[50] David C. Steinmetz, *Calvin in Context* (New York, 1995), pp. 110–21, offers a typology for the interpretation of Romans 7 in the sixteenth century. This Reformed interpretation was standard in the sixteenth century, based on the exegesis of the later Augustine. Arminius's interpretation was in step with the early church fathers, the earlier Augustine, and many medieval commentators.

describing an unregenerate person. According to Rom. 6,14, sin has no dominion over the regenerate person, for he is now under grace. Arminius pointed out that Romans 7 is describing a person who is captive under sin, that is, sin has dominion over this person (Rom. 7,14). Thus, according to Arminius, Paul is describing a person who is hopelessly losing the battle against sin, and this pessimism is transferred into the low expectations for Christian sanctification exhibited by the Reformed contemporaries of Arminius. For Arminius, the pessimism of Romans 7 describes the unregenerate and is mitigated by the optimism regarding the regenerate person who walks by the Spirit in Romans 6 and 8, a person who is free from sin.

At this point, the *"lucta* theme" enters the scene again. Arminius's opponents declared that since Rom. 7,15 describes a *lucta*, and a *lucta* of this kind can only happen in the regenerate, therefore Romans 7 describes the struggle of the regenerate. Arminius objected, affirming that Scripture depicts a *duplex lucta* against sin: "One between the flesh and the mind or conscience; the other between the flesh or sin and the Spirit."[51] The former *lucta*, which is described in Romans 7 and does not presuppose the indwelling of the Holy Spirit, may obtain in anyone who knows right from wrong, even in an unregenerate, or not yet regenerate, person. The latter *lucta* between the flesh and the Holy Spirit only obtains in those whom the Spirit indwells, the regenerate. The difference between these two *luctae* is manifest from the consequence (*ex eventus*): in the former the flesh "usually" (reading *plerumque* for *plaerunque*) conquers, but in the latter the Spirit "usually" overcomes and is superior.[52] Yes, the regenerate sometimes fulfill the lusts of the flesh, but this happens only "at times" (*aliquando*).[53] Arminius considered that his view of the state of the regenerate attributes more to the power of divine grace than his opponents were willing to recognize, for he considered their pessimism to reflect their attenuated view of sanctifying grace.[54] In the end, both Arminius and his colleagues admitted that the Christian life is a *lucta*. The difference is that Arminius thinks the regenerate Christian, through

---

[51] *Cap. VII Rom.*, in *Opera*, p. 842; *Works* 2:518–19: "una carnis et mentis sive conscientiae; altera eiusdem carnis sive peccati et Spiritus."

[52] *Cap. VII Rom.*, in *Opera*, pp. 842–43; *Works* 2:519–20. Cf. idem, *Cap. VII Rom.*, in *Opera*, pp. 868–69; *Works* 2:566–67.

[53] *Cap. VII Rom.*, in *Opera*, pp. 871–72; *Works* 2:571–72.

[54] *Cap. VII Rom.*, in *Opera*, p. 919; *Works* 2:656–57.

God's empowering grace, prevails, or ought to prevail, in the struggle more often than not. Of course, "usually" and "at times" are all relative terms, which underscores that even the practical implications of the differing interpretations of Romans 7 result in a difference of emphasis more than a fundamental contradiction.[55]

C. *The Possibility of Perfection*

Because of Arminius's more optimistic view of the life of sanctification, he was accused of holding what some understood to be Pelagian sympathies, namely, that the regenerate can perfectly (*volcomelijc*) keep God's commands in this life, living in this life without sin.[56] When the subject came up, Arminius indicated that he had never committed to one opinion and that the matter still deserved investigation.[57] As Arminius ultimately appeals to Augustine on this issue, he also cites Augustine's own reluctance to get involved in the issue. After affirming perfection in the life to come, Augustine said, "But I do not wish to contend about this life."[58] For Arminius, it is vastly more important to strive toward perfection rather than spend time debating whether it is attainable.[59]

Nevertheless, the possibility of perfection is an important question inasmuch as it was a topic of dispute between Augustine and the Pelagians. Concerning the issue of fufilling God's commands, Pelagius, according to Augustine,[60] distinguishes between *posse (possibilitas)*,

---

[55] The Leiden theologians would all agree with Zanchi's assertion that the regenerate do more good than the unregenerate, but not to the extent where they cannot sin. Cf. Zanchi, *De religione*, pp. 200–04; *H. Zanchius his confession of Christian religion, Which now at length being 70. yeares of age, he caused to bee published in the name of himselfe and his family* ([Cambridge, Eng.,] 1599), pp. 157–62.

[56] *Dec. sent.*, p. 116; *Works* 1:673–75; *Apologia*, art. 29 (9), in *Opera*, p. 178; *Works* 2:55.

[57] *Dec. sent.*, p. 116; *Works* 1:675–78.

[58] Augustine, *De natura et gratia ad Timasium et Jacobum contra Pelagium* 60.70; *PL* 44:281: "Sed ego nec de ista vita volo contendere." Cf. *Cap. VII Rom.*, in *Opera*, p. 907; *Works* 2:634.

[59] *Apologia*, art. 29 (9), in *Opera*, p. 179; *Works* 2:56.

[60] This summary of Pelagianism is according to Augustine's synthesis. This "Pelagian" synthesis, including Augustine's documented reaction to it, was a decisive influence in the subsequent history of Western theology, and particularly in the Leiden debate, and is therefore presented here in Augustine's categories. However, it is worth noting that patristic scholarship has challenged this traditional view of a dogmatically coherent Pelagianism. E.g., see Mathijs Lamberigts, 'Pelagianism: From an Ethical Religious Movement to a Heresy and Back Again,' trans. John Bowden, in *'Movements' in the Church*, ed. Alberto Melloni (London, 2003), pp. 39–48, there pp. 44–45: "In his reaction, not always correctly, he [Augustine] brought the scattered views of opponents

velle (voluntas), and *esse (actio)*. Of these three faculties, God only gives the ability (*posse*) to do good, and that through nature. A person wills (*velle*) and does (*esse*) good on her own apart from God's direct, assisting grace; good will and action are simply based on God-given capability. Therefore, Pelagius considered humanity's willing and doing good to be only indirectly God-given.[61] For Pelagius, the *possibilitas* of not sinning is implanted in nature, whose author is God.[62] The difference, then, between Augustine and Pelagius is the role of grace in the willing and doing. If only Pelagius would acknowledge the help of grace in the Christian's willing and doing in addition to the capacity, then Augustine confesses there would be no controversy between them on this issue.[63] Because of this potential common ground, the anti-Pelagian Augustine left the question of the possibility of perfection open, "For whether in this world there was, or is, or can be someone living so righteously that he has entirely no sin, there can be some question among true and pious Christians."[64] What was not open for discussion, according to Augustine, is that the fullest perfection can only be realized by the assisting grace of Christ and gift of the Spirit, contra the implanted nature proposed by Pelagius.[65]

One must recognize that the early Arminius of the Romans 7 treatise seems to allow little if any *possibility* of perfection in the regenerate. There he implies that perfection of righteousness in this life would suggest a cessation of the *lucta* between the flesh and the Holy Spirit, a struggle that he considered to be an essential part of the Christian life of sanctification.[66] Ruling out the possibility of perfection, it is no wonder

---

(not all of whom were real opponents) into a synthesis and then criticized them." On the issue of Pelagian perfection in particular, cf. the comment in idem, 'Le mal et le péché. Pélage: La rehabilitation d'un hérétique,' *Revue d'histoire ecclésiastique* 95 (2000), 97–111, there 103: "L'idée de l'*impeccantia*, si fréquemment allouée à Pélage et perçue comme une prevue de son arrogance doctrinale, se fonde sur la critique injuste émise par Jérôme."

[61] Augustine, *De gratia Christi et de peccato originali contra Pelagium et Coelestium* 3.4–4.5; *PL* 44:361–62.

[62] Augustine, *De natura et gratia* 51.59; *PL* 44:275.

[63] Augustine, *De gratia Christi* 47.52; *PL* 44:383–84.

[64] Augustine, *De natura et gratia* 60.70; *PL* 44:281: "Utrum enim in hoc saeculo fuerit, vel sit, vel possit esse aliquis ita juste vivens, ut nullum habeat omnino peccatum, potest esse aliqua quaestio inter veros piosque Christianos."

[65] Augustine, *De natura et gratia* 60.70; *PL* 44:282: "Nullo tamen modo nisi adjuvante gratia salvatoris Christi crucifixi, et dono Spiritus ejus...."

[66] *Cap. VII Rom.*, in *Opera*, p. 825; *Works* 2:489.

that Arminius at this stage categorically denied that the regenerate perfectly will, much less perfectly do, the good: "For the regenerate do not
perfectly will the good as long as they are in this mortal life."[67] Even in
1605, Arminius notes that the most perfect of the regenerate still sin.[68]
It is perhaps an indication of some theological development that the
later Arminius claims that perfect fulfillment of God's law is possible if
it is according to God's ἐπιείκεια (clemency) and if appropriate empow-
erment is given.[69] Thus, to say that it is merely possible for a regenerate
person to perform the law perfectly in this life by God's assisting grace
does not make one guilty of Pelagianism.[70] It is clear from Arminius's
disputations and apologetic treatises that, like Augustine, he regarded
God's assisting grace to be necessary along every step on the road of
sanctification.[71] At the same time, the fact that the later Arminius seems
more open to the possibility of perfection does not indicate that he
thinks it actually happens. In sum, he says that the question *de potentia*
is of no great importance as long as a person confesses with Augustine
that perfection can only be achieved by the grace of Christ.[72]

The possibility of perfection became controversial in Arminius's context because his colleagues did not consider it a question for debate,
but outright rejected the notion. It could be that Dutch Anabaptist and
spiritualist claims of perfection, so frequently denounced by Reformed
theologians and churchmen in the low countries during the 1580s and
1590s, served as a contributing factor to their antipathy toward such
ideas.[73] Any approbation of perfection in this present life could inevitably suggest a connection with the so-called "libertines." At any rate,
the other Leiden theologians were clear on the topic. For Junius, "God
indeed perfectly justifies us in this life, but does not [perfectly] sanctify."[74]

---

[67] *Cap. VII Rom.*, in *Opera*, p. 854; *Works* 2:540: "Nam regeniti bonum perfecte non
volunt dum sunt in hac mortali vita."

[68] *Disp. pub.* XV.xiii.

[69] Arminius, *Quaestiones*, resp. 9, in *Opera*, p. 186; *Works* 2:68.

[70] *Art. non.*, in *Opera*, p. 961; *Works* 2:724–25.

[71] E.g., *Disp. pub.* XV.xiv.

[72] Arminius, *Quaestiones*, resp. 9, in *Opera*, p. 186; *Works* 2:68.

[73] See Mirjam G. K. van Veen, 'Spiritualism in The Netherlands: From David Joris
to Dirck Volckertsz Coornhert,' *SCJ* 33/1 (2002), 129–50, there 140–50; idem, '"No
One Born of God Commits Sin": Coornhert's Perfectionism,' *NAKG* 84 (2004), 338–57,
there 340: "In the Low Countries this belief in the possibility of leading a perfect life
was widespread, and the Reformed Church in the Low Countries regarded it as a serious menace to the Reformed doctrines of justification and sanctification."

[74] Junius, *De differentia* (1600), xvii: "Deus igitur perfecte nos quidem in hac vita justificat, sed non sanctificat."

In their disputations on the topic of perfection, Gomarus and Kuchlinus distinguish four different types of perfection; *graduum perfectio*, that is, the highest degree of obedience that the law requires, is the kind under consideration.[75] They deny perfection of the regenerate, but do not deal with the perfection passages from Scripture or explicitly refer to Augustine on this issue.[76] In addition, they do not make an explicit distinction between possibility and actuality of Christian perfection; at times they claim that it *cannot* happen, and at other times affirm that it *does not* happen. Like the early Arminius, Gomarus and Kuchlinus assume that the presence of a *lucta* between the flesh and Spirit rules out the possibility of perfection.[77] Furthermore, according to Gomarus, good works must arise from faith, but faith is imperfect in this life, therefore even the best works of the regenerate remain imperfect in this life as well.[78] Gomarus appeals primarily to Scripture and experience to demonstrate that no one keeps the law perfectly. Therefore, our only perfection is to recognize our imperfection.[79] For Kuchlinus, the "ought" of the law implies "can," but only with reference to eschatological perfection.[80] Nevertheless, Kuchlinus emphasizes that the law is still important in this life, and that denying perfection should not lead to antinomianism, "for he will not obtain perfection in the future life, who does not have inchoate obedience in this life."[81] Likewise, Kuchlinus's disputation on original sin closes with a moral exhortation that Christians should be humbled by their imperfection, implore God's help, and contend for a "measure of perfection."[82] This exhortation is similar to Arminius's assertion that striving after perfection is to be preferred over disputing about it. In the

---

[75] Gomarus, *De perfectione* (1601), i; Kuchlinus, *De perfectione*, ii.

[76] At the conclusion of his disputation, Kuchlinus quotes Augustine, but not from the relevant documents cited above that would challenge his denial of the possibility of perfection. On the difficult passages of 1 John, cf. Theodore Beza, *Quaestionum et responsionum Christianarum libellus* (London, 1571), p. 73; *A booke of Christian questions and answers* (London, 1574), fol. 47; Taffin, *Marks*, p. 56.

[77] Gomarus, *De perfectione* (1601), vii; Kuchlinus, *De perfectione*, vi. Cf. idem, *De peccato originali* (Geesteranus, 1602), xiv–xv and xviii.

[78] Gomarus, *De perfectione* (1601), vii–viii.

[79] Gomarus, *De perfectione* (1601), x.

[80] Kuchlinus, *De perfectione*, xv. Cf. Gomarus, *De libero arbitrio* (Gruterus, 1603), xx.

[81] Kuchlinus, *De perfectione*, x: "quia perfectionem in futura vita non obtinebit, qui inchoatam in hac vita obedientiam non habet. Habenti enim dabitur."

[82] Kuchlinus, *De peccato originali* (Geesteranus, 1602), xviii: "...serio imperfectionis nostrae sensu humiliemur, ad implorandum Dei auxilium instigemur, ad propositam nobis perfectionis metam alacriter contendamus."

end, since Arminius is reluctant to affirm the actuality of perfection, there is nothing substantially contradictory among the Leiden theologians on this point, but only a difference of emphasis in the efficacy of the Spirit in sanctification.

III. *The Duration of Sanctification*

If Arminius maintained merely superficial differences from his colleagues in his thoughts on the Spirit's efficacy in sanctification, their differences on the matter of temporal duration, or perseverance, were potentially more substantial. As will be demonstrated, Arminius's distinct doctrine of grace as resistible over against Reformed irresistible grace suggests that perseverance on the road of sanctification, although a gracious gift from God, is nevertheless resistible. These respective doctrines result in consequential differences in one's view of the life of sanctification, which will in turn affect the epistemological question of the assurance of salvation. Gomarus expresses well a common assumption concerning the relationship between perseverance and assurance, "Since the certainty of salvation depends on the perseverance of the saints...."[83]

A. *Perseverance and the Possibility of Apostasy*

It would be inaccurate to claim that Arminius outright denied the doctrine of the perseverance of the saints; as was the case with other controversial Reformed doctrines, his affirmation was founded on a particular, qualified definition. In his *Declaratio sententiae*, Arminius declared his feelings regarding perseverance of the saints: "That those persons who have been grafted into Jesus Christ through a true faith, and have thus been made partakers of his life-giving Spirit, have sufficient power (*cracht*) to fight (*strijden*) against Satan, sin, the world, and their own flesh, and to gain the victory, yet not without the assistance of the grace of the same Spirit."[84] These true believers having thus implored God's help, Christ preserves them from falling, even to the degree that Satan

---

[83] Gomarus, *Theses theologicae de perseverantia sanctorum*, Iacobus Bouveritius, ad diem 19 June 1608 (Leiden, 1608), preface: "Cum ex perseverantia Sanctorum certitudo salutis dependeat...."

[84] *Dec. sent.*, p. 114; *Works* 1:664.

can by no means draw them from Christ's hands.[85] On the surface, Arminius's definition of perseverance is not significantly different from that of Gomarus, who defines perseverance of the saints thus: "It is the endurance of the truly faithful in faith, all the way to the end of life, from God's grace, because of Christ's merit, by virtue of the Holy Spirit through the ministry of the gospel, to the glory of God and salvation of persevering saints."[86] As this definition stands, it is hard to imagine Arminius finding fault with it.[87]

The real question is whether saints necessarily persevere, or if it is possible for them to fall away. When Arminius gave explicit attention to the topic of saints falling away, he usually did not commit himself to a firm opinion. In his work against Perkins early in his career, Arminius wrote that he would not easily dare to say that true and saving faith totally or finally falls away.[88] Even towards the end of his career, he seemed to remain undecided on the issue.[89] Indeed, accounts of the final conference at The Hague two months before his death show that Arminius never opposed the doctrine concerning the certain perseverance of the truly faithful (*vere fidelium*).[90] At the same time, one can easily see the inclinations of Arminius on this topic. Not only is he quick to point out that at no time in the history of the church had any particular viewpoint on this question been regarded as a necessary doctrine, but he also asserts that the majority of the Christian tradition, especially

---

[85] *Dec. sent.*, pp. 114–15; *Works* 1:664–65.

[86] Gomarus, *Theologicarum disputationum decimaoctava: de sanctorum perseverantia*, Henricus Arnoldus respondens, 5 March 1597 (Leiden, 1597), i: "Ea autem est vere fidelium in fide, ad finem usque vitae, ex Dei gratia, propter Christi meritum, virtute S. Sancti per ministerium Evangelii, perduratio, ad gloriam Dei et perseverantium sanctorum salutem." Cf. the definition in idem, *De perseverantia* (1608), ii: "Perseverantia Sanctorum est, qua, qui vinculo non solùm aternae [*sic*] electionis, sed etiam Spiritus Christi, veraeque fidei Christo copulati, in perpetuum in ipso Christo et in fide perseveraturi sunt, ita ut a fide prorsus excidere non possint: idque non propter proprias vires, aut merita, sed tum propter promissionem, et conservationem divinam, tum propter Christi intercessionem et precationem."

[87] Letham, 'Faith,' 1:314, overstates the case when he claims, "Arminius has no doctrine of perseverance."

[88] *Exam. Perk.*, in *Opera*, p. 757; *Works* 3:454.

[89] See *Dec. sent.*, p. 115; *Works* 1:667. The fifth article of the Remonstrance of 1610 is likewise indecisive on this issue because, like the fourth article, it is taken nearly verbatim from Arminius's *Declaratio sententiae*. On the relationship between Arminius's *Declaratio* and the Remonstrance of 1610, see Hoenderdaal, 'Inleiding,' pp. 36–41.

[90] *Acta Synodi*, fol. (d)1v; see also Hommius's letter to Lubbertus in Wijminga, *Hommius*, Bijlage G, p. xiv.

the fathers, would say that it is possible for believers to fall away and perish.[91] Furthermore, when Perkins argued that it is impossible for true faith to fail, Arminius eagerly and ably argued against that view.[92]

Because of Arminius's apparent vacillation on the possibility of apostasy and because of inferences made from his clearer teachings, this subject became yet another area of conflict. It was controversial at Leiden especially because of the plain teachings of his colleagues against the possibility of apostasy. According to Gomarus and Kuchlinus, betrothal to God and union of the faithful with Christ and the church are perpetual.[93] Gomarus points out that the saints are the elect who possess true faith, not the reprobate who may have temporary faith.[94] Kuchlinus is particularly adamant that the saints can neither *toti*, nor *totaliter*, nor *finaliter* abandon their faith.[95] The gift of regeneration is ἀμεταμέλητον (irrevocable), "therefore, once given, the Holy Spirit always remains."[96]

Arminius may at first appear to be uncertain with regard to the possibility of apostasy, but upon further investigation his viewpoint is actually rather straightforward. To understand Arminius's position, two points of distinction are essential. First, Arminius distinguishes between the possibility and the actuality of the faithful falling away. "I say that there ought to be a distinction between possibility and actuality (*potentiam et actum*). For it is one thing for the faithful to be able (*posse*) to defect from faith and salvation: another thing to actually defect."[97] However rarefied this distinction may appear to a modern interpreter, this distinction was important in traditional theology, as evidenced by Augustine's (and Arminius's) appeal to the same distinction in the question of Christian perfection. Arminius went on to say,

> For to be saved actually and to possibly not be saved are not contrary things, but consenting. I therefore add that I have always thus distinguished between these two, so that I have indeed sometimes said with the

---

[91] *Art. non.*, in *Opera*, p. 962; *Works* 2:725; idem, *Exam. Perk.*, in *Opera*, pp. 757–58; *Works* 3:454–55.

[92] *Exam. Perk.*, in *Opera*, pp. 757–66; *Works* 3:454–70.

[93] Gomarus, *De perseverantia* (1597), ix and xi; idem, *De fide iustificante* (1603), xvii; Kuchlinus, *De perseverantia* (1603), v and vii.

[94] Gomarus, *De perseverantia* (1608), vi.

[95] Kuchlinus, *De perseverantia* (1603), i.

[96] Kuchlinus, *De perseverantia* (1603), viii: "ergo semel datus Spiritus Sanctus semper manet." Cf. Trelcatius, Sr., *De fide* (1592), xi, who calls faith the ἀμεταμέλητον gift.

[97] *Apologia*, art. 1–2, in *Opera*, p. 136; *Works* 1:741.

added explanation, that the faithful *are able to* finally defect from faith and salvation; but I never said that the faithful do finally defect from faith and salvation.[98]

Arminius's clear affirmation that he has indeed taught that it is *possible* for believers to fall away from faith and salvation at first glance seems to contradict the equally clear statement in *Declaratio sententiae* that he never taught this possibility. The text as translated by Nichols reads, "I never taught that *a true believer can either totally or finally fall away from the faith, and perish.*"[99] Upon closer investigation of the original texts, however, this apparent contradiction is resolved, for there is no equivalent to the English "can" in the Dutch or Latin. This lack of *connen* or *posse* shows that Arminius was consistent in his teaching on this issue, and that in the *Declaratio* he was speaking of the actuality, not the possibility, of apostasy. The sentence should read, "I roundly declare that I have never taught that the true believer drifts away (*afwijcken*), either totally or finally, from the faith, and is thus lost."[100] Therefore, Arminius affirms the possibility of apostasy; whether it actually happens he seems to leave open for discussion.

The second significant distinction Arminius makes is between an elect person and a believer. He remarks that election to salvation denotes not only belief but also perseverance in that faith. Therefore, an elect person must be both a believer and a perseverer. "Believers and the elect

---

[98] *Apologia*, art. 1–2, in *Opera*, p. 136; *Works* 1:741, italics mine: "Salvari enim actu et posse non salvari contraria non sunt, sed consentanea. Addo igitur me inter ista duo huc usque ita discriminasse, ut addita explicatione aliquando dixerim quidem, fideles *posse* a fide et salute finaliter deficere; at nunquam dixisse fideles a fide et salute finaliter deficere." The italics in Nichols's English translation are confusing, as if the emphasis is on *finaliter*. The real difference is the presence and then absence of *posse*.

[99] In *Works* 1:667.

[100] *Dec. sent.*, p. 115; *Opera*, p. 123. Here lies a point of discontinuity with the later Remonstrants, who, a decade after Arminius's death, affirm not only the possibility, but also the frequent actuality, of apostasy. See *Sententiae Remonstrantium* on the fifth article, delivered at the 34th session of the Synod of Dort, in *Acta synodi nationalis, in nomine Domini nostri Iesu Christi . . . Dordrechti habitae anno M.DC.XVIII. et M.DC.XIX* (Hanau, 1620), p. 166 (emphasis mine): "Vere fideles possunt a vera fide excidere, et in istiusmodi prolabi peccata, quae cum vera et iustificante fide consistere non possunt: *nec potest hoc tantum fieri; sed et non raro fit.*" The *Sententiae Remonstrantium* are translated in *Crisis in the Reformed Churches: Essays in Commemoration of the Great Synod of Dort, 1618–1619*, ed. Peter Y. De Jong (Grand Rapids, 1968), pp. 221–29. Cf. Hoenderdaal, 'Arminius en Episcopius,' 216; Graafland, *Van Calvijn tot Barth: Oorsprong en ontwikkeling van de leer der verkiezing in het Gereformeerd Protestantisme* (The Hague, 1987), p. 175.

are not rightly taken for the same persons."[101] For Arminius, there is
certainly the category of true believers who do not persevere. By this
reasoning, the elect by definition cannot fall away, for they believe and
persevere. Believers *simpliciter* can fall away if they do not persevere, thus
demonstrating themselves not to be elect. Moreover, this judgment corresponds with Arminius's distinction between the faithful falling away
from faith and the faithful falling away from salvation. According to
Arminius, it is incoherent to simply assert that the faithful can fall away
from salvation. It is more proper to say that the faithful can fall away
from faith; then, as unbelievers, they would have no salvation. As long
as believers persevere they have salvation. "For it is impossible for the
faithful, while they remain faithful, to defect from salvation."[102]

To recall Arminius's beggar comparison, because faith is a resistible
gift—because a beggar could presumably reject the alms given to him—
true faith is not necessarily only for the elect. It is probably because of
Gomarus's different view of the irresistibility of grace and faith that
he objected to Arminius's (properly the Jesuits') theoretical distinction
between a true believer and an elect person. At the conclusion of his
disputation on perseverance, Gomarus insisted, "Also badly the Jesuits establish two species of the truly faithful and justified, namely the
elect, who persevere, and the non-elect, who defect."[103] What appears
in Arminius's system is a sort of temporary faith that, despite Gomarus's
objection, is not far different from the Reformed category of temporary faith. The practical similarity between the two systems is that both
would agree that a seemingly faithful person who apparently falls away
until the end has demonstrated that he was not one of the elect.[104] The
similar difficulty for both Arminius and his Reformed contemporaries is
that a person cannot presently tell whether he or anyone else will truly
persevere either in faith or in unbelief.

---

[101] Arminius, *Quaestiones*, resp. 8, in *Opera*, p. 186; *Works* 2:68.

[102] *Apologia*, art. 1–2, in *Opera*, p. 136; *Works* 1:741–42: "Nam impossibile est fideles,
dum fideles manent a salute deficere."

[103] Gomarus, *De perseverantia* (1597), cor. ii: "Male etiam Iesuitae vere fidelium ac
iustificatorum duas constituunt species, videlicet electos, qui perseverant: et non electos,
qui deficiunt."

[104] Cf. Kendall, *Calvin*, pp. 143–45.

B. *The Conditions of Apostasy*

A final relevant question is, given that it is possible for a true believer to fall away from faith and therefore from salvation, what conditions must obtain for such an apostasy to be actualized? Arminius neither directly asks nor responds to this question, but we may draw reasonable inferences from his statements. Because faith is the condition for salvation, Arminius makes it clear that a rejection of faith is what constitutes a falling away from salvation. Union with Christ, which Arminius's colleagues regarded as perpetual, can be nullified if the faith which effects that union is lost.[105] Just as the gift of faith is received—that is, not rejected—by free choice, so defection consists of a free choice defecting.[106] As Paul testifies in Rom. 11,20, some branches are indeed broken off because of unbelief (*infidelitas*).[107]

If it is clear that explicit rejection of faith is sufficient to constitute a falling away, it is less clear whether Arminius thinks that apostasy can be the result of sins of commission. Arminius's statement quoted above, that "it is impossible for the faithful (*fideles*) to defect from salvation as long as they remain faithful," has caused confusion regarding whether sins are a contributing factor to apostasy. One theologian interprets Arminius as saying, "The only way a Christian can lose salvation is by renouncing his or her faith in Christ."[108] Another modern interpreter, who claims to hold "the view of Jacobus Arminius himself," argues that since faith alone, and not works, makes one justified, then unbelief alone, and not sin, makes one "unjustified."[109] In other words, these theologians claim that only an overt renunciation of faith could cause a Christian to lose salvation; commission of sin *per se*, in which all believers participate, has no relation to one's salvation. Or, to put this argument more succinctly, sanctification (or lack thereof) should have no positive or negative effect whatsoever on justification.

---

[105] *Exam. Perk.*, in *Opera*, p. 762; *Works* 3:460: "But no one exists (*existit*) in Christ except by faith in Christ, which is the necessary means of our union with Christ. Because if it happens that someone defects (*deficere*) from faith, he defects from the union, and consequently from the favor of God by which he was earlier embraced in Christ."

[106] *Exam. Perk.*, in *Opera*, p. 758; *Works* 3:455: "Defectus enim est liberi arbitrii deficientis."

[107] *Exam. Perk.*, in *Opera*, p. 760; *Works* 3:458.

[108] J. Matthew Pinson, 'Introduction,' in *Four Views on Eternal Security*, ed. J. Matthew Pinson (Grand Rapids, 2002), pp. 7–19, there p. 15.

[109] Ashby, 'Reformed Arminian,' pp. 137 and 187. Kendall, *Calvin*, pp. 143–45, does not treat this important issue in any detail in his chapter on Arminius.

This idea that Arminius only allowed absolute unbelief, and not just any sin, to be the condition of apostasy seems to cohere with many of his statements. However, this view falls short, first, because it does not take into account the clear passages where Arminius does connect the commission of sin with apostasy; second, because it does not appreciate the nuances of the various causes of sin; and third, because it does not acknowledge the nuances of the nature of faith in its relation to sinful deeds.

First, Arminius, like his contemporaries, gravitated to the example of David when the issue of apostasy surfaced. Kuchlinus, for example, mentions that David's fall (*lapsus*) was not enough to dismiss the Holy Spirit from him.[110] Unlike his colleagues, however, Arminius used the example of David not only to demonstrate that a true believer can fall away, but also how sin itself, and not just unbelief, could cause a believer to fall away. Against Perkins's doctrine of perseverance, Arminius entertains the possibility that David indeed did lose the Holy Spirit after committing adultery and murder.[111] When discussing the regenerate state of humanity, Arminius says, "But if it happens that reborn persons (*renatos*) fall into sin, they neither repent nor rise again unless they are resuscitated by God through the power of his Spirit, and are renewed to repentance (*poenitentiam*), which is most firmly proved by the examples of David and of Peter."[112] Whatever Arminius has in mind, it involves a falling away from something and a rising again, and David is the prime example.

Arminius discusses this example more clearly in an article on the regenerate:

> VI. The regenerate can grieve the Holy Spirit by their sins, so that for a season, until they allow (*patiantur*) themselves to be led back to repentance, he does not exert his power and efficacy in them.
> VII. Some regenerate thus sin, thus they spoil (*vastant*) the conscience, thus they do grieve the Holy Spirit.
> VIII. If David had died at that moment in which he sinned against Uriah by adultery and homicide, he would have been damned (*fuisset condemnatus*) to eternal death.[113]

---

[110] Kuchlinus, *De perseverantia* (1603), xi.
[111] *Exam. Perk.*, in *Opera*, pp. 763–64; *Works* 3:463.
[112] *Disp. pub.* XI.xiv. Contra Ashby, 'Reformed Arminian,' pp. 182–83.
[113] *Art. non.*, in *Opera*, p. 961; *Works* 2:725.

Notice first that not only does Arminius acknowledge that the regenerate *can* grieve the Holy Spirit, but also that some in fact *do*. He still stops short of affirming that anyone has actually fallen without returning. Furthermore, Arminius says nothing of faith or unbelief in this article, but it is sin that grieves the Spirit, causing the Spirit to be ineffective. Arminius specifies that a grieved Holy Spirit who is rendered ineffective by sin is tantamount to a loss of salvation, as Arminius speculates would have happened in the case of David. It is true that the *Articuli nonnulli* originally were accompanied by indications of strong or qualified affirmation, or of strong or qualified negation; because of the absence of these indicators in the extant editions, one might question whether Arminius actually affirmed the above quotation. I conclude, however, that he did affirm this view that sin can cause a person to fall, for he explicitly corroborates it in a letter to Uytenbogaert: "But it is possible for a believer to fall into a mortal sin, as is seen in David. Therefore he can fall (*potest incidere*) at that moment in which if he were to die, he would be condemned."[114]

Second, to claim that Arminius thought sins alone cannot effect apostasy ignores the fact that Arminius acknowledges that a certain class of sins indeed can condemn a believer. Arminius affirms that not all sins are equal.[115] Although the wages of all sins is death, sins are not equal, for they are motivated by a variety of causes. Arminius enumerates four causes of sin: *ignorantia, infirmitas, malitia,* and *negligentia*. Which of these motivations for sin could cause a believer to fall? Distinct from the other three causes, sin *ex malitia* is "when something is committed with a determined purpose of mind (*animi*) and with deliberate counsel." Arminius suggests that Judas denying Christ and David having Uriah killed are examples of this sin out of malice.[116] Since Judas's condition is uncontested, and since Arminius has already revealed that David's sin caused a fall, then the sin out of malice is the kind that would cause a regenerate person to fall. In his letter on the topic of the sin against the

---

[114] *Ep. ecc.* 81, p. 151; *Works* 2:70. It is probable that the Remonstrants also had the example of David in mind at the Synod of Dort, when they talked about true believers falling into grave and most atrocious sins such as *adulteria et homicidia*. See *Sententiae Remonstrantium* 5.6.5, in *Acta Synodi*, p. 167.

[115] *Disp. pub.* VIII.ix. Modern interpreters of this issue in Arminius fail to grasp his nuanced categories and causes of sin. Cf. Pinson, 'Introduction,' p. 15; with Ashby, 'Reformed Arminian,' pp. 180–87.

[116] *Disp. pub.* VIII.v.

Holy Spirit, Arminius further defines this malice as that "by which any knowing willing person, being enticed indeed by some temptation, but which can be easily (*facile*) resisted by the will, and which the will can easily overcome, is carried to sin."[117]

Arminius next distinguishes two types of malice: "one, by which no resistance is offered to concupiscence, when it can easily be done, without great harm (*noxam*); the other, by which Christ himself is hated, either because he endeavors, by his precepts, to impede the completion of the illicit desire; or because he is not permitted to enjoy (*frui*) the same, on account of his [Christ's] cause and name."[118] The former type of malice is apparently a kind of hatred for a particular command of the law. The latter type of malice is a conscious and direct hatred for Christ himself, the one behind the command. The former type of malice produces a sin that does cause one to fall, but is also forgivable upon repentance. The latter type of malice brings about the unforgivable sin, which consists first of voluntary confession of Christ followed by rejection of Christ, then blasphemy against him, persecuting him, and blasphemy against his Spirit.[119] For Arminius, this sin in all its degrees is the only one that is irrevocable. A person who falls away by means of the former sin of malice need not remain in that state, for God's grace can bring that person to repentance.[120]

The third factor that must be considered is how these sinful deeds of malice that can cause apostasy actually relate to faith, which is the only condition of salvation. After all, Arminius says that believers, as long as they remain believers, cannot lose salvation. These *fideles* would presumably include sinful believers. The solution to this problem lies in Arminius's distinction between faith as *qualitas* or *habitus* on the one hand, and faith as *actus* on the other hand. Actual faith, or to believe actually

---

[117] *Ep. ecc.* 45, p. 93; *Works* 2:743.

[118] *Ep. ecc.* 45, p. 94; *Works* 2:745.

[119] *Ep. ecc.* 45, pp. 94-5; *Works* 2:746–47 and 750. Cf. *Disp. pub.* VIII.xi.

[120] There can be no doubt that Arminius regarded it as possible for those who have fallen away to be brought back to repentance. See *Disp. pub.* XI.xiv; *Ep. ecc.* 45, pp. 92–93; *Works* 2:740 and 742–43; idem, *Exam. Perk.*, in *Opera*, p. 759; *Works* 3:456. Contra Pinson, 'Introduction,' pp. 15-16; Ashby, 'Reformed Arminian,' pp. 181–83 and 187, who, without ever appealing to his writings on this matter, ascribe the position of irremediable apostasy to Arminius, claiming that Arminius believed a fallen person cannot be forgiven. Like Arminius, the Remonstrants also confessed that true believers who had fallen away could be restored to repentance. See *Sententiae Remonstrantium* 5.5, in *Acta synodi*, p. 166.

(*actuale credere*), is what justifies, for the act of believing is imputed for righteousness. The very capability of actual faith rests on the divinely infused *habitus* of faith; actual faith presupposes habitual faith. Arminius concludes, "And so since actual faith does not consist (*consistat*) with mortal sin, the one falling (*incidens*) into mortal sin can be condemned."[121] In other words, commission of mortal, or malicious, sin is incompatible with actual, saving faith; thus, it leads to, or at least indicates, actual infidelity. Arminius asserts that sin from infirmity weakens faith, but does not extinguish it.[122] However, there exists a sin that does extinguish faith—sin from malice. In this way, sin may be connected to unbelief (*infidelitas*), which is the prime condition of apostasy. At the same time, there is a sense in which the *habitus* of belief may still be present so that the fallen Christian retains some kind of non-justifying belief in God that fails to apprehend Christ.[123] Sin itself is a heart problem, a lack of faith and confidence in God. Although David by his sins lost actual faith and stood condemned for a time, the *habitus* of faith remained in him and, by God's grace, provided the foundation for his repentance and recovery of actual faith.

It is critically important that one should not suppose that Arminius is proposing a constant movement in and out of God's favor from day to day. Considering his reluctance to affirm that a once regenerate person is ever actually condemned, the paucity of scriptural examples of such a fall from grace, and his insistence on assurance of salvation, one gets the distinct impression that most sins of the regenerate are done out of ignorance, negligence, and especially weakness, but not malice.[124]

---

[121] *Ep. ecc.* 81, p. 151; *Works* 2:70. Cf. the *Sententiae Remonstrantium* 5.3, in *Acta Synodi*, p. 166: "Vere fideles possunt a vera fide excidere, et in istius modi prolabi *peccata, quae cum vera et iustificante fide consistere non possunt*" (italics mine). The incompatibility of sin and true faith, with different implications, was acknowledged by Junius, *De iustificatione* (1600), xiii: "Post iustificationem sequi studium obedientiae, propositum enim peccandi cum vera fide subsistere non potest."

[122] *Exam. Perk.*, in *Opera*, p. 764; *Works* 3:464: "Nam Petrus ex infirmitate peccavit, quae fidem labefactat, non exstinguit."

[123] *Exam. Perk.*, in *Opera*, p. 763; *Works* 3:463, says, contra Perkins, that the habit of faith may be lost as well. However, whether the habit may be lost is of little import, says Arminius, since it is the act of faith that apprehends Christ.

[124] Unlike Arminius, the Remonstrants forthrightly asserted that such apostasy happens frequently. See *Sententiae Remonstrantium* 5.3, in *Acta Synodi*, p. 166: "Nec potest hoc tantum fieri; sed et non raro sit."

IV. *Conclusion*

The importance of sanctification for this study of assurance is evident because assurance is a question specifically for participants in the Christian life of sanctification. Therefore, before moving on to the epistemological question of salvation, it is important to provide this full summary of the chief points of Arminius's view of the life of sanctification in comparison with the views of his colleagues as demonstrated in the disputations of the Leiden curriculum. Sanctification is a process of progressive holiness made possible by the regenerate cooperating with God's sanctifying grace given through the indwelling Holy Spirit. All the Leiden theologians agreed that good works are a necessary part of sanctification, though not a condition of justification. Thus, Arminius and his colleagues agreed that justification is not dependent on sanctification.

With regard to the call of the righteous to perfection (cf. Matt. 5,48), Arminius and his colleagues concurred that perfection of obedience to God's law is utterly impossible for the unregenerate. They also were in agreement on the fact that a change occurs in the regenerate, so that there is now a *lucta* between the flesh and the Holy Spirit. The difference in Arminius's position is seen clearly in his exegesis of Romans 7, where he claims that such a pessimistic outcome cannot describe the regenerate. Although Arminius maintains that the *lucta* remains in this life, he contends that the Holy Spirit more often prevails in this wrestling match. There is present, then, a greater sense of optimism in the efficacy of the sanctifying grace of the Spirit in the life of the truly regenerate. Because of the comparatively pessimistic outlook of the Reformed view of sanctification, Arminius's colleagues felt that Christian perfection was impossible. Arminius, in contrast, appealed to Augustine and thought that, by God's grace, it would be *possible* for a Christian to obey perfectly. However, Arminius never speculated that such perfection ever *actually* happens in this life. He was more content to call people to strive for perfection rather than to argue about its possibility. The difference on the issue of the efficacy of sanctification between Arminius and his colleagues is simply one of emphasis.

The difference of Arminius on the topic of perseverance of the saints, however, was more substantial, for this question is directly connected to one's view of predestination. Arminius affirmed perseverance of the saints in that God gives sufficient grace and power to believers in order that they might persevere. Nothing can separate true believers from God's love. Arminius is notoriously difficult to pinpoint on the issue of the possibility of apostasy. The primary difference in Arminius's doctrine is that, since he regards the gift of faith which justifies as a resistible gift, then defection from faith also may happen by free choice. The difficulty of interpretation lies in whether he considered such a fall to be possible and actual, and if so, how it happens.

Arminius's colleagues clearly asserted that true believers, the elect, could not possibly fall away from salvation. Arminius, on the other hand, by distinguishing between the elect and true believers, said it is *possible* for believers to lose faith and then be lost. Arminius was less clear regarding whether apostasy *actually* happens. Although he seems undecided in key passages, Arminius's use of David's example shows that he thought that at least one true believer actually did fall away for a time. Such a fall Arminius deemed to be reversible through repentance, unless it was precipitated by the heinous blasphemy against the Holy Spirit.

The fact that Arminius sees malicious sin against God's law, and not just renunciation of faith, as a contributing factor to apostasy raises the important question of the relationship between sanctification and justification. Did Arminius believe that sin can *unjustify* a true believer? The answer is yes, in that a sin of malice is inconsistent with actual, justifying faith. Thus, it is incorrect to say that justification is based on sanctification. However, there exists for Arminius a relationship between justification and sanctification, namely, faith; precarious as this relationship seems, it is not entirely different than the Reformed language of the necessity of good works in the regenerate. For Arminius, malicious sin contributes to apostasy inasmuch as it is an indicator of a lack of faith and trust in God.

These issues in the doctrine of sanctification are crucial to the discussion of assurance, for the epistemological question is rooted in the ontological question. Many conclusions have been drawn about assurance based on Calvinist and Arminian views of sanctification, and especially perseverance. Calvin says, "Since the heavenly Father allows none of those whom he has given to his Son to perish, our assurance and confidence are as great as his power."[125] Pierre du Moulin wonders

---

[125] John Calvin, *De aeterna Dei praedestinatione*, in *Ioannis Calvini opera*, vol. 8:275; *Concerning the Eternal Predestination of God*, trans. J. K. S. Reid (Louisville, 1997), p. 75. Cf. Seeberg, *History*, 2:423.

how Arminians can have any assurance of salvation without affirming perseverance of the saints. Those who acknowledge perseverance, he remarks, need not worry about final apostasy.[126] Thomas Fuller asserted that the doctrine that a child of God may relapse into damnation and lose saving grace is a "desperate Position [that] cuts asunder the sinewes of all Gospel-comfort."[127] As the argument goes, without a robust doctrine of perseverance, there can be no real assurance. The task of the next part of this monograph is to determine whether or to what degree this common conclusion is accurate.

---

[126] Pierre Du Moulin, *The Anatomy of Arminianisme: or The Opening of the Controversies lately handled in the Low-Countryes* (London, 1620), pp. 466–67.
[127] Thomas Fuller, *A Sermon of Assurance* (London, 1648), p. 18.

PART THREE: THE EPISTEMOLOGY OF SALVATION

CHAPTER FIVE

THE UNDERMINING OF ASSURANCE

I. *The Epistemology of Salvation*

As important as the question concerning the ontology of salvation is, the question of the epistemology of salvation is just as crucial. The questions are connected, but also distinct. It is the difference between asking, "How can one be saved?" and, "How can I know I am saved or elect?" The latter issue raised more than an academic question; it was a significant pastoral issue in the Church. This chapter will be devoted to identifying and analyzing the potential problems associated with the epistemology of salvation. Special attention will be given to comparing and contrasting Arminius's opinion about the causes that undermine assurance with the opinions of his contemporaries. This investigation will shed light on how Arminius fits into the larger Christian tradition in general and into the context of early Reformed orthodoxy in particular on this question, and it will show the significance that Arminius's vision of the problems of assurance had for his own theology. Identifying the problems will lay the groundwork for the next chapter, which will offer a description and analysis of various solutions to the problems.

The matter of the epistemology of salvation arises from Scripture, for to say that a person can know his own salvation is to say exactly what the epistle of 1 John says.[1] What is the nature of this assurance that the Bible addresses and that occupies the hearts and consciences of many believers? Before going any further, a definition of assurance ought to be considered, which often has gone undefined in similar discussions.[2] First,

---

[1] 1 Jn. 5,13: "Ταῦτα ἔγραψα ὑμῖν ἵνα εἰδῆτε ὅτι ζωὴν ἔχετε αἰώνιον." Contra Karl Barth, *The Epistle to the Romans*, 6th ed., trans. Edwyn C. Hoskyns (New York, 1933), p. 411: "'Assurance of salvation'—the phrase is of doubtful legitimacy—is not a possession which can be claimed either against or on behalf of the Church. Only complete misunderstanding of the Reformers could lead to such an opinion. The decision is God's." This chapter and the next will more clearly show that it is Barth who has misunderstood the Reformers and their successors.

[2] Although assurance is the topic of their monographs, one is hard-pressed to find a clear, succinct definition of "assurance" in Bell, *Calvin*; Kendall, *Calvin*; or Zachman, *Assurance*.

although this essay is not primarily dealing with religious epistemology in general, the epistemological certainty or assurance of salvation may be considered to be a specific type of religious epistemology. It is fair to conclude that the categories of Arminius's doctrine of assurance of salvation have wider implications for his general religious epistemology. However, since the general epistemological question is beyond the scope of this essay, I shall use the word "assurance" to specifically signify the assurance of salvation.[3] Second, in this essay, "assurance of salvation" will be reserved as a question for people who consider themselves to be Christian believers. Thus, the following discussion does not primarily relate to the issue of assurance or lack of assurance among those who are not (yet) believers.

Finally, since it should not be assumed that everyone means the same thing by assurance of salvation for believers, it is appropriate to offer a more detailed, standard definition. Beeke uses "assurance" to indicate the assurance of grace and salvation, defining it as "undoubted certainty that I personally belong to Christ, possess His saving grace, and will ultimately enjoy everlasting salvation."[4] In other words, we can sum up this definition of assurance by calling it "undoubted certainty." The remainder of the definition is simply the content of one's assurance, or certainty, which for this discussion will always be one's personal salvation, unless otherwise noted.

We must also turn to the works of the early orthodox period to discover what was meant by assurance at that time. It should first of all be noted that there is no Latin cognate of the English words "assurance" or "assured." The most common word to describe this assurance of salvation was *certitudo*, along with its adjective, *certus*. *Certitudo* was the standard vocabulary of the academic disputations and *loci communes* on this topic. Franciscus Junius defines *certitudo salutis* as follows: "We say that the certainty of this [future] salvation is πληροφορία, excited and confirmed in the hearts of the faithful by the Spirit of adoption, by which

---

[3] The importance of defining "assurance" or "certainty" is manifest by the fact that there are many specific areas of religious epistemology besides the epistemology of salvation. For example, Nichols confused these topics when, as he discussed the "assurance of salvation," he attempted to refer the reader to Arminius's comments on assurance of salvation. Instead, the passage he cited is from Arminius's *Oration on the Certainty of Sacred Theology*, which refers to the certainty of the divinity of Scripture, not the certainty of salvation. Cf. *Works* 1:667 n., with 1:383 and 397.
[4] Beeke, *Assurance*, p. 3.

they know that God is favorable and a merciful Father to themselves."[5] Πληροφορία is a reference to Heb. 10,22 (πληροφορία πίστεως), and it means the "state of complete certainty."[6] Junius's definition, unlike Beeke's, designates the cause of this assurance, namely, the Holy Spirit. Also in contrast to Beeke, Junius did not explicitly say that this *certitudo* is "undoubted." However, it is perhaps the case that Beeke is being redundant, because there is no other kind of certainty. Whether or not *certitudo* can be anything other than "undoubted" will be discussed later. It is sufficient for now to have the following working definition of *certitudo*, which is consistent with Junius and Beeke: assurance of one's personal salvation made known in one's heart by the Holy Spirit. This definition is what is intended when we use "certainty" or "assurance" in this essay.

Used in a similar mode as *certitudo* was the word *fiducia*, that is, confidence or assurance. In general, *fiducia* causes the believer to rest and put her trust in God.[7] According to Kuchlinus, the catechism teaches the following about *fiducia*: It is

> 1. A certain persuasion of the heart which is opposed to every doubt concerning God's grace, and to the dread concerning eternal torments. 2. It includes particular application of individual believers *for themselves* of the *merit* and *efficacy* of Jesus Christ. 3. Peace and internal quiet by which those who believe in God as their most kind Father rest in Christ Jesus, and they accept all things, so the prosperous as the adverse, from the most kind hand of the same with a quiet and joyful mind....[8]

Thus, *fiducia*, which is the part of faith that pertains to certainty, is a persuasion free from all doubt, which includes the application of Christ's righteousness and peace of mind. According to Gomarus, *fiducia* means

---

[5] Junius, *De certitudine* (1601), ii: "Hujus salutis [futurae] certitudinem dicimus esse πληροφορίαν a Spiritu adoptionis in cordibus fidelium excitatam, et confirmatam, qua sciunt Deum sibi esse propitium, et Patrem misericordem." Cf. Kuchlinus, *De certitudine* (1603), iii, who also defines *certitudo* as πληροφορία.

[6] Frederick William Danker, ed., *A Greek-English Lexicon of the New Testament and other Early Christian Literature*, 3rd edition (Chicago: University of Chicago Press, 2000), q.v.

[7] Kuchlinus, *De salvandis*, viii, says that by *fiducia*, "in Deo acquiesco."

[8] Kuchlinus, *De salvandis*, xiii: "I. Certam cordis persuasionem quae omni dubitationi de gratia Dei, & formidini de suppliciis aeternis opponitur. II. Includit particularem singulorum credentium *pro se* applicationem *meriti* & *Efficaciae* Iesu Christi. III. Pacem seu quietem internam qua credentes in Deo tanquam clementissimo patre suo in Christo Iesu acquiescunt, omniaque tam prospera quam adversa ex benignissima ipsius manu quieta & laeta mente accipiunt...."

a firm persuasion of the heart, by which truly faithful individuals certainly appropriate the general promise of God's grace to themselves individually.[9] Elsewhere, Gomarus calls *fiducia* a true tranquility of the heart that rests in God, establishing that God loves us. As Junius and Kuchlinus did with *certitudo*, Gomarus equates *fiducia* with πληροφορία τῆς πίστεως.[10] It should be clear that, when Arminius's colleagues employ *certitudo* and *fiducia* in this context of assurance of salvation, they use the two words nearly synonymously. The main difference, but not inconsistent with *certitudo*, is that *fiducia* is characterized more explicitly with the idea of the believer's inner peace and tranquility in God.

In his definition of *fiducia*, Arminius concurs with his colleagues: "For this *fiducia* is a certain intrinsic quiet and tranquility of the soul acquiescing in God and in Christ, because of the immutable truth of these promises."[11] He does, however, seem implicitly to draw a distinction between *certitudo* and *fiducia*. As I noted in chapter three, Arminius asserted that *fiducia* is not a component of *fides*, but consequent upon it. But *certitudo fidei*, Arminius claims, is the πληροφορία that is a part of *assensus fidei*.[12]

Just as the topic of soteriology was a major point of debate between Roman Catholics and Protestants, the question of epistemology of salvation was a point of controversy as well. The Catholic Church, with its system of indulgences and merits, was perceived by Protestants as removing all assurance of salvation from individual believers.[13] Indeed, Oberman notes that certainty of salvation was for Biel not a virtue, but a liability. Only a conjectural certainty of salvation is possible in this life.[14] It was Luther's inability to find assurance of salvation in the late

---

[9] Gomarus, *De fide iustificante* (1603), ix.

[10] Gomarus, *De fide salvifica* (1603), v.

[11] Arminius, *De fide* (1608), iii: "Fiducia .n. [enim] haec est quies quaedam intrinseca et tranquillitas animi acquiescentis in Deo et in Christo, propter promissionum istarum veritatem immutabilem."

[12] Arminius, *De fide* (1608), iv.

[13] Steven E. Ozment, *The Reformation in the Cities: The Appeal of Protestantism to Sixteenth-Century Germany and Switzerland* (New Haven, 1975), pp. 22–32, describes the "burden of late medieval religion." Cf. also Zachman, *Assurance*, p. 38. Stephen Strehle, *The Catholic Roots of the Protestant Gospel: Encounter between the Middle Ages and the Reformation* [SHCT 60] (Leiden, 1995), pp. 14–29 and 127–28, notes that the plight of late medieval Catholicism has sometimes been exaggerated from the Protestant perspective. However, the real lack of assurance that Luther felt and that later Protestants perceived (rightly or wrongly) in the Catholic Church was a motivating factor for the Protestant search for true assurance.

[14] See Oberman, *Harvest*, pp. 218–35; cf. Strehle, *Catholic Roots*, pp. 5–8.

medieval Catholic system that helped give him a new perspective on the *iustitia Dei*. Luther insisted that the lack of assurance of salvation was the common plight "of all self-justifiers (*omnium iustitiariorum*)."[15] The Protestant point was simple: if remission of sins depends in any way on the quantity and quality of one's good works, one can never be assured of salvation.

Protestant, and particularly Reformed, theology saw itself as restoring not only the true ground of justification (*sola gratia*), but along with it the personal assurance of that evangelical salvation. However, regardless of what the theologians and preachers were writing and teaching, this restoration of true assurance did not always filter down to the lay level. Despite the proclamation of salvation by grace alone through faith alone, lack of assurance of salvation continued to plague members of the Reformed churches. Because the lack of assurance was a pertinent issue requiring theological and pastoral handling, it is not surprising to find a number of treatises devoting part or all of their substance to it. Works dedicated to encouraging Christians to find more assurance ranged from long, technical theological treatises to popular, vernacular books and sermons.[16]

II. *Arminius's View of the Dialectical Problem of Assurance*

From various comments throughout his works, it is clear that Arminius had a concern for the Christian's proper certainty concerning salvation. With regard to the certainty of salvation, Arminius recognized two

---

[15] Luther, *De servo arbitrio*, in *WA* 18:783; *LW* 33:289.

[16] An example of a longer, more technical treatise is Perkins, *The Whole Treatise of the Cases of Conscience, Distinguished into Three Bookes*, in *The Workes of that Famous and Worthy Minister of Christ... Mr. William Perkins*, 3 vols. (London, 1631–35) 2:1–152. Examples of shorter, more popular books are Jean Taffin, *Of the Markes of the children of God, and of their comforts in afflictions* (London, 1590); *The Marks of God's Children* (1586), trans. Peter Y. De Jong, Classics of Reformed Spirituality (Grand Rapids, 2003); Perkins, *A Case of conscience, the greatest that ever was; how a man may know whether he be the childe of God, or no*, in *Workes of Perkins* 1:421–28. Undoubtedly, many sermons were preached on this topic; some were published separately, one example of which is Fuller, *Sermon*. For more examples of English treatises and sermons on assurance, see Michael P. Winship, 'Weak Christians, Backsliders, and Carnal Gospelers: Assurance of Salvation and the Pastoral Origins of Puritan Practical Divinity in the 1580s,' *Church History* 70/3 (2001), 462–81. The writings of Continental Reformed, especially Dutch, theologians are discussed in Graafland, *Zekerheid*.

distinct and opposite errors into which a person could fall. As the first decade of the seventeenth century progressed, he seems to have warned about these pitfalls with increasing frequency. In one place, he calls them the "pests of religion and of souls."[17] That is, these two things irritate not only true religion, but also our own personal souls. Elsewhere, he calls them the "two fiery darts of Satan,"[18] and "the two greatest evils to be avoided in all religion."[19] These two perils are *desperatio* and *securitas*, each equally dangerous to salutary certainty.[20]

A. *The Two "Pests of Religion and of Souls"*

The problem of the lack of assurance that the Protestant church faced, is, in its extreme form, *desperatio*. Its verb, *despero*, literally means to have no hope (*de spero*), and was often implicitly understood as applying to the context of certainty of salvation, namely, a lack thereof. This soteriological connotation of the word is clear from Altenstaig, who recorded the following about *desperatio*: "When either from false estimation because of sins which he does, or good things which he omits, he despairs (*desperat*) concerning God's mercy, believing that God is unwilling or not able to spare or to receive him in grace." He went on to say that it does not only mean the privation of hope, but the judgment that the desired thing, in this case, salvation, is impossible. Moreover, wrote Altenstaig, *desperatio* can be taken in a twofold mode (*potest desperatio capi dupliciter*). By one mode it is improperly taken for the firm credulity by which one believes that he must be damned (*esse damnandum*); that is, he despairs himself to be saved. By another mode it is properly taken for the firm credulity by which one believes that if he does what is in him (*si faciat quod in se est*) for possessing beatitude, he still does not have it.[21] The action of *desperatio* "is directly opposite to the action of hope."[22] In sum, the individual who suffers from *desperatio* is, for whatever reason, hopeless concerning his personal salvation.

---

[17] *Disp. priv.* XLIII.viii: "pernicies Religionis et animarum."

[18] *Dec. sent.*, p. 93; in *Works* 1:637: "twee vierighe pijlen des Satans."

[19] *Disp. priv.* XXXIX.ix: "Quae duo sunt mala maxima in omni Religione cavenda."

[20] Following Arminius, Simon Episcopius, *Institutiones theologicae* 4.2.18, in *Opera theologica* 1:303, said that security and despair "duae sunt pestes omnis Religionis."

[21] The latter describes very well the plight of the young Luther.

[22] Ioannes Altenstaig, *Lexicon theologicum quo tanquam clave theologiae fores aperiuntur* (Cologne, 1619), p. 232: "Unde talis actus est directe oppositus actui spei." Cf. *ST* Ia–IIae.xl.4 s.c.

During his time as a pastor, Arminius personally encountered cases of what he considered to be Christians suffering from a lack of assurance, or *desperatio*. In a letter to his friend Johannes Uytenbogaert, Arminius recounted his experience while ministering to church members in Amsterdam who were suffering from the deadly plague of 1602. Arminius described two true Christians, a man and a woman, unknown to each other, who could not feel in their hearts "the certainty (*certitudinem*) of the remission of sins" at the time when they needed it most. Both were overcome with grief, not that they were despairing to the point of losing their faith, but that they did not feel the certainty necessary for their salvation.[23] Although Arminius may not have been dealing here with cases of outright *desperatio*, these church members seem to have been struggling with a species of this problem. This circumstance was not unique, but is just one example of the continuing pastoral problem of assurance in the Reformed churches of the post-Reformation period. Arminius stood shoulder to shoulder with his Reformed contemporaries in contending against *desperatio*, or, as he called it in his native tongue, *wanhope*.

Because the Reformed Church understood itself in chief opposition against the Roman Church, many distinctly Reformed doctrines, however traditional they may have been, were forged in the context of reaction and polemic. To be sure, the Reformed insistence on assurance of salvation was seen as a corrective to the extreme *desperatio* that gripped many adherents of late medieval Catholicism. For the Reformed, the recovery of true assurance became not simply a happy consequence of the true proclamation of the gospel, but a necessary component of the Christian life. Under this assumption, to be a Christian is to be assured of personal salvation. It is not a far leap to conclude that the more assured one is the better Christian one is. It is here, partly in reaction to the Reformed insistence on assurance, and partly as a result of his own soteriology, that Arminius reconsidered the problem of assurance. The question underlying this revision may be proposed as follows: Is it possible to have too much assurance? Is there such a thing as an unhealthy assurance? Arminius claimed that there is, and he called it *securitas*, or *sorgloosheyt*.

---

[23] *Ep. ecc.* 56, pp. 106–07; *Works* 1:176.

Securus is etymologically from *sine cura*; thus, *securitas* is the state of being careless or without care. Again, it was pastoral experience that alerted Arminius to this problem. He observed several times in his ministry that, whenever he admonished church members to be cautious about committing sin, they would reply that it was "not necessary for them to care much about the matter or deeply to lament it."[24] To fail to have a care for something that deserves care is the essence of carelessness, or *securitas*.

In contrast to the common resistance against *desperatio* that Arminius shared with his contemporaries, he found that he was a lonely voice in the struggle against *securitas*. In fact, we find scarcely any warnings at all against *securitas* or the possibility of an unhealthy assurance in the Reformed literature of the day. For example, Taffin, whose book, *The Marks of God's Children*, encourages doubting Christians to be assured of their salvation, does not admonish against too much assurance, nor does he even acknowledge the existence of such a category in this book.[25]

B. *The Dialectic and Its History*

Although Arminius seems to be the only theologian of the era of early Reformed orthodoxy teaching about the problems of assurance in this way, the use of the dialectic of *desperatio* and *securitas* did not arise with him. As with many of his controversial doctrines, there is a patristic, medieval, and even Protestant precedent for Arminius's ideas about assurance. Therefore, it is appropriate to offer a survey of the historical background of this dialectic, granting special attention to the occasionally controversial warning against *securitas*. This historical overview will focus especially on the authors whom Arminius is known to have read or owned, and then examine in detail the treatment of the dialectic in Arminius.

---

[24] *Cap. VII Rom.*, in *Opera*, p. 921; *Works* 2:659–60: "...non magnopere hoc curandum, aut ex eo dolendum fuisse sibi...."

[25] To be sure, Taffin's primary purpose in this book was to comfort believers who were experiencing suffering and persecution. In other places, Taffin insists that election ought to result in zeal for sanctification. Cf. Taffin, *The Amendment of Life, Comprised in Fower Bookes* (London, 1595), pp. 446–48; with Graafland, *Zekerheid*, p. 170; and S. van der Linde, *Jean Taffin: Hofprediker en raadsheer van Willem van Oranje* (Amsterdam, 1982), pp. 153–55. Nevertheless, it is likely that he would have issued such a warning in *Marks* if he had thought it was an important problem in the churches.

B.1. *The New Testament and Patristic Period*

This survey must begin with the two *corpora* of literature most influential for the Reformation and Post-Reformation periods, the New Testament and patristic documents. In order to grasp the range of the terms for assurance under dispute, it is necessary to turn first to the New Testament in Greek and Latin, the primary source of theological ideas and vocabulary. Πληροφορία, the Greek word used most often to describe assurance of salvation, appears four times in the New Testament. Three times the Vulgate translates it as *plenitudo* (Col. 2,2; 1 Thess. 1,5; Heb. 10,22), and once as *expletio* (Heb. 6,11), both of which faithfully render the basic meaning of the word, "fullness."[26] *Certitudo*, the Latin word which would become the most common equivalent of assurance, never appears in the Latin Vulgate, although *certus* does several times. *Fiducia* appears 23 times in the Latin New Testament, most notably as a translation of παρρησία in 1 Jn. 3,21 and 4,17, passages specifically about the assurance of salvation. The debate in Arminius's context would be over the word *securitas*. It only appears once in the Latin New Testament, as a translation of ἀσφάλεια in 1 Thess. 5,3. The adjective *securus* also appears only once in the New Testament, as a translation of ἀμέριμνος in Matt. 28,14. *Desperatio*, the name most frequently given to the idea opposed to *securitas*, does not appear in the Latin New Testament. *Despero* appears once in Lk. 6,35 as a translation of ἀπελπίζω, and in some manuscripts of Eph. 4,19, accounting for a textual variant of the same Greek word. Although the concepts of *securitas* and *desperatio* appear throughout the pages of Scripture, these ideas are often expressed without these two words.[27] This phenomenon is curious, given that these words become the standard terminology of the dialectic.

The debates of the late sixteenth and early seventeenth centuries had a strong component of appealing not only to the New Testament, but also to the church fathers, the second major *corpus*.[28] Although the Latin terminology of *securitas* and *desperatio* is more important for the following survey, it is useful to offer an example of what an influential Greek father

---

[26] Danker, *Lexicon*, q.v., says that the meaning of fullness, rather than certainty, also merits attention.

[27] E.g., cf. the description of *securitas* in 1 Cor. 10,12 and of *desperatio* in Eph. 2,12.

[28] Cf. David Neelands, 'The Authority of St. Augustine in the Debates Leading to the Lambeth Articles,' paper presented at the Sixteenth Century Studies Conference (Pittsburgh, 31 October 2003), pp. 1–35.

said concerning the idea of *securitas*. As an illustration, I submit John Chrysostom's comments on seeking security in life. He wrote, "Therefore do not seek a life filled with freedom from fear, for it is not useful to you."[29] Ἄδεια, literally, "fearlessness," can also have the connotation of "licentiousness." In this passage, ἄδεια is translated into Latin as the adjective *securus*. Thus, even in the Greek tradition, there is evidence of security as something to avoid.

As with so much theological vocabulary, the Latin terminology is established early by the first major Latin father, Tertullian.

> Fear is the foundation of salvation, presumption the impediment of fear. Therefore it is more useful if we hope not to be able to fail, than if we presume not to be able to; for by hoping we will fear, fearing we will be cautious, being cautious we will be saved; on the contrary, if we presume neither fearing nor being cautious, we will be saved with difficulty. He who acts secure is not anxious; he does not possess safe and firm security. But he who is anxious can truly be secure.[30]

The language of presumption and security versus fear and hope will be influential throughout the tradition, as will be the paradox that one can only be secure by being anxious.

The importance of this survey of patristic opinion is evident especially with a look to Augustine. Despite Augustine's occasionally positive use of *securitas*,[31] for this most frequently cited father during the Reformation and post-Reformation period, *securitas* and *desperatio* already functioned normatively as two opposite and unsatisfactory attitudes about personal salvation. He claimed that the scriptural examples of good individuals gone bad and bad individuals turning good are there for a reason, namely, "so that the righteous may not be exalted by security into pride, nor the wicked be hardened by despair against the remedy."[32]

---

[29] John Chrysostom, *Expositio in Psalmos* 114.2; in Τα Ευρισκομενα Παντα 5:366 E: "Μὴ τοίνυν μηδὲ σὺ ζήτει τὸν ἀδείας γέμοντα βίον, οὐ γάρ ἐστί σοι λυσιτελές."

[30] Tertullian, *De cultu foeminarum* 2.2; in *PL* 1:1318: "Timor fundamentum salutis est, praesumptio impedimentum timoris. Utilius ergo, si speremus non posse delinquere, quam si praesumamus non posse; sperando enim timebimus, timendo cavebimus, cavendo salvi erimus; contra si praesumamus neque timendo neque cavendo, difficile salvi erimus. Qui securus agit, non est sollicitus, non possidet tutam et firmam securitatem. At qui sollicitus est, is vere poterit esse securus."

[31] See the discussion in Oscar Velásquez, 'From *Dubitatio* to *Securitas*: Augustine's *Confessions* in the Light of Uncertainty,' in *Studia Patristica 38, St. Augustine and His Opponents* (Leuven, 2001), pp. 338–41.

[32] Augustine, *Contra Faustum Manichaeum* 22.96; *PL* 42:464: "ut neque justi in superbiam securitate extollantur, nec iniqui contra medicinam desperatione obdurentur."

Elsewhere, with reference to the biblical examples of righteous people committing sin, Augustine wrote that the examples are not intended to generate "security of sinning," but to encourage those who fall into sin to steer clear of despair.[33] Worried that baptism might breed "the most destructive security" (*perniciosissima securitas*) in new Christians, Augustine is quick to warn them that baptism means remission of sin, not permission to sin.[34] This kind of security in sinning is dangerous enough that it can even ruin one's salvation.[35]

In his *Confessiones*, Augustine addressed God concerning the question of the possibility of assurance of salvation: "And no one ought to be secure in this life, the whole of which is called a temptation, that he who could become better from worse, might not become worse from better. One hope, one confidence (*fiducia*), one firm promise—your mercy."[36] For Augustine, there is no place for security in this life; but even after *securitas* is rightly rejected, *fiducia* remains.[37]

The two most influential bishops of Rome in the first millennium made significant contributions to what would be regarded as the tradition. Following Augustine, Leo the Great asserted that "no one is supported by so much steadfastness, that he ought to be secure concerning his own stability."[38] Gregory I, often considered by Protestants as the first true pope of Rome, was an influential promoter and distributor of a popular Augustinianism. Standing at the end of the transition from late antiquity to the medieval period, Gregory the Great helped solidify Catholic dogma for the Middle Ages, during which time he was perhaps the most widely read of the Western church fathers.[39] Commenting on Job's misery, Gregory stated that even the life of the good does not find

---

[33] Augustine, *De natura et gratia* 35.40; *PL* 44:266.

[34] Augustine, *De fide et operibus* 20.36; *PL* 40:221.

[35] Augustine, *De fide et operibus* 14.21; *PL* 40:211: "...securitate salutem suam perdant."

[36] Augustine, *Confessionum libri tredecim* 10.32.48; *PL* 32:799: "Et nemo securus esse debet in ista vita, quae tota tentatio nominatur, utrum qui fieri potuit ex deteriore melior, non fiat etiam ex meliore deterior. Una spes, una fiducia, una firma promissio, misericordia tua."

[37] Neelands, 'Authority of St. Augustine,' pp. 22–25, cites many other passages from Augustine against security about salvation and perseverance.

[38] Leo I, *Sermones in praecipuis totius anni festivitatibus ad Romanam plebem habiti* 43, *De quadrigesima* 5.3; *PL* 54:283: "Nemo est tanta firmitate suffultus, ut de stabilitate sua debeat esse securus."

[39] See Pelikan, *Christian Tradition*, 3:16.

security of salvation.[40] Nothing seems inherently negative about *securitas salutis* in this passage, except for the fact that even a righteous person like Job does not experience it. Later in the same work, Gregory declared, "Often therefore the mind of the righteous, in order to be more secure, has a greater sense of trepidation."[41] Again, although there is nothing necessarily negative about *securitas mentis*, it only comes as a result of fear and trembling. It is when people claim for themselves a fearless attitude of *securitas* that it becomes dangerous and retains the negative connotation for Gregory.

Gregory's general feeling about *securitas* is evident by the contexts in which he discussed it and in the adjectives he employed to modify the word. For example, he wrote that "our mind may dare to be elevated in pride by the presumption of its own security."[42] Moreover, because of our depravity, we turn the tranquility of human peace into the use of "vain security."[43] Gregory affirmed that the elect are not promised the confidence of *securitas salutis* in this life.[44] In fact, he noted elsewhere that humanity fell from paradise, and the angels from heaven, the most secure of places.[45]

The overall thrust of Gregory is that *securitas* as a positive state of mind with reference to assurance is a nearly unattainable, if not impossible, goal in this life. Therefore, the person who claims to possess *securitas* or manifests such an attitude has stepped beyond the appropriate boundary. The situation is analogous to the question of perfection in this life as addressed by Augustine. It is not utterly impossible that a person can keep God's law perfectly, but it is more likely that the person who claims to be free of sin has just committed a lie. Likewise, for Gregory, the person who is *securus* likely treads on the dangerous ground of arrogance, presumption, negligence, and vanity.

---

[40] Gregory I, *Moralium libri, sive expositio in librum B. Job, pars secunda* 8.10.22; *PL* 75:814.

[41] Gregory I, *Moralium libri, pars secunda* 9.45.69; *PL* 75:897: "Saepe ergo mens justi, ut magis secura sit, altius trepidat."

[42] Gregory I, *Moralium libri, pars secunda* 9.56.85; *PL* 75:906: "mens nostra in superbiam audeat praesumptione suae securitatis elevari."

[43] Gregory I, *XL Homiliarum in Evangelia libri duo* 2.35.1; *PL* 76:1260.

[44] Gregory I, *Moralium libri, pars quarta* 20.3.8; *PL* 76:139.

[45] Gregory I, *Epistolae Gregorii Magni* 7.4; *PL* 77:856.

B.2. *The Medieval Period*

Although Protestants generally appealed to the medieval fathers less frequently than to the early fathers of the church, Protestant orthodoxy
was still highly influenced by medieval scholasticism. The frequently
overt attitude of contempt toward Catholic scholasticism should not
overshadow the implicit and at times explicit admiration that Protestant
scholastics held for many of their Catholic forerunners. For example,
Bernard, the Cistercian abbot of Clairvaux, exerted a profound influence on the doctrine and piety of the high and late medieval period.
Like his predecessors, Bernard acknowledged a suitable use of *securitas*:
"What is the true and safe security of the soul, except the Lord's
attestations?"[46] *Securitas animae* rests on the promises of God. However,
Bernard also demonstrated continuity with the tradition when he employed *securitas* in a pessimistic light, directly opposite to the problem of
desperatio. Speaking of how one can tell whether Jesus dwells in a particular person, Bernard pointed to two signs. These two divine footprints
of Jesus on a person's soul are *timor* and *spes*, for the Lord is pleased by
those who fear him and hope in his mercy. Thus, Bernard urges his
audience to kiss these two feet, fear and hope, yet warns them not to
neglect either one.

> If, for instance, you feel deep sorrow for your sins along with the fear of
> judgment, you have pressed your lips on the imprint of truth and of judg-
> ment. But if you temper that fear and sorrow with the thought of divine
> goodness and the hope of obtaining his pardon, you will realize that you
> have also embraced the foot of mercy. It is clearly inexpedient to kiss one
> without the other; a man who thinks of the judgment alone will fall into
> the bottomless pit of despair, another who deceitfully flatters God's mercy
> gives birth to a most wicked security.[47]

Despair and security are both to be avoided. For Bernard, the sure way
to escape their danger is to embrace a healthy balance of fear of God
and hope in God.

---

[46] Bernard of Clairvaux, *Sermones in Cantica Canticorum* 57.3; *PL* 183:1051.
[47] Bernard, *Sermones in Cantica Canticorum* 6.8; *PL* 183:806: "Porro enim si jam do-
lore peccati, et judicii timore compungeris, veritatis judiciique vestigio labia impressisti.
Quod si timorem doloremque divinae intuitu bonitatis, et spe consequendae indulgen-
tiae temperas, etiam misericordiae pedem amplecti te noveris. Alioquin alterum sine
altero osculari non expedit; quia et recordatio solius judicii in barathrum desperationis
praecipitat, et misericordiae fallax assentatio pessimam generat securitatem."

In agreement with Augustine's warning, and following Gregory I, Bernard said, "Security is nowhere, brothers, not in heaven, not in paradise; much less in the world. For in heaven the angel fell under the presence of divinity; Adam in paradise [fell] from the place of enjoyment; Judas in the world [fell] from the school of the Savior."[48] From God's perspective, there is ontological and epistemological security, for he knows his elect. The situation is different, however, for humanity, who can never have epistemological security of personal, individual salvation.

As with his physical presence, the intellectual shadow of Thomas Aquinas looms large over the history of theology. The revival of Thomism and its various interpretations in the sixteenth century affected both Roman Catholic and Protestant theologies in profound ways. With regard to Arminius in particular, we may speak of a "modified Thomism," to the degree that he takes up the concerns and foci of Thomas.[49] Furthermore, Thomas dealt with the problems of despair and security in greater detail than his predecessors. It is therefore important to survey what Thomas believed about these issues.

First, it is necessary to place Thomas's statements on hope and its contraries into proper context, for his discussion in the *Summa theologiae* was influential on Arminius and his contemporaries. Thomas first examined hope as a passion of the sensitive appetite, according to its Aristotelian classification. Based on Aristotle, Thomas divided the individual passions of the sensitive appetite into two categories, the concupiscible and the irascible. The concupiscible passions are those which have pleasure or pain as their possible object. The irascible passions also have the acquisition of good or avoidance of evil as their object, but the possibility of their acquisition or avoidance is more arduous and difficult (*difficilis*) than with the concupiscible.[50] Under the irascible, Thomas discussed five passions: *spes* and its opposite, *desperatio*; *timor* and its opposite, *audacia*; and *ira*, which has no opposite. Hope is the movement into the good according to the reason of the good; but despair is withdrawal from the good.[51] That is, despair is not merely a privation of hope; it is

---

[48] Bernard, *Sermones de diversis* 30.1; *PL* 183:622: "Nusquam est securitas, fratres, neque in coelo, neque in paradiso; multo minus in mundo. In coelo enim cecidit angelus sub praesentia divinitatis; Adam in paradiso de loco voluptatis; Judas in mundo de schola Salvatoris."

[49] Muller, *GCP*, p. 39.

[50] *ST* Ia–IIae.xxiii.1 resp.

[51] *ST* Ia–IIae.xxv.3 resp.; Ia–IIae.xl.4 resp.

the positive turning away from a desired thing, because its attainment is deemed impossible.[52]

The other context in which Thomas examined hope is under its Pauline—as distinct from Aristotelian—classification, namely, as a theological virtue. Thomas asked whether the theological virtues, like other virtues in Aristotelian ethics, observed a mean. He answered negatively, for it is impossible to excessively love, believe in, or hope in God to the point of vice. In other words, in one sense, there is no such thing as too much hope in God.[53]

In another sense, however, Thomas affirmed that theological virtues, including hope, can be regarded as the mean between extremes, when they are considered *ex parte nostra*. From this perspective, "Hope is the mean between presumption and despair from our part" (*spes est media inter praesumptionem et desperationem ex parte nostra*). He continued, "Someone is said to presume through hoping to receive from God a good that exceeds his condition, or [to despair] by not hoping what he might be able to hope according to his condition. However, it is impossible for there to be an over-abundance of hope *ex parte Dei*, whose goodness is infinite."[54] Thus, without even using the language of *securitas*, Thomas Aquinas indicated that there are two perspectives on the question of too much hope. On the one hand, *ex parte Dei*, there is no such thing as too much hope, for one should rest securely in God's goodness and promises. The tradition before and after Aquinas was pleased to occasionally describe this hope as *securitas*, affirming a positive use of the word. On the other hand, *ex parte nostra*, the person whose excessive hope does not correspond to his actual condition suffers from presumption. Traditional theology has given the name *securitas* also to this situation, but with its more common, negative implications. Indeed, *praesumptio* and *securitas* were used interchangeably in Gregory.

In his larger discussion of the theological virtue of hope, Thomas assumed *desperatio* and *praesumptio* as the two vices opposed to *spes*. Despair is when "a person does not hope for himself to participate in God's goodness."[55] Presumption despises God's justice, which punishes sinners.[56] Despair takes away hope in God's mercy, and presumption

---

[52] *ST* Ia–IIae.xl.4 ad 3.
[53] *ST* Ia–IIae.lxiv.4 s.c.
[54] *ST* Ia–IIae.lxiv.4 resp., ad 3.
[55] *ST* IIa–IIae.xx.3 resp.
[56] *ST* IIa–IIae.xxi.1 s.c.

takes away fear of God's justice.[57] The opposition of *godly* hope and fear to *impious* presumption and despair is reminiscent of Bernard.

Both despair and presumption are sins. A person can despair and still believe, just as a believer may commit other mortal sins.[58] Since Thomas assumed that God shows goodness primarily, and secondarily shows his punishment only in view of sins, he declared that presumption is less a sin than despair, for it looks inordinately to God's mercy, as despair looks inordinately to God's punitive justice, a secondary, *a posteriori* attribute.[59] Presumption implies a certain immoderation of hope.[60] One kind of presumption relies on one's own abilities to achieve something that they are in fact incapable of achieving. The other kind of presumption relies on the divine power to also achieve something impossible, namely, to give pardon without repentance.[61]

Thomas does not give a precise explanation of security, but he does say that it excludes fear.[62] It is also clear that Thomas can see *securitas* in either a positive or a negative light. Security, he declared, "pertains to magnanimity, in so far as it repels despair."[63] A few sentences later, however, he affirmed that security is not always laudable, "but only when someone places aside care according as he ought, and in things which he ought not to fear."[64] Pious fear of God is apparently not a care that one should discard. As excluding a pious fear of God's justice, security at least has close affinities with presumption in Thomas's thought. Thomas's presupposition of the traditional dialectic is evident when he explained why it is good that the predestined do not know their status before God; if they knew for sure, "they who are not predestined [elected] might despair, and security might bring forth negligence in the predestined."[65]

---

[57] *ST* IIa–IIae.xiv.2 resp.
[58] *ST* IIa–IIae.xx.2 resp.
[59] *ST* IIa–IIae.xxi.2 resp.
[60] *ST* IIa–IIae.xxi.1 resp.
[61] *ST* IIa–IIae.xxi.1 resp.
[62] *ST* Ia–IIae.xlv.1 ad 3; IIa–IIae.cxxviii.1 ad 6.
[63] *ST* IIa–IIae.cxxix.7 resp.
[64] *ST* IIa–IIae.cxxix.7 ad 2.
[65] *ST* Ia.xxiii.1 ad 4. For a historical investigation of certainty of salvation with special attention to the Franciscan and Dominican debates, see Gustaf Ljunggren, *Zur Geschichte der Christlichen Heilsgewißheit von Augustin bis zur Hochscholastik* (Göttingen, 1921). Since Ljunggren's study does not focus much attention on the use of *securitas* vis-à-vis other certainty vocabulary, it is of limited value for the present historical survey.

To summarize the evidence up to this point in the history of doctrine, there is a common sentiment that a person can err in two ways on the question of assurance of salvation, that is, through despair or security. The word *securitas* can sometimes have a positive connotation, especially when it refers to the objective truth and firmness of God's promises and character.[66] Furthermore, from the perspective of divine omniscience, the elect are secure. More often, however, *securitas* carries a negative connotation, especially with regard to human epistemology of salvation. In fact, it is frequently associated with the sins that it "brings forth" (*parit*). Jerome wrote, "For security brings forth negligence, negligence [brings forth] contempt."[67] This line became influential in the subsequent tradition, being echoed by Isidore of Seville, Rabanus Maurus, and Thomas Aquinas.[68] In another passage which was frequently quoted in subsequent discussions of assurance, Gregory made the same point when he declared that *securitas* tends to be the *mater negligentiae*.[69] Gregory was underscoring the tradition that connects *securitas* with its fruit, *negligentia*. If there ever were attempts to promote *securitas* as a viable word to describe Christian assurance of salvation, they were not part of the larger, mainstream tradition. Following Augustine, the tradition avoids *securitas*, but still views itself as retaining true assurance as *fiducia* or *certitudo*.

B.3. *Luther and the Continental Reformed Movement*

As we approach the period of the Reformation, we find the dialectic of *securitas* and *desperatio* still in force. Erasmus, for example, spoke of the "Scylla of arrogance" and the "Charybdis of despair or indolence."[70] We have already alluded to the problem of assurance for Luther and the role that assurance played in his dissent from Catholic soteriology.

---

[66] Biel spoke of *securitas spei*, but this could never add up to *certitudo salutis*, much less *securitas salutis*. See Oberman, *Harvest*, pp. 227–30.

[67] Jerome, *Commentariorum in Isaiam Prophetam libri duodeviginti* 8; *PL* 24:301: "Securitas enim negligentiam, negligentia contemptum parit." See also Jerome, *Commentariorum in Jeremiam Prophetam libri sex* 6; *PL* 24:894: "Ubertas enim securitatem, securitas negligentiam, negligentia contemptum parit." Jerome's statements bear similarity to Cyprian of Carthage, *Epistola prima ad Donatum* 4; *PL* 4:202.

[68] Isidore of Seville, *Sententiarum libri tres* 2.13.18; *PL* 83:616–617; Rabanus Maurus, *Expositionis super Jeremiam Prophetam libri viginti* 12.23; *PL* 111:1055; and *ST* Ia.xxiii.1 ad 4.

[69] Gregory I, *Moralium libri, pars quinta* 24.11.27; *PL* 76:301. Cf. Gottfried of Admont, *Homilia XVI. in epiphaniam Domini tertia* 87; *PL* 174:693, with Aelred of Rievaulx, *Sermones de oneribus* 25; *PL* 195:463.

[70] Erasmus, *De libero arbitrio*, col. 1247 d; *On the Freedom of the Will*, p. 96.

In Luther's mind, the assurance of salvation was the most pressing pastoral problem.[71] The topic of assurance in general and this traditional dialectic in particular came up in his famous 95 theses, as he drew an analogy between hell, purgatory, and heaven, and the concepts of "despair, nearly (*prope*) despair, security," respectively.[72] Oberman notes that Luther's occasional reference to the *superbi* and *desperati* is "a traditional allusion to the two erring groups on the left and the right of the *via media* of the Church militant."[73]

With regard to the use of *securitas* itself, we see that Luther had some positive use for the word in general. For example, Luther spoke of a security that was ontological in nature; that is, the *anima fidelis* is indeed *secura* against death and hell.[74] Moreover, Luther acknowledged a kind of epistemological security when he declared that God's promise of life is "our assurance and security and consolation in all our labors and afflictions" (*nostra fiducia et securitas et consolatio in omnibus laboribus et adflictionibus nostris*). Furthermore, "The sum of our religion is this: that a man be certain and secure (*securum*) in his own conscience."[75] Although Luther sometimes used *securitas* in a favorable way, he also associated security with the lukewarm condition of the Laodicean church of Revelation 3.[76] Elsewhere, he lamented that many give themselves up to "laziness and security."[77] In this category, he included the ungodly priests and unfaithful pastors who "snore securely" (*secure stertitis*).[78] In the Heidelberg Disputation and comments on the theses, Luther contrasted *securitas* with *timor Dei*, and *praesumptio* with *vera spes*.[79] A. Kurz declares that when Luther fights violently against *securitas* in his Romans lectures, he apparently stands entirely on the side of ecclesiastical tradition.[80] We find that

---

[71] David C. Steinmetz, *Luther in Context* (Grand Rapids, 1995), p. 18. Cf. Strehle, *Catholic Roots*, pp. 8–14.

[72] Luther, *Disputatio* (1517), 16; in *WA* 1:234.

[73] Oberman, *Dawn*, p. 149.

[74] Luther, *Tractatus de libertate Christiana*, in *WA* 7:55.

[75] Luther, *Vorlesung über den 1. Timotheusbrief (4:9)*, in *WA* 26:79; *LW* 28:325.

[76] Luther, *Dictata super Psalterium (LXVIII [LXIX])*, in *WA* 3:416–17; *LW* 10:352.

[77] Luther, *Epistola ad Romanos (4:7)*, *Die Scholien*, in *WA* 56:279–80; *LW* 25:267.

[78] Luther, *De captivitate Babylonica*, in *WA* 6:538.

[79] Luther, *Disputatio Heidelbergae habita* (1518) 7 and 11, in *WA* 1:358–59. Hemmingius continues this Lutheran tradition in *Enchiridion*, p. 239: "Huius regula usus est, ut timeamus Deum, ne provocemus iram Dei nostra securitate et impoenitenti corde...."

[80] Alfred Kurz, *Die Heilsgewissheit bei Luther* (Gütersloh, 1933), p. 198. See Kurz, *Die Heilsgewissheit*, pp. 197–201, on the distinction between *certitudo* and *securitas* in Luther. Cf. Willem van't Spijker, *Luther: Belofte en ervaring* (Goes, 1983), p. 199; and Beeke, *Assurance*, p. 24, show the distinction in Luther. Zachman, *Assurance*, p. 84, notes Luther's warning against security only in passing.

Luther's use of the dialectic and its terminology corresponds well with the greater tradition.

John Calvin, whose influential theology was well known to Arminius, serves as a representative of the Continental Reformed tradition. A quick glance through the discussion of salvation in Calvin's *Institutio* reveals what he thought about *securitas*. When he discussed the nature of faith as a believer personally apprehending God's promises, he insisted that *securitas* is the fruit that follows.[81] Although it is not a security that never struggles or is affected by doubt, it is nevertheless *securitas*.[82] Calvin claimed that faith, apprehended by God's love, has solid security of all good things. Special security resides in the expectation of the future life.[83]

With Calvin's repeated use of *securitas* to describe the believer's state of mind in faith, his emphasis at first appears to be in tension with the preceding tradition. However, upon closer examination, it becomes clear that Calvin was not affirming *securitas salutis* over against its rejection by Jerome, Augustine, Gregory, Bernard, and Aquinas. First of all, throughout this section in the *Institutio* on faith, Calvin used *securitas, firmitudo, fiducia*, and *certitudo* almost interchangeably. He scarcely acknowledged any difference in these epistemological descriptions.[84] Second, his association of *securitas* with *timor (filialis) et trepidatio* in the midst of this section betrays his meaning. He declared that this connection of fear and trembling with "security of faith" is exemplified when believers, thinking about the examples of divine vengeance against the impious, "anxiously beware (*solicite cavent*)" lest they provoke God's wrath.[85] Thus, he was using *securitas* in a way consistent with Gregory's declaration that it can only be favorable if it is the result of godly fear. This *securitas* is neither the kind that Bernard said ignores God's justice nor the kind that Aquinas said excludes fear. Therefore, Calvin's acknowledgment of a positive connotation to *securitas*, along with his recognition that certainty must be accompanied by fear and trembling with regard to God's wrath, is in basic continuity with his predecessors. Furthermore, he goes

---

[81] *Inst.* 3.2.16.
[82] *Inst.* 3.2.17.
[83] *Inst.* 3.2.28.
[84] Henry Beveridge's translation also overlooks the peculiarity of *securitas*, for he variously translates *securitas, fiducia*, and *certitudo* as "security." Cf. translations offered in Kendall, *Calvin*, p. 19.
[85] *Inst.* 3.2.22.

on to make a distinction between "simple security" and *carnis securitas*, the latter of which "brings with it pride (*fastum*), arrogance, contempt of others, extinguishes humility, and reverence of God."[86]

Peter Martyr Vermigli, a Reformed contemporary of Calvin whose scholastic method anticipated the normative theological method of Reformed orthodoxy, was also represented in Arminius's library. More than Calvin, Vermigli explicitly interacted with the tradition on this point. Like Calvin, Vermigli distinguished Christian certainty from *carnis securitas*.[87] However, Vermigli also defended the use of *securitas* by appealing to Tertullian, whose little book on baptism says that "pure faith has security of salvation."[88] Furthermore, because Ambrose thanked God for our salvation and security, Vermigli said that "he asserts with us the security of salvation."[89]

G. Zanchi is one example of early Reformed orthodox thought on security. He made an explicit distinction between *securitas Spiritus* and *securitas carnis*:

> Security of the Spirit and of faith is that, by which because of such divine promises, and because of Christ's supplication and merits, we may be certain and secure concerning our perseverance in God's grace, and therefore concerning our eternal salvation: and so we take rest and sleep secure on Christ's bosom.... This security is not only good, but is also necessary for salvation.... Security of the flesh is that, by which we take rest not in God, nor in God's promises; but in our works, our powers and virtues....This security is destructive.[90]

Although not completely contradictory to the tradition, considered together, Calvin, Vermigli, and Zanchi represent a decided shift in the use of *securitas salutis*. Up to the mid-sixteenth century, Christian theology

---

[86] *Inst.* 3.24.7.

[87] Peter Martyr Vermigli, *In Epistolam S. Pauli Apostoli ad Rom. D. Petri Martyris Vermilii Florentini* (Basel, 1560), p. 320.

[88] Vermigli, *In Epistolam ad Rom.*, p. 1300: "fidem integram habere securitatem salutis."

[89] Vermigli, *In Epistolam ad Rom.*, p. 334: "eum securitatem salutis nobiscum asserere."

[90] Girolamo Zanchi, *Miscellaneorum libri tres* (London, 1605), p. 169: "Securitas Spiritus et fidei est ea, qua propter tantùm divinas promissiones, proptérque Christi precationem et merita, certi et securi simus de nostra in gratia Dei perseverantia, ideoque de aeterna nostri salute: atque ita securi in sinu Christi acquiescimus atque dormimus.... Haec securitas non solùm bona est, sed etiam ad salutem necessaria.... Securitas carnis est ea, qua non in Deo, neque in Dei promissionibus acquiescimus: sed tum nostris operibus, tum nostris viribus et virtutibus.... Securitas haec perniciosa est."

had generally underscored the harmful *securitas*, especially in the context of assurance of salvation, and had given only passing attention to its positive, acceptable use. Yet Calvin, Vermigli, and Zanchi, despite their warnings against *securitas carnis*, seem to have attempted to rescue *securitas* as a biblical and traditional position with reference to assurance of salvation, paying much less attention to its negative connotation. The need to affix a label like *carnis* to *securitas*, not known in the medieval period, shows that the normative use of *securitas* simpliciter was taking a positive turn. Therefore, their usual intention with the word *securitas* is positive; when they acknowledge the wicked *securitas*, it demands to be modified as *securitas carnis*. As will be shown below, it is a shift that will be influential in the period of early Reformed orthodoxy.

B.4. *The English Reformed Movement*
Before we deal with the views of Arminius and his Leiden colleagues, it is important for two reasons to note the state of this question in England. First, being aware of the development of this issue in England provides additional contextualization for the similar development of the problem in the low countries. Like Holland, England was influenced by the Continental Reformation both directly (by the teaching of resident aliens such as Martin Bucer, Peter Martyr Vermigli, and Peter Baro, as well as the return of the Marian exiles) and indirectly (by the imported writings of Calvin and others). Second, and more specific to Arminius, a look at England provides a background to the writings of William Perkins, whose work on predestination Arminius directly examined.

In mid-sixteenth-century Protestant England, warnings against "security" were a part of the popular piety. For example, Thomas Becon (ca. 1512–67), in his popular book on virtue and godly living, devoted a section to warning "agaynst carnall securitie and fleshly living without feare of God."[91] The biblical passages and examples he offered demonstrate that "securitie" means living without godly fear. Edwin Sandys (1519–88), archbishop of York, preached against sleeping in security and compared human life to warfare, leaving no place for security. After quoting a passage from Bernard, he said that Noah's contemporaries who were sleeping in security were awakened by the flood.[92]

---

[91] Thomas Becon, *The Governaunce of Vertue, teaching all faythfull Christians, how they ought dayly to lead their life* (London, 1578), fols. 148r–52r.
[92] Edwin Sandys, *Sermons Made by the most reverende Father in God, Edwin, Archbishop of*

This popular and traditional dialectic was given confessional status in the Church of England. In the 39 Articles of the Church of England, Article 17, on predestination, affirms a single predestination that does not at all mention reprobation. This omission in a confessional statement does not preclude double predestination. In fact, it is written is a way that does not exclude many types of unconditional predestination, and, arguably, even conditional predestination. For our purposes, what this article declares about despair and security is noteworthy. After stating that the consideration of predestination is beneficial for comforting the godly elect, the article says that the perpetual consideration of predestination is the most destructive precipice (*pernitiosissimum est praecipitium*) for curious and carnal people, for the devil uses this consideration of predestination to thrust them forth "either into despair or into the equally destructive security of a very impure life."[93] First, it is worth mentioning that this article assumes the dialectic between despair and security, and that these are both unhealthy attitudes toward salvation. Second, the article paints a remarkable picture regarding the direct connection between, on the one hand, consideration of predestination and, on the other hand, despair and security. For the curious and carnal, not only does thinking about this doctrine bring them to the brink, but it is also what the devil uses to throw them over the edge.[94]

Although the 39 Articles served as the normative confession for the Church of England, nevertheless, as the Church became increasingly influenced by the confessions and theology of the Continental Reformed churches, the English universities and their professors were increasingly intolerant of views that seemed to be underdetermined by the 39 Articles. Theological controversies were not uncommon in the churches and universities. One example of such disagreement was

---

Yorke (London, 1585), pp. 183–85. For references to and a discussion of puritan literature concerning secure believers, see Winship, 'Assurance and Puritan Practical Divinity,' 464–72.

[93] *Articuli XXXIX. Ecclesiae Anglicanae. A.D. 1562*, in Schaff, *The Creeds of Christendom* 3:486–516, art. 17: "vel in desperationem, vel in aeque pernitiosam impurissimae vitae securitatem."

[94] Cf. the similar idea in Ignatius of Loyola, *Exercitia spiritualia*, in *Institutum Societatis Iesu*, 3 vols. (Rome, 1869–86), 2: 417. For a description of one of the most influential English figures of this period, see Egil Grislis, 'The Assurance of Faith according to Richard Hooker,' in *Richard Hooker and the Construction of Christian Community*, Medieval and Renaissance Texts and Studies, vol. 165, ed. Arthur Stephen McGrade (Tempe, 1997), pp. 237–49.

the important controversy that had been brewing for years and finally broke out in Cambridge in 1595.[95] William Barrett, a divinity student, preached a *concio ad clerum* in which he railed against the increasing influence of "Calvinists." Interestingly, after Calvin, the first name Barrett mentioned was "P. Martyr," followed by, among others, Zanchi.[96] The sermon primarily was a polemic against unconditional predestination, but he also raised the distinction between *certus* and *securus*, claiming that no one "ought to be secure about his salvation" (*de salute sua debeat esse securus*). Although Barrett did not mention Augustine, this statement is almost a direct quote from *Confessiones*.[97] Nevertheless, eleven days later, the Heads of Cambridge forced Barrett to deliver a public recantation drawn up by the Cambridge theologian Robert Some, in which Barrett was made to say, among other things, that those who are justified "ought to be certain *and secure* regarding their own salvation, by the certainty of faith itself,"[98] a statement in direct contradiction with Augustine and the tradition.

However, Archbishop of Canterbury John Whitgift was not pleased with the treatment Barrett received from the Heads of Cambridge. Although he agreed with some of their points against him, nevertheless Whitgift agreed with Barrett's original use of *certus* rather than *securus*.[99] Furthermore, not all of Archbishop Whitgift's advisors were thrilled with the text of the retraction Barrett was made to read. For example, Adrianus Saravia, collaborating author of the Belgic Confession and one time theologian and rector of the University of Leiden, although

---

[95] For a more detailed account of this controversy, see Stanglin, 'Arminius *avant la lettre*'; and Elizabeth Gilliam and W. J. Tighe, 'To "Run with the Time": Archbishop Whitgift, the Lambeth Articles, and the Politics of Theological Ambiguity in Late Elizabethan England,' *SCJ* 23/2 (1992), 325–40.

[96] William Barrett, 'Recantatio Mri. Barret,' in John Strype, *The Life and Acts of John Whitgift, D.D.*, 3 vols. (1718; repr. Oxford, 1822), 3: 317–20, there 319. The text of the sermon has not survived, but this *recantatio* summarized what he recanted in the sermon.

[97] Letham, 'Faith,' 1:288, misunderstands the source of Barrett's allusion when he says, "Barrett's main contention was 'neminem debere esse securum de salute.' This assertion was dependent on his revision of the doctrine of predestination, it being based on foreknowledge." Letham, in his attempt to link Barrett's statement to a doctrine of conditional predestination, is apparently unaware that Barrett was alluding to Augustine. Letham clearly fails to take into account the controversial history of the term *securitas*, noting only that Calvin had used it approvingly (ibid., 2:153 n. 252).

[98] Barrett, 'Recantatio,' in Strype, *Life and Acts* 3:317, italics mine: "Ergo debere eos de salute sua, fidei ipsius certitudine, certos esse *et securos*."

[99] Strype, *Life and Acts* 2:238–40 and 254.

approving of some of the retractions, also agreed with Barrett's original distinction between *certitudo* and *securitas*. Saravia, in line with the tradition and then alluding to Jerome, wrote that "there is a great difference between certainty of salvation, and security. Faith brings forth certainty; presumption and arrogance [bring forth] security."[100]

Likewise, Lancelot Andrewes, another advisor of Whitgift, wrote a censure of the Heads' censure of Barrett. In addition to his appeals to scriptural examples of people in a state of security who eventually fell away, Andrewes cited Hilary, Chrysostom, Ambrose, Augustine, Leo the Great, Gregory the Great, and Bernard against security.[101] Security, according to Andrewes and following Augustine, seems to disagree both with the Christian life, which is a special work of difficulty (*militia*), and human life, which is a temptation (*tentatio*).[102] In the end, although he recognizes a difference between *carnalis et spiritualis securitas*, Andrewes wonders whether it is expedient to use the word *securitas* in these times, and he concludes that it is not.[103] In other words, for Andrewes, despite the occasional positive use of *securitas*, the word itself is not worth rescuing as a standard description of assurance.

Despite the limited support for Barrett on the certainty of salvation, in response to Barrett's sermon and insincere recantation, William Whitaker, Regius Professor of Divinity at Cambridge, drew up the Lambeth Articles, revised by several divines under Archbishop Whitgift.[104] These articles were intended as the new rule for teaching at Cambridge. Lambeth Article 6 said that a faithful person "is, by the full assurance of faith, certain regarding remission of his sins and his eternal salvation by

---

[100] Adrianus Saravia, 'Opinion of Barret's Recantation,' in Willem Nijenhuis, *Adrianus Saravia (c. 1532–1613): Dutch Calvinist, first Reformed Defender of the English Episcopal Church order on the Basis of the Ius Divinum* [SHCT 21] (Leiden, 1980), pp. 330–42, there p. 330: "Magnum discrimen est inter certitudinem de salute et securitatem. Certitudinem parit fides, securitatem presumptio et arrogantia."

[101] Lancelot Andrewes, *Censura censurae D. Barreti de certitudine salutis*, in F. G., ed., *Articuli Lambethani* (London, 1651), pp. 33–5 and 37–40.

[102] Andrewes, *Censura censurae*, p. 35.

[103] Andrewes, *Censura censurae*, p. 37.

[104] For Whitaker's original Latin articles, see W. D. Sargeaunt, 'The Lambeth Articles,' *Journal of Theological Studies* 12 (1911), 251–60, 427–36, there 427–28; for the finalized Latin articles, which changed the wording of propositions 2, 5, 6, and 7, see William Prynne, *Anti-Arminianisme: Or The Church of Englands old antithesis to new Arminianisme* ([London,] 1630), pp. 12–14; and Schaff, *The Creeds of Christendom*, 3:523–24; for both versions juxtaposed with commentary on the changes, see F. G., ed., *Articuli Lambethani*, pp. 12–19.

Christ."[105] Therefore, even these anti-Barrett articles did not approve of *securitas*, but only *certitudo*.

Although it was forbidden to preach on the controversial new articles, Whitaker proceeded to offer his interpretation in his *concio ad clerum* on 9 October 1595. This sermon, which would be his last, not only looked back to the Barrett controversy, but was also directed against the teaching of his own Cambridge colleague, the Lady Margaret Professor Peter Baro, who was Barrett's teacher and who had been teaching conditional predestination at Cambridge for over twenty years. Whitaker concluded his sermon with some points on the certainty of salvation. He implied that the doctrine of his opponents causes a believer to perpetually doubt his salvation. Then, surely much to the chagrin of Baro, and in apparent conflict with the 39 Articles and implicit conflict with the Lambeth Articles, Whitaker proceeded to give a defense of *securitas*, quoting Isa. 32,17 to support its biblical use.[106] Whitaker associated *securitas* with the New Testament words θάρσος and θαρρέω, and was not able to understand how anyone could be offended at the word *securitas*.[107] In an attempt to show that his view was not novel, he then cited Ambrose, Augustine, and a few other fathers, along with some contemporary Catholics, who used *securus* in a positive way, concluding that the testimonies supporting his viewpoint are "infinite." Whitaker's constant repetition of *securitas* and *securus* in this sermon no doubt rang in the ears of the auditors who knew what was at stake in these words. He affirmed those who "preach certain truth, and true certainty, and holy security."[108] Before ending the sermon, Whitaker went on to declare, "Securely, and in perpetuity is this perseverance secure and security persevering."[109]

---

[105] F. G., ed., *Articuli Lambethani*, pp. 16–7: "Homo vere fidelis, id est, fide justificante praeditus, certus est Plerophoria fidei de Remissione peccatorum suorum et salute sempiterna sua per Christum." "Plerophoria" was substituted for Whitaker's original "certitudine." See *Articuli Lambethani* for the rationale behind this alteration.

[106] William Whitaker, *Cygnea cantio Guilielmi Whitakeri, hoc est, ultima illius concio ad clerum... Octob. 9. anno Dom. 1595*, in *Praelectiones doctissimi viri Guilielmi Whitakeri* (Cambridge, Eng., 1599), p. 24. Peter Baro, *In Jonam Prophetam praelectiones 39. In quibus multa pié doctéque differuntur et explicantur* (London, 1579), p. 89, compared Jonah's slumbering in the boat with the tendency to sleep secure ("dormimus tamen securi").

[107] Whitaker, *Cygnea cantio*, p. 24. In view of Whitaker's claim, it is worth pointing out that the Vulgate translates θάρσος as *fiducia* and θαρρέω as *audeo* and *confido*, never as *securus* or its derivatives.

[108] Whitaker, *Cygnea cantio*, p. 25: "...certam veritatem, et certitudinem veram, et sanctam securitatem praedicant."

[109] Whitaker, *Cygnea cantio*, p. 26: "*Secure, et in perpetuum est haec perseverantia secura, et securitas perseverans.*"

Whitaker attempted to make the case that, not only is *securitas* far from being a harmful attitude, it is the biblical and proper attitude of the believer concerning personal salvation. For Whitaker, not only is there no such thing as an unhealthy assurance of salvation, but also the word that some have used to describe it, *securitas*, is really a sound word.

Having glanced at *securitas/desperatio* through English eyes by means of examples of popular piety and preaching, confessional codification of doctrine, and the struggle at Cambridge University, we are now set to examine this issue from the viewpoint of Perkins, who lived his life in all three of these spheres. No one in early orthodoxy gave more attention to the problem of the assurance of salvation than Perkins. In the preface to one of his works dealing with cases of conscience, he explained the occasion that prompts his writing: "In Gods Church commonly they who are touched by the Spirit, and begin to come on in Religion, are much troubled with feare, that they are not Gods children; and none so much as they. Therefore they often think on this point: and are not quiet till they finde some resolution."[110]

Therefore, given that Perkins saw lack of assurance as no small problem in living the Christian life, it appears that much of his work was stimulated by the need to answer doubting and despair.[111] This emphasis is evident by the amount of attention he gives to the problem. Desperation, according to Perkins, is when a person is "out of all hope of the pardon of his sinnes."[112] Perkins makes a distinction of degrees in this distress of mind that is contrary to faith.

> The lesse is a single Feare or griefe, when a man standeth in suspense and doubt of his owne salvation, and in feare that he shall be condemned. The greater distresse is Despaire, when a man is without all hope of salvation in his own sense and apprehension. I call Despaire a greater distresse, because it is not a distinct kinde of trouble of minde, (as some doe thinke) but the highest degree in every kinde of distresse. For every distresse in the minde is a feare of condemnation, and comes at length to desperation, if it be not cured.[113]

---

[110] Perkins, *A Case of Conscience*, in *Workes of Perkins* 1:422.

[111] See Perkins, *A Golden Chaine: or, the Description of Theologie*, in *Workes of Perkins* 1:114 col. 1 a. Cf. Winship, 'Assurance and Puritan Practical Divinity,' 473: "Perkins...systematically organized assurance and faith around the weak Christian."

[112] Perkins, *A Discourse of Conscience. Wherein Is Set Downe the nature, properties, and differences thereof*, 8th ed., in *Workes of Perkins* 1:536 col. 2 b–c. Cf. idem, *An Exposition of the Symbole, or Creed of the Apostles: According to the tenour of Scripture, and the consent of Orthodoxe Fathers of the Church*, in *Workes of Perkins* 1:258 col. 2 c.

[113] Perkins, *Cases*, in *Workes of Perkins* 2:22 col. 1 b–c.

Hence, there are greater and lesser degrees of distress or despair. The lesser fear, if left unchecked, will lead to the greater fear, which is properly termed despair. Perkins acknowledges that even the elect "may fall into despaire of Gods mercy for a time, and this is a dangerous sin. For he which despaires, makes all the promises of God to be false: and this sinne of all other is most contrary to true saving faith."[114]

Even if Perkins gave much more attention in his writings to the danger of despair in the Christian life, he did not completely ignore the problem of security. Like his Reformed predecessors and contemporaries, Perkins drew a distinction between carnal and spiritual security, one which apparently arose as an attempt to codify terminology for the phenomenon of the positive and the negative connotations of *securitas* throughout the tradition. "Spirituall," said Perkins, is "when a man relieth on God for his salvation, by beleeving his promises." On the other hand, there is "carnall, when a man regardeth not at all the means of his salvation, but giveth himselfe wholly to the profits and pleasures of this world."[115] Elsewhere, Perkins described carnal security as "when men upon contempt of the judgements of God, and threatnings of his Word, goe on still in their sinnes, flattering and soothing themselves."[116] The elect, just as they can commit the sin of despair, are also liable to this sin of presumption.[117] This "carnall conceit" is distinguishable from the true witness of God's Spirit.[118] Perkins denies that his doctrine of salvation encourages (carnal) security; instead, he affirms certainty. Giving attention to the means makes one fearful and careful, not secure.[119] Therefore, Perkins, unlike his Cambridge colleague Whitaker, is cautious about using the word security to describe assurance of salvation, which should always be accompanied by fear and trembling. He prefers to speak of certainty. When Perkins does employ "security," he connects it with a reliance on God's promises.

---

[114] Perkins, *A Treatise Tending unto a Declaration, whether a Man Be in the Estate of Damnation, or in the Estate of Grace*, in *Workes* 1:378 col. 1 b.

[115] Perkins, *A godly and learned Exposition or Commentarie upon the Three First Chapters of the Revelation*, in *Workes of Perkins* 3:272 col. 2 c–d.

[116] Perkins, *How to Live, and that Well: In All Estates and Times. Specially, when helps and comforts faile*, in *Workes of Perkins* 1:482 col. 1 d.

[117] Perkins, *Estate of Damnation or Grace*, in *Workes* 1:378 col. 1 b.

[118] Perkins, *Cases*, in *Workes of Perkins* 2:19 col. 1 b–c.

[119] Perkins, *Commentarie upon the Three First Chapters of the Revelation*, in *Workes of Perkins* 3:298 col. 2 c.

B.5. *Summary of the Preceding Tradition*

To summarize the progression of the whole tradition preceding Arminius, there is a dialectic present that opposes the extreme notion of careless presumption against the extreme notion of hopeless dread. *Securitas*
(along with *praesumptio*) and *desperatio* became formulaic terms to denote
the two extremes in the context of the life of salvation. Admonitions regarding both of these conditions were not an uncommon motif in treatises concerning, and exhortations directed to, the church; that is, these
were problems that concerned Christians. It is worth noting that warning against *securitas* was not a practice exclusive to conditional predestinarians. Proponents of unconditional predestination, such as Augustine
and Luther, were equally bothered by the threat of *securitas*. To caution
against *securitas* was so far from being a sign of Pelagian influence that
Augustine did so in a treatise against Pelagius.

The generally positive association of the word *certitudo*, over against
the negative association of *securitas* when it is applied to the context of
assurance of salvation, indicates that a *via media* is possible. This is not
to say that every incidence of the word *securitas* carried a negative connotation. That the connotation of *securitas* varied with its context is seen
when, on the one hand, Luther decried *securitas* as laziness, and, on the
other hand, he praised *securitas* in God's promise and being *securus* in
conscience. This positive aspect is confirmed by Altenstaig's definitions.
The elect, from the perspective of divine omniscience, are ontologically
secure in salvation. Even from the perspective of the believer in this
life, there is a sense in which he may be secure in God's promise. More
often, though, epistemological *certitudo salutis* was preferred over *securitas
salutis*.

However, in an attempt to rescue true assurance of salvation, Reformed theology saw a general shift to stronger language of assurance,
a shift that has gone largely unnoticed in the major studies of assurance
in Calvin and the Reformed tradition.[120] Vis-à-vis the larger Christian
tradition, there are two indicators of this shift. First, there was now little
room left for warning against unhealthy assurance in the period of early
orthodoxy. Besides the occasional, brief recognition of *securitas carnalis*,
it is rare to find prominent theologians of the period of early Reformed

---

[120] The lack of attention to this dialectic and to the shift in terminology in the work of
Beeke, Bell, Kendall, and Zachman justifies both the need for the preceding discussion
as well as my scarce interaction with these sources throughout that discussion.

orthodoxy who warned against the dangers of unhealthy assurance and general use of the term *securitas* without also being accused of hetero-doxy, and usually in particular, of "papism."[121]

Further indication of the shift is the increasingly positive use of *securitas* in the context of the assurance of salvation and the subtle use of the distinction between *spiritualis securitas* and *carnalis securitas*. The need to modify *securitas* with the negative *carnalis/carnis* betrays the new normal sense of positive *securitas* in Reformed churches. I have noted Calvin's overwhelmingly positive use of *securitas*, and the increasing tendency for simple *securitas* to stand for the positive, and carnal *securitas* for the nega-tive. It became more common, unless otherwise noted, to understand *securitas* (*simpliciter*) as healthy and salutary. This tendency is evidenced by Whitaker's unapologetic insistence on the propriety of the word *securitas* without any qualification or re-definition. Whitaker appealed to the stream in the tradition that recognized the positive aspect of *securitas*. Without exegeting every source cited by Whitaker and others in this pos-itive tradition, we can at least wonder whether in every case *securitas* was being directly applied—as Whitaker himself applied it—to the context of an attitude about salvation. In any case, Whitaker's idea of applying this controversial word to the believer's attitude concerning salvation did not endure in the Reformed tradition.[122] As will be demonstrated below, Reformed usage and Whitaker's insistence were not enough to rescue the negative connotation of the word *securitas* when applied in the context of the assurance of salvation. However, the core idea that *securitas* is not a genuine threat to the elect lived on after Whitaker and became a source of agitation to Arminius. This whole section provides further evidence that the concern of Arminius regarding the right doc-trine of assurance was a concern shared by early Reformed orthodoxy in general, and it was the debate over Arminius's proposed corrective to the assurance problem that culminated at the Synod of Dort.

C. *The Dialectic in Arminius and His Colleagues*

Having surveyed the use of this dialectic up to the time of Arminius, it is now suitable to examine Arminius's use of it in more detail. The fullest

---

[121] One possible exception to this is Saravia. But cf. the cases of Barrett, Baro, and Andrewes, a Baro sympathizer.

[122] See the discussion of the Leiden theology below.

discussion of this dialectic in Arminius appears in the *Declaratio sententiae*.
He defined *securitas*, or his literal translation into Dutch, *sorgloosheyt*, as
"when a person persuades himself that, however inattentive he may be
to the worship of God, he will not be damned but saved."[123] Consistent
with Altenstaig, Arminius defined *desperatio*, or his literal translation, *wanhope*, as "when he persuades himself that, whatever degree of reverence
he may evince towards God, he will not receive any remuneration."[124]
He defined *securitas* and *desperatio* this way in light of Heb. 11,6, which
says that God rewards those who seek him. Both of these conditions,
according to Arminius, are contrary to faith.[125] They represent two opposite forms of a lack of true assurance. On an Aristotelian model,
desperatio and *securitas* are two extreme vices, the most distant points in
opposite directions from the true virtue of *certitudo salutis*, the golden
mean. This *certitudo*, this *via media* between two vices, is true hope.

Arminius's discussion of despair in particular must be seen in its
Thomistic context. Arminius accepted the common Aristotelian division of the affections into the ἐπιθυμητικός, that is, concupiscible or
desiring, and the θυμοειδής, that is, irascible, which apply to humanity
and by analogy to God as well.[126] In the irascible affections, despair is
said to be the opposite of hope.[127] Hope must be confirmed in order
for despair to be removed.[128] Arminius also indicated that *desperatio* is a
consequence of the human awareness of sinfulness before God. This
awareness sometimes causes one to despair of God's mercy.[129] Despair
thus looks only to God's just punishment against sin, and not to his gracious mercy. What Arminius wrote about *desperatio* manifests complete
conformity with traditional theology.

As mentioned above, Arminius viewed *desperatio* as a serious evil and
irritant of souls, a pastoral problem that he faced in his own ministry
to others. However, Arminius regarded the threat of *securitas* as an even
more serious problem in the church. Arminius feared that, once people
have been delivered from their fall into despair, they might subsequently
fall off the other side into negligence (*negligentia*) and security. "Human-

---

[123] *Dec. sent.*, p. 93; in *Opera*, p. 114; *Works* 1:637.
[124] *Dec. sent.*, p. 93; in *Opera*, p. 114; *Works* 1:638.
[125] Arminius, *De fide* (1605), xvi.
[126] *Disp. pub.* IV.lxx; XVII.iii; *Disp. priv.* XX.ix.
[127] *Disp. pub.* IV.lxxii; *Disp. priv.* XX.xi.
[128] *Disp. priv.* XXXIX.x.
[129] *Ep. ecc.* 45, p. 96; in *Works* 2:750–51.

ity," wrote Arminius, "has a greater propensity to the latter [security] than to the former [despair]."[130] This security is "directly opposed to the most salutary fear, with which we are commanded to work out our salvation."[131] In continuity with the tradition, Arminius viewed *securitas* as a problematic attitude for a Christian. Significantly, unlike some of his Reformed contemporaries, every occurrence of *securitas* in Arminius assumes the negative, carnal *securitas*.[132] It makes no difference that he sometimes follows Reformed usage by modifying *securitas* as *carnalis*, for security is always evil for him. I am not suggesting that Arminius was unaware of or outright rejected a *securitas spiritualis*. However, his silence concerning the legitimacy of such a category reveals the intensity of his reaction to contemporary usage of his day.

The prefaces contained in Arminius's *Opera* offer further commentary regarding his feelings on the danger of *securitas*. Although the prefaces were signed by the "nine orphan children" (*liberi orphani novem*) of Arminius, these theologically and politically astute pieces of writing were probably composed not by a child, but by Arminius's friend Uytenbogaert.[133] At any rate, the prefaces written by the so-called *liberi* give an interesting insight into the interpretation of Arminius by those closest to him. They say that Arminius was worried that the Reformed doctrine of predestination would supply arguments for and prepare the way to "either security or true despair," bar many "from all care (*cura*) of Religion," and that not a few would be lulled "to a confidence

---

[130] *Disp. pub.* VIII.viii.

[131] *Art. non.* 22.4; in *Opera*, p. 962; *Works* 2:726.

[132] *Dec. sent.*, pp. 93–4; in *Works* 1:637–38; *Disp. pub.* VIII.viii; XV.xiv; *Disp. priv.* XXXIX.ix; XLIII.viii; *Art. non.* 22.4; in *Opera*, p. 962; *Works* 2:726; *De fide* (1605), xvi. The English reader should be cautious about the use of the adjective in the translation by Nichols, who obviously did not grasp the subtleties of the distinction between *securitas* and *certitudo*. E.g., "secure" in *Disp. pub.* XIV.ii is a translation of *tutus*. Moreover, this use of *tutus* refers to ontological, not epistemological, safety. The same is true of Nichols' translation of *Analysis cap. 9. ad Romanos ad Gellium Snecanum*, in *Opera*, p. 786; *Works* 3:497, where he has Arminius seemingly approving "the security of our salvation." First, the Latin phrase is "salutis nostrae firmitas," and, second, he is speaking of ontological stability.

[133] It has become common wisdom that the prefaces were not composed by any of the children, the oldest of whom was seventeen at the time of Arminius's death. None went on to become a theologian or pastor. Thus, Maronier, *Arminius*, p. 339 n. 1, states that the author is unknown. Bangs, 'Introduction,' in *Works* 1:xviii and xxviii, is convinced that the author is Uytenbogaert, which is as good a guess as any. However, since Bangs gives no evidence for his assertion, and since I am unaware of any evidence myself, I shall refer to the author as the prefaces do—the "liberi."

(*confidentiam*) not according to the Spirit."[134] The preface to *De sensu cap. VII. ad Romanos dissertatio* provides the most extensive commentary on the danger of *securitas*. Near the beginning of the preface, the *liberi* described *securitas* in the following way:

> If this admonition [to piety] ever was necessary, it is certainly the more necessary at this time; because we see impiety overflowing in every direction, like a sea raging and agitated by whirlwinds. Yet amidst all this storm, such are the stupor and ἀναιθησία [insensibility] of people, that not a few who remain exactly the same persons as they formerly were, and who indeed have not changed the least particle of the manners of their impure life, still imagine themselves to be in the class of prime Christians, and promise themselves the favor of the Supreme God, heaven, life, and of the company of Christ and of the blessed angels, with such great and *presumptuous confidence* (*praesumptuosa praefidentia*), and with such *security of soul* (*animi securitate*) that they consider themselves to be atrociously injured by those who, judging them to be deceived in this vain persuasion, order them in any way to doubt (*dubitare*) concerning it.[135]

The *liberi* went on to call this a state of "diabolical lethargy."[136] It should be noted, however, that Arminius never encouraged people to "doubt" their salvation, but to be stirred out of the presumptuous slumber of *securitas*, as the preface here seems to be saying. To the degree that later Remonstrants encouraged people to doubt their salvation in order to stir them to good works, they demonstrate their discontinuity with Arminius himself.[137]

Consistent with Arminius, the preface then proceeds to enumerate some of the signs of this carelessness. However, Arminius only claimed that, with *securitas*, vices are often dismissed as nothing to worry about;

---

[134] Preface to *Exam. Perk.*, in *Opera*, pp. 627–28; *Works* 3:257–59.
[135] Preface to *Cap. VII Rom.*, in *Opera*, p. 812; *Works* 2:473, italics mine.
[136] Preface to *Cap. VII Rom.*, in *Opera*, p. 812; *Works* 2:473.
[137] Moulin, *Anatomy*, pp. 468–69, accused Arminians of encouraging people to doubt their salvation. There can be no question that later "Arminians" did encourage doubt. In a mock dialogue between Arminius and the fictional Enthusiastus, there is a whole section on the certainty of salvation. See O. N., *An Apology of English Arminianisme or a Dialogue, betweene Iacobus Arminius, Professour in the University of Leyden in Holland; and Enthusiastus an English Doctour of Divinity, and a great Precisian* ([Saint-Ômer,] 1634), pp. 88–132. The author accurately portrays Arminius seeking assurance as a means between two extremes. However, he has Arminius proscribing *certitudo* of salvation, and instead promoting doubt and uncertainty of our election. This apology is indicative of how even the "defenders" of Arminius, past and present, have misunderstood and twisted his writings. Cf. *Canons and Decrees of the Council of Trent*, ed. H. J. Schroeder (St. Louis, 1950), pp. 35 and 38–39.

this preface goes further by claiming that the extreme form of *securitas* actually considers vices to be virtues, and virtues to be vices.

> Thus, among people, drunkenness obtains the name of hilarity; and αἰσχρολογία [foul language], that of happy παρρησία; [but] sobriety in food and drink, and simplicity in dress, that of hypocrisy. This is really to call good evil, and vice versa; and [is] to seek an occasion, by which one may cease from the practice of virtues, and devote himself to vices, not only without any reluctance of conscience, but also at the impelling and instigating of his [seared] conscience.[138]

Finally, the preface points out the disparity between the attention that *desperatio* generally received and the lack of attention to *securitas*. According to the *liberi*, "all things (*omnia*) are directed to the assurance of special mercy (*specialis misericordiae fiduciam*)...against the despair that is opposed to it; but in which all things are not directed to the necessary performance of obedience in opposition to security." They inferred that this lack of attention to security is due to the widespread assumption that despair should be more greatly feared than security. In fact, said the *liberi*, the contrary is true. In addition to the earlier assertion of the prevalence of *securitas* in the church of their time, they declared that Scripture only gives one example of someone in the state of *desperatio* (namely, Judas), but gives very many testimonies of persons in the state of *securitas*.[139] Indeed, concerning the amount of attention generally given toward these vices, they said that *desperatio* is "more familiar among us" than is *securitas carnalis*.[140]

This observation that the danger of *securitas* was generally overlooked by Arminius's contemporaries is confirmed with an examination of the Leiden disputations. After perusing all the available disputations related

---

[138] Preface to *Cap. VII Rom.*, in *Opera*, p. 814; *Works* 2:476. These examples likely reflect the context and ethical concerns of Arminius himself. For example, Schotel, *Academie*, p. 231, notes that several professors at the university, including Kuchlinus, took to drunkenness. Schotel also recounts the stories of Arminius's encounters with Dominicus Baudius, a Latinist at Leiden University known for his bad behavior. Baudius was heading across the Breedestraat (modern day Breestraat) to a bar called "de Hemel." Baudius called to Arminius, "I am going by the broad way to heaven (*per viam latam ad coelum*)," thus making a pun of the street name and turning Jesus' warning of Matt. 7,13–14 on its head. On another occasion, Arminius, seeing Baudius lying on the street drunk, said to him, "Pestis Academiae!" to which Baudius replied, "Pestis Ecclesiae!" Bangs, *Arminius*, p. 250, reports that Baudius later died of delirium tremens.

[139] Preface to *Cap. VII Rom.*, in *Opera*, p. 817; *Works* 2:480.

[140] Preface to *Exam. Perk.*, in *Opera*, p. 632; *Works* 3:263.

to the doctrine of salvation, I have discovered only two brief references to *securus* or *securitas* in this context.[141] The first comes from Junius,
who says that our confidence in God's promise renders our conscience
secure (*securam*) against all temptations.[142] However, this description of
the conscience that is secure concerning God's promise relates more to
the positive use of *securus* than to the negative connotation associated
with security directly concerning personal salvation. In accord with his
contemporaries, Junius offered no warning against *securitas de salute* or
too much assurance, but only against too little assurance.

Of more relevance is a reference to *securitas* found in a disputation on
faith by Gomarus: "Although it is imperfect, and occasionally becomes
faint and either is buried under the ashes of security, or is held back by
the difficulty of spiritual temptations, nevertheless, salvific faith once
reckoned in the elect can never plainly be extinguished or defect."[143]
This is the only pertinent use of *securitas* that I found among Arminius's
contemporary colleagues, and indeed the only *quasi* warning against
too much assurance. Gomarus's statement yields two interesting points.
First, *securitas* has retained its negative connotation, even for Gomarus.
He described it as something that tends to bury saving faith. Thus, the
implicit attempts of Reformed usage and the explicit attempt of Whitaker to rescue *securitas* as an appropriate term for describing the biblical
attitude of certainty of personal salvation apparently did not completely
succeed.[144] Moreover, the pertinent question is not whether *securitas* is an
evil to be avoided; about this both Arminius and Gomarus concurred.
The question is whether Gomarus's doctrine of salvation really generated *securitas*; Arminius would affirm that it does, and Gomarus would
naturally deny it.

The second point is that, although *securitas* retains its evil connotation,
Gomarus still insists that even *securitas* is not a genuine threat to saving
faith. It is more like a temporary weakness which seems to deserve no

---

[141] One should keep in mind that their neglect of the issue of *securitas* does not mean
that the Leiden theologians considered sanctification to be insignificant or optional in
the life of a Christian.

[142] Junius, *De certitudine* (1601), xii.

[143] Gomarus, *De fide salvifica* (1603), xv: "Quod licet imperfecta sit, et interdum langu-
escat et vel sub cineribus securitatis sepeliatur, vel mole tentationum spiritualium suppri-
matur: tamen fides salvifica semel accensa in Electis, nunquam possit plane extingui aut
deficere...."

[144] Cf. also *Canons of Dort*, 5.12–13, which denies that its soteriology makes believers
"carnaliter securos," or that it produces "lasciviam aut pietatis injuriam."

more attention than this passing reference in the thesis. Therefore, according to Gomarus, for the elect, *securitas* is really no cause of concern. This lax attitude toward something which Arminius considered to be a great danger is exactly the problem pointed out by Arminius. Not caring about carelessness would only confirm, for Arminius, the depth of the problem of *securitas*.

A final question to explore regarding this dialectic is the potential of good ever resulting from these two errors. Even with the negative aspect of *desperatio*, which attracted the ubiquitous attention of Reformed pastors and theologians who warned Christians of its danger, it was also not uncommon to see a positive use of the feeling of *desperatio*. A sort of healthy *desperatio* was acknowledged that leads one to depend on God. Luther recalled being brought "to the depth and abyss of despair" (*ad profundum et abyssum desperationis*) before realizing "how salutary that despair was and how near to grace."[145] Perkins declared, "For when a man despaireth of himselfe and of his owne power in the matter of his salvation, it tends to his eternall comfort."[146] He defined "holy desperation" as "when a man is wholly out of all hope ever to attaine salvation by any strength or goodnes of his owne: speaking and thinking more vilely of himself than any other can doe; and heartily acknowledging himselfe to have deserved not one onely, but even ten thousand damnations in hell fire with the divell and his angels."[147] Kuchlinus said that one reason for preaching the law is, "So that despairing of our own righteousness, we might more ardently seek the most perfect righteousness of Jesus Christ, which is offered in the Gospel, and applied to us by true faith."[148] Arminius claimed that the law is an instrumental cause of faith in that it drives us to a "holy despair" (*sancta desperatio*) concerning our own powers.[149] The positive function of despair in this context corresponds with the second use of the moral law. As Calvin put it, the law condemns a person in order that he "may be brought at once to know and to confess his weakness and impurity."[150] Thus, recognizing one's

---

[145] Luther, *De servo arbitrio*, in *WA* 18:719; *LW* 33:190; cf. idem, *Disputatio Heidelbergae habita* (1518) 18, in *WA* 1:361; idem, *De Libertate Christiana*, in *WA* 7:52.

[146] Perkins, *An Exposition of the Symbole*, in *Workes of Perkins* 1:258 col. 2 c.

[147] Perkins, *Estate of Damnation or Grace*, in *Workes of Perkins* 1:365 col. 1 a–b.

[148] Kuchlinus, *De perfectione*, xiii: "…de iustitia propria desperantes, iustitiam Iesu Christi perfectissimam, quae in Evangelio offertur, et per veram fidem nobis applicatur, ardentius quaeramus."

[149] Arminius, *De fide* (1605), v.

[150] *Inst.* 2.7.6; cf. *Disp. pub.* XII.iv.

own despair is a step to faith. Nevertheless, *desperatio* retains its negative import, for Arminius declared that it is "contrary to faith,"[151] inasmuch as it properly describes those unregenerate who do not possess, or have not yet been given in time, the gift of saving faith.

Since the recognition of *desperatio* can have a positive outcome, it is appropriate to ask whether *securitas* can ever be a good thing. We have already seen that Whitaker and others attempted to rescue *securitas* in the context of assurance of salvation, referring to it as *sancta securitas* or *securitas Spiritus/spiritualis*. On the contrary, although Arminius was willing to speak of *sancta desperatio*, he never spoke of *sancta securitas*, as did Whitaker. *Desperatio* is only good when it is recognized as such, and the desperate person is then able to find hope in God. *Desperatio* is holy when it functions as a direct, proximate means to true assurance. In contrast, *securitas* can never be the means to good in a comparable way. By definition, those in the state of *securitas* either do not know it, or they do not care. *Securitas* is only positive when it is recognized for what it truly is, the state of *desperatio*. The *securus* person must be brought out of his stupor in order to see his real condition of despair. According to Arminius, one use of the doctrine of predestination is to terrify the wicked (*impii*) and to drive away their *securitas*.[152] *Securitas* must be driven away. Whereas a person can be self-aware of his *desperatio* and learn to depend on God, a *securus* person is not even aware of the danger of *securitas*, and when he is made aware by something external, it is only a means to *desperatio*. Thus, *securitas* is, at best, only an indirect, improper means to the assurance of salvation.

III. *The Dialectic and Reformed Soteriology*

Arminius saw the problems of *desperatio* and *securitas* as two opposite extremes, each a manifestation of a lack of true, biblical assurance of salvation. In contrast to his Reformed contemporaries, Arminius did not think that a solution could be found by simply pointing out these problems. To encourage a doubting person to rest assured, or a pre-

---

[151] Arminius, *De fide* (1605), xvi.

[152] *Disp. pub.* XV.xiv. The Dutch translator of this disputation provides an interesting insight into the connotation of *securitas* when he renders "impii" as "godloosente" and "securitas" as "godloosheyt." See Arminius and Gomarus, *Twee disputatien*, fol. C4r.

sumptuous person to be careful, fails to address the common root of the problems. Arminius considered this dialectic of *desperatio* and *securitas* to be the direct result of certain distinctive aspects of soteriology increasingly taught and commonly accepted in the Reformed churches. Arminius's contention is that Reformed soteriology in general and predestination in particular provided fertile ground for these two pests of religion and of souls to be fruitful and multiply. Under this assumption, encouragement towards true assurance is fine, but it overlooks the underlying cause of the problem.

A. Desperatio *as the Effect of Reformed Soteriology*

Arminius implied that there are two aspects of Reformed soteriology that, in light of unconditional predestination, can lead a person to *desperatio*. Both aspects concern the doctrine of faith. The first problem regards the Reformed use of *fiducia*. This word, which was employed nearly synonymously with *certitudo*, was generally joined as a necessary component of saving *fides*, and often used synonymously with *fides*.[153] Saving faith is incomplete without assurance. As quoted above, Zanchi considered *securitas Spiritus* to be necessary for salvation. Whitaker claimed that those who deny certainty of salvation "leave us no faith."[154] In other words, if there is no certainty, it is because there is no true faith.

This Reformed doctrine of faith, which includes the element of *fiducia*, was certainly taught and defended with good intentions of restoring true assurance of salvation to God's people. However, under this assumption, if a person has belief in Christ as Savior, and believes that Christ's righteousness may be imputed to him by faith, and the person desires this salvation, yet this person lacks certainty of this salvation, then the person is inclined to begin to question his faith altogether. That is, if he is missing a key component of saving faith, then he will naturally question whether he is one of the elect; any lack of certainty in this conscientious self-examination will tend to despair. Arminius identified this precise problem in his ministry to those dying of the plague in Amsterdam. As he spoke with two different believers on their death beds, he found that they both "accounted the certainty of the remission of sins

---

[153] Cf. the discussion in chapter three, II.E.2.
[154] Whitaker, *Cygnea cantio*, p. 24: "nullam nobis fidem relinquere."

and the testimony of the Holy Spirit in the hearts of believers to be that faith by which a believing person (*homo fidelis*) is justified; and therefore, because they were at this time destitute of this assurance and testimony, [they thought] they also lacked (*carere*) faith."[155] It is clear that Arminius traced this problem of doubt to the fact that both of the sick people considered "the sense of faith itself to be the remission of sins."[156]

The standard Reformed reply to this potential problem would be to point out the weakness of the believer's saving faith in all its parts. So Calvin insists that faith as well as assurance may be affected by doubt and attacked by anxiety.[157] Perkins writes that true faith is still mingled with unbelief; true faith is weak and imperfect.[158] In fact, Perkins noted that God does not always manifest his favor to his children; sometimes he draws back so that they will appreciate his grace all the more. "Now for the time of this eclipse of the favour of God, hee not onely darkeneth his love, but makes them feele also such a measure of his wrath, as that they will often thinke themselves castawayes from the favour of God."[159] Trelcatius, Sr., admitted that true faith often languishes.[160] Junius said that infirmity concerning perseverance in faith should not make us doubt our certain hope of eternal salvation.[161] Kuchlinus wrote that true faith may be infirm and small. Infirmity does not take away its truth, nor smallness its sincerity.[162] Hence, the Reformed response corresponds to the following logic: "*Fiducia* is part of *fides*; but *fides* is weak in this life; *ergo, fiducia* is weak, too." Beeke attempts to reconcile the apparent contradiction that assurance is described as both free from doubt, yet not free, by mentioning that faith ought to be fully assured, but in reality and experience, it is not.[163]

Perhaps, then, the widespread acknowledgment that faith and assurance can be weak would suffice to remedy the tendency to despair, if

---

[155] *Ep. ecc.* 56, p. 107; in *Works* 1:176.

[156] *Ep. ecc.* 56, p. 107; in *Works* 1:178: "sensum remissionis peccatorum esse fidem ipsam."

[157] *Inst.* 3.2.17.

[158] Perkins, *A Cloud of Faithfull Witnesses: Leading to the Heavenly Canaan. Or, A Commentarie upon the Eleventh Chapter to the Hebrewes*, in *Workes of Perkins* 3:157 col. 2 c.

[159] Perkins, *Cloud of Faithfull Witnesses*, in *Workes of Perkins* 3:4 col. 1 a.

[160] Trelcatius, Sr., *De fide* (1592), xi.

[161] Junius, *De certitudine* (1601), xv.

[162] Kuchlinus, *De certitudine* (1603), x. On weak faith, cf. Taffin, *Marks*, pp. 49–67, there p. 49: "Be comforted in knowing that there is a great difference between unbelief and weak faith."

[163] Beeke, *Assurance*, pp. 54–55.

it were not for the next point about the doctrine of faith. The second problem with the Reformed doctrine of faith that weakens the connection of *fides* and *fiducia* and tends to lead people to despair is the category of temporary faith. The doctrine of temporary faith explains the fact that some people who seem to possess saving faith and presently demonstrate the signs of being a faithful person, occasionally end up demonstrating that they were really reprobate all along.[164] Calvin gives the example of Simon Magus, who is described as having believed, and genuinely thought himself to be a true believer, but later showed that he was not.[165] Calvin then says that such faith that is attributed to the reprobate is a *temporalis fides*.[166] God enlightens them for a time and then leaves them in even greater blindness.[167]

Reformed theologians agreed with Calvin on this point. Zanchi acknowledged the category of "temporary Christians."[168] He said, "Wee grant that they which beleeve by such a faith, which is in hypocrisie and onely lasteth for a time; that they are deceived, whilest they thinke that they doe truly beleeve, and yet doe not indeed: for they are like them which dreame that they are kings, when as they are very beggars...."[169] Perkins's famous chart in the *Golden Chaine* shows how the temporary marks of the reprobate closely parallel those of the elect.[170] The Leiden professors continued to affirm the category of temporary faith. Junius

---

[164] Cf. Winship, 'Assurance and Puritan Practical Divinity,' 474 n. 32: "The unconscious hypocrite was a structural necessity in Reformed doctrine, needed for explaining the gap between theoretical perseverance of the saints and the reality of backsliding."

[165] *Inst.* 3.2.10.

[166] *Inst.* 3.2.11.

[167] *Inst.* 3.24.8. Kendall, *Calvin*, pp. 21–28, passim, acknowledges Calvin's doctrine of temporary faith, but assumes that his alleged intellectualism sets him apart from the voluntaristic temporary faith of his successors. The basis of this assumption is unclear. Kendall recognizes that Arminius saw problems in Perkins's doctrine, but Kendall's claim (ibid., p. 145) that Perkins could have resolved the problems if he had "taken up Calvin's position" presupposes a discontinuity that he fails to adequately demonstrate. Kendall even leaves open the possibility that Arminius realized this putative break between Calvin and Beza. Cf. Kendall, *Calvin*, p. 146: "Whether [Arminius] perceives a substantial difference between Calvin and Beza remains unknown.... Arminius, moreover, appears to have recognized the voluntarism that was implicit in reformed theology since Beza." Arminius, along with his contemporary allies and opponents alike, certainly did not see such discontinuity between Calvin's soteriology on the one hand and that of Beza and Perkins on the other hand.

[168] Zanchi, *A Briefe Discourse*, in *Workes of Perkins* 1:429 col. 1 b.

[169] Zanchi, *A Briefe Discourse*, in *Workes of Perkins* 1:431 col. 1 b. Cf. idem, *Miscellaneorum libri tres* (London, 1605), p. 440.

[170] Perkins, *Golden Chaine*.

said that hypocritical and temporary faith will vanish and succumb to the attacks of temptations. As opposed to true faith, temporary faith is an obscure conception, a versatile opinion.[171] Gomarus described temporary faith as *notitia* of all things proposed in the Gospel concerning Christ.[172]

The reason that the category of temporary faith undermines assurance is the great correspondence between true and temporary faith. It is a likeness not only from an external observer's perspective, but also from the individual believer's own perspective. Calvin underscores the resemblance when he points out that God's goodness can be tasted by those with temporary faith, and they can even experience a *Spiritus operatio*, albeit an "inferior" one. There exists, therefore, a "great likeness and affinity (*similitudo et affinitas*)" between the elect and those with temporary faith, but the elect alone have *fiducia*.[173] Furthermore, as noted above, Calvin says that Simon Magus truly thought he was a genuine believer. Foxgrover acknowledges that this category of temporary faith in Calvin seems to undermine the doctrine of assurance: "If there is the possibility that one may confuse true faith and temporary faith, how can one be certain of his salvation?"[174] Foxgrover attempts to reconcile Calvin's statements on temporary faith and personal assurance by noting that Simon believed, and, although he was not aware of it, he was a hypocrite in his faith. Based on statements in Calvin's commentaries, Foxgrover posits two successive stages of hypocrisy: first, a "gross hypocrisy," by which the person is self-aware of his "forced," insincere belief; second, an "inward hypocrisy," by which the person is self-deceived, thinking himself to be a true believer. Therefore, Foxgrover asserts, Calvin recognized a brief period of time where Simon could have recognized his superficial faith, but, by the time he was confronted by Peter, he was not even aware of his own temporary, false faith.[175] The assumption, then, is that a person, at some point, however brief, ought to be able to distinguish between true and temporary faith.

---

[171] Junius, *De certitudine* (1601), vii–viii.

[172] Gomarus, *De fide iustificante* (1603), ii.

[173] *Inst.* 3.2.11. Cf. also *Inst.* 3.24.6–8, with the discussions in David Foxgrover, '"Temporary Faith" and the Certainty of Salvation,' *Calvin Theological Journal* 15/2 (1980), 220–32; Anthony N. S. Lane, 'Calvin's Doctrine of Assurance,' 45–47; Beeke, *Assurance*, p. 67; Bell, *Calvin*, pp. 29–30.

[174] Foxgrover, 'Temporary Faith,' 221.

[175] Foxgrover, 'Temporary Faith,' 227–31.

The problem that prevents this interpretation from rescuing assurance of salvation is that even this twofold stage of hypocrisy can, from the perspective of the troubled conscience, resemble the faith of the elect. According to Calvin and other Reformed theologians, the saving faith that is weak, always intermingled with doubt, and always suffering from attacks and temptations, may yet grow in strength and assurance. This process is hardly distinguishable from Simon Magus's initially weak, inadequate faith that grew to be a self-assured, or self-deceived, faith. Furthermore, in light of the emphasis on the similarities between true and temporary faith, the solutions and distinctions meant to help people distinguish between them tend to be too subtle to benefit the person suffering from doubt and despair. Foxgrover himself admits that "Calvin's comments on hypocrisy are quite confusing."[176] Likewise, Perkins's stress on the parallels between true and temporary faith provokes him to attempt to lay out the distinctions that will help believers who struggle. In his *Treatise Tending unto a Declaration*, the first section is appropriately titled "Certaine Propositions Declaring How Farre a Man May Goe in the Profession of the Gospel, and yet bee a wicked man and a Reprobate."[177] Demonstrating how much the reprobate may resemble the elect, Perkins proposes 36 points for distinguishing the two groups. It is a relatively safe assumption that even a well informed sixteenth-century layman would have some trouble finding comfort here.[178] At the same time, in contrast to Perkins's well-conceived points, the practical efficacy of pithy, ambiguous, subjective distinctions for examining one's own faith is debatable as well.[179]

---

[176] Foxgrover, 'Temporary Faith,' 228.

[177] Perkins, *Estate of Damnation or Grace*, in *Workes of Perkins* 1:356–62. Cf. Beeke, *Assurance*, pp. 109–10; with Kendall, *Calvin*, pp. 67–76.

[178] Cf. Winship, 'Assurance and Puritan Practical Divinity,' 474: "[Perkins] seemingly kicked out all the elaborate props he had erected to bolster the weak Christian." Furthermore, whereas Winship does not attempt to harmonize the apparent tensions in Perkins, he claims that the "lack of system points to the deeper system of Perkins's work" (ibid., 476–77), namely, a rhetorical device to meet the pastoral needs of both secure and weak believers. However, although the erudition and popularity of Perkins's works are beyond question, one cannot simply pass over the recurring issues raised by his method and critiqued by Arminius.

[179] E.g., cf. Foxgrover, 'Temporary Faith,' 224, who, summarizing Calvin, speaks of true faith as having an affection "penetrating to the heart," but temporary faith not having an affection of godliness; with Junius, *De certitudine* (1601), viii, who briefly notes the differences between true and temporary faith. Gomarus, *De fide iustificante* (1603), ii, briefly defines three types of non-justifying faith, but does not offer tips for distinguishing these three types from actual justifying faith.

Thus, to say that faith—along with its necessary ingredient assurance—can be frail is little consolation. If even the reprobate can have a temporary faith that resembles that of the elect both externally and internally, then it matters not how weak or strong one's faith and assurance seem to be at present. Both the elect and reprobate may have a measure of faith given by the Spirit and experience a measure of assurance.

For Arminius, the central issue is the unsatisfactory effect that the Reformed doctrine of unconditional reprobation has on one's assurance of salvation. That is, it is not the category of temporary faith *per se* that Arminius rejects. Conditional predestinarians and those who believe that one can fall away from God's grace would also affirm the category of temporary faith; the only difference would be that the Reformed would not call it justifying faith during that time of belief.[180] Arminius, following Augustine and Prosper of Aquitaine (among others), affirmed that some people believe without final perseverance.[181] The force of this undermining of assurance occurs when combining the doctrine of temporary faith with unconditional reprobation. Under such a system, discussions about temporary faith become more than just admonitions for the believer to persevere.[182] If a person finds himself in Simon Magus's situation of hypocritical faith, there is little recourse.

In his polemic against the doctrine that later became known as supralapsarianism, Arminius explains the link between unconditional reprobation and despair.

> [This doctrine] produces within people a despair (*wan-hope*) both of performing that which their duty requires and of obtaining that towards which their desires are directed. Because when they are taught, that the grace of God (which is necessary in order to do the good), is denied to a great portion of humanity by a precise and absolute decree of God (*precijs ende absoluydt besluyt Godes*), and that such grace is denied because, by a preceding decree equally precise, God has determined not to give them salvation but to damn; when they are thus taught, it is scarcely possible for any other result to ensue, than that the individual who cannot even with great difficulty work a persuasion within himself of his being elected, should soon consider himself included in the number of the reprobate; from which necessarily must arise a despair of doing righteousness and obtaining salvation.[183]

---

[180] See Gomarus, *De perseverantia* (1597), cor. ii.
[181] Arminius, *Apologia*, art. 1–2, in *Opera*, pp. 135–37; *Works* 1:738–42.
[182] Contra Foxgrover, 'Temporary Faith,' 232.
[183] *Dec. sent.*, p. 87; *Works* 1:632.

Therefore, the doctrine that assurance is a necessary component of saving faith inclines uncertain consciences to question their faith and salvation altogether. The response that saving faith and assurance can be weak is inadequate, for it only leads the troubled soul to worry about temporary faith. A weak feeling of faith and assurance that is ontologically salvific is hardly distinguishable from a strong feeling of faith and assurance that is ontologically temporary or self-deceivingly hypocritical. When reprobation is unconditional, as it is considered to be by all the Reformed orthodox theologians, then there is nothing the reprobate person can do to positively affect his situation. If you are reprobate, then you are "damned if you do, damned if you don't." In some ways, the consequent despair is at least as severe as the "Roman Catholic despair" against which the Reformed reacted. In the Roman Catholic system, despair often focused on the person's inability to merit salvation, which, at best, might lead one to rely on God. However, for those considering themselves to be unconditionally reprobate, the despair is focused on God's immutable decree.

B. Securitas *as the Effect of Reformed Soteriology*

Just as Arminius perceived despair to be the consequence of some aspects of the Reformed doctrine of faith and unconditional reprobation, he also believed that two aspects of the Reformed doctrine of salvation, in light of unconditional election, tended to lead some people to carnal security. Both of these aspects are connected with the doctrine of sanctification. The first doctrine that Arminius pointed to was the efficacy of the Spirit in sanctification, or, from Arminius's perspective, the Reformed doctrine of the Spirit's inefficacy. That is, if there is already a low expectation for sanctification, then a sinful, immoral person will possess an undue confidence in his own salvation. In general, Arminius was more optimistic than his Reformed contemporaries regarding progress in sanctification. An assertion like this must take the whole of his theology into account, for individual statements can be found which seem to contradict this generality. On the one hand, as was noted in chapter four, Arminius still recognized that sanctification is impeded by sin and weakness. On the other hand, his Reformed contemporaries, in certain contexts, made some relatively optimistic statements. Junius declares, "The same Spirit sanctifies believers in Christ, and renders efficacious for good works, that they might not live according to the flesh, but according to the Spirit. For since the Holy Spirit lives in believers as his temple, he cannot be idle. But he necessarily produces the fruit of sanctification."[184] Kuchlinus declared that, by the Holy Spirit, "We are truly regenerated, and from day to day we are more and more sanctified."[185] Hence, on given occasions and under various doctrinal topics, both Arminius and his colleagues could sound quite optimistic or pessimistic.

The difference is more evident when Arminius interprets Romans 7. For many Reformed theologians, Paul is clearly describing the common struggles of a regenerate person. For Arminius, however, Paul's language demonstrates that Romans 7 describes an unregenerate person who struggles with and is overcome by sin, and this is not "a property of the regenerate."[186] Arminius also describes what he saw, during his time as a pastor, to be the effects of the opposing interpretation:

> For nothing can be imagined more noxious to good morals than to assert, that it is a property (*proprium*) of the regenerate not to do the good which they will (*volunt*), and to do the evil which they do not will (*nolunt*): For therefore *it necessarily follows*, that those persons flatter (*applaudant*) themselves in their sins, who, while they sin, feel that they do so with a reluctant conscience and with a will that offered some resistance.... I truly and sacredly affirm, that this has more than once fallen within the range of my experience: When I have admonished certain persons to exercise a degree of caution over themselves and to guard against the commission of some wickedness which they knew to be prohibited by the law, they have replied, "that it was indeed their will so to refrain, but that they must declare, with the apostle that they cannot (*non posse*) perform the good which they would."[187]

According to Arminius, this low expectation in sanctification, based especially on a faulty interpretation of Romans 7, is one factor that leads to security.

The other doctrine that, according to Arminius, inclines believers toward security is the perseverance of the saints. Of course, Arminius

---

[184] Junius, *De certitudine* (1601), x: "...idem spiritus in Christum credentes sanctificat, et ad bona opera efficacos reddit, ut non secundum carnem: sed secundum Spiritum vivant. Cum enim Spiritus S. in credentibus tanquam templo suo habitet, otiosus ibidem minime esse potest: sed sanctitatis fructus proferat necesse est."

[185] Kuchlinus, *De necessitate*, xi: "mittit etiam Spiritum suum sanctum cuius virtute carnis concupiscentiae mortificantur: nos vero regeneramur, et indies magis ac magis sanctificamur."

[186] See *Cap. VII Rom.*, in *Opera*, pp. 809–934; *Works* 2:471–683.

[187] *Cap. VII Rom.*, in *Opera*, p. 921; *Works* 2:659, italics mine.

believed that the elect will persevere, and he probably would not contend much with Gomarus's definition of the doctrine: "[Perseverance] is truly the endurance of the faithful in faith, continually to the end of life, from God's grace, because of Christ's merit, by virtue of the Holy Spirit by the ministry of the Gospel, for the glory of God and salvation of persevering saints."[188] Arminius agreed that perseverance means that the Holy Spirit gives believers the strength to fight against sin, and they cannot be unwillingly dragged out of the hands of Christ.[189]

The trouble for Arminius is when perseverance is combined with unconditional election. Arminius objects to the notion that all true believers will persevere in faith to the end of life, and that they cannot abandon their faith.[190] For if a person believes he is elect and will persevere, he tends to be secure about his salvation. After all, since one is elect from eternity, there is nothing one can do in time that will separate one from the love of Christ. There will always be time for an elect believer to repent of sins. One is not saved because of deeds anyway, so one cannot be lost because of them either. Furthermore, since assurance is part of saving faith, it would be wrong to doubt one's election. In opposition to reprobation and despair, Arminius describes the effect of unconditional election: "It takes away all that salutary *fear and trembling by which we are commanded to work out our salvation*. For it states that he who is elected and believes, cannot sin with that full and entire will with which the ungodly (*Godtloose*) sin; and that they cannot either entirely or finally fall away from faith and grace.'"[191] Again, Arminius wrote,

> The persuasion by which any believer (*fidelis*) certainly persuades himself that he cannot defect from the faith, or that, at least, he will not defect from the faith, does not conduce so much to consolation against despair or doubt (*desperationem seu dubitationem*) that is adverse to faith and hope, as it does to engender security (*securitati ingenerandae*), a thing directly opposed to that most salutary fear with which we are commanded to work out our salvation, and which is exceedingly necessary in this place of temptations (*in hoc tentationum loco*).[192]

---

[188] Gomarus, *De perseverantia* (1597), i: "Ea autem est vere fidelium in fide, ad finem usque vitae, ex Dei gratia, propter Christi meritum, virtute S. Sancti per ministerium Evangelii, perduratio, ad gloriam Dei et perseverantium sanctorum salutem."

[189] *Dec. sent.*, pp. 114–15; *Works* 1:664–65.

[190] E.g., as found in Kuchlinus, *De perseverantia* (1603), i.

[191] *Dec. sent.*, p. 87; *Works* 1:632.

[192] *Art. non.* 22.4, in *Opera*, p. 962; *Works* 2:726.

This kind of security ("saved if you do, saved if you don't") reveals a person with a misplaced hope, hoping in a doctrine and a God that are really unbiblical. This person does not realize it, but he is ungodly, according to Arminius.

The idea that considering the decree of unconditional predestination tends to lead someone to either despair or security precedes Arminius. Indeed, the core of this idea gains confessional status in the 39 Articles. We have noted how Article 17 of the 39 Articles assumes a connection between consideration of the decree and the problem of despair/security. Moreover, because of Arminius's influence, this theme was reiterated after him in the United Provinces by the Remonstrants. Episcopius warned against the consequences of unconditional predestination. "If, someone says, I have been predestined, no sins could take away the kingdom of heaven for me; if reprobated, no works will be able to confer [it]."[193]

C. Implications for Reformed Soteriology

The central question, then, is whether despair and security are the natural results of Reformed soteriology. It is always possible that sinful people can take a sound doctrine and make a stumbling block out of it. In such a case, the doctrine itself is not to blame. In contrast, it is possible that God can work good in the lives of people who unwittingly adhere to an unsound doctrine of salvation. The attitudes of thinking oneself to be reprobate or of sinning so that grace may abound are not the ways Reformed theology is meant to function. Arminius is acutely aware of this point. For the Reformed, despair and security are aberrations that do not follow from their soteriology; the theology is not to blame.[194]

---

[193] Episcopius, *Institutiones theologicae* 4.5.7, in *Opera theologica* 1:415: "Si, inquit, praedestinatus sum, nulla peccata mihi poterunt regnum caelorum auferre; si reprobatus, nulla opera valebunt conferre."

[194] Cf. Peterson and Williams, *Why I Am Not an Arminian*, p. 89: "We respect the godly concerns of Arminians that 'the eternal security doctrine' will lead to license. With sorrow we admit that some have indeed presumed on God's grace and used this teaching as an excuse for not repenting of their sins. But the abuse of a doctrine does not disprove that doctrine." Cf. also Taffin, *Amendment*, p. 446: "Even so doe wee mocke with God, if we say that being elected, we need not to live vertuously, considering that contrariwise we are elected onely to this end, to be holy."

Thus, the implied solution in the 39 Articles is to simply refrain from constant consideration of the decree.

However, for Arminius and the Remonstrants, the problem is not only the improper human consideration of the decree, but also the nature of the decree itself. First of all, one cannot pretend the decree is not there. By making assurance of salvation an integral part of saving faith, the epistemological question of salvation and the decree upon which salvation is absolutely and solely based necessarily become the objects of the believer's consideration. In other words, people are driven to consider whether they are elect.[195] Furthermore, Arminius is serious about despair and security being not aberrations, but the fair implications of Reformed soteriology; and if these are validly inferred, then there is something wrong with the theology itself. As he says elsewhere, "We know something cannot be true from which something false can by good consequence be concluded."[196] He works with this same principle when he declares supralapsarianism to be wrong, because it logically implies, in spite of denials to the contrary, that God is the author of sin in a direct way.[197] Likewise, for Arminius, Reformed soteriology is flawed because it leads one to believe that there is nothing one can do to affect one's salvation, either positively or negatively. A person in such a situation finds himself in either despair or security.

---

[195] In *Inst.* 3.24.4, when Calvin warns against people inquiring about their divine election, he is warning against inquiring "out of the proper way (*extra viam*)." He does not here say that one should not consider one's own assurance of salvation, which is integral to faith. It still could be a matter for debate whether Calvin's attaching assurance to faith inadvertently encourages people to inquire about election in both proper and improper ways.

[196] *Cap. VII Rom.*, in *Opera*, p. 825; *Works* 2:490: "... sciens verum esse non posse, unde falsum bona consequentia concludi potest."

[197] For the Reformed, the efficient, or "deficiens," cause of the first sin was the will of Adam and Eve. See Kuchlinus, *Disputatio theologica de primo peccato primorum parentum Adami et Evae*, Leoninus Leone Petrus F. respondens, ad quaest. 7 catechet, in *Theo. disp.* 16, pp. 88–93, iv–vi; idem, *Theses theologicae de peccato originali*, ad quaest. 7 catechesios, Henricus Henrici Geesteranus respondens (Leiden, 1602), x. For one example of the charge of Reformed predestination making God the author of sin, see *Exam. Gom.*, pp. 154–58; *Works* 3:654–58. It should be noted that, when Arminius's opponents used the principle of *bona consequentia* to infer (semi)Pelagianism in his doctrine of faith, he then decried the practice. See *Apologia*, art. 27 (7), in *Opera*, p. 176; *Works* 2:51–52: "It is a species of injustice to attach to anyone those consequences, which one may frame out of his sayings (*dictis*), as if he felt (*sentiret*) thus; and the injustice is greater if those consequences cannot by good consequence be concluded out of the sayings." Arminius considered himself to be the victim of the latter, more flagrant injustice.

IV. *Conclusion*

We have seen that assurance of salvation was a concern of Arminius, a concern that arose while he ministered in Amsterdam. His experience taught him that there were two opposite errors that people committed with regard to assurance. Arminius, consistent with Augustine and the rest of the broad Christian tradition, warned against *desperatio* and *securitas*.[198] Arminius, like Thomas Aquinas, saw these as two vices most distant from the theological virtue of hope. It is, therefore, a question of the foundation of hope, or one's relation of dependence. On what is a person dependent? Despair is grounded on nothing, based on no foundation, and thus, is no hope. Security is grounded on a false something, based on an inadequate foundation, and thus, is a misplaced hope, which leaves the secure person in no better situation than the desperate.

In his rejection of these vices, Arminius found that the Reformed discussions of assurance had generally neglected the more dangerous of these two sins, namely, security. As Reformed theology intensified its assurance language and urged church members to flee despair and rest assured, Arminius felt that security was the more acute problem, and he followed the tradition in using this word to describe the arrogant presumption that is contrary to true faith and hope. If security is placing one's hope on a false foundation, many phantom foundations were battling for the hearts of believers. Placing hope in one's good works is certainly a misplaced hope, but at least it is possible to end in a holy despair that causes one to seek salvation in Christ alone. However, the doctrine of unconditional election and perseverance, combined with a low expectation for progress in sanctification, formed a foundation that, according to Arminius's inspection, is most deceitful, dangerous, and cannot even hold its own weight. To place hope on a *false* foundation is no better than no foundation at all; in other words, the secure person is ontologically in the same state as the desperate person, but, much worse, is not epistemically aware of it. For Arminius, true *certitudo* is about grounding hope on something solid, which will be the subject of the next chapter.

---

[198] G. J. Hoenderdaal, 'Life and Thought of Arminius,' 542–43, notes that Arminius's concern for these two errors arises out of the "practical bias" of his theology, but does not mention the impact of Arminius's actual pastoral experience on his theology.

Attempts to understand Arminius's theology in continuity and discontinuity with Reformed theology are incomplete without recognizing the important role of the doctrine of assurance. The tight causal connection Arminius drew between Reformed theology and the problematic experience of assurance among believers is one of the fundamental bases in his polemic, enabling him to connect his rejection of unconditional predestination with the Christian tradition's rejection of despair and security. Arminius claimed that Reformed soteriology inclined people to these two vices and was thus fraught with irremediable problems. His polemic against Reformed theology and construction of a distinctive system must therefore be seen in light of the problems he identified in the doctrine of the assurance of salvation.

CHAPTER SIX

THE GROUNDING OF ASSURANCE

Having analyzed Arminius's critique of Reformed soteriology and, as he perceived it, its consequent errors with regard to the assurance of salvation, we may now turn to his positive doctrine of assurance. For, as should be evident by this point in the essay, underneath Arminius's polemic there was a conception of God, creation, and salvation operating that was at many points similar to, yet at other key points quite distinct from, the Reformed theology of his contemporaries. It should also be evident that the issues on both sides of the questions are considerably more nuanced than much of the current literature has indicated. This chapter begins with a brief description of certainty in the context of Arminius's religious epistemology in general. The next section will seek to describe Arminius's solution to the primary problem of this study, the epistemological question of salvation, namely, "How can one know he is saved?" The grounds of assurance may be considered in two different modes, either *a posteriori* or *a priori*. We shall examine the question from these distinct angles and compare the solutions proposed by Arminius and his contemporaries, again employing the academic disputations of the Leiden theologians as indications of the agreements and disagreements.

I. *Certainty*

A. *Certainty in General*

In his oration on the certainty of sacred theology, Arminius begins with a concise overview of *certitudo* in general. "Therefore, certainty," he says, "is a property of the mind or intellect, and a mode of cognition, according to which the mind knows (*cognoscit*) an object as it is, and knows itself to know it [the object] as it is (*novit se id nosse prout est*)."[1] In

---

[1] Arminius, *Orationes tres, Oratio tertia*, in *Opera*, p. 56; *Works* 1:375.

other words, certainty involves a second order knowing and is therefore properly concerned with epistemology.[2] This certainty resides primarily in the intellect, which is the faculty that apprehends the object as true; for this reason, *certitudo* is distinguished from *fiducia*, which is primarily affective. Arminius's definition of *certitudo* is in agreement with the standard scholastic definition of certainty as primarily intellective and secondarily affective.[3]

Arminius then divides certainty into three types, corresponding to the causes that produce certainty in the mind. The first is the certainty of experience, which is when particular objects fall under the senses. The second type is the certainty of knowledge (*scientiae*), which is when general conclusions are deduced from known *principia*, that is, when objects fall under reason. The third type is the certainty of faith, which involves things that are remote from the senses or reason; this certainty is wrought by divine revelation.[4] The certainty of theology falls under the certainty of faith, for it is based on the revelation of God's word.[5]

B. *The Nature of the Certainty of Salvation*

For the purposes of this essay, the main reason for noting Arminius's general epistemology is simply to point out that there are degrees of certainty. Arminius does not specify under which type of certainty the assurance of salvation falls. He does, however, mention that certainty of salvation is not on an equal level with the certainty by which we know that there is a God or that Christ is the Savior of the world. The reason for this lesser assurance is that God is greater than our hearts, and he is the ultimate judge.[6] It may also simply be that certainty of salvation is based on God's existence and Christ's work; therefore, certainty of salvation cannot be stronger than the foundation on which it is constructed.

---

[2] Cf. Dekker, *Rijker*, p. 43 n. 133: "Met andere woorden, Arminius geeft hier een nauwkeurige definitie van zekerheid in termen van tweede-orde kennis: zeker weten betekent dat je weet dat je iets weet."

[3] Altenstaig, *Lexicon*, p. 131.

[4] Arminius, *Orationes tres, Oratio tertia*, in *Opera*, pp. 57–58; *Works* 1:377. These categories roughly correspond to Altenstaig's division of natural, moral, and supernatural certainty. See Altenstaig, *Lexicon*, p. 131. Cf. Oberman, *Harvest*, pp. 461–62.

[5] Arminius, *Orationes tres, Oratio tertia*, in *Opera*, p. 60; *Works* 1:382.

[6] *Dec. sent.*, p. 116; *Works* 1:668–71.

As noted in chapter five, my working definition of certainty of salvation that is consistent with Reformed orthodoxy and modern interpreters is "the assurance of one's personal salvation made known in one's heart by the Holy Spirit." Despite the claims of his opponents, certainty of salvation was an issue of great significance to Arminius. He affirmed that a Christian believer "can be certain (*verseeckert*), and is certain if his heart does not condemn him, that he is God's child and stands in the grace of Christ."[7]

In searching for the grounds of a person's assurance, the epistemological question of salvation can be considered and resolved from two different perspectives. Let two Leiden theologians suffice to establish this distinction. First of all, Arminius writes the following in a letter to Uytenbogaert:

> Let there be a distinction (*Distinguatur*) between being constituted as Savior, and to actually (*actu*) save; for the former notes the power, will, and authority (*potentiam, voluntatem et potestatem*) of saving; the latter [notes] the very execution and bestowing of salvation. If therefore I believe, as I am bound to do, that Christ is constituted as Savior, that is, he has the authority, power, will of saving, and I thus by faith surrender (*trado*) myself to him, then I shall actually obtain salvation from him, that is, remission of sins, the Spirit of grace, and eternal life. Therefore in these words, "I believe that Christ is the Savior of the world, or rather of the faithful (*fidelium imo*), and my Savior," these [thoughts] are not included, "I believe that my sins have been remitted, I believe that I have eternal life."[8]

Although Arminius is here speaking of the ontology of salvation, this distinction applies directly to the epistemology of salvation as well. In other words, there are two related yet distinct epistemological questions: "How do I know Christ has the ability and will to save me?" and "How do I know I am actually saved?" It is the difference between *potentia* and *actus*.[9]

Junius describes the same distinction more directly in his disputation on the assurance of salvation. Two things are required for this assurance: "one is that we know the foundation of our salvation is firm and

---

[7] *Dec. sent.*, p. 115; *Works* 1:667.

[8] *Ep. ecc.* 81, p. 152; *Works* 1:179–80, note.

[9] It is not so much a difference between grounds of salvation and grounds of assurance, as Beeke implies (*Assurance*, pp. 81 and 102 n. 202). Rather, the distinction is between the ground for knowing God has made salvation possible and the ground for knowing this salvation has been actually applied to me.

unmoved; the other, that same [salvation] pertains to us as individuals."[10] That is, in dealing with the question of grounding assurance, we must distinguish between the foundation of salvation and whether salvation actually pertains to a certain individual. This distinction that is explicit in both Junius and Arminius is correspondingly implicit, even if at times somewhat blurred, in Reformed orthodoxy generally.[11]

The former way to consider the epistemological question may be stated, "How can I know that salvation is really true in the first place or even possible for me?" From this angle, the inquirer seeks assurance by examining the very foundation of salvation. Instead of gathering evidence from human conditions, the seeker considers how the doctrine of God—especially his power and will—impacts the question of assurance. We shall refer to this line of examination as the *a priori* epistemological question; it is objective and external to the inquirer. The *a priori* question properly concerns the ground of assurance by considering the true *fundamentum* of salvation and assurance. Moreover, after analyzing the thought of Arminius vis-à-vis that of his Reformed contemporaries, their distinct solutions to the *a priori* question will become clear.

From the latter perspective, the inquirer searches for signs or proofs in his own life in order that he might discover his ontological status before God. This query may be phrased, "Is there any evidence in my Christian life that demonstrates my actual salvation?" We shall refer to this line of examination as the *a posteriori* epistemological question; it is subjective and internal to the inquirer. Instead of looking to the potential of salvation, it is *a posteriori* in the sense that the object of investigation is one's own life, particularly the testimony consequent upon a person's actual ontological status. Stacking up *a posteriori* evidence is the familiar method for resolving this question. Albeit in an improper sense, nevertheless this *a posteriori* question concerns the grounds of assurance, for positive testimony should serve to bolster one's assurance. By comparing Arminius with his Reformed contemporaries, I shall demonstrate

---

[10] Junius, *De certitudine* (1601), iv: "unum est, ut sciamus fundamentum nostrae salutis firmum, et immotum esse: alterum, illam ipsam ad nos singulos pertinere."

[11] For examples of the explicit distinction, see Heinrich Heppe, *Reformed Dogmatics Set Out and Illustrated from the Sources*, ed. Ernst Bizer, trans. G. T. Thomson (London, 1950), pp. 175–78. The blurring occurs when all the testimonies, *a priori* as well as *a posteriori*, are mentioned together without distinction. As will be shown below, the traditional threefold division of the testimonies which is present in Gomarus, Kuchlinus, and Perkins is an alternative, but not contradictory, categorization.

that their respective solutions to the *a posteriori* question are quite similar, although not in every case identical.

Grasping the distinction between the *a priori* and *a posteriori* epistemological questions is essential for analyzing and assessing the similarities and differences between Arminius and the Reformed soteriology of his day, given that it is with regard to the *a priori* question that the major differences arise.[12] This distinction provides therefore the best template for our purposes. I shall begin, however, with the *a posteriori* question before moving to the more fundamental *a priori* question, because the *a posteriori* gets more attention in discussions of assurance and is the more obvious of the two problems.

II. A Posteriori *Grounding: Subjective Confirmation of Salvation*

A. *The Testimonies of Salvation*

A.1. *Vocabulary*

The variety of terminology that was employed to describe the marks of a person's status before God reveals something about the function of these marks in assurance. Perhaps the most common word was *testimonium*.[13] Considered as testimony, these indicators were called on to provide evidence of or bear witness to a person's true status. Other common words employed were *signum* and *nota*.[14] As signs or marks, their

---

[12] Cf. a similar distinction in Zachman, *Assurance* (foundation and confirmation of salvation). As Zachman remarks (ibid., p. 6), it is the difference between asking, "Do I have a gracious God?" and "Is my faith in the grace of God sincere or hypocritical?" Cf. also Paul Helm, *Calvin and the Calvinists* (Carlisle, PA, 1982), p. 28; and Beeke, *Assurance*, pp. 108–09. Beeke acknowledges the distinction and appropriately differentiates between objective and subjective assurance. However, noting that Perkins implicitly employs such a distinction, Beeke claims that it is a Perkinsian novelty. In contrast to Beeke, I note that since Perkins's contemporaries in Leiden were utilizing the distinction explicitly, and since the epistemological distinction is the logical development of the *potentia/ actus* distinction, the distinction is certainly not an invention of Perkins. Beeke (*Assurance*, p. 12) admits as much when he traces the seed of the notion back to Augustine.

[13] E.g., Kuchlinus, *De certitudine* (1603), vi, uses "testimonium." Perkins, *Cases*, in *Workes of Perkins* 2:19 col. 1, uses "testimonie." Fuller, *Sermon*, p. 12, uses the alternate translation, "witness."

[14] E.g., Arminius, *De iustificatione* (1603), xxxiii. Perkins, *Cases*, in *Workes of Perkins* 2:20, uses "sign." Cf. Oberman, *Harvest*, p. 229 n. 119.

function was to point the person's conscience away from fear and to the peace of assurance. A less commonly used word, but just as important, was τεκμήριον,[15] which denotes a positive proof. In addition to being testimonies and signs, then, these indicators were regarded as *a posteriori* proof of one's status before God.[16] Thus, these indicators carried great epistemological weight with respect to the question of salvation in early Reformed orthodoxy.

A.2. *The Inventory of Testimonies*

In view of the fact that assurance of salvation was a key pastoral and theological problem in early Reformed orthodoxy, Arminius and his contemporaries considered and documented the various testimonies to which a troubled conscience ought to appeal in times of doubt.[17] As Beeke has noted, there is in Reformed theologians evidence of a threefold testimony: the promise of the gospel, the internal testimony of the Holy Spirit, and the effects of sanctification.[18] The first of these three categories is external and objective, falling under the *a priori* question of the foundation of salvation and its assurance. The latter two are *a posteriori* and relate more directly to the so-called *syllogismus practicus*. That such a division of categories was known in Leiden is clear from Kuchlinus's and Gomarus's disputations.[19] However, since the external, objective testimony concerns the *a priori* question and is better left to the next section, here we shall treat only the testimonies that are subjective and personal.

---

[15] Arminius, *De iustificatione* (1603), xxxiii; Gomarus, *De fide iustificante* (1603), xx. Cf. New Testament usage in Acts 1,3 with LSJ, q.v.

[16] Perkins, *Cases*, in *Workes of Perkins* 2:20 col. 1, calls the signs infallible.

[17] I am not suggesting that Reformed orthodoxy obsessed over this problem much more than did medieval Catholicism, but that there were a reason and new context for its continued discussion. For an indication of the late medieval gathering of testimonies, see the list of eleven *signa praedestinationis* in Altenstaig, *Lexicon*, pp. 729–30.

[18] Beeke, *Assurance*, pp. 81 and 107–08. Cf. Beza, *Quaestionum libellus*, pp. 133–34; *Booke of questions*, fols. 87–88; with Jacobus Kimedoncius, *Of the redemption of mankind three bookes* (London, 1598), p. 381: "But there is for the most part a threefold revelation of election: first, by the most certaine effects of election it selfe: secondly, by the word of promise: and thirdly, by the seale of the holy Ghost." In contrast to Reformed statements, the list of the causes of certainty of election given by Hemmingius is quite different. Cf. Hemmingius, *Enchiridion*, pp. 244–46. Recall again that the relevance of these works cited throughout this study is based on their influence in early Protestant orthodoxy and their appearance in Arminius's personal library.

[19] Kuchlinus, *De certitudine* (1603), xi–xiii, speaks of the *testimonium externum*. Gomarus, *De Praedestinatione* (1604), xxxii, speaks of *revelatio externa* as an indicator of salvation.

The *a posteriori* evidence in particular, as indicated in the threefold testimony mentioned above, generally fell under the latter two categories, namely, the testimony of the Holy Spirit and the effects of the Holy Spirit on the human spirit. Based on their usage in Reformed orthodoxy, I shall call this a distinction between the *a posteriori* internal evidence and the *a posteriori* effects. Perkins shows this distinction from Rom. 8,16 by distinguishing two testimonies. Concerning the internal testimony, he writes, "Againe, the holy Ghost gives testimonie, by applying the promise of remission of sinnes, and life everlasting by Christ, particularly to the heart of man, when the same is generally propounded, in the ministerie of the word."[20] This *a posteriori* internal evidence is about the application of salvation. The *a posteriori* effects on the human spirit are known by grief over sin, a resolution to obey God, and favoring spiritual things.[21]

After perusing the various disputations of the first decade of the seventeenth century in Leiden, the striking discovery is the agreement among the faculty on these *a posteriori* proofs—namely, agreement on their identification and their number, four. In Junius, although we see that these proofs are not neatly enumerated and, like Kuchlinus's discussion, they are mixed in with the *a priori* question, they are nevertheless all present. As we come to the Leiden theologians during the Arminius years, the explicit division between *a posteriori* internal evidence and *a posteriori* effects remains in tact explicitly only in Kuchlinus, but in the professors implicitly by the order of testimonies. Invariably, the first two testimonies mentioned are faith and the testimony of the Holy Spirit (in either order), that is, the internal proofs; and the last two proofs are the effects, namely, the inner peace and struggle along with the external fruit of sanctification.[22]

---

[20] Perkins, *Cases*, in *Workes of Perkins* 2:19 col. 1 a.

[21] Perkins, *Cases*, in *Workes of Perkins* 2:19 col. 1 c–d. See also the signs of the sanctifying Spirit, faith, and holiness of life in Perkins, *Cases*, in *Workes of Perkins* 2:20–1. Taffin, *Marks*, pp. 35–40, distinguishes between external and internal marks, but his list differs from that of Perkins and the Leiden theologians.

[22] Cf. the substantially identical lists of Arminius and Gomarus. Arminius, *De fide* (1605), xv: "Hanc autem Fidem vere fideles habere se sciunt. 1. Ex ipso sensu Fidei, quod docent insignia attributa & nomina, quibus insignitur Fides in Scripturis. Tribuitur enim illi πληροφορία, παρρησία, πεποίθησις, dicitur ὑπόστασις, ἔλεγχος, quae fidei non competunt, si credens ignoret se credere. 2. Ex Spiritus Sancti in illis habitantis testimonio, testatur .n. una cum spiritu nostro quod sumus Filii Dei. At Filii Dei non nisi per Fidem in nomen Christi sumus. 3. Ex lucta Fidei cum dubitationibus & spiritus cum carne: Denique ex effectis spei & charitatis erga Deum & proximum, operumque ex illa charitate promanantium." Idem, *De fide* (1608), xvi: "...tum minorem pro certa habe-

A.3. Sensus Fidei

The very sense of faith itself is an important testimony of salvation, the one to which Reformed writers often pointed first.[23] The *sensus fidei* is one's own second order consideration of whether one is a believer, known sometimes as the *actus reflectus* of faith.[24] In this context, Junius says that the assurance of salvation is attributed to those who are faithful.[25] This faith he defines as the certain (*certa*) cognition of divine benevolence towards us and a firm persuasion and apprehension of the gracious promise in Christ; whoever experiences these parts of faith can stand assured.[26] Kuchlinus places faith as the secondary *a posteriori* internal testimony of salvation.[27] Likewise, Gomarus acknowledges the importance of the sense of faith, "for the one believing knows himself to believe."[28] This sense of faith and repentance confirms that we are faithful (*fideles*) and penitent.[29] Arminius also makes it clear that a person knows that he has justifying faith by the sense of faith itself.[30] By such a *mentis reflexio* we believe that we have this true and salvific faith and we are certain that we have remission of our sins.[31] It simply cannot

---

mus, non modo ex fidei ipsius sensu, et testimonio tum Spiritus S. testificantis et conscientiae nostrae, sed etiam ex lucta fidei in dubitationibus, illiusque victora, et tota vita nostra...." Gomarus, *De fide iustificante* (1603), xx: "Hac fide justificante qui sunt praediti, etiam se ea praeditos esse certo cognoscere possunt, et ex certis hisce τεκμηρίοις cognoscunt: Primum est *Internum* Spiritus Sancti *Testimonium*; Secundum *Verus* ipsius fidei *Sensus*, credens enim scit se credere; Tertium *Mutua* Carnis et Spiritus *lucta*, Quartum *Omnia* Posteriora et pleraque etiam Priora fidei *Effecta*; posito enim Effectu ponitur causa."

[23] E.g., see Zanchi, *De religione*, p. 72; *Confession*, p. 17: "si quis tamen velit de certa sui electione fieri certior, huic recurrendum esse ad fidem, et ad conscientiae testimonium an sentiat se vere in Christum credere, sinceróque amore affectum esse erga Deum et proximum, nec ne sentiat."

[24] Cf. Beeke, *Assurance*, pp. 34, 113, and 159–69, passim. Kendall, *Calvin*, p. 33, distorts the reflex act by saying it is based on works or effects of faith. On the contrary, the reflex act is simply a reflection on one's own belief. This reflex act *per se* has nothing to do with works.

[25] Junius, *De certitudine* (1601), iii.

[26] Junius, *De certitudine* (1601), viii.

[27] Kuchlinus, *De certitudine* (1603), ix.

[28] Gomarus, *De fide iustificante* (1603), xx: "credens enim scit se credere."

[29] Gomarus, *De praedestinatione* (1604), xxxii. Cf. Graafland's summary of Gomarus's doctrine of faith in Graafland, *Zekerheid*, p. 98: "De geloofszekerheid rust dus op de geloofservaring, die het geloof begeleidt en zijn waarachtigheid kenmerkt."

[30] Arminius, *De fide* (1605), xv. Cf. also idem, *De iustificatione* (1603), xxxviii: "Cum igitur justificemur non ex operibus, sed ex fide, colligimus nos sane certos esse posse satisfactionem Christi a Deo nobis imputari, quia scimus nos esse in fide, ideoque non esse dubitandum de nostra justificatione."

[31] Arminius, *De fide* (1608), xvi: "Distinguimus fidem hanc ab illa fide, qua post peractum judicium de hac fide per mentis reflexionem in eandem, credimus, nos hanc veram

be that a believer who knows he believes could doubt concerning his salvation.[32] Even for Arminius, this is not a historical faith, but justifying faith that looks to Christ for salvation, after which *fiducia* inevitably follows. Thus, all agree that a person knows he has salvation by the very fact that he is a believer.

A.4. Testimonium Spiritus Sancti

Based on Rom. 8,16, Junius affirmed that the Holy Spirit then approaches from God into the hearts of the faithful (*fidelium*), bearing witness to our spirit that we are God's sons. The Spirit does not simply bear witness, but also seals our hearts for the purpose of greater certainty (*ad majorem certitudinem*).[33] For Junius, certainty of salvation is already present, but the Spirit's testimony confirms what the believer already knows, leading to greater certainty. For Kuchlinus, this testimony of the Holy Spirit is the primary internal testimony; it is also at the top of Gomarus's list.[34] Arminius agrees that the Holy Spirit testifies that we are his sons; this is one of the benefits that flows from union and communion with Christ.[35] In his disputation on faith, however, Arminius adds that we are not God's sons except by faith in the name of Christ.[36] Arminius's emphasis on faith here is probably why he listed faith before the testimony of the Holy Spirit, whereas Kuchlinus and Gomarus list the Holy Spirit before faith.

A.5. Lucta

Moving on to the *a posteriori* effects of salvation, the first is strictly internal in its termination. Kuchlinus includes three testimonies under these internal effects—a sense of God's love, a contrite heart, and the *lucta* between the Spirit and flesh.[37] However, his colleagues generally

---

et salvificam fidem habere: et per quam de remissione actuali peccatorum nostrorum certi sumus." Indeed, contra Kendall, *Calvin*, 148, Arminius does employ this technical term.

[32] Arminius, *Quaestiones*, resp. 7, in *Opera*, p. 186; *Works* 2:67: "fieri nequit, ut qui credit, et credere se novit, de sua salute dubitet...."

[33] Junius, *De certitudine* (1601), ix.

[34] Kuchlinus, *De certitudine* (1603), vii; Gomarus, *De fide iustificante* (1603), xx; cf. idem, *De praedestinatione* (1604), xxxii. Cf. Taffin, *Marks*, p. 38: "The fruits and the activities both of the Holy Spirit and of faith are the most exceptional and the most powerful signs of our adoption as God's children."

[35] *Disp. priv.* XLVII.v.

[36] Arminius, *De fide* (1605), xv.

[37] Kuchlinus, *De certitudine* (1603), xiv. Cf. Beza, *Quaestionum libellus*, p. 136; *Booke of questions*, fol. 89r.

summed up these internal effects under one heading, the *lucta* between the Spirit and flesh, for the sense of love and penitence mentioned by Kuchlinus may be considered as effects of the Spirit who is wrestling with the flesh. According to Junius, although faith may be weak at times, it finally overcomes in this *lucta* between *fiducia* and doubt.[38] Gomarus refers to this proof of salvation as the *lucta* between the flesh and Spirit.[39] In concurrence with Junius and Gomarus, Arminius characterizes this testimony as a *lucta* of faith with doubts and of the Spirit with the flesh.[40] Faith wins the victory over doubts in this *lucta*.[41] Interestingly, this *a posteriori* effect that serves as a testimony of salvation provides a sense of the wide use of the *lucta* theme in early orthodoxy. As noted in chapter four, the *lucta* between the Spirit and flesh was cited by the Leiden theologians as proof that perfection only happens in the next life.[42] Therefore, this same *lucta* simultaneously proves one's utter imperfection and one's salvation.

A.6. Bona Opera

Following the internal witnessing and sealing of the Holy Spirit, writes Junius, the Spirit then sanctifies believers (*credentes*), rendering them efficacious for good works. Since the Holy Spirit lives in believers, he cannot be idle. He necessarily produces the fruit of sanctification.[43] The language of Kuchlinus is equally forceful, asserting that sanctification is necessary.[44] Gomarus calls these works the posterior and prior effects of faith.[45] For Arminius, these works are the effects of hope and love towards God and neighbor.[46] All the Leiden theologians would agree with Arminius that love, fear, and obedience towards God make one's calling, faith, and election solid (*firmam*).[47] Indeed, one purpose of good works is to make one "more certain" of faith and election.[48] The clear

---

[38] Junius, *De certitudine* (1601), viii, xvi.
[39] Gomarus, *De fide iustificante* (1603), xx. Cf. idem, *De perseverantia* (1608), xii.
[40] Arminius, *De fide* (1605), xv.
[41] Arminius, *De fide* (1608), xvi.
[42] E.g., see Kuchlinus, *De perfectione*, vi.
[43] Junius, *De certitudine* (1601), x. This point is, of course, typical of Reformed orthodoxy. E.g., see Polanus, *Partitiones*, p. 60; *Substance*, p. 99: "Regenerationis testimonium est, sancta et justa vita."
[44] Kuchlinus, *De certitudine* (1603), xv; cf. idem, *De salvandis*, xix.
[45] Gomarus, *De fide iustificante* (1603), xx.
[46] Arminius, *De fide* (1605), xv.
[47] *Disp. priv.* XLII.viii; idem, *De bonis operibus* (1603), ii.
[48] Arminius, *De bonis operibus* (1603), x; idem, *De bonis operibus* (1609), ix.

Figure 1: A Comparison of the Grounds of Assurance[1]

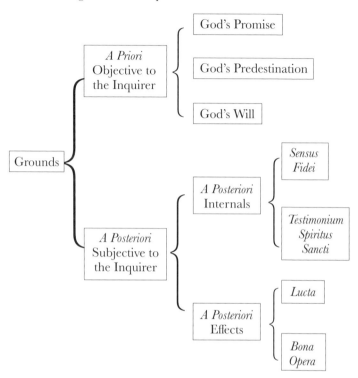

---

[1] In the *a posteriori* grounding, there is fundamental agreement between Arminius and the Reformed. In the *a priori* grounding, however, there is fundamental dissimilarity.

implication is that, here at the last of the *a posteriori* testimonies, there is already a degree of certainty present in the believer that the good works simply confirm.[49]

Having compared Arminius and the other Leiden theologians, the remarkable feature of the inventories of *a posteriori* testimonies of salvation is the similarity among them (see Figure 1). In fact, their likeness on this point may be more profound than other similarities in the *ordo salutis*, which use the same terminology but have deep differences on a couple of points. The resemblance of Arminius to his colleagues on *a posteriori* proof of salvation demonstrates their similarity in practical

---

[49] Cf. Beeke, *Assurance*, p. 74.

issues of the Christian life, even if their respective foundational theologies are distinct. At this point, we must stress that, with regard to these four *a posteriori* testimonies, Arminius did not differ from his contemporaries, neither did he offer an attenuated assurance of salvation vis-à-vis Reformed theology.[50]

B. Syllogismus Practicus

In the context of the assurance of salvation, early Reformed orthodoxy employed the *syllogismus practicus*. This practical syllogism simply and explicitly works out the relationship between the testimonies of salvation and the assurance of salvation itself in a logical manner.[51] Whether it is explicitly stated or implicitly deduced, anytime the question of the epistemology of salvation is raised, a person utilizes some form of syllogistic reasoning to arrive at a conclusion to the problem. Therefore, that Reformed orthodoxy separated the *syllogismus practicus* as a topic for explicit theological discussion does not reflect a harsh ratiocination of the doctrine of assurance; rather, it is merely an attempt to describe what actually takes place within the human conscience.

Although the practical syllogism is commonly associated with Puritan or *Nadere Reformatie* piety, it was not unknown to the Leiden theologians. Gomarus notes that use of the testimonies of salvation presupposes the use of the *syllogismus practicus*.[52] Arminius employed it as a pastoral tool when he worked amid dying bodies and troubled consciences during the Amsterdam plague of 1602. Arminius underscored that faith is imputed for righteousness, of which faith remission of sins is the fruit, and thus a sense of the remission of sins, that is, assurance, necessarily follows.[53] For Arminius, the use of the *syllogismus practicus* is based on the

---

[50] Contra the implication of, among others, Letham, 'Faith,' 1:311–20, passim. Indeed, with regard to the similarities, in *Exam. Gom.*, p. 151; *Works* 3:652, Arminius found Gomarus's list a bit too "Arminian" to be consistent with Gomarus's own theology; specifically, he accuses Gomarus of attempting to make faith both the condition *and* the effect of election.

[51] E.g., "God will save believers. But I believe. Therefore, God will save me." Cf. Beeke, *Assurance*, p. 160; Kendall, *Calvin*, p. 8.

[52] Gomarus, *De praedestinatione* (1604), xxxii; idem, *Disputationum theologicarum quinto repetitarum trigesima quarta: de Dei praedestinatione*, Casparus Sibelius respondens, ad diem 15 July 1609 (Leiden, 1609), cxxii.

[53] *Ep. ecc.* 56, p. 107; *Works* 1:177–78.

consideration of oneself as a believer in Christ.[54] In a disputation *de fide*, Arminius declares that it is by a reflex act of the mind (*mentis reflexio*) that we believe we have true and salvific faith and are certain of the remission of our actual sins. Then he offers this syllogism: "Everyone who believes in Christ has a kind God and will be saved, I believe in Jesus Christ; therefore."[55]

It should be clear, then, that the focus of the *syllogismus practicus* was not merely on good works, nor was it necessarily external or empirical. A syllogism can be made out of any of the *a posteriori* testimonies, and even in conjunction with *a priori* grounding.[56] In addition, when the topic of the syllogism is good works, this testimony is not to be separated from the other three testimonies or the *a priori* grounding. For example, the testimony of good works is always qualified by the recognition of the *lucta*, which acknowledges the continued weakness of the flesh. The reason that good works is the last mentioned testimony is partially due to the fact that this testimony is considered the least important and is based on all the testimonies preceding it. To imply that early Reformed orthodoxy taught a works-based assurance of salvation would be to de-contextualize the place of works in its *a posteriori* position.[57]

Even so, some modern interpreters are guilty of putting undue emphasis on the place of works in the early orthodox use of *syllogismus practicus*. Furthermore, along with this assumption often appears the claim that the *syllogismus* itself assumed a foundational character in assurance. After describing the *syllogismus practicus*, Kendall concludes, "Thus the method of achieving assurance of salvation is to scrutinize the claim of faith in oneself."[58] According to Bell, Scottish Calvinists relied on self-examination and syllogistic deduction to gather assurance.[59] Most interpreters who perpetuate these notions believe that this shift in the importance of good works and the foundational place of the *syllogismus* happened after Calvin was succeeded by Beza. Zachman claims,

---

[54] *Exam. Gom.*, pp. 148–53; *Works* 3:650–54.

[55] Arminius, *De fide* (1608), xvi: "Omnis credens in Christum, habet Deum propitium et salvus erit, ego credo in Iesum Christum; ergo."

[56] Moreover, the possible range of syllogisms would include both the *syllogismus practicus et mysticus*. For this distinction, see Beeke, *Assurance*, pp. 159–69.

[57] Beeke, *Assurance*, pp. 72–78 and 113, agrees.

[58] Kendall, *Calvin*, p. 9.

[59] Bell, *Calvin*, p. 8.

By saying that the testimony of the good conscience confirms both our faith and our eternal election, they [Luther and Calvin] left the door open for the possibility that the foundation of faith might be reversed, as indeed happened immediately after the death of Calvin in the theology of Beza, with the emergence of the *practical syllogism (syllogismus practicus) as the foundation of faith and assurance*.[60]

These writers have misunderstood the function of the syllogism in at least two ways. First of all, as affirmed above, the syllogism, or call it simple logical reasoning, inevitably operates anytime one considers one's own status before God. This syllogistic reasoning, in its implicit or explicit form, is not—contra the implication of Kendall, Bell, and Zachman—a Bezan invention.[61] Just because it is not spelled out as a logical sentence in earlier thinkers does not mean it is not functioning intuitively in a thinker's mind. If someone is to blame, it could very well be the writer of 1 John, who repeatedly appeals to the testimonies of faith, works, and the Holy Spirit for the purpose of instilling assurance.

Second, the fact that the syllogism simply operates does not entail that it functions in a strictly foundational way. In other words, mentioning or writing a treatise on the testimonies of salvation does not as such indicate a "foundational" role for the *syllogismus practicus*, any more than writing a treatise on predestination is evidence of one's "central dogma." None of the sixteenth- and seventeenth-century theologians under consideration in this monograph ever referred to the *syllogismus practicus* itself as the "foundation" of faith and assurance.

Therefore, modern interpreters who feel the need to censure early orthodoxy's use of the *syllogismus practicus* have generally failed to note the syllogism's proper context or let the documents speak for themselves. As noted above, the syllogism was never understood to function independently of the *a priori* ground on which salvation is based or to isolate one testimony to the exclusion of the others. Properly understood as the source from which causality flows, moreover, *fundamentum* is antithetical to anything *a posteriori*, the latter of which approaches more proximately to *terminus* instead.[62] To use an analogy, the *a posteriori* proofs of salva-

---

[60] Zachman, *Assurance*, pp. 6–7, italics mine. Cf. Bray, *Beza's Doctrine*, pp. 59 and 106–10. Strehle, *Catholic Roots*, pp. 38–41, traces the doctrine to Beza and Zanchi.

[61] Kendall, *Calvin*, p. 211, claims that use of the practical syllogism is the necessary consequence of a voluntaristic view of saving faith.

[62] E.g., Kimedoncius, *Redemption*, pp. 381 and 388–89, who explicitly calls these testimonies *a posteriori*, compares consideration of them to Moses viewing God's back, thus putting these effects in their proper place.

tion are meant to operate similarly to the *a posteriori* proofs of God's existence. The proofs do not create assurance or belief, but confirm the belief. To the degree that the *a posteriori* proofs become the foundation for religious epistemology they have been de-contextualized and their value has been overestimated. Such de-contextualization was generally not the case in early orthodoxy with respect to either knowledge of God or knowledge of salvation. The assumption that *a posteriori* testimonies of assurance are indeed subordinate and subsequent is why early orthodox writers said that the testimonies make us "more certain" of our election; that is, they build on an *a priori* certainty already present.[63] However, considering the citations above, the silence of Kendall and Bell regarding anything but the syllogism implies their assumption that *a posteriori* proof was foundational in Reformed orthodoxy, an assumption that Zachman overtly declares. I would agree with Zachman that the very mention of confirmation of salvation opens the *possibility* that someone will treat it as the foundation of assurance. However, this potential abuse does not render the distinction unusable for those who would employ it rightly.[64] Furthermore, people have been building their epistemology on inadequate foundations long before and independent of this alleged post-Calvin turn; the blame cannot all fall on Beza, or even on Luther and Calvin. As long as the assurance of salvation is a topic of discussion, as it certainly was in the late medieval and early modern periods, some will examine the effects of grace as if they are the foundations. The practical syllogism *per se* is not an indicator of sudden shifts in soteriology as many modern interpreters have assumed.

---

[63] Junius, *Theses theologicae, de aeterna Dei electione*, Lucas Trelcatius, Jr., respondens, 13 March 1593 (Leiden, 1593), xiv; Arminius, *De bonis operibus* (1603), x. Neither Arminius nor his Reformed orthodox contemporaries granted *a posteriori* testimonies a higher place than did Calvin himself. Contra Kendall, *Calvin*, pp. 27–28; Zachman, *Assurance*, pp. 6–7 and 211; and Strehle, *Catholic Roots*, pp. 38–39, who all assume that Calvin is set apart from his successors because he gives these testimonies only a subordinate place, while the testimonies are primary for his followers. Indeed Strehle, *Catholic Roots*, p. 39 n. 41, admits the true position of these *a posteriori* testimonies when he notes how Beza exhorts believers not to cling to "secondary testimonies."

[64] I therefore disagree with Zachman (*Assurance*, p. 87) that Luther's distinction between the foundation of assurance and its confirmation is "inherently unstable." Moreover, the distinction belongs to Luther no more than it belongs to the writer of 1 John.

C. *Lack of Testimony*

One problem with the subjective confirmation of salvation is the fact that the elect often waver in their confidence. Given that faith is in a constant *lucta* with doubt, and that faith is imperfect in this life, it is not surprising that one would experience doubt. However, what if the testimonies that are intended as weapons in this battle against doubt are missing in action? Since *fiducia*, for Reformed theologians, is a necessary component of saving *fides*, then how can a faithful person ever doubt?

Joel Beeke's monograph is a significant contribution to the topic of assurance in Reformed orthodoxy, and particularly with respect to this problem of assurance despite a lack of testimony. As Beeke contends, Calvin contributes to the problem when he offers apparently contradictory statements about faith.[65] In an attempt to resolve the inconsistencies, one option is to appeal to an implicit distinction in Calvin. When Calvin defines faith as consisting of assurance and then says that faith lacks assurance, he is distinguishing faith as it ought to be and faith as it really is in life. Thus, he qualifies his own definition of faith by asserting that it does fluctuate. According to Helm, Calvin's definition of faith as assurance is merely a "recommendation" for how it ought to be.[66] Apparently, though, the assumption is that there is always a measure of assurance in the faithful person, however tiny it may be, for assurance is essential to faith.[67]

Another option for harmonizing Calvin, though not necessarily contradictory to the preceding one, is posed by Beeke in conjunction with the first. In dealing with the phenomenon of a troubled conscience that has no apparent assurance, Beeke declares Calvin teaches that the "smallest germ of faith contains assurance in its very essence, even when the believer is not always able to grasp this assurance due to weakness in being conscious of his faith."[68] Thus, according to Beeke, the believer still has assurance "regardless of the believer's consciousness of his assurance."[69] Furthermore, for Beeke, this is the point where Calvin and the Calvinists merge:

---

[65] See Beeke, *Assurance*, pp. 54–72.
[66] Helm, *Calvin*, pp. 24–26. Beeke, *Assurance*, pp. 54–56, follows this solution and quotes Helm approvingly.
[67] Beeke, *Assurance*, p. 61.
[68] Beeke, *Assurance*, p. 60.
[69] Beeke, *Assurance*, p. 61.

Assurance may be possessed without being known. That is, the notion that assurance belongs in essence to every believer though he may not feel the "sense" of it, is a bridge which unites the two varying emphases qualitatively.[70]

The problem with Beeke's solution is not that assurance fluctuates with faith, for this was a common assumption, but rather the claim that assurance may be present with faith without the believer being conscious of its presence. Rather, this description is problematic for three reasons. First, if assurance of salvation may be neither consciously known nor felt by the elect, then it flatly contradicts Beeke's own definition of assurance as "undoubted certainty."[71] If certainty is "knowing that you know," that is, a conscious, second-order knowing, then how can this knowledge be unknown and still be called "certainty" without doing violence to the very definition of what it means to be certain? How can one be assured without knowing it? As defined, assurance entails an epistemological or experiential feeling of salvation, but he has here redefined it to the extent that it no longer has to do with epistemology.

The first problem implies the second, namely, that Beeke has confused the ontological question with the epistemological question. Let it be assumed for now, as Beeke states, that some people may not even be aware of the little germ of faith they do have, like the unbelieving disciples on the way to the empty tomb.[72] However, the question of whether they actually *had* faith is the ontological question, which in this case is answered affirmatively. The question of whether they were *aware* of their faith or salvation is the epistemological question of assurance, which in this case must be denied. The lack of the *sense* of faith, that is, the reflex act of faith, is what keeps the person from being assured. Thus, Beeke's assumption appears to be that the ontological and epistemological questions are equivalent to the extent that an affirmative answer to the ontological question entails an affirmative answer to the epistemological question. Unfortunately, it is far from clear exactly how this condition could coherently obtain.[73]

---

[70] Beeke, *Assurance*, p. 62. Cf. *Canons of Dort*, 5.5, which admit that the elect may for a time lose *sensum gratiae*, but do not say that the elect is still assured without conscious assurance, which is Beeke's claim about Calvin. Cf. also Seeberg, *History*, 2:423.

[71] Beeke, *Assurance*, pp. 3–4.

[72] Beeke, *Assurance*, pp. 53 and 60–61.

[73] Whether Beeke is accurate in his representation of Calvin and the Calvinists is another question. I acknowledge that this way of speaking about assurance is a point of agreement between these two parties (as I will demonstrate by examining Perkins). At this point I am only arguing that Beeke's attempt to harmonize their views *per se* is

Third, on a more practical and historical note, the apparent inco-
herence of the category of *unconscious assurance* confirms the problem
of assurance in the Reformed churches to which Arminius responded.
From his perspective, on the one hand, there were true believers who
were not completely assured and, for this reason, doubted the genuine-
ness of their faith itself.[74] On the other hand, there were people who possessed neither assurance nor, significantly, any testimonies confirming
assurance (presumably including faith and good works), who were nevertheless being told to be assured. For Arminius, it would be presumptuous to believe something if there were no testimony to support it; such
an unfounded hope is an indication of *securitas* itself. Therefore, when
Reformed theologians claimed that assurance can be strong, weak, or
completely and unknowingly latent in the elect, at that point assurance
itself as an epistemological category nearly became impractical.

Beeke's interpretation of Calvin and Reformed orthodoxy along with
the problems Arminius identified can be confirmed to a certain extent
in the writings of Perkins. Again, the problem is not the admission that
faith and assurance can be weak at times,[75] which all acknowledge, but
rather the contention that assurance is actually present even when the
believer is completely unconscious of it. Returning to Perkins's two testimonies from Rom. 8,16, he mentions the testimony of the Holy Spirit
and the testimony of our spirit or conscience through penitence and
obedience, testimonies which correspond respectively to the *a posteriori*
internals and to the *a posteriori* effects (that is, encompassing all four testimonies of the Leiden theology).[76] Perkins then proceeds to assert that
if we lack the former testimony of the Holy Spirit, then the latter testimony, the sanctification of the heart, will suffice to assure us.[77] Hence,
a person does not need the testimony of the Holy Spirit to be assured.
Furthermore, says Perkins, even if the Holy Spirit's testimony is lacking
and our sanctification is uncertain, we must have recourse to first beginnings, namely, being displeased with sin, grieving when we offend God,
using good means, and praying for grace.[78] Finally, the interlocutor asks,

---

unsuccessful. Of course, one could choose to allow for inconsistencies or incomplete
formulations in the Reformed doctrine of faith, especially as stated by Calvin. Beeke
and Helm choose instead to attempt to harmonize it.

[74] *Ep. ecc.* 56, pp. 106–07; *Works* 1:176–78.
[75] E.g., see Perkins, *Cloud of Faithfull Witnesses*, in *Workes of Perkins* 3:157 col. 2 c.
[76] Perkins, *Cases*, in *Workes of Perkins* 2:19 col. 1.
[77] Perkins, *Cases*, in *Workes of Perkins* 2:19 col. 1 d.
[78] Perkins, *Cases*, in *Workes of Perkins* 2:19 col. 1–2.

what must be done if both testimonies are lacking? Perkins responds, "Men must not despaire, but use good meanes, and in time they shall be assured."[79]

In this passage from Perkins we do not see the claim put as clearly as argued by Beeke that a believer can have assurance without being conscious of it. Thus, there is nothing patently incoherent about Perkins's position here. However, the contention of Perkins is that, even if all *a posteriori* testimony and assurance are lacking, then the person should somehow still be assured that he will eventually be assured of salvation, which is different from saying he is presently assured of salvation. Arminius, who assumed that at least the testimony of the sense of faith would need to be present, would probably find it presumptuous to believe something with no testimony. To be sure, Perkins encourages the use of good means, which mitigates against the antinomian fear that Arminius wanted to avoid. Yet, if Perkins's "good meanes" or good works are not present to be counted as the testimony of sanctification, it is questionable whether this would completely satisfy Arminius's fear of *securitas carnis*.

Arminius's definition of *fides* sans *fiducia* opens the possibility that a person can ontologically possess saving faith without being epistemologically assured of it. Compared to Arminius's contemporaries and Beeke's interpretation in particular, this phenomenon presents fewer difficulties for Arminius's definition of faith and his view of the practical experience of the Christian life. However, since he says that *fiducia* necessarily follows *fides*, a faithful person without assurance is still problematic, though less so than for his contemporaries who claimed that *fiducia* is a component of *fides* itself. That a person can have faith without knowing it, the so-called unconscious seed or germ of faith, is the assumption of Beeke and consistent with the claim of Perkins. For Arminius, though, faith must be consciously present to the believing subject for assurance also to be present.

> Therefore since we are justified not by works, but by faith, we gather that we can be sensibly certain that Christ's satisfaction is imputed by God to us, because we know that we are in faith, and therefore there must be no doubting concerning our justification, as the *Pontificii* falsely teach from the opinions of the Scholastics, inasmuch as faith and the peace of consciences generated by justification are diametrically opposed to doubt.[80]

---

[79] Perkins, *Cases*, in *Workes of Perkins* 2:19 col. 2 b.
[80] Arminius, *De iustificatione* (1603), xxxviii: "Cum igitur justificemur non ex operibus,

Arminius presupposes that, at the very least, faith will be consciously present, and thus the reflex act of faith to which he appealed in pastoral situations will always be possible as a testimony of salvation. Accordingly, Arminius says it is impossible for a believer who knows he believes to simultaneously doubt concerning his salvation.[81] In addition, given Arminius's assumption that faith and the Spirit usually prevail in the *lucta* with doubt and the flesh, it further demonstrates the unlikelihood of a person having saving faith without being able to point to some evidence of it. Moreover, even Arminius's colleagues spoke of the sense of faith as if it would always be present to the believer reflecting on the question. In sum, for Arminius, although faith wrestles with doubt and fluctuates in one's life, *a posteriori* testimony is always present to the true believer who is seeking it, contra Perkins, who acknowledges a complete lack of testimony for some of the elect. This subtle difference may be due to the fact that, for Arminius, faith is a condition for election and is therefore necessarily present in the elect; for Perkins, faith is a consequence of election, and may not necessarily be present yet in the elect.[82]

III. A Priori *Grounding: The Objective Foundation of Salvation*

All the *a posteriori* proofs of salvation presuppose knowledge of the *a priori* foundation of salvation. Epistemological awareness of the foundation of salvation is the principal ground of assurance, without which the secondary *a posteriori* testimonies crumble.[83] The *a posteriori* testimonies, therefore, are only as strong as the *a priori* foundation. This objective foundation is external to the believer, and so its force does not depend on the life of the believer. One way to locate what a certain thinker considered to be the foundation of salvation is simply to search

---

sed ex fide, colligimus nos sane certos esse posse satisfactionem Christi a Deo nobis imputari, quia scimus nos esse in fide, ideoque non esse dubitandum de nostra justificatione, ut falso Pontificii ex Scholasticorum placitis docent, siquidem fides et orta ex justificatione pax conscientiarum ex diametro cum dubitatione pugnant."

[81] Arminius, *Quaestiones*, resp. 7, in *Opera*, p. 186; *Works* 2:67.

[82] Nevertheless, both Arminius and Perkins would agree that the elect are infallibly known to God, and in time an elect person may be either regenerate or not yet regenerate.

[83] Cf. Zachman, *Assurance*, pp. 210–23.

soteriological discussions for *fundamentum* language, which was reserved
for *a priori* grounding, but not used to describe the *a posteriori* testimonies. A *fundamentum* in relation to an efficient cause, more than what is
commonly thought of as a basis, is where causal development properly
begins. As will be demonstrated, Reformed orthodoxy spoke of many
fundamenta with respect to salvation; because of the range of such language in Arminius and his colleagues, it is somewhat difficult to clarify
the systematic relationship among the *fundamenta* in the thought of a
given theologian. In this section, I shall first discuss each *fundamentum* on
its own terms principally from the perspective of Arminius's Reformed
contemporaries, and then, by gathering, contextualizing, and showing
the systematic relationship of Arminius's *fundamenta*, I shall explain the
different priorities represented in Arminius's soteriology with respect to
the remote, or ultimate, foundation, in which we find the chief point of
difference. This elaboration on the contrasts between Arminius's system
and what was then becoming Reformed orthodoxy will also confirm the
findings from chapters three and four.[84]

A. *The Promise of God*

God's promise of life has long been the source of confidence and comfort for his people.[85] Kuchlinus speaks of the external word of God as an
external testimony of salvation. By this he means the evangelical promises, the foremost being that the one who believes in the Son has eternal
life.[86] According to Junius, "This promise, although by itself unmoved,
is confirmed by the oath of God."[87] When this promise of salvation is
applied to us, it is impossible for firm *fiducia* not to exist in our souls.[88] For
Gomarus, it is by *fiducia* that believers appropriate the general promise
of grace for themselves individually.[89] At this point the *a priori* grounding

---

[84] Because of the lack of extant scholarship on Arminius's doctrine of the assurance
of salvation, this point of comparison and contrast has not received due consideration.

[85] E.g., see Luther, *Vorlesung über den 1. Timotheusbrief (4:9)*, in *WA* 26:79; *LW* 28:325.

[86] Kuchlinus, *De certitudine* (1603), xi–xii. Cf. idem, *De perseverantia* (1603), ii and iv.

[87] Junius, *De certitudine* (1601), v: "Promissio haec, per se alioquin immota, juramento
Dei confirmatur."

[88] Junius, *De certitudine* (1601), xii: "Cùm itaque fundamentum salutis, cum respectu
Dei promittentis, tum nostri promissionem ejus nobis applicantium certum et immotum
sit, non potest non statim in nostris animis existere firma fiducia...."

[89] Gomarus, *De fide iustificante* (1603), ix and xvii. Cf. idem, *De fide salvifica* (1603), vii;
idem, *De perseverantia* (1597), x; idem, *De perseverantia* (1608), xv; with Trelcatius, Sr., *De
fide* (1592), x.

is joined with the *a posteriori* testimonies of salvation because the promise of God is appropriated by faith; thus, the promise is assuring by the reflex sense of faith. Without faith, which for Arminius is the most important subjective testimony, the promise does not apply to anyone. God's promise of eternal life to all who believe in Christ, combined with faith in Christ, is sufficient to assure someone.[90] To doubt the certainty of God's power and promises is contrary to faith and closer to despair.[91] The same view is held by Perkins, who stresses the connection of despair and nullification of God's promises as contrary to true faith.[92] Elsewhere, Perkins offers a solution for despair: "...we must draw our arguments from the *promise* of God, and from the *power* of God; we must joyne the promise and power of God together."[93]

The promise of God is not without its own confirmation. In order to further seal and confirm the promise, God added the sacraments.[94] For Junius, inasmuch as the sacraments contain both the sign and the divine promise, they are visible signs of invisible grace to the faithful that render them more certain about the truth of the promise. Those who were circumcised under the old covenant and by true faith looked for the coming Messiah ought to have been certain concerning grace and righteousness. Junius then refers to the new covenant sacraments of baptism and the Lord's Supper as *certissima testimonia*.[95] Thus, one can look for assurance to the external promise of God that he saves by grace through faith, a promise that is appropriated through faith, and further assurance then comes by recalling one's baptism and participating regu-

---

[90] Arminius, *Quaestiones*, resp. 7, in *Opera*, p. 186; *Works* 2:67. The Reformed authors agree with this statement *per se*. Cf. Kimedoncius, *Redemption*, p. 383, calls this God's "universall promise." He then shows its link to the reflex act of faith and practical syllogism.

[91] Arminius, *De fide* (1605), xvi.

[92] Perkins, *Estate of Damnation or Grace*, in *Workes of Perkins* 1:378 col. 1 b: "For he which despaires, makes all the promises of God to be false: and this sinne of all other is most contrary to true saving faith."

[93] Perkins, *Cloud of Faithfull Witnesses*, in *Workes of Perkins* 3:120 col. 1 b; cf. idem, *Cases*, in *Workes of Perkins* 2:22 col. 2 b.

[94] Junius, *De certitudine* (1601), vi; Kuchlinus, *De certitudine* (1603), xiii.

[95] Junius, *De certitudine* (1601), vi: "Promissioni porro juramento confirmatae Sacramenta addidit idem Deus, (non ut Sermonem suum firmarent: sed ut invisibilis gratiae, visibilia signa fidelibus exstarent, simulque eos de promissionis veritate certiores redderent) in veteri quidem Testamento circumcisionem, quae ob id signaculum justitiae fidei dicitur, quod de gratia et justitia certi esse deberent, qui circumcisi vera fide futurum Messiam expectarent: in novo autem Baptismum et Coenam Dominicam...certissima sunt testimonia."

larly in the Lord's Supper. This evangelical promise, though, is not the ultimate *fundamentum*, for there is an antecedent decree supporting it.[96]

B. *The Predestination of God*

For Arminius's colleagues, behind the promise of God lies the decree of God to elect certain people for salvation. In his disputation on the assurance of salvation, Junius identified election as the "foundation on which our salvation rests."[97] Kuchlinus grounds assurance in the same manner: "But the salvation of the faithful is in itself certain, with respect to the foundation, the gracious election made into adoption by God the Father in Jesus Christ, from infinite love."[98] This last phrase raises the important connection between God's predestination and his love. Elsewhere, Kuchlinus distinguishes between intellectual and volitional foreknowledge (πρόγνωσις). After discussing the former type which is taken more broadly, he said that the latter type "is used for knowledge joined with approval, in which sense it pertains more to the will than to the intellect. Rom. 8,29: *Whom he foreknew these he predestined*, that is, whom he loved and acknowledged for his own."[99] God's love enjoyed a similar connection with predestination in the thought of Perkins. Perkins wrote, "In the decree of election the first act is a purpose, or rather a part and beginning of the divine purpose, whereby God doth take certaine men which are to be created (*creandos*), unto his everlasting love (*amorem*) and favour, passing by the rest, and by taking maketh them vessels of mercie and honour."[100] Perkins counseled those in despair to "marke the tokens of Gods love unto us, and that will fortifie our faith."[101]

---

[96] Kendall, *Calvin*, p. 148, asserts that the reflex act of faith is for Perkins and Arminius the "ultimate appeal." In reality, the evangelical promise appropriated by faith is built on something more foundational.

[97] Junius, *De certitudine* (1601), iv: "Fundamentum cui innititur nostra salus est electio Dei gratuita εἰς υἱοθεσίαν in Christo Iesu."

[98] Kuchlinus, *De certitudine* (1603), iv: "Est autem salus fidelis in se certa, respectu fundamenti, electionis gratuitae a Deo Patre in I. Christo factae εἰς υἱοθεσίαν, ex amorem infinito."

[99] Kuchlinus, *De praedestinatione* (1600), iii: "usurpatur pro notitia conjuncta cum approbatione; quo sensu ad voluntatem magis, quam ad intellectum pertinet. Rom. 8,29. *Quos praescivit hos praedestinavit*, h.e. quos amavit et pro suis agnovit."

[100] Perkins, *De praedestinationis modo et ordine: et de amplitudine gratiae divinae... desceptatio* (Cambridge, Eng., 1598), p. 9; *A Treatise of the Manner and Order of Predestination*, in *Workes of Perkins* 2:607–08.

[101] Perkins, *Commentarie upon the Three First Chapteres of the Revelation*, in *Workes of Perkins* 3:367 col. 1 b. According to Gomarus, *De fide salvifica* (1603), v, *fiducia* establishes that God loves us.

C. *The Will of God*

Because the love of God and the predestination of God are so tightly interwoven in the thought of Arminius's Reformed contemporaries, the implication is that the salvific love of God extends only as far as the election to salvation; therefore, this divine love is, like election, unconditional. It is based on the will of God alone, and is assuring because it rests in God's hands alone without the threat of being overturned.[102] After speaking of the divine purpose to elect some and pass by others, Perkins remarks that "this act is of the sole (*mera*) will of God, without any respect either of good or evil in the creature."[103] That God's will is behind predestination was the common understanding of early orthodoxy. All four Leiden theologians agreed that the *beneplacitum* of God is the impulsive efficient cause of election. The divine will, therefore, with respect to the *ordo salutis*, can rightly be called *fundamentum*.

It is not enough, though, for the distressed conscience to know that God has the authority to save, and that he saves graciously without regard to human works. The next logical step for the conscience seeking assurance is to ask what, if not meritorious works, determines the divine will to save. Or, to put it more mildly, is there any indication that God is willing to extend his grace to elect and save me personally? What is really behind God's will to elect? Arminius's colleagues give few indications. Gomarus notes that the *beneplacitum* concerning election is connected with God's gracious love, but that the *beneplacitum* itself as the impulsive cause is internal to God and antecedent.[104] For Gomarus, the divine *beneplacitum* is not only the cause of election, but is also causally related to reprobation.[105] Similarly, Trelcatius places the *beneplacitum* of God in

---

[102] Cf. Seeberg, *History*, 2:388 and 407.

[103] Perkins, *De modo*, p. 9; *Treatise of Predestination*, in *Workes of Perkins* 2:608 col. 1 a.

[104] Gomarus, *De praedestinatione* (1604), xx: "Causa impulsiva est beneplacitum voluntatis Dei et dilectio gratuita." Idem, *De praedestinatione* (1609), xlvi: "...causa etiam efficientem impulsivam non esse externam; secuturam videlicet creandorum dignitatem, vel obedientiae et inobedientiae conditionem; sed internam, antecedens, et a nulla conditione suspensum Dei, de creabilibus, beneplacitum." Cf. idem, *De iustificatione* (1605), x: "Causa impulsiva [iustificationis] duplex, interna, externa: interna, est pura puta Dei gratia, et dilectio ega genus humanum: tum ratione beneplaciti, praedestinantis nos in adoptionem filiorum...."

[105] Gomarus, *De praedestinatione* (1604), xxiii; idem, *De praedestinatione* (1609), lxxxv. Cf. William Ames, *Medulla s.s. theologiae, ex sacris literis, earumque interpretibus, extracta, et methodice disposita* (London, 1630), p. 32; *Marrow of Sacred Divinity, Drawne out of the Holy Scriptures and the Interpreters thereof, and brought into Method* (London, 1642), p. 27.

election in relation to the benevolent affection of God in Christ, but
offers no comment on the *voluntas* that impulsively causes reprobation.[106]
Kuchlinus remarks that some people ask why God elects some and reprobates others. He says that the impulsive cause is connected to the final
cause, such that God elects some and reprobates others for the disclo-
sure of his grace and justice, respectively, and of his glory in both. The
more specific second question that is frequently asked is, "Why did God
elect this one, say Jacob or Peter, and reprobate that one, say Esau or
Judas?" Kuchlinus responds that no other reason can be assigned than
the free *beneplacitum* of God.[107] By his refusal to speculate about the possible motives or inclinations of the divine will to predestine, Kuchlinus
exemplifies the standard Reformed hesitancy to define the *beneplacitum*,
appealing instead to mystery. For Reformed theology, God's sovereignty
means he has a right to do with creation whatever he wills, and he is
righteous in so doing.[108] Warnings against prying too deeply into the
divine will and decree of predestination are ubiquitous in the piety of
Reformed theology.[109] This ultimate agnosticism regarding God's volition in the extent of salvation, this *voluntas* itself being a *fundamentum* of
salvation, on the one hand preserves the free, absolute sovereignty of
God in salvation, but on the other hand can cause anxiety for the soul
that is already weak.

---

[106] Trelcatius, *De praedestinatione* (1606), xii: "Impulsiva est divinum beneplacitum, seu
benevolus affectus Dei in Christo...." Ibid., xx: "Causa ergo efficiens hujus praedestinationis [reprobationis—KDS] primaria est Deus, impulsiva voluntas, et justitia ipsius."
This is consistent with Trelcatius's distinction between *beneplacitum* (God's will to elect)
and *placitum* (God's will to reprobate). See Trelcatius, *Scholastica*, pp. 27–28; *Common
Places*, p. 71.

[107] Kuchlinus, *De praedestinatione* (1600), xv. Ibid., xi, describes *beneplacitum* as *liberri-
mum*. This line of questions and answers is identical to the discussion in the work of the
Heidelberg theologian, Kimedoncius, *Redemption*, pp. 269–71 and 299. Kuchlinus may
not be depending on Kimedoncius here, but he does have obvious ties to Heidelberg.

[108] Beza, *Quaestionum libellus*, p. 127; *Booke of questions*, fols. 82v–83r, says that the cause
of God's ordaining some to hatred "sit nobis *occulta* (excepto gloriae ipsius fine) tamen
iniusta esse nequit, quum *voluntas Dei sit unica iustitiae regula*" (italics mine). Kimedoncius,
Redemption, p. 314, echoes the assumption that what humanity considers unjust may
not be so for God. Note the re-wording in his application of 1 Cor. 1,25 in *Redemption*,
p. 394: "For the foolishnes of God is wiser than men: and likewise the *unrighteousness
of God* is more righteous than men. With this answere the godly are content" (italics
mine).

[109] E.g., cf. *Inst.* 3.24.3; *Articuli XXXIX*, art. 17; Musculus, *Common places*, fol. 386v;
Kimedoncius, *Redemption*, p. 387; *Canons of Dort*, 1.12. Cf. also Brian Armstrong, *Calvin-
ism and the Amyraut Heresy: Protestant Scholasticism and Humanism in Seventeenth-Century France*
(Madison, 1969), pp. 163–68.

D. *Arminius and the* Duplex Dei Amor

In the *Declaratio sententiae* stands the mature and very clear statement of Arminius on the true foundation of the Christian religion and the assurance of salvation. Arminius argues that the supralapsarian type of predestination undermines this very foundation, which he calls the *tweederley liefde Godes,* the *duplex Dei amor,* namely, God's primary love for righteousness and secondary love for humanity. Such undermining of this twofold love results in the two spiritually fatal errors with regard to assurance, that is, security and despair. In contrast to supralapsarianism and its effect on assurance, Arminius considered the doctrine of conditional predestination, based on the certainty of God's antecedent love for all people, to suit this foundation well and provide more assurance than could the hidden divine *beneplacitum.* But what is the origin of Arminius's idea of God's twofold love, and how did Arminius view the divine love in relation to God's will, predestination, and assurance?[110]

D.1. *Background of the* Duplex Dei Amor

In several places throughout the writings of Arminius, he assumes two objects of the divine love. The topic arises in Arminius's discussions of God's will and the affections therein. Arminius affirms that God primarily loves himself and the good of righteousness, and he secondarily loves the creature and its blessedness.[111] In other places, Arminius notes the distinction in passing and builds an argument on the assumption.[112] In these early works, Arminius does not yet specify this distinction as *duplex Dei amor,* although this category underlies his thought from an early stage.

The origin of Arminius's notion of God's twofold love as an affection can be grasped only by examining his doctrine of the divine will, which he developed to a much greater extent than did his Leiden colleagues.[113] It begins with the assertion that God's will, which is logically subsequent to his intellect, is carried (*fertur*) to the known good.[114] Because

---

[110] Cf. the following discussion with Muller, *PRRD* 3:561–69; Heppe, *Reformed Dogmatics,* pp. 95–96.

[111] *Disp. pub.* IV.lxvii; *Disp. priv.* XX.iv–v.

[112] *Disp. pub.* XII.iv; XVII.iv; idem, *Art. non.,* in *Opera,* p. 949; *Works* 2:707.

[113] Cf. *Disp. pub.* IV.xlvii–lxxvii; *Disp. priv.* XVIII–XXI; with Trelcatius, *Disputationum theologicarum quinto repetitarum sexta de attributis divinis essentialibus secundi generis,* Isaacus Iunius respondens, ad diem 5 May 1607 (Leiden, 1607), xi–xxi. Cf. also Muller, *GCP,* pp. 168–69.

[114] *Disp. pub.* IV.xlix; *Disp. priv.* XVIII.ii.

of the infallibility of God's prior knowledge, what God knows to be good is infallibly good and is therefore the proper object of his will. But there are two kinds of good, namely, the chief good, which is the divine essence itself, and any other subordinate good willed by God.[115] Arminius proceeds to clarify a basic distinction in God's will with respect to these two objects. According to the mode of nature, God's will inclines (*tendit*) toward himself; by the mode of liberty, his will inclines toward other things.[116]

For Arminius, of the many affections of God's will, love and goodness are foremost (*primitivi*). In the doctrine of God's will, Arminius elevates love above the other volitional affections by removing it from its Aristotelian and Thomistic classification as a concupiscible passion of human will and discussing it separately.[117] In this context, Arminius defines God's love as "an affection of union in God, whose objects are God himself and the good of righteousness, the creature and its happiness."[118] The connection between God's will and love is clear, inasmuch as the chief and subordinate objects of both are identical. In the extended presentation of the private disputation, Arminius mentions that God loves the creature as it relates to the image or vestige of God. He elaborates on this distinction of love, showing its correspondence to the distinction between the *amor complacentiae* and the *amor amicitiae*. Arminius, in line with his contemporaries, said that God loves himself with the love of complacency, the affection that is carried "to enjoying and having" (*ad fruendum habendumque*) the object, that is, his essence; he loves creatures with the love of friendship, the affection carried "to benefiting" (*ad benefaciendum*) the object, that is, the creature.[119] Moreover, Arminius goes on to say that God may be said in some degree to "enjoy" (*frui*) his actions *ad extra*; that is, he loves the creature and its righteousness to the extent of "having" it (*ad illam habendam*).[120] The indication, then, is that Arminius views God's love of humanity as something more than mere means (*uti*) towards the goal of his own glory, but as approaching enjoyment (*frui*), the beatitude of the creature as an end that God enjoys. Arminius

---

[115] *Disp. pub.* IV.l; *Disp. priv.* XVIII.iii.

[116] *Disp. pub.* IV.lvi; *Disp. priv.* XIX.ii. Cf. Muller, *GCP*, pp. 167–81.

[117] Cf. *Disp. pub.* IV.lxxi; *Disp. priv.* XX.x; with *ST* Ia–IIae.xxvi.1.s.c., resp.

[118] *Disp. pub.* IV.lxvii; "affectus unionis in Deo, cujus objecta sunt Deus ipse et bonum Iustitiae, Creatura et felicitas illius." Cf. *Disp. priv.* XX.iv.

[119] *Disp. priv.* XX.iv.

[120] *Disp. priv.* XX.iv.

is not suggesting that creation is primarily to be considered as an end in itself or in any way on a plane with God, but that the beatitude of creation itself achieves the status of a subordinate end in the divine will. Since the creature as God's image is an indication of God's perfection proceeding from his free will, then the creature can be rightly enjoyed as such.[121]

In sum, Arminius's reasoning appears to proceed in the following way: God's will tends toward himself and his creation; but God's will is loving, and his love is volitional; therefore, God's love, as his will, tends toward himself and his creation.[122] Furthermore, the primary love is directed not only toward God's essence, but also specifically toward the attribute of divine righteousness. The secondary love is directed not only toward creation, but also specifically toward creation's beatitude and its good. The implication is that God's nature as loving will tends toward the good of the creature. Not only had Arminius developed a matrix which directly affected his theology proper, Christology, and soteriology, but, by 1608 and into his last conference in August, 1609, he had also defined and explicitly designated this notion as *duplex Dei amor*, raising it to the level of *fundamentum*.[123]

D.2. *Creation and Love*

Duplex Dei amor in itself is not an idea unique to Arminius,[124] but, insofar as it is qualified by his conception of God's prior relationship to creation, it differed from the common Reformed understanding. This relationship between Creator and creation is manifest in God's purpose for creating humanity, specifically, that man "might acknowledge God his Creator, love, worship, and live blessed (*beatus*) with him forever."[125] Humanity was created for fellowship with God, an affirmation that Arminius's

---

[121] This assertion does not contradict *Disp. priv.* XIX.cor.iii. It may, however, be in tension with the traditional notion that love of a finite object as an end is the impure *amor concupiscentiae*. On this distinction, cf. Trelcatius, *De attributis* (1607), xix; with Muller, *DLGT*, p. 31.

[122] The general shape of this theology of divine will and love and its relationship to creation is Thomistic in character. Cf. Seeberg, *History*, 2:107. It is also typical of Reformed orthodoxy. Cf. Muller, *PRRD* 3:564–65.

[123] *Disp. pub.* XIV.xvi (31 March 1608); *Dec. sent.*, pp. 90–4; *Works* 1:634–38 (30 October 1608); report of Hommius in Wijminga, *Hommius*, Bijlage G, pp. xii and xiv (12–22 August 1609).

[124] Cf. Altenstaig, *Lexicon*, p. 41.

[125] *Disp. priv.* XXVI.x.

opponents did not predicate to all humanity. Trelcatius asserted that creation, as the first external action of God, is "for his glory, the good of the universe, and the salvation of the elect," but he is noticeably silent about God's goal for the reprobate.[126] Against Gomarus's patent view that creation in righteousness is a *via reprobationis*, Arminius claims creation in this right state to be "the most certain sign of the benevolence and love of God toward those whom he has created such."[127] God's act of creation is itself an act of love. For this reason, God "cannot hate things as far as they have some likeness of God, that is, [as far as] they are good; albeit he is not necessarily bound to love them."[128] Because of his love of righteousness and the creature, God freely—not of necessity—obliges himself to creation with the result that he sets limits on the possibility of his own actions toward creation. Therefore, asserts Arminius,

> God's first action toward some object, whatever it may be, cannot be its casting away or reprobation to eternal misery. Because God is the highest good, therefore his first volition, by which he is engaged with some object, is the communication of good.[129]

This conception of the Creator-creation relationship is directly opposed to the thought of Arminius's colleagues. It also differs from Perkins, who, after remarking that God passes by those he does not elect, claims that God does no injury to the reprobate, "because he is obliged to no one."[130]

---

[126] Trelcatius, *Disputationum theologicarum quinto repetitarum nona de creatione*, Ioannes LeChantre respondens, ad diem 4 July 1607 (Leiden, 1607), iii: "ad gloriam suam, universi bonum, et electorum salutem." Cf. also Ursinus, *Compendium*, pp. 303–04; *Summe*, p. 367.

[127] *Exam. Gom.*, p. 87; *Works* 3:599: "certissimum signum benevolentiae et amoris Dei erga illos quos tales creavit."

[128] *Disp. priv.* XIX.ii: "quia non potest odisse res quatenus simllitudinem [*sic*] aliquam Dei habent, id est, bonae sunt; quanquam amare eas necessario non teneatur...." Arminius would no doubt reject Beza's attempt to escape the difficulty. Beza, *Quaestionum libellus*, p. 127; *Booke of questions*, fol. 82v: "Verum aliud est odisse, aliud iusto odio destinare."

[129] *Exam. Gom.*, p. 76; *Works* 3:590: "Prima Dei in aliquod objectum qualecumque id sit actio, non potest esse ejus abjectio seu reprobatio ad aeternam miseriam. Quia Deus est summum bonum, itaque prima ejus qua circa aliquod objectum versatur volitio est communicatio boni."

[130] Perkins, *De modo*, p. 9; *Treatise of Predestination*, in *Workes of Perkins* 2:607–08: "quia nemini obligatus est."

It should now be clear why Arminius, particularly contra supra-lapsarianism, cannot allow reprobation to be God's first act toward any part of creation. He loves good before hating evil, and only hates evil because he first loves good.[131] God has a prior, but free, obligation to his creation as the object of his will and love. Since love is an act of union, reprobation of the creature without consideration of its sin would be to Arminius an impossible act of separation. The relationship between creation and the rightful state of the creature is explicit in Arminius's rejection of Perkins's supralapsarianism. Because of God's obligation, he has no right (*jus*) to eternally punish humanity without regard to sin. Arminius then proceeds:

> For these four things—to be, not to be, to be happy, to be miserable (*esse, non esse, faelicem esse, miserum esse*)—are so related among themselves that, as it is better to be happy than [merely] to be, so it is worse to be miserable than not to be... [Matt. 26,24]. For which reason the right of God does not permit (*permittit*) that he may inflict miserable existence (*miserum esse*) on a person to whom he gave existence, except upon the perpetration of that by whose opposite he could have arrived at the felicity opposed to that misery. Therefore, insofar as he does not elect all, he does injury to no one, if the non-elect only lack the good not owed to them; but if also they ought to suffer unmerited evil (*malum non meritum pati debent*) from non-election or reprobation, injury is already done to them, because *the right of God does not extend itself over them as far as this* (*eo quod jus Dei in illos eousque se non extendat*).[132]

Because of God's love of righteousness and his obligation to creation, he relinquishes any "right" to choose to inflict punishment unequally. This notion parallels the distinction between *potentia absoluta* and *potentia ordinata*. Commenting on Romans 9, Arminius wrote:

> The term "power" (*potestas*) used here signifies not "ability" (*potentia*) but "right" (*jus*) and "authority" (*autoritas*). For it is ἐξουσία, not δύναμις.

---

[131] *Exam. Gom.*, p. 59; *Works* 3:574–75: "Deus prius amat quam odit, amat bonum quam odit malum: quia enim bonum amat, hinc malum odit, prius obedeientiae vult praemium quam inobedientiae poenam." The Reformed used language similar to that of Arminius here. E.g., see Kuchlinus, *Theses theologicae de liberatione hominis a miseria*, Valerius Valerii Tophusius respondens, in *Theo. disp.* 23, pp. 130–34, iv: "[Deus] Est *summe misericors*, cuius bonitas gloriatur contra iudicium, propensior est ad misericordiam praestandam quam iustitiam." The greater importance of creation theology in Arminius's doctrine of predestination is evident in *Dec. sent.*, pp. 80–2; *Works* 1:626–27. On God and his relationship to creation, see Muller, 'God, Predestination,' 431–46; and Witt, 'Creation,' pp. 261–315.

[132] *Exam. Perk.*, in *Opera*, p. 656; *Works* 3:302, italics mine.

Therefore it is not here concerned about absolute power (*potentia*) by
which [God] can [do] something, but about the right by which it is lawful
for him [to do] something.[133]

God certainly has the absolute power, but, by his own ordination, he
freely relinquishes the right and authority to simply (*simpliciter*) make a
person a vessel for dishonor and wrath.[134] Arminius's Reformed contemporaries, for the most part, did not share his enthusiasm for this
concept of self-limited divine sovereignty.[135]

D.3. *Antecedent and Consequent Love*

Arminius underscores the priority of God's love in his willing and decree.
Yet, by means of a distinction familiar to traditional theology, Arminius
distinguishes God's general love of humanity from his love in Christ.
God's general love is that by which he loved the world and sent his Son;
this love is different from the love that is the cause of predestination.[136]
God's general love and gracious affection are uniform towards all those
to be created, but a sinner can actually be saved only by the love and
affection that are considered in Christ.[137] Moreover, the relation of this
distinction to God's twofold love of righteousness and the creature is
easily applied, for example, when God only continues to love the sinful
creature based on the presence of consequent righteousness, whether or
not it is imputed. Such a connection is implied when Arminius writes:

> III. God loves righteousness and creatures, yet righteousness more than
> creatures: from which two things follow.
> IV. First, God does not hate the creature, except because of sin.
> V. Second, God loves no creature absolutely for eternal life, except con-
> sidered as righteous, either by legal or evangelical righteousness.
> VI. God's will is distinguished, both rightly and usefully, into antecedent
> and consequent.[138]

---

[133] Arminius, *Analysis*, in *Opera*, p. 794; *Works* 3:510: "*Potestatis* vox hic usurpata significat non *potentiam* sed *jus* et *autoritatem*. Est enim ἐξουσία non δύναμις. non igitur hic
agitur de *absoluta potentia* qua potest aliquid, sed de *jure* quo licet illi aliquid."
[134] Arminius, *Analysis*, in *Opera*, p. 797; *Works* 3:514.
[135] E.g., cf. Beza, *Quaestionum libellus*, p. 127; *Booke of questions*, fols. 82v–83r.
[136] *Amica col.*, in *Opera*, pp. 614–15; *Works* 3:241; idem, *Exam. Perk.*, in *Opera*, p. 658;
Works 3:304–05.
[137] *Exam. Perk.*, in *Opera*, p. 655; *Works* 3:300. Cf. Muller, *PRRD* 3:562.
[138] *Art. non.*, in *Opera*, p. 949; *Works* 2:707: "III. Deum amare justitiam, et creaturas,
magis tamen justitiam quam creaturas: unde duo sequuntur. IV. Primum, Deum creaturam non odisse, nisi propter peccatum. V. Secundum, Deum nullam creaturam prae-
cise ad vitam aeternam amare; nisi consideratam ut justam, sive justitia Legali, sive

In light of the predominant themes of God's love and human faith in Arminius's soteriology, one can begin to detect an order in God's willing, an order which anticipates the order of decrees as articulated in the *Declaratio sententiae*. According to Arminius, God's decree of giving the mediator and saving believers by the mediator is prior to the decree of predestination.[139] Thus, in contrast to the thought of his colleagues, the promise and will of God precede particular election and reprobation. Furthermore, it is God's general love for the world that inspired the mission of his Son as a mediator. This love, however, is not the love by which God actually bestows eternal life. Faith intervenes between God's general love and his granting of eternal life.[140] Just as Arminius connects God's love with the divine will, this distinction in love parallels the well-known distinction between the divine antecedent and consequent will. Inasmuch as God's general love is the basis of the Son's advent, Arminius calls it preceding love. The love that follows and is the basis of salvation he calls consequent love.[141]

The acknowledgment that God's will is circumscribed principally by his twofold love, along with Arminius's description of God's will, yield insight into the divine *beneplacitum*. Like his colleagues, Arminius understood God's *beneplacitum* to be the impulsive cause of election.[142] Yet he defines this *beneplacitum* as "benevolent affection."[143] For Arminius, the divine *beneplacitum* is not so much hidden and unknown as it is based on God's prior love and human faith. "The *beneplacitum* of God's will to salvation is toward the faithful only."[144] It directly corresponds to God's consequent will to elect believers.[145]

Evangelica. VI. Voluntas Dei et recte, et utiliter in Antecedentem, et consequentem distinguitur."

[139] *Exam. Perk.*, in *Opera*, p. 679; *Works* 3:337. Cf. *Dec. sent.*, pp. 104–06; *Works* 1:653–54. By "predestination" here he means the decree of electing and reprobating certain individuals.

[140] *Exam. Perk.*, in *Opera*, p. 653; *Works* 3:296–97. Jn. 3,16 was one of many texts Arminius employed to support this distinction between God's will and love for the salvation of all and his actual salvation of those who believe.

[141] *Exam. Gom.*, p. 139; *Works* 3:642. On antecedent and consequent will, see *Disp. pub.* IV.lx–lxii; *Disp. priv.* XIX.vi. For more on the connection between antecedent/consequent will and antecedent/consequent love, cf. also idem, *Exam. Perk.*, in *Opera*, pp. 743–44; *Works* 3:432–35. For commentary on Arminius's use of antecedent/consequent will and the Thomistic background, see Dekker, *Rijker*, pp. 122–24.

[142] *Exam. Gom.*, p. 66; *Works* 3:581.

[143] *Disp. pub.* XV.iv.

[144] *Exam. Gom.*, p. 67; *Works* 3:582: "Beneplacitum voluntatis Dei ad salutem est erga fideles solos."

[145] *Exam. Perk.*, in *Opera*, p. 669; *Works* 3:321.

A definite, logical order is revealed in God's will and love that differs markedly from the Reformed order. Assuming the created order and the fall into sin permitted by God, there follows 1) God's general antecedent love and will, 2) the giving of Christ as mediator, 3) human faith foreseen, 4) God's consequent love and will in Christ (or, *beneplacitum*), and 5) particular election and reprobation. From an examination of Arminius's contemporaries, they are clearly more hesitant than Arminius to describe God's affection toward all humanity as "love." Although they would not necessarily be opposed to speaking of God's common love, the chief difference is that, for Arminius, even this general, antecedent love of God has the salvation of humanity as its goal:

> For since by his providence [God] has given to all creatures necessary and sufficient means by which they can arrive at their end (*finem*); but the end of man created in God's image is eternal life; thus it follows that *all persons have been loved (amatos esse) by God to eternal life by the antecedent will*; nor can God without change of his purpose deny eternal life to persons, without respect of sin; which denial, consequent (*consequens*) on the action of a person, will be of the consequent will.[146]

Like God's antecedent will, his preceding love for all people comes logically before any actions of particular individuals; like his consequent will, his consequent love logically follows an individual's acceptance of God's grace. For the opponents of Arminius, God's common love for all humanity extends only to general benefits, but not to spiritual salvation.[147] For Arminius, although not all are consequently saved, all are equally loved antecedently and desired by God for the goal of eternal fellowship. Both God's general love and his love in Christ are intended for salvation; the former is potential, whereas the latter is actual.[148]

---

[146] *Exam. Perk.*, in *Opera*, p. 744; *Works* 3:434–35, italics mine. Cf. ibid., in *Opera*, pp. 674–75; *Works* 3:329–30.

[147] Gomarus, *De perseverantia* (1608), xvi, distinguishes between, on the one hand, God's love, grace, and general benevolence shown commonly to all, and, on the other hand, God's grace and infinite love conferred in Christ. Although it parallels Arminius's distinction between God's general and saving love, Gomarus's general love is not for the purpose of saving. As Gomarus comments on 1 Tim. 2,4 in *Proeve van M. P. Bertii Aenspraeck* (Leiden, 1610), p. 30: "God wil oock dat alle, dat is, allerley soorten van menschen, salich worden." Cf. Itterzon, *Gomarus*, p. 184. Gomarus's interpretation of 1 Tim. 2,4 as synecdoche is the classic explanation of Augustine and Calvin as well. See, among other places, Augustine, *Enchiridion ad Laurentium sive de fide, spe et caritate* 103, in *PL* 40:280–81; Calvin, *Inst.* 3.24.16; Perkins, *De modo*, pp. 77–88; *Treatise of Predestination*, in *Workes of Perkins* 2:623–25. Arminius interprets this verse by appealing to God's antecedent will (per John of Damascus) in *Exam. Perk.*, in *Opera*, pp. 740–41; *Works* 3:429–30. On the scholastic uses and distinctions of *amor Dei*, see Muller, *DLGT*, pp. 31–32.

[148] Some modern interpreters have indeed pointed out that "Arminianism" defines

D.4. *Love and the* Fundamenta

As has been observed, Arminius insisted that predestination is the "foundation of Christianity, of salvation, and of the certainty of salvation."[149] Furthermore, against his Reformed contemporaries, he asserted that Christ is the *fundamentum electionis*.[150] How do these two *fundamenta*—predestination and Christ—relate to one another, and, more importantly, how do they relate to *duplex Dei amor*, which he calls the *fundamentum* of religion and of the Christian religion?

First of all, with regard to the "fundamental" nature of predestination, it is essential to point out what part of "predestination" Arminius considered to be foundational to salvation and assurance. In *Articuli nonnulli*, he specifies that the actual foundation is the second of his four predestination decrees, namely:

> II. The second decree is that by which God resolves to receive into grace those who repent and are faithful and who persevere, to save [them] in Christ, because of Christ, and through Christ. But to leave the impenitent and unbelievers under sin and wrath, and to condemn [them] as aliens from Christ....
> VI. That second decree is predestination to salvation, which is the foundation of Christianity, salvation, and of the assurance of salvation, the matter of the gospel, the sum of apostolic doctrine.[151]

This foundational decree to save penitent believers and condemn impenitent unbelievers is another way for Arminius to articulate the function of the consequent will of God. This evangelical promise, taken on its own, was also acknowledged by the Leiden theologians as an external, *a priori* testimony of salvation and, therefore, a ground of assurance. Thus, the "foundation" of salvation and of the assurance

---

God's will by his love and that "Calvinism" defines God's love by his will, but without attempting to analyze Arminius and his colleagues on their own terms. E.g., see Walls and Dongell, *Why I Am Not a Calvinist*, pp. 198–203 and 216–21.

[149] "Fundamentum Christianismi, salutis, et certitudinis de salute." For references, see above, pp. 89–90.

[150] *Disp. priv.* XL.v; *Dec. sent.*, pp. 85–86; *Works* 1:630–31.

[151] *Art. non.*, in *Opera*, p. 957; *Works* 2:719: "II. Secundum decretum est, quo Deus statuit Resipiscentes et Fideles in gratiam recipere, eousque perseverantes salvare in Christo, propter Christum, et per Christum. Impoenitentes vero et incredulos sub peccato, et ira relinquere, et condemnare tanquam a Christo alienos....VI. Illud secundum decretum est Praedestinatio ad salutem, quae est Fundamentum Christianismi, salutis et certitudinis de salute, Materia Evangelii, Summa Apostolicae doctrinae." Cf. *Dec. sent.*, p. 104; *Works* 1:653. See these places for all four decrees as well.

of salvation is the promise that God will save believers. It runs counter
to the typical Reformed notion that God elects certain persons without
regard to faith or repentance.

Next, concerning the "fundamental" character of Christ, it is only
reasonable—given Arminius's order of decrees and his affirmation that
the second decree concerning election only obtains in, because of, and
through Christ (*in Christo, propter Christum, et per Christum*)—that the foundation of election is Christ, "ordained by God as priest and mediator
through the blood of his cross, redeemer from the captivity of sin and
Satan, and author and giver of eternal salvation."[152] This early statement unmistakably parallels Arminius's first divine decree in which
God resolves to constitute Jesus Christ as "Savior, Mediator, Redeemer,
Priest."[153] Because Christ is ready and willing to save all people, this
first decree is another way for Arminius to articulate God's antecedent
will. Therefore, the foundation of salvation and assurance, the promise to save penitent believers (second decree), is itself founded on and
made possible only by the foundational person and work of Christ (first
decree).

It is necessary now to demonstrate Arminius's application of the
duplex Dei amor so that its foundational nature and connection with predestination in Christ can be established. According to Arminius, *duplex
Dei amor* is the foundation of religion in general and of the Christian
religion in particular. With respect to religion in general, God's love
of the reasonable (*redelijcke*) creature is qualified by and second only to
his love of righteousness (*gherechticheyt*). The consequence of this twofold love in its proper order is that God will indeed condemn a person
on account of sin and never condemn a person without regard to sin.
Supralapsarianism, however, inverts this proper order when it asserts
that God wills to save a certain person without regard to obedience or
righteousness, thus placing God's love of the creature above his love
of righteousness. At the same time, when a person is reprobated for a
reason other than unrighteousness, it completely extinguishes the love
for the creature, even when this love is not in conflict with the love for
righteousness.[154]

---

[152] *Exam. Perk.*, in *Opera*, pp. 657–58; *Works* 3:303–04: "ordinato a Deo Sacerdote et
Mediatore per sanguinem crucis suae, salvatore ex peccatis, redemptore ex captivitate
peccati et satanae, salutisque aeternae auctore et datore."
[153] *Art. non.*, in *Opera*, p. 957; *Works* 2:718–19: "Salvatorem, Mediatorem, Redemp-
torem, Sacerdotem." Cf. *Dec. sent.*, p. 104; *Works* 1:653.
[154] *Dec. sent.*, pp. 90–91; *Works* 1:634–36.

With regard to the Christian religion in particular, the difference (*weynich anders*) being that Arminius here assumes humanity as fallen and an enemy of God, God's love is directed primarily toward righteousness and secondarily toward sinful humanity. Again, the only factor that can supersede God's love for sinners is his primary love for righteousness. Arminius then describes the divine love for sinful creatures in two ways. The first is the love by which God gave his Son for them and constituted him a savior of those who obey him. The second love of sinners is that by which he graciously and gently (*sachtmoedelijck*) requires obedience, with the added promise of remission of sins for those who repent.[155]

Although Arminius does not elaborate on these categories in this passage, in light of the preceding analysis we can see from his brief description that this first love of sinners corresponds to the general, antecedent love of God, which in turn corresponds to the first decree of predestination. As noted above, this first decree, which considers the mission of the Son, is for Arminius the *fundamentum electionis*. The second love of sinners corresponds to the consequent love of God in Christ, which in turn corresponds to the second decree of predestination. It is the second decree, the evangelical promise to save the faithful, which comprises the *fundamentum Christianismi, salutis, et certitudinis de salute*. Thus, the very foundation of the Christian religion, God's twofold love, merges with the other two *fundamenta* in the first two decrees of predestination, for they proceed directly from God's loving volition toward fallen creation (see Figure 2).

From Arminius's position, Reformed predestination equally undercuts the twofold love that he takes to be foundational to the Christian religion in particular. First, the Reformed position has God loving some sinners and saving them logically before he had given satisfaction (*hebbe ghenoech gedaen*) to his own righteousness, thus inverting the twofold love by subordinating his love for righteousness to his love for sinners.[156] Second, God wills to damn some sinners without regard to whether the sinner would continue impenitent, thereby abolishing his love for sinners even when satisfaction has been made.[157] According to one report,

---

[155] *Dec. sent.*, pp. 91–92; *Works* 1:636.

[156] Whether Arminius still intends to directly attack the doctrine later known as supralapsarianism is unclear. His present polemic about God's love of sinners assumes an infralapsarian position and thus applies more appropriately to the types of predestination that he discusses later in the speech.

[157] *Dec. sent.*, pp. 92–93; *Works* 1:636–37. For Arminius's connection of the *duplex amor* to the atonement, see also *Disp. pub.* XIV.xvi.

Figure 2: *Tria Fundamenta*—Arminius's *A Priori* Grounding of Assurance

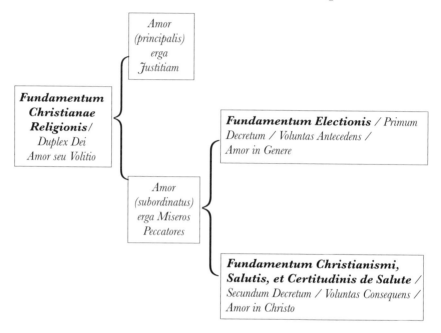

Arminius stated his opinion of the predestination doctrine of his opponents and its relation to the *duplex Dei amor* more succinctly in his final conference of 1609:

> Not only is the doctrine contending with God's word, but it also ought in no way to be allowed in the church,
>
> I. Because it overturns all Religion: for the foundation of all Religion is the twofold love of God. 1. Love of righteousness. 2. Love of humanity. This [foundation] is overturned by [this] doctrine of predestination.
>
> II. Because it overturns the Christian Religion whose foundation indeed is the twofold love. The love of righteousness demands that God save no one except the faithful, damn no one except the unfaithful. The love of humanity [demands] that he does not damn a person except as a sinner. [This] Predestination overturns this [foundation] as well.[158]

---

[158] As reported in Hommius's letter, in Wijminga, *Hommius*, Bijlage G, p. xii: "…esse doctrinam non tantum cum verbo Dei pugnantem sed etiam in Ecclesia nullo modo ferendam I. Quia evertit omnem Religionem: nam fundamentum omnis Religionis est duplex Amor Dei. 1. Amor justitiae. 2. Amor Hominis. Uterque evertitur doctrina de

In the previous chapter, we described the opposite dangers of *securitas* and *desperatio*, and how Arminius perceived them to be the logical consequences of Reformed soteriology. It now remains to demonstrate how Arminius's conception of *duplex Dei amor* functions to ground assurance and chart a middle way between *securitas* and *desperatio*. Arminius's chosen text in his *Declaratio* is Heb. 11,6 ("Die tot Got gaet, moet ghelooven datter een God is, ende dat hy een verghelder is der ghener die hem soecken"), with special attention to the last phrase (namely, God rewards those who seek him), which contains the twofold foundation—the twofold love of God—against the two fiery darts of Satan, *securitas* and *desperatio*. First, Arminius demonstrates how consideration of God's love of righteousness eliminates *securitas*. If one truly believes that God will give eternal life to no one except those who seek him, a belief that is based on God's love of righteousness, which love is greater than God's love for any impenitent person, then security is prevented (*wordt verhoedet*).[159] A person can never rest in security of the flesh or the doctrine of unconditional perseverance without being attentive to the righteousness that God loves and imputes to those who seek him. Second, Arminius shows how consideration of God's love of sinners takes away *desperatio*. If one truly believes that God will certainly (*seeckerlijck*) reward those who diligently seek him, a belief that is based on God's great love for humanity that cannot hinder God from saving, then there is no room for despair.[160] In other words, the faithful person need not worry about an unknown divine will to reprobate, for God is eager to reward the faithful. The agnosticism concerning the Reformed doctrine of God's secret will for certain individuals is mitigated by Arminius's contention that God's *beneplacitum* can indeed be known concerning his will to save all people. As Graafland indicates, this is a "deeply radical variation" in the doctrine of God.[161]

Praedestinatione. II. Quia evertit Religionem Christianam cujus fundamentum idem duplex amor est. Amor justitiae exigit ut Deus neminem salvet nisi fidelem, neminem damnet, nisi infidelem. Amor hominis ut hominem non damnet nisi peccatorem. Utrumque evertit Praedest."

[159] *Dec. sent.*, pp. 93–94; *Works* 1:638.

[160] *Dec. sent.*, p. 94; *Works* 1:638.

[161] According to Graafland, *Van Calvijn tot Barth*, pp. 92–93, Arminius connects the God of revelation with the hidden, unknown God, while Perkins maintained a greater sense of mystery concerning the latter.

IV. *Comparison*

A. *Implications for Assurance and Doubt*

From Arminius's perspective, the supralapsarian order of the decrees undermines the *a priori* foundation of salvation and its assurance. If, as the Reformed taught, God's *beneplacitum* and particular predestination are unconditional and unknown, then it would lead to agnosticism concerning the *a priori* grounding of assurance, that is, whether God is willing to save me.[162] For Arminius, however, God's consequent will and particular election are conditioned not only by human faith, but also by the recognition that, antecedent to any human action, God truly loves all humanity (including "me") for the purpose of eternal life. There can be no question as to God's desire for each person's salvation; to think otherwise would implicate God as showing favoritism and unjust inequality.[163] It is true that Arminius and his colleagues all affirmed the same *a posteriori* testimonies of salvation, and that the *a posteriori* testimonies are only as strong as the *a priori*. For this reason, on the one hand, the Reformed testimonies, from Arminius's point of view, are based on *a priori* doubt about God's will to save. On the other hand, for Arminius, God's *a priori*, antecedent love for salvation lends more credibility to the *a posteriori* testimonies, especially the sense of faith.

In sum, for Arminius, the true ground of assurance, the foundation to which a Christian should look for assurance, is rooted in the doctrine of God and his twofold love. To the one suffering from despair, this twofold love means the absolute certainty that God has obliged himself to his creation and loves each person for the goal of salvation. To the one slumbering in false security, it means that God will by no means save someone who has not been imputed with righteousness through true, saving faith. God's love simply did not function in this way for Arminius's colleagues.

---

[162] Even if one accepts Kendall's argument for Christ's universal death and particular intercession in the thought of Calvin, it is ultimately unclear how this genuinely resolves the problem of epistemological assurance of the saving intercession. See Kendall, *Calvin*, pp. 17–18.

[163] See comments favoring universal grace versus unjust inequality in Hemmingius, *Enchiridion*, pp. 235–37. See Beza's response to this charge in Beza, *Quaestionum libellus*, pp. 127–29; *Booke of Questions*, fols. 83r–84r.

This difference in *a priori* grounding likewise indicates the location of doubt in the thought of Arminius and of his Reformed opponents. Each system admitted the *lucta* between confidence and doubt, thereby implying that doubt has a place in the Christian life—albeit an unwanted place. On the one hand, for Arminius, doubt appears with regard to the future. "No one," Arminius writes, "can believe that future sins will also be remitted to him, unless he knows (*sciat*) that he will believe to the end."[164] A person is not privy to this kind of knowledge, though God is. A person can be completely consoled at the present time simply by the sense of faith, but this present faith does not guarantee the future. On the other hand, for the Reformed, although the elect individual who is presently assured need not concern himself about a future apostasy, there is doubt with regard to the *fundamentum* itself. Therefore, if a person inquires into the extent of God's *a priori* will to save a certain person, a firm answer is impossible, leading to an *a priori* agnosticism that can undermine present assurance for the person who, from Arminius's perspective, can do nothing about his status.

In the estimation of Arminius, then, the belief that one cannot fall away inspires carnal security, but the possibility of apostasy actually inspires consolation, even if the comfort is limited to the present.

IV. The persuasion by which any believer certainly persuades himself that he cannot defect from the faith, or that, at least, he will not defect (*non defecturum*) from the faith, does not conduce so much to consolation against despair or doubt (*dubitationem*) that is adverse to faith and hope, as it engenders security, which is directly opposed to the most salutary fear by which we are commanded to work out (*operari*) our salvation, and which is exceedingly necessary in this place of temptations.

V. He who is of opinion that he can defect from the faith, and therefore is afraid (*metuit*) lest he should defect, is neither destitute of necessary consolation, nor is he, on this account, tormented with anxiety of the soul (*animi*). For it suffices to inspire consolation and to exclude anxiety for him to know that by no force (*vi*) of Satan, of sin, or of the world, and by no affection or weakness of his own flesh will he defect from the faith, unless he of his own accord and willingly (*ultro volens*) falls to temptation, and neglects to work out salvation from the conscience.[165]

---

[164] *Ep. ecc.* 81, p. 151; *Works* 2:70.
[165] *Art. non.*, in *Opera*, p. 962; *Works* 2:726.

For Arminius, then, it is not necessary to affirm unconditional perseverance in order to retain assurance. Comfort still exists because the believer still has a say in the acceptance or refusal of faith.[166] For the believer, there is no external force, including any unknown *beneplacitum*, that can lead to condemnation.

B. *Faith and Hope*

When comparing and contrasting Reformed and Roman Catholic views of the assurance of salvation, Perkins observes that the primary difference is that certainty of salvation for the Reformed is by faith, whereas certainty of salvation for Roman Catholics is by hope.[167] Perkins seems to mean that, for the Reformed, faith itself entails assurance. Since for Arminius *fides* does not entail *fiducia*, but *fiducia* is the consequence of faith, he may fall under Perkins's Roman Catholic category of placing assurance in hope. Certainly, as I have shown, Arminius located true assurance between *securitas* and *desperatio*, which are extreme vices most distant from the theological virtue of hope. For Arminius, this hope is founded on God's love for creation and his will to save all sinners.

It is interesting, though, that Perkins goes on to mention that even the "papists" ought to have infallible assurance if it is based on true hope. He then says that "the true hope followeth faith, and presupposeth certainty of faith; neither can any man truly hope for his salvation, unless by faith hee bee certainly assured thereof in some measure."[168] Perkins admits that even assurance based on hope should be as strong as that based on faith, for there is a strong connection between faith and hope. Calvin likewise affirms the inseparability of true faith and hope.[169] He also claims that, since faith does not promise health and wealth, "its

---

[166] Again, Letham, 'Faith,' 1:315, exaggerates the case against Arminius: "*Precisely because Arminius inverts the order of the decrees and so makes perseverance conditional, so he destroys the doctrine of the assurance of salvation.*" Of course, from Arminius's perspective, it is supralapsarianism that has inverted the decrees and destroyed assurance.

[167] Perkins, *A Reformed Catholike or, A Declaration Shewing How Neere Wee may come to the present Church of Rome in sundrie points of Religion: and wherein we must for ever depart from them*, in *Workes of Perkins* 1:563 col. 1 b–c. It should be clear that the doctrine of unconditional predestination *per se* does not guarantee the claim of necessary assurance as found in Reformed soteriology. E.g., Aquinas still only allowed a conjectural certainty of salvation. On the variety of Catholic views, see Seeberg, *History*, 2:121, 202, 435, and 437.

[168] Perkins, *Reformed*, in *Workes of Perkins* 1:565 col. 2 c–d.

[169] *Inst.* 3.2.42–43. Cf. also Ursinus, *Compendium*, pp. 239–40; *Summe*, pp. 278–79.

chief (*praecipua*) security resides in the expectation of future life."[170] On the actual basis of assurance, Arminius is not so far from his Reformed contemporaries. To the degree that assurance of salvation is oriented toward the future, it is by hope. The difference lies in the divergent conceptions of the foundation of that hope, the doctrine of God.

---

[170] *Inst.* 3.2.28.

CHAPTER SEVEN

CONCLUSION

This essay has been an attempt to describe and analyze Jacobus Arminius's doctrine of salvation in general and his doctrine of the assurance
of salvation in particular, thus supplementing current scholarship on
Arminius and on Reformed soteriology. In view of this goal, Arminius and his theology have been placed in their academic context at the
University of Leiden and his views of the ontology of salvation and the
epistemology of salvation have been examined. Throughout the essay,
I have provided a comparative analysis of Arminius and his closest
Reformed contemporaries that demonstrates both the similarities and
the differences in their systems, thus further illuminating the roots of the
Arminian debate in Leiden and the low countries. This final chapter
will recapitulate some of the chief conclusions of the essay and reiterate
the position of assurance in the overall thought of Arminius.

I. *Ontology and Epistemology of Salvation*

The most basic distinction pertinent to this study of Arminius's soteriology is the difference between the ontology and the epistemology of
salvation. The two categories must not be confused. Given the epistemological consequences of the fall, it can be easily imagined that one
may be ontologically elect but epistemically unaware of it, or, in contrast, one may be ontologically reprobate but epistemically assured of
salvation. In brief, this is the problem of the assurance of salvation.
The doubt that plagued the late medieval church was not eliminated in
the Reformed church, and, for that matter, this problem of assurance
goes back at least to the first epistle of John and extends into the 21st
century.

Although these categories are distinct, they are nevertheless inti-
mately related to and mutually influential on one another. A particular
conception of how salvation is achieved and applied will directly affect
the mode and extent of the assurance of the personal application of
salvation. Likewise, one's assumptions about what constitutes a healthy,

biblical assurance of salvation will affect one's opinion of any soteriological system that tends to generate what appears to be unhealthy, unbiblical assurance. These theoretical and practical considerations regarding soteriology are at stake in the Arminian controversy.

II. *Arminius's Soteriology in the Context of Reformed Orthodoxy*

The tendencies characterizing much of twentieth-century scholarship on Arminius—namely, inattention to the original languages and primary works of Arminius and his colleagues; imposing the thoughts of later Enlightenment Remonstrantism, American revivalism, or Continental existentialism on Arminius; and using Arminius to bolster a modern theological viewpoint before pausing to understand him—must be superseded by more contextual examinations of the man and his thought. This monograph is intended as a step in the right direction. As mentioned in chapter one, theological application is a legitimate and profitable use of the inquiry into the history of theology, but the history must first be understood on its own terms if the application is to be at all accurate or meaningful. In order to understand the Leiden debate and the literature from the pens of its participants in any depth, Arminius must be examined within the context of early Reformed orthodoxy and interpreted in relation to the Protestant scholasticism from which he learned and to which he contributed. Furthermore, specific attention must also be given to his colleagues in the Staten College at Leiden. Kuchlinus and Gomarus in particular, with varying degrees of hostility, resisted Arminius before his arrival and throughout his tenure. At the same time, Arminius himself was increasingly hostile—if not to the persons—at least to the views of his colleagues on some matters relevant to soteriology and predestination. The stage was set for a theological conflict that initially took place by and large in an academic, university context; and in matters regarding soteriology, the debate often gravitated to the causes and order of salvation. The language of the debate was Latin and the means were public disputations, which, as the substantive work of the professors, provided an occasion for publicizing their respective views, with students sometimes getting caught in the crossfire. The academic disputations employed in the present essay are a portion of this large *corpus* that, despite its importance for contextualizing the theology and controversy at Leiden, has not been examined by previous scholarship.

Despite all the controversy, however, there was an ambience of collegiality at Leiden that fluctuated opposite to the waxing and waning of the intensity of the debates. In the end, these theologians were associates who not only agreed on most of the fundamental points of doctrine and presupposed the heuristic value of scholastic methodology, but who also were united in the common cause of training pastors in the premier theological seminary of Holland. Even in the disputations, there was sufficient room for ambiguity so that agreement in terminology could exist even if there was underlying diversity of definition. The repetitions of public disputations in the Staten College, despite the polemic of the era, demonstrate the agreement of the faculty on the progression of theological *loci*. The fourth repetition, planned and executed by Gomarus, Arminius, and Trelcatius, Jr., demonstrates similarity of content not only with the fifth repetition that was planned by the same group, but also with the third repetition, with which Arminius and Trelcatius apparently had no hand in planning. The congruence of the third repetition with the later ones shows that Arminius and Trelcatius assimilated themselves to the Leiden theology. The university curators intentionally kept the Leiden faculty diverse up to the Synod of Dort, and the thought represented in the *Syntagma* of the fourth repetition of disputations is an example of the shape of the Leiden theology, parts of which remained influential at Leiden beyond Dort.

When comparing the Leiden disputations on soteriology, the similarity of content between Arminius and his colleagues is striking. The disputations on significant Protestant topics such as justification, for example, are in virtual harmony. They agreed that faith is the instrumental cause of justification, and that union with Christ is the goal of salvation for the elect. According to Arminius, he confessed that grace is necessary for the commencement and continuation of good. These emphases that Arminius and his colleagues held in common have often been overlooked by scholarship. I have isolated two primary differences that have repercussions throughout Arminius's system. First, although Arminius described the operations of grace in the same manner as did his colleagues, he asserted that grace is resistible. Second, eternal election to salvation is conditional upon a person's acceptance of God's gift of faith, that is, a person's refusal to refuse God's grace; reprobation to condemnation is conditional upon a person's rejection of grace and continued impenitence. The other noteworthy point for this study that arises out of Arminius's doctrine of predestination is that his doctrine upholds what he perceived to be true assurance of salvation. This would have an impact throughout his theology and soteriology.

In matters of sanctification, the Leiden theologians agreed that justification is not dependent on sanctification, and that perfection in this life is not a reality, even if Arminius thought it was a possibility. The continual *lucta*, or wrestling, between the Spirit and flesh is characteristic of the life of the regenerate. On the issue of apostasy, however, Arminius affirmed that it is possible for a true believer to fall from grace either through abandonment of faith or through sin, inasmuch as certain sins can demonstrate the absence of faith in God. Grace, therefore, is resistible all along the way of life's journey. In contrast to some modern interpretations of Arminius, he did think that a regenerate person could fall away through sin, and that this person could be restored by God's grace.

In matters relating to epistemology of salvation, Arminius expressed genuine concern that he saw Reformed orthodoxy shifting to stronger language of the assurance of salvation than the tradition warranted. From Arminius's perspective, the language of *securitas* reflected an unhealthy attitude of negligence in the Christian life of sanctification. Arminius's vigorous battle against both *securitas* and *desperatio* in Reformed churches was an attempt on his part to remain faithful to the tradition and to provide an alternative that avoided these two dangers.

Arminius, in continuity with Reformed theology, pointed to *a posteriori* proofs of salvation and to the use of the practical syllogism as a means to healthy assurance. Indeed, the testimonies to which he pointed were identical to those of his colleagues. Moreover, these thinkers consistently employed the *a posteriori* testimonies, including the *syllogismus practicus*, in the context of and in subordination to the *a priori* grounding of assurance. It is here in the foundation of assurance that the point of divergence is evident. For Arminius, God's *duplex amor* toward righteousness and the sinful creature is the foundation of the Christian religion, and thus, of salvation and assurance as well. The knowledge that God will reward the righteous by faith is evidence of the twofold love and is enough to remove both security and despair. Furthermore, God obliges himself to his creation and loves the sinful creature to the extent that he antecedently wills and enjoys (*frui*) its salvation. This divine love defines the divine will.

A common critique of Arminius, past and present, is that his soteriology results in the removal of any hope of genuine assurance of salvation since he considers it possible for the regenerate to fall away from grace.[1] However Arminius's doctrine of salvation is evaluated, though, two things must be acknowledged by interpreters. First, one must recognize that he was attempting to restore true assurance, not remove it. Of course, this point alone does not prove he succeeded, but is an affirmation of his intention that often goes unheeded. Second, if one in fact compares his system with that of the Reformed, then one would be hard pressed to demonstrate that his system actually does undermine assurance to any greater degree than the Reformed way. Room for doubt exists in both systems. The Reformed doctrine of unconditional predestination combined with an unknowable divine will, in conjunction with the allowances of temporary faith in some reprobate and complete lack of conscious testimony in some elect, can undercut assurance as much as Arminius's possibility of apostasy. Insofar as the opponents of Arminius truly affirmed such a category as unconscious assurance or assurance with no testimony, we see even more clearly the context and object of Arminius's polemic.

In sum, attempts to show that Arminius's doctrine of assurance, in comparison with the Reformed doctrine, is attenuated either in intention or in actual result are unfounded. If there is a difference between basing assurance on faith and basing it on hope, Arminius's assurance of hope is arguably as robust as the Reformed assurance of faith. For true hope is based on the loving nature of the God who desires all people to be saved and who, albeit counterfactually, grants equal distribution of grace and equal opportunity of salvation to all.

As various interpreters have noted, Arminius and his Reformed opponents shared much in common theologically, and even regarding the topic of soteriology, they shared many practical similarities. Although

---

[1] This popular, common criticism of Arminius is put most starkly by Letham, 'Faith,' 1:319 (italics mine): "Absent entirely from Arminius' thinking on faith is the element of assurance of salvation. *His theology has totally undermined assurance* since perseverance has been cast into the quicksands of contingency. He is left with faith as a self-conscious act of free-will aided by grace which can equally be resisted and negatived [*sic*]. The price of his realignment of the decree of election is the *overthrow of assurance*. A more thorough-going anthropocentrism than Bullinger or Musculus ever envisaged (but one which in a certain sense emanated from their covenantal ideas) has made salvation dependent on man's effort rather than on God's promise. The gospel, even the promise itself, is conditional through and through. As a result, *faith (inevitably bereft of assurance of salvation) is seen in an extreme naturalistic mould and becomes a mere human act.*" The inaccuracies in Letham's description of Arminius are heightened only by his persistent hyperbole.

Arminius and his opponents might have been able to pastor in the same congregation and oversee the same disputation on justification, however, the differences are especially evident on a more theoretical level, specifically in the doctrine of God. Reformed theology underscored the unlimited sovereignty of God over creation and the inscrutability of the divine will toward creation, whereas Arminius stressed the freely limited sovereignty of God over creation and the definition of the divine will by God's loving enjoyment of creation, enabling greater mutuality and freedom for response from the creature.

Although this essay has intentionally juxtaposed Arminius with the "Reformed," the question of whether Arminius's soteriology in general and doctrine of predestination in particular can be accurately labeled "Reformed" is a complicated question.[2] On the one hand, it cannot be denied that Arminius considered himself to be a Reformed pastor and theologian and that, even if his views were controversial, he died in good standing as a Reformed theologian at the University of Leiden. To think of him as excluded from the Reformed church of his day would be a post-Dort anachronism. He deemed his views of predestination to fit within the confessional bounds applicable to him. Furthermore, Arminius was in some ways part of the non-Calvinistic Dutch Protestant tradition that goes back to the spirit of Anastasius Veluanus.[3] Based on such evidence, C. Bangs concludes that "Arminius is indeed one of the theologians of the Dutch Reformed Church and cannot be properly understood under the category of dissenter, outsider, schismatic, or heretic."[4] On the other hand, Arminius himself noted that the

---

[2] See the comment of Bangs in 'Review of Richard Muller, *God, Creation, and Providence*.' *Church History* 66/1 (1997), 118–20, there 119. Muller, notes Bangs, speaks of "Arminius and Reformed theologians," whereas Bangs himself prefers to speak of "Arminius and other Reformed theologians." This representation seems to be an accurate description of the difference between these perspectives. The work of Hoenderdaal, perhaps more than that of Bangs, never fails to point out the similarities between Calvin and Arminius, even positing that Arminius would have been accepted by Calvin. On this last point, see Hoenderdaal, 'Arminius en Episcopius,' 213: "Had Arminius 50 jaar eerder geleefd, in een tijd dat het gezag van Genève nog niet zo sterk was gevestigd en de theologie in de lage landen nog niet was toegesnoerd over de calvinistische leer, zoals die door Beza nader was gevormd, hij zou bij Melanchton, Bucer, Bullinger en anderen niet uit de toon zijn gevallen." See also idem, 'Theologische betekenis,' 96.

[3] Therefore, when Kendall, *Calvin*, pp. 150 and 212, repeatedly asserts that Arminius has "stolen" Calvin's idea that Christ died for all, it is not only an infelicitous way of making a point, but the alleged origin of Arminius's doctrine is also incorrect.

[4] Carl Bangs, 'Arminius as a Reformed Theologian,' in *The Heritage of John Calvin: Heritage Hall Lectures, 1960–70*, ed. John H. Bratt (Grand Rapids, 1973), pp. 209–22,

older, milder Dutch theologians came under fire for their doctrines of
predestination.[5] Even if the catechism was ambiguously stated, he had
access to the intention of Ursinus.[6] His soteriology, although similar to
Reformed terminology and definitions at many points, is constructed
around a fundamentally different doctrine of God and creation.

Once Arminius is seen within the context of early orthodoxy and
is viewed as part of the development and codification of doctrine, the
complexity of his relationship to Reformed theology becomes more
apparent. Working with a similarly wide range of sources from Scripture through Aristotle through Augustine through Thomas to Suárez
(and any legitimate sources in between), not to mention the Protestant
and particularly Reformed precedents embodied especially in the Belgic Confession and Heidelberg Catechism, Arminius was seeking to
broaden the definitions whereas his colleagues were seeking to narrow
them. Arminius was offering a system that he thought could be true to
a generous interpretation or slight revision of the Reformed standards,
and at the same time move toward a reconciliation of divine grace,
omniscience, and human freedom. He at least thought that if Gomarus's predestinarian view (supralapsarianism) could fall under the confessional umbrella, his view could also be a Reformed option. Arminius
wanted to define "Reformed" broadly as being anti-Pelagian, which he
noted does not mean being Gomarist.[7]

Although Arminius was well aware of the opposition that conditional predestinarians had encountered in the low countries in the latter decades of the sixteenth century, he nevertheless must have thought
there was a possibility that his more precise and careful doctrine of conditional predestination had a chance of survival. A simple answer cannot be given to whether Arminius was Reformed. Based on the evidence
discussed throughout the present essay, Arminius cannot be considered
as merely a dissenter; but at the same time, his views (and their precedents) indeed dissented from what was becoming the theological norm

---

there p. 221. In a certain sense, no one doubts that Arminius was a theologian of the
Dutch Reformed Church, just as no one disputes that young Martin Luther was a theologian of the Catholic Church. Furthermore, Arminius certainly was no outsider. The
only controversial portion of Bangs's conclusion is whether Arminius is *properly* understood as a "dissenter."

[5] *Dec. sent.*, pp. 95–6; *Works* 1:643–44.
[6] See *Auction Catalogue*, p. 4.
[7] *Exam. Gom.*, pp. 155–56; *Works* 3:655–56.

in his own context and, right or wrong, he was viewed as a "dissenter" by many of his colleagues. Perhaps it is enough to note that modern theologians who think Arminianism is simply another brand of Calvinism—as well as those who claim that Arminianism has no affinities whatsoever to Reformed theology—have not understood the nuances of either Arminius or his colleagues.

III. *Assurance as a Principal Point of Departure*

It is appropriate to reiterate what this essay has discovered to be the underlying forces driving Arminius's thought, especially with respect to the points where his theology presented a clear alternative to what has been considered historically Reformed. First, Arminius dealt with the problem of evil and wanted to reconcile divine omniscience, grace, and human freedom. His doctrine of predestination, in conjunction with the Molinist *scientia media*, was an attempt to resolve this age-old theological problem. His doctrine of predestination was accompanied by a stringent rejection of what became known as supralapsarianism. His primary critique of this latter formulation—and, to a lesser degree, of the other types of unconditional predestination that he connected with supralapsarianism—was that it logically depicted God as being responsible for sin. Of course, Arminius's system does not completely relieve God of such culpability, for he still actualized a world that he knew would fall. Arminius's system, however, attempts to make the culpability more remote from God and permissive than does the Reformed system. These aspects have been explicitly or implicitly identified by many interpreters.

In connection with this factor, this essay has further revealed the possible connection between Arminius's polemic against supralapsarianism and his academic context in Leiden. Although Arminius certainly disapproved of Beza's (and Calvin's) doctrine, Arminius's polemic was not instigated by the allegedly heavy hand of his professor in Geneva. In addition to the factors considered above, it is more than likely that the social factors in Leiden contributed to the intensity of Arminius's attack on supralapsarianism. All of his theological colleagues in Leiden, in addition to the Leiden pastor Hommius, taught supralapsarianism and rejected Arminius's critiques. In the years just preceding and during Arminius's tenure, supralapsarianism was the norm at Leiden. Hence, it was not so simple as Arminius versus Gomarus, as is often imagined.

In Leiden, for a few years, it was Arminius versus almost everyone, a challenge from which he did not back down.

Finally, and most relevant to this monograph, interpreters must begin to acknowledge the importance of the assurance of salvation as a practical issue that was formative in Arminius's theology. It is clear that Arminius intended a healthy doctrine of assurance to be the primary practical application of the doctrine of predestination; thus, any system of theology that in any way undercuts true assurance needs to be reconsidered and revised. As he put it, the doctrine of predestination should comfort afflicted consciences on the one hand, and on the other hand it should overthrow the impious and drive away their security. Arminius's pastoral background in Amsterdam illuminates the theological polemic, and indeed his personal experience should not be overlooked as a contributing factor in the development of his doctrine of assurance.[8] His first-hand pastoral experience with cases of *securitas* and *desperatio*, which he perceived to be the logical consequences of Reformed theology and soteriology, led him to articulate more clearly a doctrine of salvation and assurance that would steer clear of these problems and that would at the same time be consistent with the doctrine of God and the divine twofold love and will that Arminius was working out.

The doctrine of assurance functions for Arminius as a sort of litmus test for evaluating a particular doctrine of predestination and salvation; therefore, assurance, not predestination *per se*, moved Arminius toward his dissent from the Reformed theology of his colleagues. More than simply one of many practical implications of Arminius's theology, in some ways then, assurance of salvation is both the point of departure and the conclusive goal of his system, to the degree that his system developed differently from that of his Reformed orthodox opponents. Although it is by no means the sole explanation in understanding Arminius's departure from his Reformed opponents, historians and theologians who seek to grasp the contours of Arminian/Calvinist debates, past and present, would do well to consider the pivotal place of the forgotten factor of assurance.

---

[8] A similar observation about the connection between pastoral problems and the doctrine of assurance in puritan theology is noted in Winship, 'Assurance and Puritan Practical Divinity,' 470: "Puritan practical divinity began to take on its later contours as ministers tried to adjust their theology to these problems." One of Winship's points is that the rise of assurance literature and theology in England was due to more than simply ecclesiastical politics.

FOURTH REPETITION OF THEOLOGICAL
DISPUTATIONS AT LEIDEN

1. *De sacra scriptura.* Gomarus. Ioannes Casimirus Iunius. 4 December 1604.
2. *De sufficientia et perfectione s. scripturae, contra traditiones.* Arminius. Abrahamus Christiani F. Vliet. 18 December 1604.
3. *De essentia Dei et eius attributis.* Trelcatius. Ionas Volmaer. 15 January 1605.
4. *De unitate personarum in una Dei essentia.* Gomarus. Ioannes Felix Nemanuensis. 29 January 1605.
5. *De persona Patris et Filii.* Arminius. Petrus de la Fite. 23 February 1605.
6. *De Spiritu Sancto.* Trelcatius. Alardus de Vries. 9 March 1605.
7. *De creatione mundi.* Gomarus. Ricardus Ianus Neraeus. 19 March 1605.
8. *De angelis bonis et malis.* Arminius. Andreas Knutius Vesalius. 30 March 1605.
9. *De creatione hominis ad imaginem Dei.* Trelcatius. Isaacus Ioannis F. 23 April 1605.
10. *De providentia Dei.* Gomarus. Ioannes Vasianius. 30 April 1605.
11. *De iustitia et efficacia providentiae Dei in malo.* Arminius. Rodolphus de Zyll. 14 May 1605.[1]
12. *De peccato primo et peccato originali.* Trelcatius. Matthaeus Cotterius. 15 June 1605.
13. *De peccatis in universum.* Gomarus. Bernherus Vezekius. 13 July 1605.
14. *De libero hominis arbitrio eiusque viribus.* Arminius. Paulus Leonardi F. de Leonardis. 23 July 1605.

---

[1] *LA*, 221, incorrectly dates this disputation to 4 May 1605. However, Bertius, *Aenspraeck*, B4r, confirms 14 May 1605. Furthermore, in *Ep. ecc.* 76, p. 143, Arminius, writing to Uytenbogaert on 2 May 1605, mentions that this very disputation will be conducted from the order "post aliquot dies." This evidence also points to 14 May 1605.

15. *De lege Dei*. Trelcatius. Philippus Pynacker. 17 September 1605.

16. *De evangelio*. Gomarus. Ioannes Herperus. 1 October 1605.

17. *De legis et evangelii comparatione*. Arminius. Petrus Cunaeus. 19 October 1605.

18. *De incarnatione Filii Dei*. Trelcatius. Iacobus ad Portum. 29 October 1605.

19. *De officiis Filii Dei incarnati*. Gomarus. Daniel Guerinellus. 9 November 1605.

20. *De perpessionibus Christi*. Arminius. Laurentius Pauli. 19 November 1605.

21. *De exaltatione Christi*. Trelcatius. Hermannus Keckius. 29 November 1605.

22. *De merito Christi et efficacia eius*. Gomarus. Alardus de Vries. 10 December 1605.

23. *De fide*. Arminius. Richardus Ianus Neraeus. 21 December 1605.

24. *De iustificatione hominis coram Deo per solam fidem*. Trelcatius. Bernherus Vezekius. 21 January 1606.[2]

25. *De resipiscentia*. Gomarus. Matthaeus Cotterius. 1 February 1606.

26. *De indulgentiis et purgatorio*. Arminius. Philippus Adr. F. Pynacker. 22 February 1606.

27. *De bonis operibus et meritis eorum*. Trelcatius. Ricardus Ianus Neraeus. 4 March 1606.

28. *De cultu adorationis*. Gomarus. Petrus Cunaeus. 15 March 1606.

29. *De invocatione sanctorum*. Arminius. Jacobus ad Portum. 8 April 1606.

30. *De aeterna Dei praedestinatione*. Trelcatius. Dan Guerinellus. 19 April 1606.

31. *De vocatione hominis ad salutem*. Gomarus. Laurentius Pauli. 29 April 1606.

32. *De resurrectione carnis et vita aeterna*. Arminius. Hermannus Keckius. 27 May 1606.

33. *De ecclesia catholica*. Trelcatius. Esaias Pratensis. 7 June 1606.

34. *De ecclesia visibili*. Gomarus. Samuel Hochedaeus de la Vigne I. F. 17 June 1606.

35. *De notis ecclesiae*. Arminius. Ioannes Casimirus Iunius F. F. 1 July 1606.

---

[2] This disputation shows a publication year of 1605.

36. *De ministeriis ecclesiasticis et ministrorum vocatione.* Trelcatius. Ricardus Ianus Neraeus. 12 July 1606.

37. *De capite ecclesiae.* Gomarus. Alardus de Vries. 21 July 1606.

38. *De potestate ecclesiae in fidei dogmatis, legibus ferendis, et iurisdictione.* Arminius. Bernherus Vezekius. 29 July 1606.

39. *De disciplina ecclesiastica.* Trelcatius. Laurentius Pauli. 20 September 1606.

40. *De ieiunio et votis.* Gomarus. Esaias Pratensis. 14 October 1606.

41. *De sacramentis in genere.* Arminius. Nathan Vaius. 25 October 1606.

42. *De baptismo.* Trelcatius. Ludovicus Costanus. 4 November 1606.

43. *De paedobaptismo.* Gomarus. Johannes Capdeville. 15 November 1606.

44. *De s. coena Domini.* Arminius. Ludovicus Michael. 25 November 1606.

45. *De missa papali.* Trelcatius. Isaacus Iunius F. F. 6 December 1606.

46. *De falsis quinque sacramentis.* Gomarus. Casparus Wiltens Conradi F. 16 December 1606.

47. *De magistratu.* Arminius. Ioannes Le-Chantre. 13 January 1607.

ARMINIUS, *DE BONIS OPERIBUS* (HELLERUS, 1603)

DISPUTATIONUM THEOLOGICARUM
VIGESIMA-SEPTIMA,
DE
BONIS OPERIBUS,
ET MERITIS EORUM,
Quam
FAVENTE DEO OPT. MAX.
Auctoritate
Reverendi Ordinis Theologici,
Praeside
Clarissimo, Doctissimoque Viro,
D. IACOBO ARMINIO, SS. Theologiae
Doctore ac Professore ordinario in illustri
Batavorum Academia,
publice examinandam proponit
CHRISTOPHORUS HELLERUS Bremensis,
Ad d. XVII. *Decemb. Anno* M. D. CIII.
Horis locoque solitis.

LUGDUNI BATAVORUM,
Ex Officina Ioannis Patii. Anno M.D.CIII.

THESES THEOLOGICAE
DE
BONIS OPERIBUS,
ET MERITIS EORUM.

Cum superioribus Disputationibus κατασκευαστικῶς, *& ἀνασκευαστικῶς*
actum sit de iis, quae ad veram nostri coram Deo Iustificationem pertinent, ordo
postulare videtur, ut de iis, quae Iustificationem nostram consequuntur, Bonis sc.
Operibus agamus.

THESIS I

Acturi de Bonis hominum in hac vita post Adami lapsum Operibus, quae sunt actiones, praecognoscere oportet, actiones alias esse naturales, quas omnes homines faciunt, easque bonas, quatenus a Natura communi procedunt: alias vero supranaturales, quae a renatis virtute Spiritus S. sanctificantis proficiscuntur, ex gratia singulari, ad gloriam divini nominis, & nostram in Christo salutem: Nos illis omissis, harum naturam Definitione, ejusque per causas analysi investigabimus.

II

Definimus igitur Bona Opera esse tales supernaturales actiones, quae a Regeneratis, vi Spiritus S. ex fide secundum Legem Dei fiunt, ad gloriam Dei, fidei & electionis nostrae confirmationem, & proximi aedificationem.

III

Causam Efficientem statuimui duplicem, primariam aliam, aliam vero secundariam. Primaria est Deus Pater in Filio per Spiritum S.[1] mentes nostras verbo suo illuminans, & corda in obsequium flectens, ut voluntati Dei cognitae pareamus, & paulatim malum odisse, & bonum persequi ex Legis ipsius praescripto incipiamus.

IV

Efficiens secundaria sunt Regenerati, qui (renovati non solum mente, ut regni coelestis mysteria intelligant & apprehendant, sed etiam voluntate, ut recti amorem ac conatum concipiant) actiones bonas producunt, quae ita sunt Spiritus Sancti, ut etiam nostra dicantur, tanquam a nobis ex principio regenerationis nostrae producta, juxta Augustinum[2] dicentem: *Certum est, nos renatos velle, quae volumus, sed ille facit ut velimus, qui operatur velle: Certum est, nos facere, quae facimus, sed ile facit, ut faciamus, qui operatur efficere.*

---

[1] In margin: Eph. 1.18; Phil. 2.13; Ioan. 15.5.
[2] In margin: de Grat. & lib. Arbit. cap. 16.

V

Instrumentalis est Fides, cui hoc respectu tribuitur, quod *fide purificentur corda nostra*:[3] quod *Christus per fidem habitet in cordibus nostris*:[4] quod *per fidem vivere dicamur*:[5] quod *fides per charitatem efficax sit*:[6] quod *per fidem sancti operari dicantur justitiam*:[7] quod *fides sit victoria nostra, qua mundum vincimus*.[8]

VI

Materia bonorum operum est, quicquid Lege Dei praescribitur,[9] cujus Deus ipse Legislator est, & quam nobis praescripsit normam & regulam, secundum quam malum a bono dignoscere possumus. hoc autem cum dicimus, non propterea rejicimus omnia, quae totidem literis & syllabis in Lege non sunt scripta, nec excludimus a bonis operibus, in quib. Deus renatos vult exercere obedientiam, ἀδιάφορα ista, quae fundamentum in Lege habent, & ordini, decoro, & aedificationi Ecclesiae Dei inserviunt, & ita proponuntur, ut non pugnent cum libertate Christiana, *hoc est*, ut non observentur vel proponantur cum opinione necessitatis, cultus & meriti: sed tantum illa, quae hisce conditionibus carent, ualia sunt secundum Pontificios, mandata Ecclesiae, quae multa & vana suis praescribunt, & necessario observanda proponunt,[10] ut peregrinationes, cultus sanctorum, confessiones auriculares, & insinita [sic] alia, quae fundamentum nullum in Scriptura, imo nullam cum bonis operibus cognationem habent, sed nuda voluntate hominum nituntur.

VII

Forma bonorum operum est perfecta conformitas cum Lege Dei,[11] nam sicut mali operis ratio & forma est ἀνομία & aberratio a Lege, sic ἐννομία & conformitas nostrae actionis ad Legem Dei, tum secundum externam speciem, tum etiam secundum internam veritatem, est

---

[3] In margin: Act 15.9.
[4] In margin: Eph. 3.17.
[5] In margin: Gal. 2.20.
[6] In margin: Gal. 5.6.
[7] In margin: Hebr. 11.33.
[8] In margin: 1. Ioan. 5.4.
[9] In margin: Phil. 4.8; Deut. 12.8.32; Ezec. 20.18.
[10] In margin: Concil. Trid. sess. 6. can. 20.
[11] In margin: Deut. 27.26; Gal. 3.10.

forma boni operis: cum enim natura Legis sit spiritualis,[12] requirit non solum externam, sed etiam internam obedientiam, & Deus, qui est καρδιογνώστης, non judicat secundum externam speciem, & secundum modum nostrum, sed secundum modum suum, & veritatem.[13]

VIII

Unde apparet, cum ea sit Legis natura, & tale examen Deus secundum eam instituat, in ipsis operibus nostris desiderari semper aliquid, quod debita bonitate careat: circumferimus enim nobiscum, quamdiu in hoc stadio ad coronam repositam currimus, veterem nostrum hominem, & reliquias peccati,[14] nec Legem, ut opus est, implemus, ideoque necessum est, imperfectionem operum nostrorum remitti, & quod ipsis adest malum, gratuita Dei misericordia tegi.

IX

Hinc etiam liquet, cum renatorum opera Deo placeant, non fieri hoc propterea, ut Pontificii volunt,[15] quod sint justa perfecta impletione legis, ita ut coram judicio Dei consistere possint: sed I. propter Christum,[16] & quia persona Deo per fidem reconciliata ipsi placet, sic enim dicitur, *Dominus respexisse ad Abelem, & ad munus ipsius, ad Caïnum vero & ipsius munus non respexisse.*[17] II. quia producuntur in conspectum Dei adspersa sanguine Christi, & justitiae ejus vestimento tecta. III. quia Deus illa, ut sui Spiritus effecta, & ut in fide Christi facta considerat. IV. quia ab ipso Christo illi offeruntur.[18]

X

Finis operum est triplex pro diversitate objectorum, Dei, nostri, & proximi: *Dei*, ut tanquam Deus Opt. Max. glorificetur inter homines:[19] *Nostri*, ut de fide & electione nostra, tanquam ex fructibus certiores simus,

---

[12] In margin: Ro. 7.14.
[13] In margin: Rom. 2.2.
[14] In margin: Gal. 5.17.
[15] In margin: Concil. Trid. sess. 6. can. 25; Bellarm. de Iustif. lib. 4 cap. 11. & seqq.
[16] In margin: 1 Pet. 2.5.
[17] In margin: Gen. 4.4; Hebr. 11.5.
[18] In margin: Hebr. 13.15.
[19] In margin: Matth. 6.16.

firmam reddamus vocationem nostram, & ut Evangelio & vocationi nostrae convenienter vivamus.[20] *Proximi*, tum respectu infidelium, ut nostro exemplo & vita ad fidem & pietatem provocentur, & ad similia praestanda excitentur:[21] tum etiam respectu fidelium, ut in pietate & fide confirmentur.

XI

His positis facile videre est, nullius esse veritatis Pontificiorum dogma de Merito Operum, quodcunque etiam sit, sive Congrui, sine Condigni:[22] S. Scriptura enim illud nomen non agnoscit, imo tantum abest, ut istud in Scriptura reperiatur, ut id etiam in ea invenias, quod prorsus repugnat & evertit illud, quod Meriti nomine significatur, *si enim per gratiam, non ex peribus, alioqui gratia non esset gratia.*[23] Ratio etiam est evidentissima, nam cum inter mercedem & opera. 1. non sit proportio aequalitatis. 2. cum opera non propria, sed Spiritus S. efficacitate fiant. 3. cum sint debita. 4. denique imperfecta, quomodo ullam meriti rationem habere poterunt?

XII

Nec hoc pro ipsis quicquam facit, quod operibus nostris in S. Scriptura Merces tribuatur, nam haec merces non datur ex debito, multo minus ex merito, sed ex gratia, quod ipsum Scriptura nobis declarat, cum quod uno loco[24] *mercedem* vocavit, altero[25] *gratiam* appellat: & haec Merces cum gratia Dei consistere potest, nec derogat quicquam ipsius justitiae.

XIII

Denique male etiam Pontificii inde concludunt, cum dicimus bona opera non esse meritoria, omne bonorum operum studium a nobis rejici & damnari, nam non valet Consequentia, si bona opera non sunt necessaria ut causa. Ergo nullo modo: Scriptura enim nos ad ea adhortatur,[26] & nos

---

[20] In margin: Eph. 4.1.
[21] In margin: 2 Cor. 9.10.11.12.13; Tit. 3.14.
[22] In margin: Bell. de Iustif. lib. 5.c.1. & 16. & seqq.
[23] In margin: Ro. 11.6; Eph. 2.8.9; Tit. 3.5; 2 Tim. 1.9; Rom. 4.2; &c.
[24] In margin: Matth. 5.46.
[25] In margin: Luc. 6.32.
[26] In margin: Mat. 5.16; Rom. 8.12.

creatos esse in Iesu Christo dicit ad bona opera, quae Deus praeparavit, ut in iis ambulemus, quo respectu etiam Bernhardus optime dixit,[27] *esse viam regni, non causam regnandi:* quamdiu igitur hîc in terris commoramur, per viam bonorum operum currere debemus, donec ad Christum caput nostrum veniamus, eoque in altera vita plene perfecteque fruamur.

Cui cum Patre & Spiritu S. sit laus & gloria
in saecula.

FINIS.

---

[27] In margin: lib. de Lib. Arbit.

ARMINIUS, *DE FIDE* (NERAEUS, 1605)

DISPUTATIONUM THEOLOGICARUM
QUARTO REPETITARUM VIGESIMA-TERTIA
DE
FIDE.
Quam
FAVENTE DEO OPT. MAX.
Ex auctoritate & decreto
Reverendi Ordinis Theologici,
Praeside
Clarissimo Praestantissimoque Viro
D. IACOBO ARMINIO, Rectore Magni-
fico SS. Theologiae Doctore & Professore
ordinario in inclyta Lugd. Bat. Acad.
publice examinandam proponit
RICARDUS IANUS NERAEUS,
Ad diem XXI. *Decembris. Anno* M. D. C. V.
Horis locoque solitis.

LUGDUNI BATAVORUM,
Ex Officina Ioannis Patii. An. M.D.C.V.

THESES THEOLOGICAE
DE FIDE.

Quum disputationibus aliquot superioribus de Christo eiusque officiis,
statu tum humiliationis tum exaltationis & merito actum sit; Ordo
postulat ut agamus de Fide qua ipsius & omnium bonorum illius
participes fimus.

THESIS I

Fidei vocabulum πολύσημον est: significat enim primo, plenam eorum revelationem quae olim sub ceremoniarum obscuritate latebant:[1] 2. Articulos Fidei.[2] 3. Evangelii doctrinam & justitiae per id annunciatae patefactionem.[3] 4. Dei erga nos[4] aut hominum[5] inter se veritatem aut constantiam tam in dictis quam in factis. 5. Certitudinem potentiae Dei veracis & ejus judiciorum.[6] 6. Nudam historiae de Deo Christoque & Fiduciae expertem notitiam.[7] 7. Notitiam & assensum persuasionemque de Dei gratia, sed temporariam & evanidam, ut quae in Christo radices non agat.[8] 8. Persuasionem de Futuro aliquo effectu miraculoso, ex revelatione, pro missione singulari, aut Spiritus sancti motu conceptam.[9] 9. Pietatis studium.[10] 10. Ministerii erga pauperes & aegrotos curandos professionem.[11] 11. Conscientiam per Evangelii doctrinam confirmatam.[12] 12. Declarationem de Christo omnibus factam.[13] 13. Doctrinae Evangelicae exactam & Christianae libertatis cognitionem.[14] 14. Graciosae promissionis & divinae virtutis in Christo ante & post incarnationem patefactae, apprehensionem.[15] 15. Denique assensum animi a Spiritu S. per Evangelium in peccatoribus & peccata per legem agnoscentibus productum, quo Iesum Christum servatorem sibi a Deo destinatum & datum agnoscunt, ex quo assensu exurgit fiducia in illum & per illum Fides & Fiducia in Deum.[16] Et ita hîc sumitur.

---

[1] In margin: Gal. 3.13.
[2] In margin: Heb. 6.1.
[3] In margin: Gal. 3.15.
[4] In margin: Psal. 33.4; Esai. 11.3; Thren. 3.23; Ose. 2.20.
[5] In margin: Gen. 19.16; Ierem. 7.28. & 42.5; Mat. 23.23; 1 Tim. 2.7.
[6] In margin: Mar. 10.22; Ose. 5.9.
[7] In margin: Iacob. 2.24.
[8] In margin: Luc. 8.13; Actor. 8.13.
[9] In margin: Mat. 17.20. & 21.21; Act. 14.9; 1. Cor. 12.9. & 13.21.
[10] In margin: Luc. 18.8; 2. Cor. 10.15.
[11] In margin: 1. Tim. 5.12.
[12] In margin: 2. Cor. 1.24.
[13] In margin: Act. 17.31.
[14] In margin: Act. 6.5. & 11.24; Ro. 14.22.23.
[15] In margin: Math. 9.2. & 15.28; Marc. 2.5. & 5.34. & 10.52; Hebr. 11.4. & 7; Iacob. 1.6.
[16] In margin: Habac. 2.4; Math. 8.10; Act. 3.6; Rom. 1.1. & 4.5.6.9.11.16; 1. Cor. 15.14.17; Gal. 2.16.20; Ephes. 2.8.

II

Causa effic. Fidei est aut principalis aut instrumentalis: illa est Deus Pater in Filio per Spiritum sanctum;[17] indivisa namque sunt opera Trinitatis ad extra. Est opus & donum supernaturale non naturale; Virtus Theologica & a Spiritu infusa, non per rationcinationem humanam ex principiis secundum naturam notis acquisita; imo superat omnem intellectum & omnia principia naturalia transcendit. Itaque Fides tum initii tum incrementi confirmationisque ratione est a Deo.

III

Spiritum S. hujus infusionis auctorem statuimus qui & intus nobis offert Christum & mentem nostram lumine suo illustrat animumque testificatione sua obsignat, ut Christum oblatum videamus, in illumque certa Fide, ut servatorem nostrum credamus.

IV

Instrumentalis est ordinaria aut extraordinaria. Ordinaria I. Est verbum[18] tum legale tum Evangelicum. Illud, indirectum, sed ejus antecedens necessarium: Hoc, directum & immediate producens Fidem, hinc verbum Fidei & vitae semenque incorruptibile appellatur.[19] II. Sacramenta Fidem verbo accensam magis excitantia, foventia & confirmantia.[20]

V

Hanc a. efficit verbum, quando homini in peccatis mortuo, & de salute ne cogitanti quidem, extrinsecus per ejus administros annunciatur.[21] Lex primo litera occidens & occisione sua ad Spiritum vivificum & ministerium justitiae & vitae deducens, cum ostendit peccata & illorum poenam

---

[17] In margin: Ioan. 6.29; Act. 16.14; Rom. 12.3; Phil. 1.29; Luc. 24.32.45; Hebr. 12.2; 2 Cor. 4.13.
[18] In margin: Rom. 10.17; Ioan. 57.16 [sic]; Act. 10.44; Rom. 1.16; Isa. 53.1. & 54.7.
[19] In margin: Rom. 10.8; Act. 13.26; 1 Pet. 1.23.
[20] In margin: 1.Ioan. 3.5; 1 Cor. 10.16. & 11.24.
[21] In margin: Ezech. 16.6; Gen. 6.5; Rom. 8.7; 2 Cor. 2.14; Ephes. 2.2; Col. 2.13; Ioan. 3.3; Ephes. 2.10.

damnationem,[22] hinc compunctio cordis[23] & de propriis viribus sancta desperatio. Sed ne hoc quidem facit lex sine spiritu, videlicet servitutis & metus, qui spiritus adoptionis & charitatis Dei praecursor statuitur. Secundo, Evangelium salutem in Christo cum conditione Fidei offerens, exhibens praestans & obsignans.[24]

VI

In ortu hujus fidei ergo haec omnia concurrere & necessario requiri dicimus. Notitiam Evangelii per illuminationem Spiritus sancti.[25] attentam promissionum Evangelicarum ex intimo sensu inopiae suae considerationem.[26] Fidem generalem in illuminatis Evangelio assensum praebentem, quam, si plenior & perfectior sit, vocat Apostolus πληροφορίαν τῆς συνέσεως,[27] spem veniae & remissionis peccatorum:[28] Esuriem & vehementem in Christo oblatae expetitionem.[29] Accessum[30] cum humillima peccatorum confessione[31] & deprecatione pro eorum remissione cum gemitibus inexplicabilib. & cum perseverantia,[32] ad thronum gratiae, ut apprehenso ibidem Christo inveniatur misericordia apud Deum. Denique specialem[33] persuasionem a Spiritu Sancto per verbum impressam, qua promissiones Evangelicas in Iesu Christo etiam & amen esse firmiter cognoscimus, I. Cor. 11.2.

VII

Extraordinaria, sunt Miracula, opera Dei praeter & supra naturam facta. Non enim negamus quin absque mediis ordinariis spiritus S. Fidem in cordibus electorum gignere possit: sed ideo dicimus, quia Deo sapienti & bono visum est, nos iis alligar, nostram obedientiam explorare & sese nostrae infirmitati accommodare nobisque συγκαταβαίνειν.

---

[22] In margin: Rom. 3.20. & 5.20; Gal. 3.19; 2 Cor. 3.7.
[23] In margin: Act 2.37.38.39. &c.
[24] In margin: 1 Ioan. 2.27; Act. 17.14; Psalm. 40.6; Esai. 54.7.
[25] In margin: Esa. 53.11.
[26] In margin: Heb. 4.2; Math. 11.28.
[27] In margin: Col. 2.2; Rom. 14.14; 1.Thess. 1.5; Luc. 1.1.
[28] In margin: Luc. 15.18.19.
[29] In margin: Ioan. 6.35. & 7.37; Apoc. 21.6.
[30] In margin: Heb. 4.16.
[31] In margin: Psal. 32.5; 2.Sam. 12.13; Luc. 25.2.
[32] In margin: Luc. 15.21; Act. 8.22; Rom. 8.26.
[33] In margin: Math. 9.2. & 15.28.

VIII

Objectum, Fidei est commune & universale aut Speciale et Proprium adaequatumque. Illud est in genere verbum Dei nobis in Scriptura declaratum, ultra hoc se non extendit fides,[34] estque illius fundamentum & fulcrum, a quo si declinat, corruit. Hoc, non est lex ostendens & arguens peccata, aut comminationes continens:[35] in ea enim non potest gratiam aut reconciliationem quaerere fides: nec praecipiens obedientiam & promissionem de remuneratione operum ex debito continens. Lex namque est ex Fide, & sine ea manifestata est justitia Dei. Est ergo doctrina Evangelii reconciliationem & sanctificationem per & propter Mediatorem Christum offerentis & conferentis.[36]

IX

In hoc haec omnia complectimur; Dei Patris gratiam, Misericordiam, dilectionem, benignitatem, humanitatem, beneplacitum, omniaque beneficia ejus; Christum ipsum in incarnatione, cruce, resurrectione, ascensione & sessione ad dextram Patris, gratuitam reconciliationem, remissionem peccatorum, imputationem justitiae Christi, gratuitam acceptationem coram Deo, adoptionem, liberationem a Lege peccati & mortis, ab execratione legis, propitiationem pro peccatis nostris, salutem, vitam aeternam, communicationem cum Deo, haereditatem vitae, salutis, pacem, gaudium, spemque Dei gloriae. Denique Spiritum S. & omnes illius salutares actiones & immensum gratiarum, virtutum, donorum ejus cumulum.

X

Fidei ergo objectum non est omne mandatum Ecclesiae cognitum aut incognitum, explicitum aut implicitum declaratum jam aut postmodum obtrudendum, & auctoritate alicujus Concilii, Ecclesiae, quae nulla

---

[34] In margin: Rom. 10.17; Ioan. 10.4.5. [In theses viii–xiv, the marginalia are not connected to a specific point in the text by a letter, so I have attempted to place them in an appropriate position—KDS.]

[35] In margin: Gal. 3.17; Rom. 10.5.6; Rom. 3.21.27.

[36] In margin: Rom. 3.22. & 26. & 4.24; Phil. 3.9; Act. 10.43; 13.39; Ioan. 3.15.16.18; 1. Ioan. 4.7. & 15. & 5.13.

est nisi vocem sponsi audiat & sequatur, ad credendum Fide expressa, proponendum, neque quorundam articulorum, praetermissis aliis, cognitio.[37] Fides namque univoce dicta, est cognitio veritatis, non ignorantio ex Ecclesiae reverentia, sed explicita Dei & propitiae voluntatis ipsius erga nos Christique in justitiam sanctificationem, sapientiam & redemptionem nobis a Patre dati cognitio, quae ex Dei verbo tantum percipitur.[38]

XI

Materiam in qua seu subjectum commune animum humanum & in eo rationales & principales facultates, mentem & voluntatem dicimus. Objectum namque fidei non solum ut verum; sed etiam ut bonum agnoscere debemus. quapropter non ad intellectum theoreticum tantum sed practicum etiam seu potius affectivum, quem sensum nobis appellare liceat, pertinere arbitramur.[39]

XII

Subjectum cui, est homo peccator animo & corpore constans & peccata agnoscens. Est namque Fides illa ad salutem necessaria illi cui infunditur. At non est necessaria non peccatori & justo: unde nemo nisi peccator in Christum credere jubetur: nemo etiam nisi peccatorem se agnoscat, Christum pro servatore suo agnoscere potest: est enim servator tantum peccatorum.[40] Qua de causa Iudaei justitiam ex lege quaerentes, in lapidem offendiculi impegisse dicuntur.

XIII

Forma fidei est ejus legitima ad objectum suum proprium & adaequatum, Christum; ordinatio, secundum quam qui credit objecto isti

---

[37] In margin: Bellarm. de Iustificat. lib. 1. Cap. 7. Rossens. contra Lutherum. Remenses supra 1. Corinth. Melan. tract. 5. Cap. 30. conclus. 12. Ban nes. 2. quaest. 2 art. 7. tribuit hanc opinionem Gulielmo parisiensi & Altisidorensi.

[38] In margin: 1. Tim. 2.4; Tit. 1.1; Ioan. 3.3; 2. Cor. 2.16; 1. Cor. 1.30.

[39] In margin: Luc. 24.45; Ephes. 4.25; Act. 16.14; Rom. 10.10; Act. 8.37; Psal. 28.7. & 112.2; Prov. 3.5.

[40] In margin: Ioan. 8.24; Mat. 11.28; Marc. 1.15; Math. 9.12; Math. 1.21; Rom. 9.31.32 & 10.3.

arctissime unitur; adeo ut unum cum Christo factus, omnium illius
bonorum communionem habeat secundum demensum a Deo ordina-
tum: Itaque Charitas non minus fidem comitans quam calor lucem solis,
non est magis forma Fidei quam corpus animae per quod operatur, aut
effectus causae. Charitas enim de corde puro & conscientia bona est
ex fide non ficta,[41] & quidem ut causa charitatis producendae necessaria, sufficiente & efficaci. Ergo merito rejicimus Fidem scholasticorum
informem, quam dicunt sine charitate esse posse:[42] utpote quae hominem salvare non possit, Iacob. 2.

XIV

Finis denique est duplex, Summus & Proximus: ille, gloria Dei sive cele-
bratio justitiae bonitatis & misericordiae divinae: ut a cujus gratia tantum beneficium profluit, ad ejus gloriam maxime illustrandam referatur.
Hic, salus & vita aeterna, justitia, pax, reconciliatio, filiatio, redemptio,
accessus cum fiducia, & omnis generis benedictiones spirituales: quo sit
ut in singulis tam requiratur haec fides ad salutem procurandam, quam
ipsa salus est necessaria, ex aeterno Dei decreto.[43]

XV

Hanc autem Fidem vere fideles habere se sciunt. 1. Ex ipso sensu Fidei,
quod docent insignia attributa & nomina, quibus insignitur Fides in
Scripturis. Tribuitur enim illi πληροφορία,[44] παρρησία,[45] πεποίθησις,[46]
dicitur ὑπόστασις,[47] ἔλεγχος,[48] quae fidei non competunt, si credens
ignoret se credere. 2. Ex Spiritus Sancti in illis habitantis testimonio,[49]
testatur .n. una cum spiritu nostro quod sumus Filii Dei. At Filii Dei non

---

[41] In margin: 1. Tim. 1.5.
[42] In margin: Bellarm. lib. 1. de Iustif. cap. 15.
[43] In margin: 1. Pet. 1.9; Rom. 10.10. & 5.1.11; Ioan. 1.12; Ephes. 1.7. & 3.12; Rom. 8.15; Hebr. 11.6; Gal. 3.9.
[44] In margin: Rom. 4.21; Col. 2.2; Hebr. 6.11. & 10.22.
[45] In margin: Ephe. 3.12; 2. Ioa. 2.28; Heb. 3.6.4. & 10.35.
[46] In margin: Ephe. 3.12; Phil. 3.4.
[47] In margin: Heb. 11.1; 2. Cor. 9.4. & 11.17.
[48] In margin: Heb. 11.1.
[49] In margin: Ephes. 1.17.18; 1. Ioan. 5.10; Rom. 8.16; 1. Cor. 2.12; 2. Tim. 1.12; 2. Cor. 4.1.

nisi per Fidem in nomen Christi sumus. 3. Ex lucta Fidei cum dubitationibus & spiritus cum carne: Denique ex effectis spei & charitatis erga
Deum & proximum, operumque ex illa charitate promanantium.

XVI

Contraria Fidei sunt incredulitas, credendi tarditas, disceptatio de Dei
potentia & promissionibus,[50] securitas carnis, confidentia in carne &
propriis viribus, operibus, meritis in justitia & dignitate nostra, brachii
carnis fiducia, disputationes & dubitationes Academiae de Deo, illius
voluntate promissionumque ejus certitudine, desperatio, diffidentia,
haeresis; quae omnia Deus Opt. Max. Fidei dator a nobis avertere
dignetur per Dominum nostrum Iesum Christum virtute Spiritus sui
sancti. Amen.

COROLLARIUM

An fides Patrum sub pactis promissionis eadem fuerit quod ad substan-
tiam attinet cum nostra sub Novo Testamento. Affir. Nam Iesus Christus
heri hodie idem & in secula.

FINIS.

---

[50] In margin: Rom. 4.

A COMPARISON OF CAUSALITY IN ARMINIUS, KUCHLINUS, AND GOMARUS[1]

In Arminius[2]

I. Causa Efficiens.
   A. Efficiens Primaria. Principalis.
   B. Efficiens Secundaria.[3]
   C. Caussa impulsiva.
      1. Προηγουμένη.[4] Interne movens.
      2. Προκαταρκτική.[5] Externe movens.
   D. Instrumentalis. Instrumentum.
      1. Ordinaria.
      2. Extraordinaria.
   E. Caussa exsecutrix. Administra.[6]
   F. Obsignans. Conservans.[7]
   G. Dispositiva.[8]

---

[1] Cf. the discussion on pp. 72–75. This table is not an exhaustive collation of every term used, but a basic representation intended to provide a general sense of the use of causality in these authors. The vocabulary is taken directly from the respective authors. The primary obstacle to an accurate interpretation is that the authors were not always explicit about the relationship among the various causes they mentioned. For definitions of some of the vocabulary of cause and effect, see Muller, *DLGT*; Altenstaig, *Lexicon*; LSJ.

[2] Arminius's use of causality is collated primarily from *Disp. pub.* XVIII; XX; *Disp. priv.* XL; XLII; L; *De fide* (1605); *De iustificatione* (1603); *De bonis operibus* (1603).

[3] According to *De bonis operibus* (1603), iv–v, the *efficiens secundaria* is clearly distinct from the *instrumentalis.*

[4] This participle from the verb προηγέομαι means "preceding."

[5] This adjective means "predisposing."

[6] According to *Disp. priv.* L.vi–vii, the *caussa exsecutrix* is distinct from the *caussa impulsiva.*

[7] According to *Disp. pub.* XX.iii, the *obsignans et conservans* is identified distinctly from the *causa efficiens primaria, impulsiva,* and the *instrumentum.*

[8] The *causa dispositiva* may correspond to Burgersdijk's *forma disponens,* or, according to its position in *Disp. priv.* XLII.iii, may correspond to the προκαταρκτική.

II. Materialis. Materia.
  A. Materia in qua. Subjectum recipiens.[9]
  B. Subjectum cui.
  C. Materia circa quam. Objectum.
  D. Remota.
  E. Propinquior.
  F. Proxima.
III. Forma.[10]
IV. Finis.
  A. Finis cuius. Summus. Ultimus. Remotus.
  B. Finis cui. Subordinatus. Proximus.

In Kuchlinus[11]

I. Caussa Efficiens.
  A. Prima. Primaria. Principalis.
  B. Caussa Impulsiva.[12]
    1. Προηγουμένη.
    2. Προκαταρκτική. Materia circa quam, Obiectum, Efficiens meritoria.[13]
  C. Instrumentalis Caussa.
    1. Per quam.

---

[9] On *materia in qua* and *materia circa quam* in general, see M. Karskens, 'Subject, Object and Substance in Burgersdijk's Logic,' in *Franco Burgersdijk (1590–1635): Neo-Aristotelianism in Leiden*, ed. E. P. Bos and H. A. Krop [Studies in the History of Ideas in the Low Countries 1] (Amsterdam, 1993), pp. 29–36, there pp. 32–34.

[10] Our authors rarely developed the formal cause with any precision. Exceptions include Gomarus, *De iustificatione* (1609), xxxiii, *forma communis et propria*, and Trelcatius, *De iustificatione* (1606), xix, who speaks of *negativa* and *affirmativa* under formal cause. At any rate, the formal cause was kept comparatively simple.

[11] Kuchlinus's use of causality is collated primarily from *De praedestinatione* (1600); *De iustificatione; De natura iustificationis* (1603); *De conditionibus*.

[12] According to Kuchlinus, *De praedestinatione* (1600), xv, the "caussa impulsiva" pertains to the efficient cause ("caussa impulsiva, quae ad efficientem pertinet"), but also resembles the final cause ("finis"), which is "first by intention." This statement demonstrates the overlap of the final with the efficient cause. This kind of overlap and interrelationship among the causes is not unusual, and shows some flexibility within the model.

[13] Kuchlinus, *De iustificatione*, ix, gives these alternate names for προκαταρκτική, again indicating the overlap among some of the causes.

II. Materia.
    A. Materia in qua. Subiectum.
    B. Materia ex qua.
    C. Materia circa quam.
III. Forma.
IV. Finis.
    A. Finis οὗ. Remotus. Summus. Architectonicus.
    B. Finis ᾧ. Proximus. Subordinate.

In Gomarus[14]

I. Causa Efficiens.[15]
    A. Principalis. Caussa activa. Proxima. Propria.
    B. Causa Impulsiva. Remota. Minus propria.[16]
        1. Προηγουμένη. Interna. Intrinseca. Causa intus movens.
        2. Προκαταρκτική. Externa. Extrinseca. Causa externa movens.[17]
    C. Instrumentalis.
        1. Primaria.
        2. Secundaria.
        3. Ordinaria.
            a. Interna.
            b. Externa.
        4. Extraordinaria.
        5. Instrumentalis remota.

---

[14] Gomarus's use of causality is collated primarily from *De fide iustificante* (1603); *De fide salvifica* (1603); *De iustificatione* (1603); *De iustificatione* (1604); *De iustificatione* (1605); *De iustificatione* (1608); *Disputationum theologicarum quinto repetitarum vigesima-sexta de iustificatione hominis coram Deo*, Tobias Regius respondens, ad diem 21 January 1609 (Leiden: Ioannes Patius, 1609); *Disputationum theologicarum duodecima de primo peccato Adami, et peccato originali*, Samuel Bouchereau respondens, 19 February 1603 (Leiden: Ioannes Patius, 1603); *De perseverantia* (1597); *De resipiscentia* (1606).

[15] In Gomarus, *De iustificatione* (1608), xiii–xvi, and *De iustificatione* (1609), xiii–xx, their similar distinctions of efficient causality do not easily fit into the schema here, demonstrating again the flexibility of the method.

[16] Gomarus, *De primo peccato* (1603), ix, like Kuchlinus, also sees the "causa impulsiva" as a less proper efficient.

[17] Gomarus, *De iustificatione* (1604), xi, like Kuchlinus, associates the "causa externa movens" also with the "materia."

II. Materia.
    A. Materia in qua. Subjectum. Materia passiva.
        1. Proxima. Propinqua.
        2. Remota. Communis.
    B. Materia ex qua.
    C. Materia circa quam. Objectum.
III. Forma.
    A. Communis.
    B. Propria.
IV. Finis.
    A. Supremus. Primarius. Remotus. Summus.
    B. Subordinatus. Secundarius. Proximus. Propinquus.

WORKS CITED

I. *Disputations*

(excluding those appearing in Arminius's *Opera theologica*)

Arminius, Jacobus. *Disputatio theologica de peccato originali*, Gilbertus Iacchaeus respondens, 5 November 1603 (Leiden, 1603).
——. *Disputationum theologicarum quarto repetitarum vigesima-tertia de fide*, Ricardus Ianus Neraeus respondens, 21 December 1605 (Leiden, 1605).
——. *Disputationum theologicarum quinto repetitarum vigesima-nona, de bonis operibus et meritis eorum*, Christianus Sopingius respondens, ad diem 28 February 1609 (Leiden, 1609).
——. *Disputationum theologicarum quinto repetitarum vigesima-quinta, de fide*, Iacobus Massisius respondens, ad diem 26 July 1608 (Leiden, 1608).
——. *Disputationum theologicarum vigesima-quarta, de iustificatione hominis coram Deo per solam fidem*, Theodorus Carronus respondens, 4 Calend. November 1603 (Leiden, 1603).
——. *Disputationum theologicarum vigesima-septima, de bonis operibus, et meritis eorum*, Christopherus Hellerus respondens, ad diem 17 December 1603 (Leiden, 1603).
——. *Theses theologicae de imaginis Dei in nobis restitutione*, Theodorus Tronchinus respondens, ad diem 2 July 1605 (Leiden, 1605).
——. *Theses theologicae de vera humana Christi natura*, Sebastianus Damman respondens, 31 July 1604 (Leiden, 1604).
Gomarus, Franciscus. *Disputatio theologica de hominis coram Deo per Christum iustificatione*, Ioannes Perreus respondens, ad diem 26 April 1608 (Leiden, 1608).
——. *Disputatio theologica de libero arbitrio*, Gilbertus Iacchaeus respondens, 28 June 1603 (Leiden, 1603).
——. *Disputationum theologicarum decima-quarta, de libero arbitrio*, Samuel Gruterus respondens, 19 March 1603 (Leiden, 1603).
——. *Disputationum theologicarum duodecima de primo peccato Adami, et peccato originali*, Samuel Bouchereau respondens, 19 February 1603 (Leiden, 1603).
——. *Disputationum theologicarum quarto repetitarum trigesima-prima de vocatione hominis ad salutem*, Laurentius Pauli respondens, ad diem 29 April 1606 (Leiden, 1606).
——. *Disputationum theologicarum quarto repetitarum vigesima-quinta de resipiscentia*, Matthaeus Cotterius respondens, 1 February 1606 (Leiden, 1606).
——. *Disputationum theologicarum quinto repetitarum decima-sexta de libero arbitrio*, Hieronymus Vogellius respondens, ad diem 24 November 1607 (Leiden, 1607).
——. *Disputationum theologicarum quinto repetitarum trigesima quarta: de Dei praedestinatione*, Casparus Sibelius respondens, ad diem 15 July 1609 (Leiden, 1609).
——. *Disputationum theologicarum quinto repetitarum vigesima-sexta de iustificatione hominis coram Deo*, Tobias Regius respondens, ad diem 21 January 1609 (Leiden, 1609).
——. *Disputationum theologicarum repetitarum decima quinta, de creatione hominis ad imaginem Dei*, Symeon Ruytingius respondens, 29 July 1598 (Leiden, 1598).
——. *Disputationum theologicarum repetitarum trigesima sexta, de bonis operibus et meritis eorum*, Iacobus Vervestius respondens, 14 July 1599 (Leiden, 1599).
——. *Disputationum theologicarum vigesima-tertia, de fide iustificante*, Henricus H. Geisteranus, Jr., respondens, ad diem 15 October 1603 (Leiden, 1603).
——. *Theologicarum disputationum decimaoctava: de sanctorum perseverantia*, Henricus Arnoldus respondens, 5 March 1597 (Leiden, 1597).
——. *Theses theologicae de fide salvifica*, Elias de Monier respondens, Kal. March 1603 (Leiden, 1603).

———. *Theses theologicae de hominis perfectione in hac vita*, Cornelius Burchvliet respondens, 18 March 1601 (Leiden, 1601).

———. *Theses theologicae de iustificatione hominis coram Deo*, Laurentius Boenaert respondens, 12 March 1603 (Leiden, 1603).

———. *Theses theologicae de iustificatione hominis coram Deo*, Isaacus Diamantius respondens, ad diem 20 March 1604 (Leiden, 1604).

———. *Theses theologicae de iustificatione hominis coram Deo*, Henricus Slatius respondens, ad diem 19 February 1605 (Leiden, 1605).

———. *Theses theologicae de perseverantia sanctorum*, Iacobus Bouveritius, ad diem 19 June 1608 (Leiden, 1608).

———. *Theses theologicae de praedestinatione Dei*, Samuel Gruterus respondens, ad diem 31 October 1604 (Leiden, 1604).

Junius, Franciscus. *Disputatio theologica de iustificatione peccatoris coram Deo*, Benjamin Basnageus respondens, 16 November 1600 (Leiden, 1600).

———. *Disputatio theologica de salutis fidelium certitudine pro asserenda fiducia*, Ioannes vander Haghe respondens, 3 February 1601 (Leiden, 1601).

———. *Theses theologicae, de aeterna Dei electione*, Lucas Trelcatius, Jr., respondens, 13 March 1593 (Leiden, 1593).

———. *Theses theologicae de differentia inter iustificationem et sanctificationem*, Lambertus de Riick respondens, 12 July 1600 (Leiden, 1600).

Kuchlinus, Johannes. *Disputatio ἐλεγτικὴ;*[sic] *de meritis bonorum operum*, Isebrandus Guilielmius respondens, in *Theologicae disputationes* 84, pp. 522–32.

———. *Disputatio ἐλεγτικὴ;*[sic] *de perfectione hominis in hac vita*, ad quaest. catechet. 114 & 115, Ioannes Narsius respondens, in *Theologicae disputationes* 129, pp. 818–23.

———. *Disputatio theologica de fidei iustificantis causa efficiente, et instrumentali. Et de sacramentis in genere*, complectens explicationem quaestionum catecheticarum 65. 66, Tobias a Gellinchuisen respondens, in *Theologicae disputationes* 85, pp. 532–42.

———. *Disputatio theologica de primo peccato primorum parentum Adami et Evae*, Leoninus Leone Petrus F. respondens, ad quaest. 7 catechet., in *Theologicae disputationes* 16, pp. 88–93.

———. *Theses theologicae continentes exegesin et assertionem theorematis hodie controversi, sola fide absque operibus nos iustificari coram Deo*, Ioannes Arnoldus respondens, March 1603 (Leiden, 1603).

———. *Theses theologicae de bonorum operum conditionibus*, expl. quaest. 91 catech., Ioannes Arnoldus respondens, in *Theologicae disputationes* 83, pp. 516–22.

———. *Theses theologicae de bonorum operum necessitate*, Ioannes Arnoldus respondens, in *Theologicae disputationes* 82, pp. 510–16.

———. *Theses theologicae de certitudine salutis fidelium*, Isaacus Ioannis F. respondens (Leiden, 1603); also in *Theologicae disputationes* 145, pp. 915–20.

———. *Theses theologicae de divina praedestinatione*, M. Gerardus Vossius respondens (Leiden, 1600); also in *Theologicae disputationes* 65, pp. 385–94.

———. *Theses theologic* [sic] *de iustificatione hominis coram Deo*, quaest. catech. 59. 60. 61, Raphael ab Allendorp Clivius respondens, in *Theologicae disputationes* 74, pp. 459–65.

———. *Theses theologicae de liberatione hominis a miseria*, Valerius Valerii Tophusius respondens, in *Theologicae disputationes* 23, pp. 130–34.

———. *Theses theologicae de natura iustificationis in caussis*, Ioannes Arnoldus respondens, March 1603 (Leiden, 1603); also in *Theologicae disputationes* 75, pp. 465–75.

———. *Theses theologicae de peccato originali*, ad quaest. 7 catechesios, Henricus Henrici Geesteranus respondens (Leiden, 1602); also in *Theologicae disputationes* 18, pp. 100–06.

———. *Theses theologicae de peccato originali*, Lambertus de Riick respondens, in *Theologicae disputationes* 19, pp. 107–12.

———. *Theses theologicae, de primo peccato Adami*, Elia Ioannes a Campen respondens, in *Theologicae disputationes* 15, pp. 82–87.

——. *Theses theologicae de salvandis et fide*, Henricus Adamus Billichius respondens, in *Theologicae disputationes* 76, pp. 476–80.

——. *Theses theologicae de sanctorum perseverantia in fide*, ad quaestionem catech. 58, Iacobus Paulides respondens (Leiden, 1603); also in *Theologicae disputationes* 73, pp. 453–58.

——. *Theses theologicae de statu hominis non regeniti post lapsum*, ad quaest. 8 catecheseos, Franciscus Petri respondens (Leiden, 1603); also as *De libero arbitrio in homine non regenerato post lapsum*, in *Theologicae disputationes* 21, pp. 117–22.

Trelcatius, Lucas, Jr. *Disputatio theologica de iustificatione hominis coram Deo*, Ioannes Bocardus respondens, 21 January 1604 (Leiden, 1604).

——. *Disputationum theologicarum quarto repetitarum vigesima-quarta de iustificatione hominis coram Deo*, Bernherus Vezekius respondens, 21 January 1605 [1606] (Leiden, 1605 [1606]).

——. *Disputationum theologicarum quarto repetitarum vigesima-septima de bonis operibus et meritis eorum*, Ricardus Ianus Neraeus respondens, ad diem 4 March 1606 (Leiden, 1606).

——. *Disputationum theologicarum quarto repetitarum trigesima de aeterna Dei praedestinatione*, Daniel Guerinellus respondens, ad diem 19 April 1606 (Leiden, 1606).

——. *Disputationum theologicarum quinto repetitarum nona de creatione*, Ioannes Le-Chantre respondens, ad diem 4 July 1607 (Leiden, 1607).

——. *Disputationum theologicarum quinto repetitarum sexta de attributis divinis essentialibus secundi generis*, Isaacus Iunius respondens, ad diem 5 May 1607 (Leiden, 1607).

——. *Disputationum theologicarum trigesima-prima, de vocatione hominum ad salutem*, Hermannus H. Montanus, ad diem 18 February 1604 (Leiden, 1604).

Trelcatius, Lucas, Sr. *Theses theologicae de fide electorum*, Lucas Trelcatius, Jr., respondens, 14 March 1592 (Leiden, 1592).

II. *Other Primary Sources*

Acta synodi nationalis, in nomine Domini nostri Iesu Christi…Dordrechti habitae anno M.DC.XVIII. et M.DC.XIX (Hanau, 1620).

Aelred of Rievaulx. *Sermones de Oneribus*, in *PL* 195.

Altenstaig, Ioannes. *Lexicon theologicum quo tanquam clave theologiae fores aperiuntur* (Cologne, 1619).

Ames, William. *Marrow of Sacred Divinity, Drawne out of the Holy Scriptures and the Interpreters thereof, and brought into Method* (Lonsdon, 1642).

——. *Medulla s.s. theologiae, ex sacris literis, earumque interpretibus, extracta, et methodice disposita* (London, 1630).

Andrewes, Lancelot. *Censura censurae D. Barreti de certitudine salutis*, in F. G., ed., *Articuli Lambethani*, pp. 33–40.

Aristotle. *Metaphysics* [Loeb Classical Library] (Cambridge, Mass., 1961).

——. *Physics* [Loeb Classical Library] (Cambridge, Mass., 1963).

Arminius, Jacobus. *Opera Theologica* (Leiden, 1629). [the following works appear in order as found in the *Opera*]

——. *Oratio de sacerdotio Christi habita a D. Iacobo Arminio cum publice doctor s. theologiae crearetur*, in *Opera*, pp. 9–26.

——. *Orationes tres de theologia, quas ordine habuit auctor cum lectiones suas auspicaretur*, in *Opera*, pp. 26–71.

——. *Oratio de componendo dissidio religionis inter Christianos, habita ab auctore VIII. Feb. 1605 cum rectoratum deponeret*, in *Opera*, pp. 71–91.

——. *Verclaringhe Iacobi Arminii saliger ghedachten, in zijn leven professor theologiae binnen Leyden: aengaende zyn ghevoelen* (Leiden, 1610).

——. *Verklaring van Jacobus Arminius, afgelegd in de vergadering van de staten van Holland op 30 Oktober, 1608*, ed. G. J. Hoenderdaal (Lochem, 1960).

———. *Declaratio sententiae I. Arminii de praedestinatione, providentia Dei, libero arbitrio, gratia Dei, divinitate Filii Dei, et de iustificatione hominis coram Deo*, in *Opera*, pp. 91–133.

———. *The Just Mans Defence, or, The Declaration of the Judgement of James Arminius... concerning the principal points of religion... to which is added, Nine Questions Exhibited by the Deputies of the Synod...*, trans. Tobias Conyers (London, 1657).

———. *Apologia D. Iacobi Arminii adversus articulos quosdam [XXXI] theologicos in vulgus sparsos*, in *Opera*, pp. 134–83.

———. *Quaestiones numero novem cum responsionibus et anterotematis, nobiliss. DD. curatoribus Academiae Leidensis exhibite a deputatis synodi... mense Novembri anni 1605*, in *Opera*, pp. 184–86.

———. *Disputationes publicae de nonnullis religionis Christianae capitibus*, in *Opera*, pp. 197–338.

———. *Disputationes privatae, de plerisque Christianae religionis capitibus, incoatae potissimum ab auctore ad corporis theologici informationem*, in *Opera*, pp. 339–457.

———. *Amica cum D. Francisco Iunio de praedestinatione, per litteras habita collation*, in *Opera*, pp. 445–619.

———. *Examen modestum libelli, quem D. Gulielmus Perkinsius... edidit ante aliquot annos de praedestinationis modo et ordine*, in *Opera*, pp. 621–777.

———. *Analysis cap. 9. ad Romanos ad Gellium Snecanum*, in *Opera*, pp. 778–807.

———. *De vero et genuino sensu Cap. VII. Epistolae ad Romanos dissertation*, in *Opera*, pp. 809–934.

———. *Epistola ad Hippolytum a Collibus*, in *Opera*, pp. 935–47.

———. *Articuli nonnulli diligenti examine perpendendi, eo quod inter ipsos Reformatae Religionis professores de iis aliqua incidit controversia*, in *Opera*, pp. 948–966.

———. *Examen thesium D. Francisci Gomari de praedestinatione* ([Amsterdam,] 1645).

———. *The Works of James Arminius*, London ed., trans. James Nichols and William Nichols, 3 vols. (1825, 1828, 1875; repr. Grand Rapids, 1986).

Arminius, Jacobus, and Franciscus Gomarus. *Twee disputatien vande goddeliicke predestinatie* (Leiden, 1610).

Articuli Arminiani sive Remonstrantia, in Schaff, *The Creeds of Christendom* 3:545–49.

Articuli XXXIX. Ecclesiae Anglicanae. A.D. 1562, in Schaff, *The Creeds of Christendom* 3:486–516.

Athanasius of Alexandria. *Contra Gentes and de incarnatione*, ed. Robert W. Thomson (Oxford, 1971).

The Auction Catalogue of the Library of J. Arminius, a fascimile edition with an introduction by Carl O. Bangs (Utrecht, 1985).

Augustine, Aurelius. *Confessionum libri tredecim*, in *PL* 32.

———. *Contra Faustum Manichaeum*, in *PL* 42.

———. *Contra secundam Juliani responsionem imperfectum opus*, in *PL* 45.

———. *De continentia*, in *PL* 40.

———. *De fide et operibus*, in *PL* 40.

———. *De gratia Christi et de peccato originali contra Pelagium et Coelestium*, in *PL* 44.

———. *De natura et gratia ad Timasium et Jacobum contra Pelagium*, in *PL* 44.

———. *De utilitate jejunii sermo*, in *PL* 40.

———. *Enchiridion ad Laurentium sive de fide, spe et caritate*, in *PL* 40.

———. *Sermones ad populum omnes*, in *PL* 38.

Baillie, Robert. *A Scotch Antidote against the English Infection of Arminianism* (London, 1652).

Baro, Peter. *In Jonam prophetam praelectiones 39. In quibus multa pie docteque differuntur et explicantur* (London, 1579).

———. *Summa trium de praedestinatione sententiarum*, in *Ep. ecc.* 15, pp. 29–32.

Barrett, William. 'Recantatio Mri. Barret,' in Strype, *Life and Acts* 3:317–20.

Becon, Thomas. *The Governaunce of Vertue, teaching all faythfull Christians, how they ought dayly to lead their life* (London, 1578).

Bernard of Clairvaux. *Sermones de diversis*, in *PL* 183.

——. *Sermones in Cantica Canticorum*, in *PL* 183.

Bertius. *Aen-spraeck aen D. Fr. Gomarum op zijne bedenckinghe over de lijck-oratie ghedaen na de begraefenisse van D. Jacobus Arminius zaligher* (Leiden, 1601 [1610]).

——. *De vita et obitu reverendi et clarissimi viri D. Iacobi Arminii oratio. Dicta post tristes illius exsequias XXII. Octob. Anno M.D.C.IX. in Auditorio Theologico*, in Arminius, *Opera theologica*, fols. 001–0004.

Beza, Theodore. *A booke of Christian questions and answers* (London, 1574).

——. *Quaestionum et responsionum Christianarum libellus* (London, 1571).

Burgersdijk, Franco. *Institutionum logicarum libri duo ad juventutem Cantabrigiensem* (Cambridge, Eng., 1637).

——. *Monitio logica, or, An abstract and translation of Burgersdicius his logick by a gentleman* (London, 1697).

Calvin, John. *Concerning the Eternal Predestination of God*, trans. J. K. S. Reid (Louisville, 1997).

——. *De aeterna Dei praedestinatione*, in *Ioannis Calvini opera*, vol. 8.

——. *Ioannis Calvini opera quae supersunt omnia*, ed. G. Baum, E. Cunitz, and E. Reuss (Brunswick, 1863–1900).

——. *Institutio Christianae religionis* (1559), in *Ioannis Calvini opera*, vol. 2.

——. *Institutes of the Christian Religion*, trans. Henry Beveridge (1845; repr. Grand Rapids, 1994).

Canons and Decrees of the Council of Trent, ed. H. J. Schroeder (St. Louis, 1950).

Canons of the Synod of Dort, in Schaff, *The Creeds of Christendom* 3:550–97.

Curcellaeus, Stephen. 'Praefatio Christiano Lectori,' in Arminius, *Examen thesium Gomari*, fols. 02r–04v.

Cyprian of Carthage, *Epistolae*, in *PL* 4.

Episcopius, Simon. *Institutiones theologicae privatis lectionibus Amstelodami traditae*, in *Opera theological*, 2nd ed. (London, 1678).

Erasmus, Desiderius. *De libero arbitrio diatribh sive collation*, in *Desiderii Erasmi Roterodami opera omnia*, 10 vols. (Leiden, 1703–06), 9: cols. 1215–48.

——. *On the Freedom of the Will: A Diatribe or Discourse*, trans. E. Gordon Rupp, in *Luther and Erasmus: Free Will and Salvation* [Library of Christian Classics 17] (Philadelphia, 1969), pp. 35–97.

Fuller, Thomas. *A Sermon of Assurance* (London, 1648).

G., F., ed. *Articuli Lambethani* (London, 1651).

Gomarus, Franciscus. *Bedencken over de lyck-oratie van Meester P. Bertius*, in *Verclaringhe, over de vier hooftstucken, der leere, waer van hy met sijn weerde mede—Professore D. Iacobo Arminio, gheconfereert heeft, voor de E. E. moghende Heeren Staten van Hollandt ende Westvrieslandt: overghelevert den achtsten Septembris* [Leiden, 1609], pp. 41–49.

——. *Locorum communium theologicorum, epitome* [ed. Adolphus Sibelius] (Amsterdam, 1653).

——. *Opera theologica omnia, maximam partem posthuma; suprema autoris voluntate a discipulis edita* (Amsterdam, 1644).

——. *Proeve van M. P. Bertii aenspraeck* (Leiden, 1610).

——. *Waerschouwinghe over de vermaninghe aen R. Donteclock* (Leiden, 1609).

Gottfried of Admont. *Homilia XVI. in epiphaniam Domini tertia*, in *PL* 174.

Gregory of Nazianzus. Λογοι θεολογικοι, ed. Joseph Barbel (Düsseldorf, 1963).

Gregory I the Great. *Epistolae Gregorii Magni*, in *PL* 77.

——. *Moralium libri, sive expositio in Librum B. Job*, in *PL* 75.

——. *XL homiliarum in Evangelia libri duo*, in *PL* 76.

Grotius, Hugo. *Ordinum hollandiae ac westfrisiae pietas (1613)*, trans. Edwin Rabbie (Leiden, 1995).

Harvey, Gideon. *Archelogia philosophica nova, or New Principles of Philosophy* (London, 1663).

The Heidelberg Catechism, in Schaff, *The Creeds of Christendom*, 3:307–55.

Hemmingius, Nicolaus. *Enchiridion theologicum, praecipua verae religionis capita breviter et simpliciter explicata continens* (London, 1580).

Ignatius of Loyola. *Exercitia spiritualia*, in *Institutum societatis Iesu*, 3 vols. (Rome, 1869–86), 2:365–418.

Isidore of Seville. *Sententiarum libri tres*, in *PL* 83.

Jerome. *Commentariorum in Isaiam prophetam libri duodeviginti*, in *PL* 24.

——. *Commentariorum in Jeremiam prophetam libri sex*, in *PL* 24.

John Chrysostom. Τα ευρισκομενα παντα, 13 vols. (Paris, 1834–38).

Junius, Franciscus. *Opera theologica* (Geneva, 1607).

Kimedoncius, Jacobus. *Of the redemption of mankind three bookes* (London, 1598).

Kuchlinus, Johannes. *Ecclesiarum Hollandicarum et Westfrisicarum Catechismus... disputationibus theologicis, a quaestionum et responsionum catecheticarum initio ad finem, in unum volumen redactis* ([Geneva,] 1612).

——. *Oratio reverendi doctissimique viri D. Iohannis Kuchlini, Ecclesiae Amstelrodamensis pastoris, electi et vocati primi praesidis Collegii Theologici* (Leiden, 1593).

——. *Theologicae disputationes de religionis Christianae capitibus praecipuis: in Collegio Theologico Illustr. DD. ordinum Hollandiae et Westfrisiae* ([Geneva,] 1613).

Leo I. *Sermones in praecipuis totius anni festivitatibus ad Romanam plebem habiti*, in *PL* 54.

Limborch, Philip van. *Historical Relation concerning the Origin and Progress of the Controversies in the Belgic League, upon Predestination and its Connected Heads*, in L.W. P., 'Arminian Controversy in the Low Countries,' *Methodist Review* 26 (1844), 425–60 and 556–87.

Luther, Martin. *D. Martin Luthers Werke: Kritische Gesamtausgabe*, 66 vols. (Weimar, 1883–1987).

——. *Disputatio pro declaratione virtutis indulgentiarum* (1517), in *WA* 1:233–38.

——. *Disputatio Heidelbergae habita* (1518), in *WA* 1:353–74.

——. *In Epistolam Pauli ad Galatas M. Lutheri commentarius* (1519), in *WA* 2:443–618.

——. *Dictata super Psalterium I–LXXXIII [LXXXIV]*, in *WA* 3.

——. *De captivitate Babylonica Ecclesiae praeludium*, in *WA* 6:497–573.

——. *Tractatus de libertate Christiana*, in *WA* 7:49–73.

——. *De servo arbitrio*, in *WA* 18:600–787.

——. *Vorlesung über den 1. Timotheusbrief*, in *WA* 26:1–120.

——. *Epistola ad Romanos, die scholien*, in *WA* 56:155–528.

——. *Luther's Works*, American ed., 56 vols., ed. Jaroslav Pelikan and Helmut Lehmann (St. Louis, 1955–86).

Melanchthon, Philip. *Loci Communes 1543*, trans. J. A. O. Preus (St. Louis, 1992).

——. *Loci praecipui theologici* (1543), in *Corpus doctrinae Christianae. Quae est summa orthodoxi et catholici dogmatis* (Lipsiae, 1565), pp. 299–672.

Migne, J. P., ed. *Patrologia Latina cursus completus, sive bibliotheca universalis... omnium S.S. patrum, doctorum, scriptorumque ecclesiasticorum qui ab aevo apostolico ad Innocentii III tempora floruerunt* (Paris, 1878–90).

Molina, Luis de. *On Divine Foreknowledge (Part IV of the* Concordia), trans. Alfred J. Freddoso (Ithaca, 1988).

Moulin, Pierre du. *The Anatomy of Arminianisme: or The Opening of the Controversies lately handled in the Low-Countryes* (London, 1620).

Musculus, Wolfgang. *Common places of the Christian Religion* (London, 1563).

N., O. *An Apology of English Arminianisme or a Dialogue, betweene Iacobus Arminius, Professour in the University of Leyden in Holland; and Enthusiastus an English Doctour of Divinity, and a great Precisian* ([Saint-Omer,] 1634).

Origen. *In Lucam homiliae*, in *Origenis opera omnia*, vol. 4 (Berlin, 1834).

Perkins, William. *The Workes of that Famous and Worthy Minister of Christ... Mr. William Perkins*, 3 vols. (London, 1631–35).

——. *Armilla aurea, id est, theologiae description*, 2nd ed. (Cambridge, Eng., 1591).

——. *A Golden Chaine: or, the Description of Theologie*, in *Workes of Perkins* 1:9–116.

———. *An Exposition of the Symbole, or Creed of the Apostles: According to the tenour of Scripture, and the consent of Orthodoxe Fathers of the Church*, in *Workes of Perkins* 1:117–322.

———. *A Treatise Tending unto a Declaration, whether a Man Be in the Estate of Damnation, or in the Estate of Grace*, in *Workes of Perkins* 1:353–420.

———. *A Case of Conscience, the greatest that ever was: How a man may know whether he be the childe of God, or no*, in *Workes of Perkins* 1:421–28.

———. *How to Live, and that Well: In All Estates and Times. Specially, when helps and comforts faile*, in *Workes of Perkins* 1:475–86.

———. *A Discourse of Conscience. Wherein Is Set Downe the nature, properties, and differences thereof*, 8th ed., in *Workes of Perkins* 1:515–54.

———. *A Reformed Catholike or, A Declaration Shewing How Neere Wee may come to the present Church of Rome in sundrie points of Religion: and wherein we must for ever depart from them*, in *Workes of Perkins* 1:555–624.

———. *De praedestinationis modo et ordine: et de amplitudine gratiae divinae ... desceptatio* (Cambridge, Eng., 1598).

———. *The Whole Treatise of the Cases of Conscience, Distinguished into Three Bookes*, in *Workes of Perkins* 2:1–152.

———. *A Treatise of the Manner and Order of Predestination*, in *Workes of Perkins* 2:603–41.

———. *A Cloud of Faithfull Witnesses: Leading to the Heavenly Canaan. Or, A Commentarie upon the Eleventh Chapter to the Hebrewes*, in *Workes of Perkins* 3:1–190.

———. *A godly and learned Exposition or Commentarie upon the Three First Chapters of the Revelation*, in *Workes of Perkins* 3:207–370.

Piscator, Johannes. *A learned and profitable treatise of mans iustification* (London, 1599).

Polanus a Polansdorf, Amandus. *Partitiones theologicae iuxta naturalis methodi leges conformatae duobus libris* (London, 1591).

———. *The substance of Christian religion, Soundly Set Forth in two bookes, by definitions and partitions* (London, 1595).

Praestantium ac eruditorum virorum epistolae ecclesiasticae et theologicae, 2nd ed., preface by Philip van Limborch (Amsterdam, 1684).

Prynne, William. *Anti-Arminianisme: Or The Church of Englands old antithesis to new Arminianisme* ([London,] 1630).

Rabanus Maurus. *Expositionis super Jeremiam prophetam libri viginti*, in *PL* 111.

Sandys, Edwin. *Sermons Made by the most reverende Father in God, Edwin, Archbishop of Yorke* (London, 1585).

Saravia, Adrianus. 'Opinion of Barret's Recantation,' in Nijenhuis, *Adrianus Saravia*, pp. 330–42.

Sententiae Remonstrantium, in *Acta synodi nationalis*, pp. 159–60 and 163–67; also trans. in Peter Y. De Jong, ed., *Crisis in the Reformed Churches*, pp. 221–29.

Spencer, Thomas. *The art of logick delivered in the precepts of Aristotle and Ramus* (London, 1628).

Suárez, Francisco. *Disputationes metaphysicae*, in *Disputaciones metafisicas*, 7 vols., ed. Sergio Rábade Romeo, et al. (Madrid, 1960–66).

———. *On Creation, Conservation, and Concurrence: Metaphysical Disputations 20, 21, and 22*, trans. Alfred J. Freddoso (South Bend, 2002).

———. *On Efficient Causality: Metaphysical Dispuations 17, 18, and 19*, trans. Alfred J. Freddoso (New Haven, 1994).

Syntagma disputationum theologicorum, in Academia Lugduno-Batava quarto repetitarum ... Francisco Gomaro, Iacobo Arminio, et Luca Trelcatio Iuniore (Rotterdam, 1615).

Taffin, Jean. *The Amendment of Life, Comprised in Fower Bookes* (London, 1595).

———. *The Marks of God's Children* (1586), trans. Peter Y. De Jong [Classics of Reformed Spirituality] (Grand Rapids, 2003).

———. *Of the Markes of the children of God, and of their comforts in afflictions* (London, 1590).

Tertullian of Carthage. *De cultu foeminarum*, in *PL* 1.

Thomas Aquinas. *Summa theologiae*. 61 vols. (London, 1964–1981).

Trelcatius, Lucas, Jr. *A briefe institution of the common places of sacred divinitie* (London, 1610).

——. *Oratio funebris in obitum reverendi et clarissimi viri D. Iohannis Kuchlini*, ad diem 5 July 1606 (Leiden, 1606).

——. *Scholastica, et methodica, locorum communium s. theologiae institutio* (London, 1604).

Ursinus, Zacharias. *Doctrinae christianae compendium: seu, commentarii catechetici* (Cambridge, Eng., 1585).

——. *The summe of Christian religion: Delivered by Zacharias Ursinus in his Lectures upon the Catechism* (Oxford, 1587).

Ursinus, Zacharias, and Caspar Olevianus. *The Heidelberg Catechism*, in Schaff, *The Creeds of Christendom* 3:307–55.

Veluanus, Ioannes Anastasius. *Kort bericht in allen principalen punten des Christen geloves... und is des halven genant der leken wechwyser* (1554), in *Bibliotheca Reformatoria Neerlandica: Geschriften uit den tijd der hervorming in de Nederlanden*, ed. S. Cramer and F. Pijper, vol. 4 (The Hague, 1906), pp. 123–376.

Vermigli, Peter Martyr. *In Epistolam S. Pauli Apostoli ad Rom. D. Petri Martyris Vermilii Florentini* (Basel, 1560).

Virgil. *Georgicon* [Loeb Classical Library] (Cambridge, Mass., 1953).

Wallis, Johannes. *Institutio logicae, ad communes usus acommodata* [sic] (Oxford, 1687).

Whitaker, William. *Cygnea cantio Guilielmi Whitakeri, hoc est, ultima illius concio ad clerum... Octob. 9. Anno Dom. 1595*, in *Praelectiones doctissimi viri Guilielmi Whitakeri* (Cambridge, Eng., 1599).

Zanchi, Girolamo. *A Briefe Discourse*, in *Workes of Perkins* 1:429–38.

——. *H. Zanchius his confession of Christian religion, Which now at length being 70. yeares of age, he caused to bee published in the name of himselfe and his family* ([Cambridge, Eng.,] 1599).

——. *Hier. Zanchii miscellaneorum libri tres* (London, 1605).

——. *De religione Christiana, fides* (London, 1605).

III. *Secondary Works*

Ahsmann, Margreet J. A. M. *Collegia en Colleges: Juridisch onderwijs aan de Leidse Universiteit 1575–1630 in het bijzonder het disputeren* (Groningen, 1990).

Armstrong, Brian. *Calvinism and the Amyraut Heresy: Protestant Scholasticism and Humanism in Seventeenth-Century France* (Madison, 1969).

Ashby, Stephen M. 'A Reformed Arminian View,' in *Four Views on Eternal Security*, ed. J. Matthew Pinson (Grand Rapids, 2002), pp. 135–87.

Bakhuizen van den Brink, J. N. 'Arminius te Leiden,' *Nederlands Theologisch Tijdschrift* 15 (1960), 81–89.

Bangs, Carl. *Arminius: A Study in the Dutch Reformation* (1971; repr. Eugene, OR, 1998).

——. 'Arminius and Socinianism,' in *Socinianism and Its Role in the Culture of the XVIth to XVIIIth Centuries*, ed. Lech Szczucki (Warsaw, 1983), pp. 81–84.

——. 'Arminius as a Reformed Theologian,' in *The Heritage of John Calvin: Heritage Hall Lectures, 1960–70*, ed. John H. Bratt (Grand Rapids, 1973), pp. 209–22.

——. 'Introduction,' in *Works* 1:vii–xxix.

——. 'Review of Richard Muller, *God, Creation, and Providence*,' *Church History* 66/1 (1997), 118–20.

Bangs, Nathan. *The Life of James Arminius, D.D., Compiled from His Life and Writings, as Published by Mr. James Nichols* (New York, 1843).

Bantjes, A. A., ed. *De Leidse hoogleraren en lectoren 1575–1815. 1. De theologische faculteit* (Leiden, 1983).

Barth, Karl. *The Epistle to the Romans*, 6th ed., trans. Edwyn C. Hoskyns (New York, 1933).

Beeke, Joel R. *Assurance of Faith: Calvin, English Puritanism, and the Dutch Second Reformation* (New York, 1991).

Bell, M. Charles. *Calvin and Scottish Theology: The Doctrine of Assurance* (Edinburgh, 1985).

Berkouwer, G. C. *Faith and Justification*, trans. Lewis B. Smedes [Studies in Dogmatics] (Grand Rapids, 1954).

Biografisch lexicon voor de geschiedenis van het nederlandse protestantisme, ed. D. Nauta, et al., 6 vols. (Kampen, 1978–2006).

Biographisch woordenboek van protestantsche godgeleerden in Nederland, ed. J. P. de Bie and J. Loosjes, 6 vols. (The Hague, 1919–49).

Blacketer, Raymond A. 'Arminius' Concept of Covenant in Its Historical Context,' *NAKG* 80/2 (2000), 193–220.

Bos, E. P. and H. A. Krop, eds. *Franco Burgersdijk (1590–1635): Neo-Aristotelianism in Leiden* [Studies in the History of Ideas in the Low Countries 1] (Amsterdam, 1993).

Bradley, James E., and Richard A. Muller. *Church History: An Introduction to Research, Reference Works, and Methods* (Grand Rapids, 1995).

Brandt, Caspar. *The Life of James Arminius, D.D.*, trans. John Guthrie, with an intro. by T. O. Summers (Nashville, 1857).

Brandt, Gerard. *The History of the Reformation and Other Ecclesiastical Transactions in and about the Low-Countries*, 4 vols. (London, 1720–23).

Bray, John S. *Theodore Beza's Doctrine of Predestination* (Nieuwkoop, 1975).

Brown, William Kenneth. 'An Analysis of Romans 7 with an Evaluation of Arminius' Dissertation on Romans 7' (Ph.D. diss., Bob Jones University, 1984).

Cameron, Charles M. 'Arminius—Hero or Heretic?' *Evangelical Quarterly* 64 (1992), 213–27.

Clarke, F. Stuart. 'Arminius's Understanding of Calvin,' *Evangelical Quarterly* 54 (January–March 1982), 25–35.

Clotz, Henrike L. *Hochschule für Holland: Die Universität Leiden im Spannungsfeld zwischen Provinz, Stadt und Kirche, 1575–1619* (Stuttgart, 1998).

Copleston, Frederick. *A History of Philosophy*, 9 vols. (Garden City, 1962–75).

Cossee, Erik Henri. *Arminius en de eerste Remonstranten in hun betrekkingen tot Rome* (Leiden, 1973).

Danker, Frederick William, ed. *A Greek-English Lexicon of the New Testament and other Early Christian Literature*, 3rd ed. (Chicago, 2000).

De Jong, Peter Y., ed. *Crisis in the Reformed Churches: Essays in Commemoration of the Great Synod of Dort, 1618–1619* (Grand Rapids, 1968).

De Vries, Herman, ed. *Genève Pépinière du Calvinisme Hollandais*, vol. 2 (The Hague, 1924).

Dekker, Evert. 'Jacobus Arminius and His Logic: Analysis of a Letter,' *Journal of Theological Studies* 44 (1993), 118–142.

——. *Rijker dan Midas: Vrijheid, genade en predestinatie in de theologie van Jacobus Arminius, 1559–1609* (Zoetermeer, The Netherlands, 1993).

——. 'Was Arminius a Molinist?' *SCJ* 27/2 (1996), 337–352.

Dell, Robert Thomas. 'Man's Freedom and Bondage in the Thought of Martin Luther and James Arminius' (Ph.D. diss., Boston University Graduate School, 1962).

Dibon, Paul Auguste Georges. *L'Enseignement philosophique dans les universités néerlandaises à l'époque pré-cartésienne (1575–1650)* (Amsterdam, 1954).

Eekhof, Albert. *De theologische faculteit te Leiden in de 17de eeuw* (Utrecht, 1921).

Ellis, Mark Alan. 'Simon Episcopius's Doctrine of Original Sin' (Ph.D. diss., Dallas Theological Seminary, 2002).

Fiering, Norman. *Moral Philosophy at Seventeenth-Century Harvard: A Discipline in Transition* (Chapel Hill, 1981).

Foxgrover, David. '"Temporary Faith" and the Certainty of Salvation,' *Calvin Theological Journal* 15/2 (1980), 220–32.

Freddoso, Alfred J. 'Introduction,' in Molina, *On Divine Foreknowledge (Part IV of the Con-cordia)*, trans. Alfred J. Freddoso (Ithaca, 1988), pp. 1–81.

——. 'Introduction,' in Suárez, *On Creation, Conservation, and Concurrence: Metaphysical Dis-putations 20, 21, and 22*, trans. Alfred J. Freddoso (South Bend, 2002), pp. xi–cxxiii.

Gilliam, Elizabeth, and W. J. Tighe. 'To "Run with the Time": Archbishop Whitgift, the Lambeth Articles, and the Politics of Theological Ambiguity in Late Elizabethan England,' *SCJ* 23/2 (1992), 325–40.

Glasius, B. *Godgeleerd Nederland: Biographisch woordenboek van Nederlandsche godgeleerden*, 3 vols. ('s-Hertogenbosch, 1851–56).

Godbey, John C. 'Arminius and Predestination,' *Journal of Religion* 53 (1973), 491–98.

Graafland, C. *Van Calvijn tot Barth: Oorsprong en ontwikkeling van de leer der verkiezing in het Gereformeerd Protestantisme* (The Hague, 1987).

——. *De zekerheid van het geloof: Een onderzook naar de geloofsbeschouwing van enige vertegenwoor-digers van reformatie en nadere reformatie* (Wageningen, 1961).

Grislis, Egil. 'The Assurance of Faith according to Richard Hooker,' in *Richard Hooker and the Construction of Christian Community*, ed. Arthur Stephen McGrade [Medieval and Renaissance Texts and Studies 165] (Tempe, 1997), pp. 237–49.

Groenewegen, H. Y. *Jacobus Arminius op den driehonderd-jarigen gedenkdag van zijnen dood* (Leiden, 1909).

Hakkenberg, Michael Abram. 'The Predestinarian Controversy in the Netherlands, 1600–1620' (Ph.D. diss., University of California at Berkeley, 1989).

Harper, George W. 'Calvin and English Calvinism to 1649: A Review Article,' *Calvin Theological Journal* 20/2 (1985), 255–62.

Harper, J. Steven. 'A Wesleyan Arminian View,' in *Four Views on Eternal Security*, ed. J. Matthew Pinson (Grand Rapids, 2002), pp. 209–55.

Harrison, A. W. *The Beginnings of Arminianism to the Synod of Dort* (London, 1926).

Haussleiter, Johannes. *Aus der Schule Melanchthons: Theologische Disputationen und Promo-tionen zu Wittenberg in den Jahren 1546–1560* [Festschrift der Königlichen Universität Greifswald zu Melanchthons 400 jährigem Geburtstag] (Greifswald, 1897).

Helm, Paul. *Calvin and the Calvinists* (Carlisle, PA, 1982).

Heppe, Heinrich. *Reformed Dogmatics Set Out and Illustrated from the Sources*, ed. Ernst Bizer, trans. G. T. Thomson (London, 1950).

Hicks, John Mark, 'The Righteousness of Saving Faith: Arminian versus Remonstrant Grace,' *Evangelical Journal* 9 (Spring 1991), 27–39.

——. 'The Theology of Grace in the Thought of Jacobus Arminius and Philip van Limborch: A Study in the Development of Seventeenth-Century Dutch Arminian-ism' (Ph.D. diss., Westminster Theological Seminary, 1985).

Hoenderdaal, G. J. 'Arminius en Episcopius,' *NAKG* 60 (1980), 203–35.

——. 'Arminius, Jacobus (Hermansz),' in *BLGNP* 2:33–37.

——. 'The Debate about Arminius outside the Netherlands,' in *Leiden University in the Seventeenth Century: An Exchange of Learning*, ed. Th. H. Lunsingh Scheurleer and G. H. M. Posthumus Meyjes (Leiden, 1975), pp. 137–59.

——. 'Inleiding,' in *Verklaring van Jacobus Arminius, afgelegd in de vergadering van de staten van Holland op 30 Oktober, 1608*, ed. G. J. Hoenderdaal (Lochem, 1960), pp. 8–41.

——. 'The Life and Struggle of Arminius in the Dutch Republic,' in Gerald McCulloh, ed., *Man's Faith and Freedom*, pp. 11–26.

——. 'The Life and Thought of Jacobus Arminius,' *Religion in Life* 29/4 (1960), 540–47.

——. 'De theologische betekenis van Arminius,' *Nederlands Theologisch Tijdschrift* 15 (1960), 90–98.

Holk, Lambertus Jacobus van. 'From Arminius to Arminianism in Dutch Theology,' in Gerald McCulloh, ed., *Man's Faith and Freedom*, pp. 27–45.

Huggins, Ronald Vincent. 'Romans 7 and the Ordo Salutis from Arminius to Iron-side (1591–1928): With Special Emphasis on the American Revivalist Tradition in Its Trans-Atlantic Connection' (Th.D. diss., Wycliffe College [Canada], 1996).

Israel, Jonathan. *The Dutch Republic: Its Rise, Greatness, and Fall, 1477–1806* (Oxford, 1995).

Itterzon, Gerrit Pieter van. *Franciscus Gomarus* (1929; repr. Groningen, 1979).

——. 'Gomarus, Franciscus,' in *BLGNP* 2:220–25.

——. 'Hommius, Festus,' in *BLGNP* 2:251–54.

Janssen, H. Q., and J. J. van Toorenenbergen, eds. *Werken der Marnix-Vereeniging III/4: Brieven uit Onderscheidene Kerkelijke Archieven* (Utrecht, 1880).

Jorgenson, James, 'Predestination according to Divine Foreknowledge in Patristic Tradition,' in *Salvation in Christ: A Lutheran-Orthodox Dialogue*, ed. John Meyendorf and Robert Tobias (Minneapolis, 1992), pp. 159–69.

Karskens, M. 'Subject, Object and Substance in Burgersdijk's Logic,' in *Franco Burgersdijk (1590–1635): Neo-Aristotelianism in Leiden*, ed. E. P. Bos and H. A. Krop [Studies in the History of Ideas in the Low Countries 1] (Amsterdam, 1993), pp. 29–36.

Keefer, Luke L. 'Arminian Motifs in Anabaptist Heritage,' *Brethren in Christ History and Life* 13 (1990), 293–323.

Kendall, R. T. *Calvin and English Calvinism to 1649*, 2nd ed. [Paternoster Biblical and Theological Monographs] (Carlisle, Cumbria, 1997).

Kenny, Anthony, and Jan Pinborg. 'Medieval Philosophical Literature,' in *The Cambridge History of Later Medieval Philosophy*, ed. Norman Kretzmann, et al. (Cambridge, Eng., 1982), pp. 11–42.

Kolb, Robert. 'Teaching the Text: The Commonplace Method in Sixteenth Century Lutheran Biblical Commentary,' *Bibliothèque d'Humanisme et Renaissance* 49 (1987), 571–85.

Kooi, Christine. *Liberty and Religion: Church and State in Leiden's Reformation, 1572–1620* [Studies in Medieval and Reformation Thought 82] (Leiden, 2000).

Krop, H. A. 'Natural Knowledge of God in Neo-Aristotelianism. The Reception of Suarez's Version of the Ontological Argument in Early Seventeenth Century Leiden,' in *Franco Burgersdijk (1590–1635): Neo-Aristotelianism in Leiden*, ed. E. P. Bos and H. A. Krop [Studies in the History of Ideas in the Low Countries 1] (Amsterdam, 1993), pp. 67–82.

Kurz, Alfred. *Die Heilsgewissheit bei Luther: Eine entwicklungsgeschichtliche und systematische Darstellung* (Gütersloh, 1933).

Kuyper, Abraham. *De Leidsche professoren en de executeurs der Dordtsche nalatenschap* (Amsterdam, 1879).

Lake, Donald M. 'He Died for All: the Universal Dimensions of the Atonement; Jacob Arminius' Contribution to a Theology of Grace,' in *Grace Unlimited*, ed. C. H. Pinnock (Minneapolis, 1975), pp. 223–42.

Lamberigts, Mathijs. 'Le mal et le péché. Pélage: La rehabilitation d'un hérétique,' *Revue d'histoire ecclésiastique* 95 (2000), 97–111.

——. 'Pelagianism: From an Ethical Religious Movement to a Heresy and Back Again,' trans. John Bowden, in *'Movements' in the Church*, ed. Alberto Melloni (London, 2003), pp. 39–48.

Lamping, A. J. 'Kuchlinus (Cuchlinus), Johannes,' in *BLGNP* 5:317–19.

Lane, Anthony N. S. 'Calvin's Doctrine of Assurance,' *Vox Evangelica* 11 (1979), 32–54.

Letham, Robert. 'Saving Faith and Assurance in Reformed Theology: Zwingli to the Synod of Dort' (Ph.D. diss., University of Aberdeen, 1979).

Liddell, Henry George, Robert Scott, and Henry Stuart Jones. *A Greek-English Lexicon*, new ed. (Oxford, 1940).

Lindberg, Carter. *The European Reformations* (Oxford, 1996).

Linde, S. van der. *Jean Taffin: Hofprediker en raadsheer van Willem van Oranje* (Amsterdam, 1982).

Ljunggren, Gustaf. *Zur Geschichte der Christlichen Heilsgewißheit von Augustin bis zur Hochscholastik* (Göttingen, 1921).

Lohr, Charles H. 'Jesuit Aristotelianism and Sixteenth-Century Metaphysics,' in *Paradosis: Studies in Memory of Edwin A. Quain*, ed. G. Fletcher and M. B. Schuete (New York, 1976), pp. 203–20.

McCulloh, Gerald O., ed. *Man's Faith and Freedom; the Theological Influence of Jacobus Arminius* (New York, 1962).

McSorley, Harry J. 'Was Gabriel Biel a Semipelagian?' in *Wahrheit und Verkündigung*, ed. Leo Scheffczyk, et al. (Munich, 1967), pp. 1109–20.

Marenbon, John. *Later Medieval Philosophy (1150–1350): An Introduction* (New York, 1987).

Maronier, Jan Hendrik. *Jacobus Arminius: Een Biografie* (Amsterdam, 1905).

Mbennah, Emmanuel D., and J. M. Vorster. 'The Influence of Arminian Conception of Predestination on the 18th-century Wesleyan Revival,' *Studia Historiae Ecclesiasticae* 24 (1998), 161–87.

Molhuysen, P. C. *Bronnen tot de geschiedenis der Leidsche Universiteit*, 7 vols. (The Hague, 1913–24.)

Morsink, Gerrit. *Joannes Anastasius Veluanus (Jan Gerritsz. Versteghe, levensloop en ontwikkeling)* (Kampen, 1986).

Muller, Richard A. *After Calvin: Studies in the Development of a Theological Tradition* [Oxford Studies in Historical Theology] (New York, 2003).

———. 'Arminius and the Scholastic Tradition,' *Calvin Theological Journal* 24/2 (1989), 263–77.

———. 'The Christological Problem in the Thought of Jacobus Arminius,' *NAKG* 68 (1988), 145–63.

———. *Dictionary of Latin and Greek Theological Terms: Drawn Principally from Protestant Scholastic Theology* (Grand Rapids, 1985).

———. 'The Federal Motif in Seventeenth-Century Arminian Theology,' *NAKG* 62/1 (1982), 102–22.

———. *God, Creation and Providence in the Thought of Jacob Arminius: Sources and Directions of Scholastic Protestantism in the Era of Early Orthodoxy* (Grand Rapids, 1991).

———. 'God, Predestination, and the Integrity of the Created Order: a Note on Patterns in Arminius' Theology,' in *Later Calvinism*, ed. Fred W. Graham (Kirksville, MO, 1994), pp. 431–46.

———. 'Grace, Election, and Contingent Choice: Arminius' Gambit and the Reformed Response,' in *The Grace of God and the Bondage of the Will*, ed. Thomas Schreiner and Bruce Ware, 2 vols. (Grand Rapids, 1995), 2: 251–78.

———. 'Perkins' *A Golden Chaine*: Predestinarian System or Schematized *Ordo Salutis?*' *SCJ* 9/1 (1978), 68–81.

———. *Post-Reformation Reformed Dogmatics*, 4 vols. (Grand Rapids, 2003).

———. 'The Priority of the Intellect in the Soteriology of Jacob Arminius,' *Westminster Theological Journal* 55 (1993), 55–72.

———. *The Unaccommodated Calvin: Studies in the Foundation of a Theological Tradition* [Oxford Studies in Historical Theology] (New York, 2000).

Neelands, David. 'The Authority of St. Augustine in the Debates Leading to the Lambeth Articles' (paper presented at the Sixteenth Century Studies Conference, Pittsburgh, 31 October 2003), 1–35.

Nieuw Nederlandsch biografisch woordenboek, ed. P. C. Molhuysen and Fr. K. H. Kossman, 10 vols. (Leiden, 1911–1937).

Nijenhuis, Willem. *Adrianus Saravia (c. 1532–1613): Dutch Calvinist, first Reformed Defender of the English Episcopal Church order on the Basis of the Ius Divinum* [SHCT 21] (Leiden, 1980).

Nuttall, Geoffrey F. 'The Influence of Arminianism in England,' in Gerald McCulloh, ed., *Man's Faith and Freedom*, pp. 46–63.

Oberman, Heiko A. *The Dawn of the Reformation: Essays in Late Medieval and Early Reformation Thought* (1986; repr. Grand Rapids, 1992).

———. *The Harvest of Medieval Theology: Gabriel Biel and Late Medieval Nominalism* (1963; repr. Grand Rapids, 2000).

———. *The Reformation: Roots and Ramifications*, trans. Andrew Colin Gow (Grand Rapids, 1994).

Olson, Roger E. *The Story of Christian Theology: Twenty Centuries of Tradition and Reform* (Downers Grove, 1999).

Otterspeer, Willem. *Groepsportet met Dame I. Het bolwerk van de vrijheid: De Leidse universiteit, 1575–1672* (Amsterdam, 2000).

———. 'Leiden, University of,' in *The Dictionary of Seventeenth and Eighteenth-Century Dutch Philosophers*, vol. 2, (Bristol, Eng., 2003), pp. 603–14.

Ozment, Steven E. *The Reformation in the Cities: The Appeal of Protestantism to Sixteenth-Century Germany and Switzerland* (New Haven, 1975).

Pannenberg, Wolfhart. *Jesus—God and Man*, 2nd ed., trans. L. Wilkins and Duane A. Priebe (Philadelphia, 1977).

Paulsen, Friedrich. *The German Universities and University Study*, trans. Frank Thilly and William W. Elwang (New York, 1906).

Pelikan, Jaroslav. *The Christian Tradition: A History of the Development of Doctrine*, 5 vols. (Chicago, 1971–89).

Peterson, Robert A., and Michael D. Williams. *Why I Am Not an Arminian* (Downers Grove, 2004).

Petit, Louis D. *Bibliographische lijst der werken van de Leidsche hoogleraren van de oprichting der Hoogeschool tot op onze dagen: Faculteit der godgeleerdheid*, Eerste Aflevering (Leiden, 1894).

Pinson, J. Matthew. 'Introduction,' in *Four Views on Eternal Security*, ed. J. Matthew Pinson (Grand Rapids, 2002), pp. 7–19.

Platt, John. *Reformed Thought and Scholasticism: The Arguments for the Existence of God in Dutch Theology, 1575–1650* [SHCT 29] (Leiden, 1982).

Poelgeest, L. van, ed. *Addenda Hoogleraren en Lectoren Theologie, Regenten Statencollege, Regenten Waals College, Bibliothecarissen, Secretarissen van de Curatoren* (Leiden, 1985).

Praamsma, Louis. 'The Background of the Arminian Controversy (1586–1618),' in *Crisis in the Reformed Churches*, ed. Peter Y. De Jong (Grand Rapids, 1968), pp. 22–38.

Rabbie, Edwin. 'Introduction,' in Grotius, *Ordinum Hollandiae ac Westfrisiae Pietas (1613)*, trans. Edwin Rabbie (Leiden, 1995), pp. 1–92.

Reed, Rodney L. 'Calvin, Calvinism, and Wesley: The Doctrine of Assurance in Historical Perspective,' *Methodist History* 32 (Oct. 1993), 31–43.

Rieu, W. du, ed. *Album studiosorum Academiae Lugduno Batavae MDLXXV–MDCCCLXXV, accedunt nomina curatorum et professorum* (The Hague, 1875).

Ritschl, Otto. *Dogmengeschichte des Protestantismus: Grundlagen und Grundzüge der theologischen Gedenken- und Lehrbildung in den protestantischen Kirchen*, 4 vols. (Leipzig/Göttingen, 1908–27).

Ruler, J. A. van. 'Franco Petri Burgersdijk and the Case of Calvinism within the Neo-Scholastic Tradition,' in *Franco Burgersdijk (1590–1635): Neo-Aristotelianism in Leiden*, ed. E. P. Bos and H. A. Krop [Studies in the History of Ideas in the Low Countries 1] (Amsterdam, 1993), pp. 37–65.

Sargeaunt, W. D. 'The Lambeth Articles,' *Journal of Theological Studies* 12 (1911), 251–60 and 427–36.

Schaff, Philip. *The Creeds of Christendom, with a History and Critical Notes*, 3 vols., 6th ed. (1931; repr. Grand Rapids, 1998).

Schneppen, Heinz. *Niederländische Universitäten und Deutsches Geistesleben von der Gründung der Universität Leiden bis ins späte 18. Jahrhundert* (Münster, 1960).

Schotel, G. D. J. *De Academie te Leiden* (Haarlem, 1875).

Seeberg, Reinhold. *Text-book of the History of Doctrines*, 2 vols., trans. Charles E. Hay (Grand Rapids, 1977).

Sell, Alan P. F. *The Great Debate: Calvinism, Arminianism and Salvation* (Grand Rapids, 1983).

Sirks, G. J. *Arminius' pleidooi voor de vrede der kerk* [Referatenreeks uit Remonstrantse Kring 11] (Lochem, 1960).

Slaatte, Howard A. *The Arminian Arm of Theology: The Theologies of John Fletcher, First Methodist Theologian, and His Precursor, James Arminius* (Washington, D.C., 1978).

Smalley, Beryl. *The Study of the Bible in the Middle Ages* (New York, 1952).

Spijker, Willem van't. *Luther: Belofte en ervaring* (Goes, 1983).

Stanglin, Keith D. ' "Arminius *avant la lettre*": Peter Baro, Jacob Arminius, and the Bond of Predestinarian Polemic,' *Westminster Theological Journal* 67 (2005), 51–74.

Stanglin, Keith D. and Tom McCall. 'S. M. Baugh and the Meaning of Foreknowledge,' *Trinity Journal*, n. s. 26 (2005), 19–31.

Steinmetz, David C. *Calvin in Context* (New York, 1995).

———. *Luther in Context* (Grand Rapids, 1995).

Strehle, Stephen. *The Catholic Roots of the Protestant Gospel: Encounter between the Middle Ages and the Reformation* [SHCT 60] (Leiden, 1995).

Strype, John. *The Life and Acts of John Whitgift, D.D.*, 3 vols. (1718; repr. Oxford, 1822).

Studebaker, Richard F. 'The Theology of James Arminius,' *Reflections* 4 (1996), 4–17.

Veen, Mirjam G. K. van. ' "No One Born of God Commits Sin": Coornhert's Perfectionism,' *NAKG* 84 (2004), 338–57.

———. 'Spiritualism in The Netherlands: From David Joris to Dirck Volckertsz Coornhert,' *SCJ* 33/1 (2002), 129–50.

Velásquez, Oscar. 'From *Dubitatio* to *Securitas*: Augustine's *Confessions* in the Light of Uncertainty,' in *Studia Patristica 38, St. Augustine and His Opponents* (Leuven, 2001), pp. 338–41.

Venemans, B. A. 'Junius, Franciscus (François du Jon),' in *BLGNP* 2:275–78.

Walls, Jerry L., and Joseph R. Dongell. *Why I Am Not a Calvinist* (Downers Grove, 2004).

White, Peter. *Predestination, Policy, and Polemic: Conflict and Consensus in the English Church from the Reformation to the Civil War* (Cambridge, Eng., 1992).

Wijminga, P. J. *Festus Hommius* (Leiden, 1899).

Winship, Michael P. 'Weak Christians, Backsliders, and Carnal Gospelers: Assurance of Salvation and the Pastoral Origins of Puritan Practical Divinity in the 1580s,' *Church History* 70/3 (2001), 462–81.

Witt, William Gene. 'Creation, Redemption and Grace in the Theology of Jacob Arminius' (Ph.D. diss., University of Notre Dame, 1993).

Wolgast, Eike. 'Das Collegium Sapientiae in Heidelberg im 16. Jahrhundert,' *Zeitschrift für die Geschichte des Oberrheins* 147 (1999), 303–18.

Wood, Arthur Skevington. 'The Declaration of Sentiments: The Theological Testament of Arminius,' *Evangelical Quarterly* 65 (April 1993), 111–29.

Zachman, Randall C. *The Assurance of Faith: Conscience in the Theology of Martin Luther and John Calvin* (Minneapolis, 1993).

Zilverberg, S. B. J. 'Bertius, Petrus,' in *BLGNP* 2:63–64.

NAME INDEX

SUBJECT INDEX